No Armor for the Back

MERCER
UNIVERSITY PRESS

Endowed by
TOM WATSON BROWN
and
THE WATSON-BROWN FOUNDATION, INC.

No Armor for the Back

Baptist Prison Writings, 1600s—1700s

Keith E. Durso

MERCER UNIVERSITY PRESS
MACON, GEORGIA
AND
THE BAPTIST HISTORY & HERITAGE SOCIETY
ATLANTA, GEORGIA

First Edition.

Books published by Mercer University Press are printed on acid
free paper that meets the requirements of American National
Standard for Information Sciences—Permanence of Paper for
Printed Library Materials.

MUP: H747//P374

ISBN
978-0-88146-091-9 (HB)
978-0-88146-096-4 (PB)

Library of Congress Cataloging-in-Publication Data

Durso, Keith E.
No armor for the back : Baptist prison writings, 1600s-1700s / Keith E.
Durso.
p. cm.
Includes bibliographical references and index.
ISBN-13: 978-0-88146-091-9 (hardback : alk. paper)
ISBN-10: 0-88146-091-5 (hardback : alk. paper)
ISBN-13: 978-0-88146-096-4 (pbk. : alk. paper)
ISBN-10: 0-88146-096-6 (pbk. : alk. paper)
1. Baptists—England—History—17th century. 2. Baptists—
England—History—18th century. 3. Persecution—England—History—17th
century. 4. Persecution—England—History—18th century. 5. England—Church
history—17th century. 6. England—Church history—18th century. I. Title.
BX6276.D87 2007
272'.8--dc22
2007039593

For Pam, of whom it can truly be said:
"Many are the women of proven worth,
but you have excelled them all."
(Prov 31:29; NAB)

Contents

Preface

While writing a book on Baptists in the United States, which I co-authored with my wife, I had the opportunity to research John Waller, an eighteenth-century Virginia Baptist preacher. During one of his imprisonments for preaching his Baptist beliefs, Waller wrote two letters describing that prison experience. Those letters led me to consider writing an article on the prison writings of Baptists in the seventeenth and eighteenth centuries. At one point, I asked my wife, Pam, "Wouldn't it be funny to write an article titled 'Letters from Baptist Cons'?" "A book!" she exclaimed. Thus, I decided not to write an article, but to take my wife's suggestion to write a book.

My first title for the book was *Letters and Papers from Baptist Cons*. Yet I continually had to explain this title, saying something like this: "No, not 'cons' as in 'con *men*'; 'cons' as in 'con*victs*.'" A title that must be explained repeatedly is not a good title.

Another title I considered using was *When Baptists Really Had Something to Whine About*, and I planned to compare the statements and circumstances of early Baptists with those of modern Baptists, particularly those in the United States. Reading the statements of some current-day Baptists in America, one would think that they faced constant persecution and oppression and were living in deplorable conditions, being dragged away from their hearths and homes, and being imprisoned in state and federal prisons. By studying early Baptists, I learned that, unlike current-day Baptists in the United States, they really did have something about which to whine. Yet Baptists of the seventeenth and eighteenth centuries stated their cases without any self-pity and interpreted their persecutions as the natural consequence of professing their faith in Christ. In the end, I decided to focus (except for one example below) on the writings of those early Baptists and leave the comparing and contrasting for others.

Why write a book on the writings of seventeenth- and eighteenth-century Baptists who had trouble staying out of prison? Many reasons could be given, but foremost among them is the importance of remembering and passing along the stories of our Baptist forebearers. From prison on 25 September 1675, Thomas Hardcastle, a Baptist preacher in Bristol,

England, and a man who knew well the inside of a prison, reminded his congregation about the necessity of remembering the past: "Treasure up your experiences of the Lord's goodness, and power, and faithfulness, that they may be useful if you should hereafter meet with the like temptations. The people of Israel of old had very bad memories (see Judg. 8:34; Pss. 78:42; 106:7). It would not be strange if the stories of persecution, of informers, disturbances, prelate imprisonment, etc., should grow out of date in Bristol and be forgotten. Greater afflictions and deliverances than ours have been forgotten by a professing people (Lam. 3:18, 37)."[1]

The need for Baptists to remember their past was reiterated again in 1845 when a group of English Baptists founded the Hanserd Knollys Society, which was dedicated to the republishing of the writings of early English Baptists. In its prospectus, the society lamented that many Baptists in England had lost their sense of denominational legacy. The society noted, "It is to be feared that as a body we are too ignorant of our own history, and of the great and good men who lost all in the maintenance of our principles. Our young people especially need information on these points. Moreover they [the works of early Baptists] are needed for the libraries of our ministers."[2] English Baptists, apparently, had lost interest in "the opinions and the bitter trials of those men to whom the Baptist body owes its existence in this country:—in whose stripes, and bonds, and death, was laid the foundation of that liberty we now enjoy."[3] Like the Hanserd Knollys Society, this book is an attempt to keep alive the stories of the Baptist men and women who paid a heavy price for expressing their understanding of what it meant to be a Christian.

As in 1845, historical amnesia appears to be a common ailment at the beginning of the twenty-first century. In 2003, C. Truett Baker, president emeritus of the Arizona Children's Services, stated, "The paranoia and persecution complex mentality of earlier centuries is not appropriate in the

---

[1] Thomas Hardcastle's seventh letter to Broadmead Church, 25 September 1675, in *The Records of a Church of Christ, Meeting in Broadmead, Bristol, 1640–1685*, ed. Edward Bean Underhill (London: J. Haddon, 1847) 282.

[2] See Edward Bean Underhill, *Tracts on Liberty of Conscience and Persecution, 1614–1661*, Elibron Classics Series (London: J. Haddon, 1846; repr. Chestnut Hill MA: Adamant Media Corporation, 2003) 3. The prospectus is placed before Underhill's historical introduction.

[3] Ibid., 2.

21st century." He wondered, "Why can't church and state work together without feeling that one will dominate the other? The state has a role in health and safety and the church has a role in pursuing its spiritual mission. In fact, the state has a responsibility to protect churches.... Again, the state has a place in organized religion and the church has a place in the public square. This can be done by each respecting the venue of the other and neither attempting to dominate the other."[4]

Seventeenth- and eighteenth-century English and American Baptists were "paranoid" because the ecclesiastical authorities, blessed and backed by the power of the state, and the civil authorities, blessed and backed by the church, utterly despised Baptists and enthusiastically sought to put many of them in prison, if not in the grave. In reality, however, early Baptists were not paranoid, for paranoid people are delusional, believing that everyone and everything is out to do them harm. John Murton, a seventeenth-century English Baptist, described his reality, not his paranoia, when he wrote:

> No mortal man may make a law to the conscience and force [people] to [obey] it by persecutions, and consequently [he] may not compel [anyone] to any religion where faith is wanting.... But the learned of this land see it not, or rather will not practice it; but, for our not submitting herein, [they] procure [their] temporal sword to persecute us, by casting us in prisons, where many of us have remained many years in lingering imprisonment, deprived of all earthly comforts, as wives, children, callings, etc., without hope of release, until God, for the practice of whose commandments we are thus persecuted, persuades the hearts of your majesty, your highness, your honors, your worships, to take pity upon us, our poor wives and children, or his heavenly Majesty release us by death.[5]

---

[4] C. Truett Baker, "Response to Brent Walker's Review," *Christian Ethics Today* 9/3 (Summer 2003): 14. See Brent Walker, "Response to C. Truett Baker," *Christian Ethics Today* 9/3 (Summer 2003): 14–15.

[5] [John Murton], *A Most Humble Supplication of Many of the King's Majesty's Loyal Subjects, Ready to Testify All Civil Obedience, by the Oath of Allegiance, or Otherwise, and That of Conscience; Who Are Persecuted (only for Differing in Religion), Contrary to Divine and Human Testimonies* (n.p., 1620) in Underhill, *Tracts on Liberty of Conscience and Persecution*, 210–11.

Murton was not delusional in thinking that people were out to get him; they had already gotten him. He wrote these words in London's Newgate Prison, which prisoners described, without exaggerating, as a hell on earth.

In 2009, many Baptists will celebrate the 400th anniversary of their beginning. Four hundred years have provided ample time to allow the memory of those who preceded us to be completely ignored, if not forgotten. "History," as the German theologian Otto Weber observed, "is a 'city of the dead.' But 'we awaken' the dead, and 'we deal with them....' Historical research itself demonstrates that history is not 'dead' in every sense of the word. It processes 'memories' and prevents forgetting.... The present is determined by the past."[6] Looking back does not mean that we ignore the present, but studying the past will help remind us of the men and women who suffered and who laid the foundation for who Baptists are today. The stories of these Baptist cons (con*victs*, not con *men*) need to be resurrected and retold. I hope I have done that.

The following pages will demonstrate at least two truths. First, early Baptists learned the tragic truth expressed in Pascal's dictum that "men never do evil so completely and cheerfully as when they do it from religious conviction."[7] Indeed, those who persecuted Baptists did their work joyfully and zealously and apparently with few, if any, pangs of a guilty conscience. They truly believed that they were doing God's work, and their fear of losing control compelled them to use temporal force to achieve spiritual goals. Yet the following pages also illustrate the truth of F. F. Bruce's observation that "where love is the compelling power, there is no sense of strain or conflict or bondage in doing what is right: the man or woman who is compelled by Jesus' love and empowered by his Spirit does the will of God from the heart. For (as Paul could say from experience) 'where the Spirit of the Lord is, there the heart is free' (2 Corinthians 3:17)."[8] Early Baptists would have agreed with Bruce's observation. They, like their persecutors and opponents, fervently believed that they were doing God's work. Yet,

---

[6] Otto Weber, *Foundations of Dogmatics*, trans. Darrell L. Guder, 2 vols., Grand Rapids MI: William B. Eerdmans Publishing Company, 1983) 2:91.

[7] Blaise Pascal, *Pensées*, no. 895, http://www.ccel.org/p/pascal/pensees/pensees 15.htm (accessed 16 June 2004).

[8] F. F. Bruce, *Paul: Apostle of the Heart Set Free* (Grand Rapids MI: William B. Eerdmans Publishing Company, 1977) 21. Bruce quoted the Basic English Version.

unlike their detractors, imprisoned Baptists claimed that compelling anyone to worship against the dictates of his or her conscience was a sin, and they believed that, despite being imprisoned, they were much freer than the people who jailed them.

Throughout the book, I have used the term Baptist to describe all of the prisoners, even though, as will be demonstrated in the text, that particular term was not used to describe them until 1640s, and it was not until 1650s that the Baptist label stuck.

I have included in this book people who were Baptists when they wrote documents while in prison or who wrote about their prison experiences. Not every Baptist prisoner or every Baptist prison document is included, but the stories of a great majority of the early imprisoned Baptists are found in the pages that follow. Some people might question whether all the prisoners included in the book were Baptists. Although I consulted numerous sources, two were particularly helpful: Leon McBeth's *English Baptist Literature on Religious Liberty to 1689* and W. T. Whitley's *A Baptist Bibliography*.[9] If a question exists about the Baptistness of a particular person, I have included sources to which anyone can consult for a more in-depth study.

Except for minor alterations, I have left the titles of documents as they appeared when published. However, to make those documents more readable, and therefore hopefully more useable, I have added quotation marks and have changed the spelling and grammar to conform to modern usage. Poems quoted throughout the book have not been altered.

Two institutions provided assistance during the writing this book. Vanderbilt University Divinity School in Nashville, Tennessee, allowed me to use its library, for which I am grateful. The Southern Baptist Historical Library and Archives (SBHLA) in Nashville, Tennessee, also made its resources available and provided me with a Lynn May, Jr., Study Grant to help defray some of the costs of writing the book. The SBHLA's staff—Jean

---

[9] Harry Leon McBeth, *English Baptist Literature on Religious Liberty to 1689* (Ph.D. diss., Southwestern Baptist Theological Seminary, 1961; repr., New York: Arno Press, 1980); W. T. Whitley, *A Baptist Bibliography, Being a Register of the Chief Materials for Baptist History, Whether in Manuscript or in Print, Preserved in Great Britain, Ireland, and the Colonies*, vol. 1, 1526–1776 (London: The Kingsgate Press, 1916).

Forbis, Taffey Hall, Bill Sumners, and Kathy Sylvest—provided invaluable help.

I am grateful to Charles W. Deweese, executive director-treasurer of the Baptist History and Heritage Society, who first expressed his support for this project and who then read the manuscript, correcting mistakes, providing encouragement, and offering suggestions along the way. I am also grateful to Walter B. Shurden, professor of Christianity and executive director of the Center for Baptist Studies at Mercer University, who also read the manuscript and whose comments were helpful and encouraging.

Last, but certainly not least, my wife helped and encouraged me throughout the entire process of the writing of this book. She read the manuscript more than once, and her suggestions have saved me from many embarrassing mistakes. Words of gratitude seem so inadequate to express my thoughts and feelings. So Pam, when I first mentioned an article about Baptist prison writings, you exclaimed, "A book!" Well, here it is.

Chapter 1

Counting the Cost

In one of the great ironies of history, the most famous persecutor of the Christian church became both the most famous preacher of the gospel and the gospel's most famous prisoner. To the Christians afflicted by his religiously-motivated persecution, he was Saul of Tarsus; to the Christians who eventually welcomed his ministry, he was the apostle Paul. He was the man who, on a mission to arrest Christians, turned from "violently persecuting the church of God" (Gal. 1:13), to being "an apostle of Christ Jesus" (1 Cor. 1:1), and finally to ministering as "an ambassador in chains" (Eph 6:20).[1] "I suffer hardship," Paul told his associate Timothy, "even to the point of being chained like a criminal. But the word of God is not chained" (2 Tim 2:9). Paul's attitude was this: Rome could incarcerate the gospel messenger, but it could not imprison the gospel message, for he could fight "his battles with his pen and prayers."[2] And fight he did. Paul never stopped preaching, teaching, or defending the gospel. Nor did he stop exhorting Christians to remain loyal to Christ and to lead a life pleasing to God.

The number of Paul's imprisonments remains a mystery, as does the number of letters he wrote while a prisoner.[3] Yet his suffering for the cause of Christ did not surprise him, nor did he consider his experience to be an anomaly. In his letter to the church at Rome, Paul reminded believers that if

---

[1] Unless otherwise indicated, all scripture verses come from the NRSV. However, verses quoted by seventeenth- and eighteenth-century authors have been left as they appear in the documents.

[2] A. T. Robertson, *Epochs in the Life of Paul: A Study of Development in Paul's Career* (New York: Charles Scribner's Sons, 1914) 278.

[3] The New Testament contains five of Paul's prison letters: Philippians, Ephesians, Colossians, Philemon, and 2 Timothy. Many scholars believe that Ephesians, Colossians, and 2 Timothy are pseudonymous. However, for the sake of argument, I will assume Pauline authorship of all these letters.

they were God's children, they were also "heirs of God and joint heirs with Christ—if, in fact, we suffer with him" (Rom. 8:17), and he warned Timothy that "all who want to live a godly life in Christ Jesus will be persecuted" (2 Tim 3:12). Paul had done both: he had striven to lead a godly life and he had suffered for doing so. Paul's words on this point echoed those of Jesus, who, in the Sermon on the Mount, warned his disciples about the cost of discipleship: "Blessed are those who are persecuted for righteousness' sake, for theirs is the kingdom of heaven. Blessed are you when people revile you and persecute you and utter all kinds of evil against you falsely on my account. Rejoice and be glad, for your reward is great in heaven, for in the same way they persecuted the prophets who were before you" (Matt 5:10–12).

As one who followed the teachings of Jesus, Paul refused to let his outward circumstances destroy his faith or his sense of mission, for he had learned to be content in every circumstance, even in prison (Phil 4:11–13). Whereas some people would have bemoaned the loss of their freedom, Paul saw his imprisonments as opportunities for good. From Rome, he wrote to the Philippians, "I want you to know, beloved, that what has happened to me has actually helped to spread the gospel, so that it has become known throughout the whole imperial guard and to everyone else that my imprisonment is for Christ" (Phil 1:12–13). Paul's optimism, faith, and courage were contagious. Other Christians drew strength from him: "Most of the brothers and sisters, having been made confident in the Lord by my imprisonment, dare to speak the word with greater boldness and without fear" (Phil 1:14).

Despite the unnamed Christians who hoped to make his imprisonment in Rome more painful, Paul still rejoiced that they preached the gospel: "What does it matter? Just this, that Christ is proclaimed in every way, whether out of false motives or true; and in that I rejoice" (Phil 1:18). This note of joy is a recurrent theme in Paul's letter to the Philippians, a letter in which he used "joy" or "rejoice" fourteen times. His joy was "a defiant 'nevertheless.'"[4] Paul might have been imprisoned and his life might have been in danger, but he would not let ill will toward his captors or fear for his

---

[4] Karl Barth, *The Epistle to the Philippians*, trans. J. W. Leitch (Richmond VA: John Knox Press, 1962) 120.

life detract him from preaching to those who wanted to hear his message and even to those who did not.

Despite his intense, deep faith, the stress and pressures of being a pastor, a missionary, and a prisoner took a heavy toll on Paul. "Besides other things," he noted in one letter, "I am under daily pressure because of my anxiety for all the churches. Who is weak, and I am not weak: who is made to stumble, and I am not indignant?" (2 Cor 11:28).[5] Near the end of his life, Paul wrote to Timothy, noting that he was "being poured out as a libation, and the time of" his "departure" had come. Yet Paul could look back at his life and confidently proclaim, "I have fought the good fight, I have finished the race, I have kept the faith" (2 Tim 4:6–7).

The Church's Painful Beginning

Paul's teaching that Christians should expect to be persecuted proved to be true. The book of Acts and several of the New Testament letters contain accounts of persecution of Christians first by Jews in Judea and then by groups of citizens throughout the Roman Empire.[6] Although Acts described official persecution under Herod Agrippa, which appears to have been organized by Jewish religious leaders (12:1–5), much of the persecution described in the New Testament seems to have been sporadic and waged by groups of local citizens, rather than a systematic, organized policy by the Roman government.[7]

Organized persecution of the church by the Roman government appears to have begun under Nero (r. 54–68) when, in AD 64, fire destroyed much of the city of Rome.[8] Roman senators blamed Nero for the fire, who in turn blamed Christians in order to deflect suspicion from himself. Nero had some Christians ripped to death by animals; others he had publicly burned. According to church tradition, the apostles Peter and Paul suffered martyrdom during Nero's reign.[9] During Domitian's reign (r. 81–96),

---

[5] For these "other things," see 2 Corinthians 6:4–10.

[6] See the book of Acts, James 1:2–3; Hebrews 10:32–37; 1 Peter 3:13–17; and the book of Revelation.

[7] See Steven Sheeley, "Persecution in the New Testament," *Mercer Dictionary of the Bible*, ed. Watson E. Mills et al. (Macon GA: Mercer University Press, 1990) 668.

[8] "R" in dates refers to that person's "reign."

[9] Bo Reicke, *The New Testament Era: The World of the Bible from 500 B.C. to A.D. 100* (Philadelphia: Fortress Press, 1968) 249–50.

persecution of the church continued in localities other than in Rome, and many scholars believe that the New Testament book of Revelation was composed during this time.

Persecution of the church became more widespread during Trajan's reign (r. 98–117). Trajan established the following imperial policy toward Christians: Roman authorities were not to seek Christians out for persecution; however, authorities were to punish any Christians who were brought before them and who refused to recant their faith. Persecution during this period was sporadic and depended on the initiative of local authorities.[10]

Roman emperors continued Trajan's policy into the fourth century.[11] Under Diocletian (r. 284–305) occurred "the most cruel of all the persecutions that the ancient church had to endure."[12] Diocletian ordered that Christians be expelled from the army and government jobs, demanded the destruction of church buildings and Bibles, and called for the imprisonment of church leaders. The emperor also required that Christians offer sacrifices to pagan gods. Refusal to obey this decree resulted in torture and sometimes death.

The Church's Turn to Persecute

For the first three centuries and part of the fourth, the relationship between the church and the Roman government can only be characterized as hostile. The church was a persecuted minority as well as an illegal organization. That relationship changed, however, when Constantine (r. 306–337) became emperor.

Prior to his retirement, Diocletian divided his empire into two parts: Constantius (r. 305–306) ruled the Western Empire, and Licinius (r. 308–324) ruled the Eastern Empire. After Constantius died, his son Constantine sought to gain control of the Western Empire, and during this

---

[10] Justo L. González, *The Story of Christianity: The Early Church to the Dawn of the Reformation*, 2 vols. (San Francisco: HarperSanFrancisco, 1984) 1:40–41. For an example of one governor's dealings with Christians and Trajan's reaction, see Pliny's letter to Trajan and the emperor's response in Henry Bettenson, ed., *Documents of the Christian Church*, 2nd ed., (London: Oxford University Press, 1963) 3–4.

[11] See González, *The Story of Christianity*, 1:43–48, 82–88, 102–106.

[12] Ibid., 1:104.

quest for domination, he defeated his rival Maxentius at the battle of Milvian Bridge in 312. Prior to this battle, Constantine prayed to God for help and then claimed that Christ appeared to him in a dream, commanding him to place on his soldiers' shields the sign God had given him. The next day Maxentius foolishly led his forces outside the fortifications of Rome, resulting in victory for Constantine, who then attributed his good fortune to the Christian God. That battle had significant ramifications for the church because, as J. Philip Wogaman observed, "The great watershed, so far as Christian relationship to the state is concerned, occurred with the rise to power of Constantine in A.D. 313. The first Christian emperor absolutely reversed the political status of Christians."[13]

In 313 Constantine and Licinius ended the persecution of the church with the issuing of the Edict of Milan, in which the co-emperors

> resolved…to grant both to the Christians and to all men freedom to follow the religion which they choose, that whatever heavenly divinity exists may be propitious to us and to all that live under our government. We have, therefore, determined, with sound and upright purpose, that liberty is to be denied to no one, to choose and to follow the religious observances of the Christians, but that to each one freedom is to be given to devote his mind to that religion which he may think adapted to himself, in order that the Deity may exhibit to us in all things his accustomed care and favor.[14]

Although the edict did not make Christianity the official Roman religion, it guaranteed Christians a place in the empire. Prior to Constantine, Christians "had been at best tolerated and at worst persecuted. Now they were favored."[15] Soon, however, the church's favored status evolved into an official one.

---

[13] J. Philip Wogaman, *Christian Perspectives on Politics*, rev. and exp. (Louisville KY: Westminster John Knox Press, 2000) 38.

[14] Eusebius Pamphilus, "Church History," in *A Select Library of the Nicene and Post-Nicene Fathers of the Christian Church*, ed. Philip Schaff and Henry Wace, 2nd series, 14 vols. (Grand Rapids MI: Wm. B. Eerdmans Publishing Company, n.d.) 1:379, http://www.ccel.org/ccel/schaff/npnf201.iii.xvi.v.html (accessed 9 March 2005).

[15] Wogaman, *Christian Perspectives on Politics*, 38.

The co-emperorship ended in 324 when Constantine defeated and then executed Licinius. As the sole ruler of the empire, Constantine instituted new policies that affected the church. He helped the church erect buildings for worship, granted Christian ministers tax exemption, and, despite the Edict of Milan's granting all people the "freedom to follow the religion which they choose," prohibited the worship of pagan gods.[16] Constantine established the precedent that church and state could and should accommodate themselves to one another for the benefit of both. The church would support the policies of the state, and in return the state would support the church through legislative and, if necessary, coercive means.

As a result of the Barbarian invasions in the fourth and fifth centuries, the Roman Empire was again divided, severing the West from the East and from the control of the emperor. The Catholic Church filled the political vacuum left in the West, and Catholic leaders soon reinterpreted the relationship between the church and state. In a letter to Emperor Anastasius (r. 491–518) written in 494, Pope Gelasius I wrote:

> There are two powers, august emperor, by which this world is chiefly ruled, namely, the sacred authority of the priests and the royal power. Of these that of the priests is the more weighty, since they have to render an account for even the kings of men in the divine judgment. You are also aware, dear son, that while you are permitted honorably to rule over human kind, yet in things divine you bow your head humbly before the leaders of the clergy and await from their hands the means of your salvation. In the reception and proper disposition of the heavenly mysteries you recognize that you should be subordinate rather than superior to the religious order, and that in these matters you depend on their judgment rather than wish to force them to follow your will.[17]

This belief that the spiritual authority had precedent over the temporal authority was in place when Christianity took a firm hold in Britain.

---

[16] See J. H. Barber, "Constantine in Relation to Christianity," *Review and Expositor* 9/1 (January 1912): 63–82.

[17] Pope Gelasius I to Emperor Anastasius, 494, Internet Medieval Sourcebook, http://www.fordham.edu/halsall/source/gelasius1.html (accessed 13 May 2005).

Henry's Dilemma

When Christianity first arrived in Britain is unknown, although Tertullian (c. 160–c. 230) and Origen (185?–254) mentioned that Christians lived among the Celts and Britons.[18] Clearly, however, Christianity had been established in Britain by the end of the sixth century. In 597, Pope Gregory I sent forty monks to Britain to evangelize and bring the churches in Britain under the authority of Rome.

By the time the Protestant Reformation began in 1517, Rome had been ruling the English church for nearly nine hundred years. That reformation came to Europe when, after years of internal struggle, the Augustinian monk Martin Luther arrived at his answer to how a worthless, damnable sinner like himself could be accepted by a holy, righteous God. Luther concluded that God accepted sinners by grace through faith, not because of works, not through the teachings of the Catholic Church, and certainly not through the mediations of its minions, the priests. Luther's conclusions contrasted sharply with those of Rome. In the early sixteenth century, Catholic priests held great power over the laity, as Simon Schama has so amply described: "The priest…was the indispensable man, and there was no getting to heaven but through his hands. Only the priest's hands could touch the bread and wine [during the Eucharist] and consecrate them, changing them through the sacrament into the flesh and blood of Christ. These were the hands that gave meaning to 'good works,' whether that meant buying wax or founding a college. They made the difference between salvation and perdition."[19] Against such power, Luther, one of "the apostles of the new Christianity—the Christianity of the word, not of spectacle," revolted.[20] Luther's story of rebellion against the political and ecclesiastical powers of Europe is one of courage and one that depicts a man, and eventually many like-minded others, who was willing to die for his faith.

Compared with the story of Luther's reforming the church in Germany, the story of the beginning of the Reformation in England is almost an embarrassment. Whereas in Germany Luther was on his knees,

---

[18] Carl A. Volz, *The Medieval Church: From the Dawn of the Middle Ages to the Eve of the Reformation* (Nashville: Abingdon Press, 1997) 32.

[19] Simon Schama, *A History of Britain: At the Edge of the World?: 300 BC–AD 1603*, 3 vols. (New York: Hyperion, 2000) 1:282.

[20] Ibid.

asking how he could be freed from the sin and guilt that tormented his soul, in England, Henry VIII was on his throne, asking how he could be freed from his wife, who had not borne him a male heir to his throne. Henry pondered that question more than once during his reign.

The succession of Henry VIII (r. 1509–1547) to the throne of England launched that country into an ecclesiastical ping-pong match. In 1509, when Henry took the throne, England was firmly ensconced in the Catholic faith. During his reign, Henry and Rome worked together for the benefit of both parties. In gratitude for his support of its struggle against Luther and other reformers and at Henry's request, the Catholic Church bestowed on the English monarch the title "Defender of the Faith" and confirmed his ecclesiastical appointments, allowing him to rule England freely. A breach between Henry and Rome developed, however, when the Catholic Church refused to grant him an ecclesiastical sanction for a divorce from his wife, Catherine, and an endorsement of his marriage to Anne Boleyn, one of Catherine's attendants. Therefore, to leave Catherine, Henry first had to leave Rome, converting his status as the "Defender of the Faith" into a new role: the "Defector of the Faith."

Henry's dilemma was that after eighteen years of marriage, he and Catherine, his brother's widow, had produced only one child, Mary. With no son, Henry did not have a legitimate, male successor. He had, however, fathered a son out of wedlock. One cardinal suggested that the son wed Mary, but Henry rejected the plan, suggesting instead that the church annul his marriage to Catherine, which would free him to marry someone who might produce a male heir. He maintained that his marriage to Catherine was illicit and therefore annullable. In his appeal to Pope Clement VII, Henry cited Leviticus 20:21: "If a man takes his brother's wife, it is impurity; he has uncovered his brother's nakedness; they shall be childless."[21] The

---

[21] However, since Henry wanted to apply a Bible verse to his situation, a more applicable passage would have been Deuteronomy 25:5–10. Verses 5 and 6 state: "When brothers reside together, and one of them dies and has no son, the wife of the deceased shall not be married outside the family to a stranger. Her husband's brother shall go into her, taking her in marriage, and performing the duty of a husband's brother to her, and the firstborn whom she bears shall succeed to the name of the deceased brother, so that his name may not be blotted out of Israel." Verses 7–10 heap scorn upon men who refuse to fulfill their duty. Obviously, this passage supports, not weakens, the legitimacy of Henry's marriage to Catherine.

pope refused to grant the annulment, but Henry found several Catholic scholars who supported his position. In 1533 he secretly married the already pregnant Anne Boleyn and had Thomas Cranmer, the archbishop of Canterbury, annul his marriage to Catherine. As head of the Church of England, Henry could now be granted what Clement had refused him—an annulment. Once this was done, Henry publicly declared his marriage to Anne. The pope quickly excommunicated Henry, but the king responded in 1534 by issuing the Act of Supremacy.

The Act of Supremacy officially severed all ties with Rome and not only made Henry "the only supreme head in earth of the Church of England, called *Anglicans Ecclesia* [Anglican Church]," but the act also made "his heirs and successors" head of the English church. As sovereign of both church and state, Henry accepted the responsibility to "increase" the "virtue in Christ's religion within this realm of England, and to repress and extirpate all errors, heresies, and other enormities and abuses heretofore used in the same," all of which was to be done "to the pleasure of Almighty God, the increase of virtue in Christ's religion, and for the conservation of the peace, unity, and tranquility of" England.[22]

Although remaining staunchly Catholic, Henry enacted several pro-Protestant policies. In 1537 Henry allowed the publication of English versions of parts of the Bible, and then in 1539 he issued the Great Bible and had it placed in every parish church so that the Bible would be more accessible to his people.[23] He even permitted his subjects to read the Bible in the privacy of their own homes. Henry also closed Catholic monasteries, confiscating the Catholic Church's lands and giving much of those lands to nobles in exchange for their support.

Despite his pro-Protestant actions, "What Henry wanted," according to A. C. Underwood, "was Popery without the Pope."[24] Henry's "Popery" is evident in the Act of Six Articles (1539). Called "the bloody whip with six strings" by Protestants, the act, among other things, made it a capital offense

---

[22] "Act of Supremacy (1534)," in *A Reformation Reader: Primary Texts and Introductions*, ed. Denis R. Janz (Minneapolis: Fortress Press, 1999) 285.

[23] F. F. Bruce, *The Books and the Parchments: Some Chapters on the Transmission of the Bible*, rev. ed. (Old Tappan NJ: Fleming H. Revell Company, 1963) 224.

[24] A. C. Underwood, *A History of the English Baptists* (London: The Carey Kingsgate Press Limited, 1947) 28.

to deny the doctrine of transubstantiation or to preach against communion, clerical celibacy, the inviolability of monastic vows, private confessions, and private masses.[25]

Henry's break with Rome gave him the power that he desired. His marriage to Anne, however, did not produce the son that he coveted, although she did give birth to one child, Elizabeth. Still lacking a legitimate male heir and having already played the annulment card once, Henry freed himself from Anne by accusing her of adultery and then by having her beheaded in 1536. Once liberated from Anne, Henry married Jane Seymour, one of Anne's maids. In 1573 Jane gave birth to Henry's long-awaited male heir, Edward.[26]

Edward's Move toward Protestantism

Upon Henry's death in 1547, ten-year-old Edward VI (r. 1547–1553) took the throne. During Henry's life, Reformation principles had spread slowly, but Protestantism took a firmer hold on England during Edward's reign. The young king declared that the pope was "the true son of the Devil, an anti-Christ and an abominable tyrant,"[27] a description many believed fit Edward's father better than it fit the pope. To further Reformation principles in England, Cranmer, one of Edward's main advisors, recognized "that one of the most effective ways of changing what people think is to change the way they worship."[28] Therefore, Edward had the *Book of Common Prayer* printed in English, had worship services conducted in English instead of Latin, rejected the doctrine of transubstantiation, allowed clergy to marry, abolished private confessions, and permitted the laity to receive both the bread and wine at communion.[29]

---

[25] "Act of Six Articles (1539)," in Janz, *A Reformation Reader*, 285–94.

[26] Justo L. González, *The Story of Christianity: The Reformation to the Present Day*, 2 vols. (San Francisco: HarperSanFrancisco, 1985) 2:74–75.

[27] Quoted in Schama, *A History of Britain*, 1:322.

[28] Alister E. McGrath, *Reformation Thought: An Introduction*, 3rd ed. (Oxford: Blackwell Publishers, 1999) 257.

[29] González, *The Story of Christianity*, 2:75–76; McGrath, *Reformation Thought*, 253; John Dillenberger and Claude Welch, *Protestant Christianity Interpreted through Its Development* (New York: Charles Scribner's Sons, 1954) 69.

Mary's Support of Catholicism

When Edward died, Mary Tudor (r. 1553–1558), the daughter of Henry and Catherine, became queen of England. A staunch Catholic, Mary set out to return England to the Catholic fold. She reestablished the pope's authority, returned the lands taken by the Crown to the Catholic Church, ordered married clergy to divorce their wives, and restored feast days to the saints.[30] Though her official title was Queen Mary I, she is best known for her ignominious title, "Bloody Mary." During her reign, the Crown persecuted dissenters, burning nearly 300 of them, imprisoning hundreds more, and driving approximately 800 into exile.[31] Fortunately for dissenters, Mary reigned only five years. Though married, she had no heir to succeed her when she died in 1558.

Elizabeth's Middle Way

Elizabeth I (r. 1558–1603), the daughter of Henry and Anne, succeeded Mary on 17 November 1558. Unsatisfied with either Mary's Catholicism or Edward's Protestantism, Elizabeth advocated a moderate form of Protestantism, a *Via Media*, or a middle way between Catholicism and radical Protestantism. Many of the Maryan exiles returned to England, bringing with them Reformed and Lutheran ideas and continuing the work begun during Mary's reign.

In April 1559 Parliament passed the Act of Supremacy and the Act of Uniformity. The first act required that anyone employed by the government, "every archbishop, bishop, and all and every other ecclesiastical person, and other ecclesiastical officer and minister," publicly declare Elizabeth to be the "supreme governor of this realm, and of all other her highness's dominions and countries, as well in all spiritual or ecclesiastical things or causes, as temporal, and that no foreign prince, person, prelate, state or potentate, has, or ought to have, any jurisdiction, power, superiority, preeminence, or authority ecclesiastical or spiritual, within this realm."[32]

---

[30] See "The Marian Injunctions (1554)," in Janz, *A Reformation Reader*, 310–11.

[31] González, *The Story of Christianity*, 2:76–77.

[32] "Elizabeth's Supremacy Act, Restoring Ancient Jurisdiction, A.D., 1559," in *Documents Illustrative of English Church History*, ed. Henry Gee and William John Hardy (London: Macmillan and Co., Ltd., 1914) 449.

The title change from "supreme head" to "supreme governor" of the church was an attempt to mollify people who insisted that Christ or the pope was the head of the church on earth, although Elizabeth rejected papal authority and considered herself to be the head of both state and church. The act gave her and her "heirs and successors, all manner of jurisdictions, privileges, and pre-eminences, in any wise touching or concerning any spiritual or ecclesiastical jurisdiction, within" their realms "to visit, reform, redress, order, correct, and amend all such errors, heresies, schisms, abuses, offences, contempts, and enormities whatsoever, which by any manner spiritual or ecclesiastical power, authority, or jurisdiction, can or may lawfully be reformed, ordered, redressed, corrected, restrained, or amended, to the pleasure of Almighty God, the increase of virtue, and the conservation of the peace and unity of this realm."[33] From these powers, Elizabeth established a new court, the Commission for Causes Ecclesiastical, known as the High Commission, to investigate, judge, and punish heresy.

The Act of Uniformity made worship services uniform by reinstating the use of the *Book of Common Prayer*, which Mary had removed. Ministers had to use the Prayer Book and to administer the sacraments in the proscribed manner. Ministers who defamed the Prayer Book, used other prayers, or refused to participate in any rite established by law were subject to a six-month imprisonment and to the loss of all their benefits. The act also required lay people to attend Sunday and holiday worship services or else be fined.[34]

In 1563 the Church of England revised Edward's Forty-Two Articles and issued instead the Thirty-Nine Articles (1563), which formed the foundation of the Church of England and established a moderate form of Protestantism.[35] Neither Catholics nor many Protestants could accept these articles of faith, forcing both groups to worship in secret.[36]

During the latter part of Elizabeth's reign, many people began to question the queen's middle way in religion, believing that she had not gone far enough to rid England of Catholic influences or to instill a more

---

[33] Ibid., 448.

[34] "Elizabeth's Act of Uniformity, A. D. 1559," in Gee and Hardy, *Documents Illustrative of English Church History*, 458–67.

[35] "The Thirty-nine Articles (1563)," in Janz, *A Reformation Reader*, 317–23.

[36] González, *The Story of Christianity*, 2:79–80.

dogmatic Protestantism in the Anglican Church. Called Puritans for their attempt to purify the doctrines and worship of the established church, this group sought to reform the church from within by simplifying worship patterns, modifying governance, and adopting more reformed, Calvinistic doctrines. They opposed many of the traditional elements of worship that the Church of England had retained from Catholicism, such as making the sign of the cross at baptism, the wearing of priestly vestments by the clergy, bowing at the name of Jesus, and kneeling at communion.[37] The Puritans emphasized preaching more than ceremony as the best way to inform the faithful and criticized the "dumb dogs" and "destroying drones" who, in their opinion, preached in most Anglican pulpits. Even worse than these pathetic preachers were the immoral parsons who spent much of their time getting drunk, playing cards, and fathering children out of wedlock.[38]

Puritans also insisted on the need for living a more disciplined life. For example, they denounced drunkenness and condemned theater attendance. With such an unspiritual and largely immoral clergy leading the Anglican Church, it was no wonder that, according to the Puritans, most church members could not articulate their religious beliefs. Most Puritans also objected to the state's control of religion, preferring instead for the church to use the state to protect and promote the Christian (Puritan) religion. They also opposed the office of bishop, the heart of Anglicanism, a position they said was unbiblical. Instead, Puritans believed that presbyters or elders elected by individual congregations should govern churches. Responding to the growing influence of Puritanism, Parliament passed the Act against Puritans in 1593, which instituted the punishment of people who did not attend the worship services of the Church of England as well as people who attended services held at conventicles (illegal worship services).[39]

Sometime around 1580, a small group of Puritans concluded that trying to reform the Anglican Church from within was a lost cause, and rather than remain in the church and fight a losing battle, these Puritans

---

[37] Ibid., 2:150; Edwin S. Gaustad, *Roger Williams*, Lives and Legacies (Oxford: Oxford University Press, 2005) 3.

[38] Edmund S. Morgan, *Visible Saints: The History of the Puritan Idea* (Ithaca NY: Cornell University Press, 1963) 7–9.

[39] "The Act against Puritans, A. D. 1593," in Gee and Hardy, *Documents Illustrative of English*, 492–98.

separated themselves, formed their own congregations, chose their own leaders, and practiced a congregational church governance. Because of their actions, members of this group were called Separatists.

Elizabeth, the "virgin queen," died in 1603, leaving no direct heir to the throne, but she had previously declared that James Stuart, the son of her cousin Queen Mary of Scotland, was to be her successor. Having been forced by Scottish Protestants to abdicate her throne in 1567, Mary had fled to England, where she was beheaded in 1587 for her role in a plot to overthrow Elizabeth.

James's Promise

In July 1567, when Mary's son James was just thirteen months old, he became James VI, King of Scotland. Several men and a tutor, who abhorred his mother, raised him, teaching him "too much theology and too little morals," according to Will and Ariel Durant.[40] James's main tutor was George Buchanan, a staunch Calvinist and the leading political theorist among Scotch Presbyterians.[41] In his book *De juri regni apud Scotos* (1579), Buchanan justified the forced abdication of Queen Mary, arguing that monarchs who fail to serve their people should be removed from the throne. Buchanan's view of James in particular and of sovereigns in general was perhaps best expressed in his response to the Countess of Mar, who protested one of Buchanan's paddlings of the toddler king: "Madam, I have whipt his arse, you may kiss it if you please."[42] Buchanan's influence on James was so strong that even after the king had "banned Buchanan's books, the old flogger continued to haunt his royal pupil, visiting his dreams as late as 1622" and predicting a hellish end for the sovereign.[43]

---

[40] Will Durant and Ariel Durant, *The Story of Civilization*, part 7, *The Age of Reason Begins: A History of European Civilization in the Period of Shakespeare, Bacon, Montaigne, Rembrandt, Galileo, and Descartes: 1558–1648* (New York: Simon and Schuster, 1961) 131.

[41] See Herbert L. Osgood, "The Political Ideas of the Puritans, I," *Political Science Quarterly* 6 (March 1891): 10–11, http://www.dinsdoc.com/osgood–5.htm (accessed 20 March 2005).

[42] Simon Schama, *A History of Britain: The Wars of the British, 1603–1776*, 3 vols. (New York: Hyperion, 2001) 2:25.

[43] Ibid., 2:26.

Upon Elizabeth's death, James (now James I of England [r. 1603–1625]) made his way from Edinburgh to London, knighting many people along the route. In a speech to Parliament shortly after arriving in England, James recounted the worshipful reception he had received from his adoring subjects:

> Shall I ever? No, can I ever be able, or rather so unable in memory, as to forget your unexpected readiness and alacrity, your ever memorable resolution, and your most wonderful conjunction and harmony of your hearts in declaring and embracing me as your undoubted and lawful king and governor? Or shall it ever be blotted out of my mind, how at my first entry into this kingdom, the people of all sorts rid and ran, no rather flew to meet me? Their eyes flaming nothing but sparkles of affection, their mouths and tongues uttering nothing but sounds of joy, their hands, feet, and all the rest of their members in their gestures discovering a passionate longing, and earnestness to meet and embrace their new sovereign.[44]

Of course, many Londoners had enthusiastically greeted Queens Mary and Elizabeth when they had entered the capital city to begin their reigns, but James was the kind of person who would have interpreted those receptions as originating solely from a sense of duty. He interpreted the crowd's response to him, however, as something special, a love and adoration expressed to someone who deserved such love and adoration.

James's attitude toward religion is discussed further in the next chapter, but for now suffice it to say that he firmly believed, as did his predecessors and successors, that as monarch he ruled both church and state. Nonconformists could "conform, at a great cost to" their consciences, "or…enter prison, at great cost to their welfare and perhaps their lives."[45] As

---

[44] James I, "A Speech, As It Was Delivered in the Upper House of the Parliament to the Lords Spirituall and Temporall, and to the Knights, Citizens and Burgesses there assembled, on Monday the 19th Day of March 1603. Being the First Day of the first Parliament," in *King James VI and I: Selected Writings*, ed. Neil Rhodes, Jennifer Richards, and Joseph Marshall (Aldershot, Hants England: Ashgate Publishing Company, 2003) 293–94. In the old style (Julian) calendar, March 25 was the beginning of the New Year. In the new style (Gregorian) calendar, the New Year begins on January 1, so under this calendar, James delivered this speech in 1604.

[45] Gaustad, *Roger Williams*, 4.

for people who chose neither conformity nor prison, James promised to run them out of England, and he spent much of his time making good on that promise.[46]

The Baptists' Beginning

Among the many British subjects who helped fulfill James's promise to drive nonconformists out of England were John Smyth (c. 1570–1612) and Thomas Helwys (1550? or 1575?–c. 1616).[47] Smyth had embraced Puritan teachings while attending Christ's College in Cambridge from 1586 to 1593. After graduating with an MA in 1593, he became a teaching fellow at the college and in 1594 was ordained as a minister in the Church of England by the bishop of Lincoln.[48] In 1598 Smyth married and left his position at Christ's College. Apparently, he spent the next two years as a parish minister.[49] In 1600 the city of Lincoln elected Smyth as lecturer,[50] a position

---

[46] Christopher Hill, *The Century of Revolution, 1603–1714*, The Norton Library History of England (New York: W. W. Norton & Company, Inc., 1961) 9, 81.

[47] Biographical information on Smyth and Helwys can be found in any general work on the history of Baptists, in biographical dictionaries, and in the following: for Smyth, see Walter H. Burgess, *John Smith the Se-Baptist, Thomas Helwys and the First Baptist Church in England, with Fresh Light upon the Pilgrim Fathers' Church* (London: James Clarke & Co., 1913) 27–106; James Robert Coggins, *John Smyth's Congregation: English Separatism, Mennonite Influence, and the Elect Nation*, Studies in Anabaptist and Mennonite History, no. 32 (Waterloo Ontario: Herald Press, 1991); Jason K. Lee, *The Theology of John Smyth: Puritan, Separatist, Baptist, Mennonite* (Macon GA: Mercer University Press, 2003) 41–95; James E. Tull, *Shapers of Baptist Thought* (Valley Forge PA: Judson Press, 1972) 13–15; W. T. Whitley, "Biography," in *The Works of John Smyth, Fellow of Christ's College, 1594–8*, 2 vols. (Cambridge: University Press, 1915) 1:xvii–cxxii; for Helwys, see Burgess, *John Smith the Se-Baptist, Thomas Helwys and the First Baptist Church in England*, 107–119; J. Glenwood Clayton, "Thomas Helwys: A Baptist Founding Father," *Baptist History and Heritage* 8/1 (January 1973): 2–8; F. W. Clonts, "Thomas Helwys and His Book, *The Mistery of Iniquity*," *Review and Expositor* 41/4 (October 1944): 373–76; Richard Groves, introduction to *A Short Declaration of the Mystery of Iniquity (1611/1612)*, by Thomas Helwys, Classics of Religious Liberty 1 (Macon GA: Mercer University Press, 1998) xix–xxvi; and W. T. Whitley, "Thomas Helwys of Gray's Inn and of Broxtowe Hall, Nottingham," *Baptist Quarterly* 7/6 (April 1935): 241–55.

[48] Tull, *Shapers of Baptist Thought*, 13.

[49] Whitley, "Biography," 1:xxxvi–xxxvii.

he held for only two years because his church fired him for preaching sermons critical of some of the city's leading citizens.[51]

What Smyth did the next three years is unknown, but in 1606 he moved Gainsborough, approximately 132 miles north of London, where he lectured and also practiced medicine, a profession that required only a few weeks of study.[52] He also became a minister of a Separatist congregation that John Robinson, William Brewster, and William Bradford had organized. As the hostility toward Separatists increased, so did the size of the Gainsborough congregation. By 1607 Smyth's church at Gainsborough had grown too large to meet openly and safely. The church chose to divide into two groups, one led by Robinson, Brewster, and Bradford; the other by Smyth. Sometime in 1607 or 1608, the two groups fled to Holland, a haven for religious dissenters. The Robinson-Brewster-Bradford group went first to Amsterdam, then to Leyden; the Smyth group settled at Amsterdam. Helwys, a wealthy layman, partially funded the Smyth group's passage to Holland.

Helwys most likely encountered Puritan and Separatist teachings while a student in London at Gray's Inn, a law school that also provided general education for the sons of wealthy landowners.[53] In fleeing to Holland, Helwys left behind his wife, Joan, and seven children. Although Helwys escaped English authorities, his wife was not so fortunate. Shortly after the Smyth group fled, Joan was arrested and jailed for refusing to swear her loyalty to the Church of England. Apparently, she was released within several weeks because she returned to court a few months later.[54] Her fate after this court appearance is unknown.

In Amsterdam, Smyth's group rented a bakery owned by Jan Munter, a wealthy Mennonite merchant.[55] Smyth's congregation met Dutch Mennonites, who advocated religious liberty and baptized believers only, not infants. The influence of these Mennonites on the congregation is

---

[50] Robert G. Torbet, *A History of the Baptists*, 3rd ed. (Valley Forge PA: Judson Press, 1963) 33. Lecturers spoke to congregations outside of a formal worship setting.

[51] Ibid.

[52] Whitley, "Biography," 1:lvi.

[53] Clayton, "Thomas Helwys: A Baptist Founding Father," 3.

[54] Groves, introduction to *A Short Declaration of the Mystery of Iniquity*, xxi.

[55] Coggins, *John Smyth's Congregation*, 72.

debatable.[56] However, Smyth's followers did change some of their theological beliefs after arriving in Holland.

After studying the Bible again, particularly the New Testament, Smyth's followers concluded that a true church should be made up of believers who publicly confessed Christ as Lord and who then experienced believer's baptism. Consequently, they also concluded that theirs was not a true church, so they disbanded and proceeded to plan a baptismal service that occurred either in late 1608 or early in 1609. Because none of the group had been baptized as believers, Smyth baptized himself, probably by pouring water over himself, and then the others, thereby forming a new church.[57] Thus, the people called Baptists began as a group of English men and women who met in a bakery owned by a Dutch Mennonite. General Baptists, those who believed that Christ died for all people, trace their

---

[56] Baptist historians disagree about the antecedent influences on the Baptist faith. Some historians trace Baptist beginnings to the English Separatist movement. Other scholars have linked Baptist origins to the Anabaptist movement, and although they acknowledge that the Baptist faith grew out of the English Separatist movement, they also recognize the influence of the Anabaptists on early Baptists. See Coggins, *John Smyth's Congregation*, 69–107; W. R. Estep, "Anabaptists and the Rise of English Baptists," *Quarterly Review* 28/4 (October-December 1968): 43–53 and 29/1 (January–March 1969): 50–62; William R., Estep, Jr., "On the Origins of English Baptists," *Baptist History and Heritage* 22/2 (April 1987): 19–26; William R. Estep, *The Anabaptist Story* (Grand Rapids MI: William B. Eerdmans Publishing Company, 1975) 206–30; Winthrop S. Hudson, "Baptists Were Not Anabaptists," *Chronicle* 20/1 (October 1953): 171–79; Lonnie D. Kliever, "General Baptist Origins: The Question of Anabaptist Influence," *Mennonite Quarterly Review* 36/4 (October 1962): 291–321; Bill J. Leonard, *Baptist Ways: A History* (Valley Forge PA: Judson Press, 2003) 18–43; Kenneth Ross Manley, "Origins of the Baptists: The Case for Development from Puritanism-Separatism," *Baptist History and Heritage* 12/4 (October 1987): 34–46; H. Leon McBeth, *The Baptist Heritage: Four Centuries of Baptist Witness* (Nashville: Broadman Press, 1987) 49–60; James D. Mosteller, "Baptists and Anabaptists I: The Genius of Anabaptism," *Chronicle* 20/1 (January 1957): 3–27; James D. Mosteller, "Baptists and Anabaptists II: John Smyth and the Dutch Mennonites," *Chronicle* 20/3 (July 1957): 100–114; and Earnest A. Payne, "Who Were the Baptists?," *Baptist Quarterly* 16/8 (October 1956): 339–42.

[57] John Robinson claimed that members of Smyth's congregation told him about this event. John Robinson, *Of Religious Communion, Private and Public* (n.p., 1614), in *The Works of John Robinson, Pastor of the Pilgrim Fathers*, ed. Robert Ashton, 3 vols. (London: John Snow, 1851) 3:168.

beginning to this congregation. Another type of Baptists known as Particular Baptists began in England in the 1630s and taught that Christ died to save only those persons whom God had elected to salvation.

When Smyth came in contact with the Waterlander Mennonite congregation in Amsterdam in 1609, he determined that this group comprised a true church, and he concluded that he should have sought baptism from one of their ministers. After much soul-searching, Smyth questioned the validity of his self-baptism. Controversy then arose in the new church concerning the succession of the Christian ministry from apostolic times. Most members agreed with Smyth that only ministers who had been properly baptized could administer baptism. Helwys and ten to twelve others disagreed.[58] As a result, the church split into two groups over this issue, and in 1610 a minority led by Helwys excommunicated Smyth and thirty-one others.[59] The Smyth group eventually joined the Waterlander Mennonite congregation in January 1615,[60] but long after Smyth died on 20 August 1612, probably from tuberculosis.

The Helwys group decided in 1611 to return to England to bear witness to their Christian faith. Before returning home, Helwys authored a confession titled *A Declaration of Faith of the English People Remaining at Amsterdam in Holland*. The confession is notable for many things, but one article stands out. Article 11 stated that "particular congregations" should gather "to pray, prophecy, break bread, and administer in all the holy ordinances" even if they do not have any "officers, or that their officers

---

[58] For Helwys's position, see Coggins, *John Smyth's Congregation*, 97–103, 147; Whitley, "Thomas Helwys of Gray's Inn," 249; Thomas Helwys, *An Advertisement or Admonition unto the Congregations* (n.p., 1611) 20–55, available at http://www.baptist libraryonline.com/library/Helwys/admonition.pdf.; Thomas Helwys, *A Declaration of Faith of English People Remaining at Amsterdam in Holland* (n.p., 1611), in *Baptist Confessions of Faith*, ed. William L. Lumpkin (Philadelphia: Judson Press, 1959) 120, article 11; and Thomas Helwys et. al. to the Waterland Church, 12 March 1609/1610, in the following sources: Champlin Burrage, *The Early English Dissenters in the Light of Recent Research: Illustrative Documents*, 2 vols. (Cambridge: University Press, 1912) 2:184–86; Benjamin Evans, *The Early English Baptists*, 2 vols. (London: J. Heaton & Son, 1862) 1:209–10; and Coggins, *John Smyth's Congregation*, 171.

[59] Clonts, "Thomas Helwys and His Book, *The Mistery of Iniquity*," 375.

[60] Whitley, "Biography," 1:cxiv–cxv.

should be in prison, sick, or by any other means hindered from the church."[61]

Helwys had perhaps already printed his book *A Short Declaration of the Mystery of Iniquity* before returning to England. In the appendix of *The Mystery of Iniquity*, he declared that no one should think that, in returning to England, he and his church were "altogether ignorant, what building, and warfare we take in hand, and that we have not sat down and in some measure thoroughly considered what the cost and danger may be."[62] Considering that Helwys died in an English prison, an event discussed in the next chapter, one might say that Helwys's statements were prophetic. Yet he did not have to be a prophet to know that he and his church would encounter persecution if they returned to England.

When the small band of Baptists returned home in 1611, they returned to a land where monarchs hardly ever demonstrated any tolerance toward religious dissenters. Yet monarchs are powerless unless some of their people are willing to enforce conformity. Many Englanders in Helwys's day held the same zealous opinions of the anonymous author of *Against Universall Libertie of Conscience*. Writing in the early 1640s, the author stated that if God called him to suffer for the truth, he would suffer gladly. If, however, God called him "to fight for the truth," he would willingly wield the sword to honor God and to save souls.[63] The author also quoted what he considered to be a wise saying: "It is better to live in that commonwealth where nothing is lawful, than where everything [is lawful]." He applied this saying to the religious situation in England, stating, "I had rather live among Barbarians, amongst whom nothing of the true religion is suffered, than

---

[61] *A Declaration of Faith of English People Remaining at Amsterdam in Holland*, 120.

[62] Thomas Helwys, *A Short Declaration of the Mystery of Iniquity (1611/1612)*, Classics of Religious Liberty 1, ed. Richard Groves (Macon GA: Mercer University Press, 1998) 154. A 1612 edition of this book is available at http://www.baptistlibraryonline.com/library/Helwys/mystery.pdf. Helwys derived his title from 2 Thessalonians 2:7 (KJV): "For the mystery of iniquity doth already work: only he who now letteth will let, until he be taken out of the way."

[63] *Against Universall Libertie of Conscience, Being Animadversions upon Two Letters Written to a Friend Pleading for It* (London: printed for Thomas Underhill, 1644) 5.

anywhere in the world [where] all religions [are] suffered."[64] Here is an example of someone who was not only willing to die for his faith; he was willing to force people to conform to that faith. For people like him, Baptists provided numerous opportunities to wield the temporal sword.

Particularly in the 1640s, the opponents of Baptists accused them of practically every sin imaginable, such as:

1. Baptists preached heresy, by rejecting infant baptism, limiting baptism to believers only and re-baptizing people who had been baptized as infants.

2. Baptists met secretly, which many of their opponents rightly interpreted as demonstrating that they held themselves to be religiously superior. Many people suspected that Baptists used these meetings to plot rebellion.

3. Most Baptist ministers lacked any theological education and had not been ordained, which meant that they were intellectually and spiritually unfit to preach.

4. Baptists demanded religious liberty or liberty of conscience, which endeared them to no one except perhaps a few other dissenting groups.[65]

In summary, opponents of Baptists accused them of being anarchists who endangered the very existence of England; they were heretics who threatened the purity of the Christian religion; and they were a lazy, deceitful, morally decadent group.

Contrary to their opponents' characterization of them, Baptists claimed to preach not heresy but the truth:

1. Preaching a believers' church, most Baptist churches only accepted people who had confessed their faith in Christ.

2. Professing a gathered church, Baptists argued that people should choose rather than be forced to attend church.

3. Practicing a congregational form of church government, Baptists churches contended that they could choose whomever they wanted to be their pastor, even uneducated and unordained men.

---

[64] Ibid. See also James VI, "The Trew Law of Free Monarchies: Or the Reciprock and mutuall duetie betwtixt a free King, and his naturall Subjects," in Rhodes, Richards, and Marshall, *King James VI and I*, 275.

[65] See Gordon Kingsley, "Opposition to Early Baptists (1638–1645)," *Baptist History and Heritage* 4/1 (January 1969) 18–30, 66.

4. Advocating religious liberty, Baptists denied the state's and the Church of England's attempts to force people to worship in any manner against their consciences.

Such beliefs and practices comprise part of what have been called "convictional" or "spiritual genes" that have shaped and continue to shape Baptists.[66] No genome, however, is perfect. For example, each person carries four to five defective genes and perhaps ten or more that are moderately flawed.[67] Most non-Baptists in the seventeenth and eighteenth centuries considered the Baptist "genes" to be genetic defects, ones that had to be eliminated from the body of Christ lest they be "inherited" by others. To rid the church and the state of such defective "genes," many government and church leaders called for radical surgery. The civil magistrates and ecclesiastical leaders used the power of the secular government to harass, fine, and imprison Baptists. As the early Baptist historian Joseph Ivimey

---

[66] See the report of the Commission on Denomination of the American Baptist Churches, U. S. A., in the entire issue of the *American Baptist Quarterly* 6/2 (June1987). For a summary of the report, see Walter B. Shurden, *The Baptist Identity: Four Fragile Freedoms* (Macon GA: Smyth & Helwys Publishing, Inc., 1993) 117–19. Concerning Baptist "genes," see William H. Brackney, *A Genetic History of Baptist Thought: With Special Reference to Baptists in Britain and North America* (Macon GA: Mercer University Press, 2004) 527–38, and Walter B. Shurden, "The Baptist Identity and the Baptist *Manifesto*," in *Not an Easy Journey: Some Transitions in Baptist Life*, by Walter B. Shurden (Macon GA: Mercer University Press, 2005) 45–46. Shurden's article is also available at http://www.centerforbaptiststudies.org/ shurden/Baptist%20Manifesto.htm, (accessed 13 July 2007). The term "gene," of course, cannot be taken literally, nor is it intended to be, for beliefs are not transmitted physically. Beliefs are what the biologist Richard Dawkins termed "memes," which are ideas that pass from "brain to brain" rather from "gene to gene." See Holmes Rolston, III, *Genes, Genesis and God: Values and Their Origins in Natural and Human History*, The Gifford Lectures, University of Edinburgh, 1997–1998 (Cambridge: University Press, 1999) 145–46, 332. In his *A Genetic History of Baptist Thought*, Brackney illustrated this point clearly: "Ideas pass from one pastor to another, or from tract to a treatise. These enduring ideas are the 'genes' of Baptist thought" (528). Although technically "memes" is a more correct term, "genes" communicates better, for who would want to read, let alone understand, a book titled *A Memetic History of Baptist Thought?*

[67] Francis S. Collins, "The Human Genome Project," in *Genetic Ethics: Do the Ends Justify the Genes?*, ed. John F. Kilner, Rebecca D. Pentz, and Frank E. Young (Grand Rapids MI: William B. Eerdmans Publishing Company, 1997) 100.

observed, "Most of our county jails have been consecrated by the residence of the suffering servants of Christ."[68]

Jailing Baptists, however, did not silence them because even in prison Baptists continued to preach and to write letters, poems, and books. Only death could ultimately silence their voices and pens, yet even then other Baptists were ready to take their place and continue to preach the Baptist faith and message.

---

[68] Joseph Ivimey, *A History of the English Baptists*, 4 vols. (London: printed for the author, 1814) 2:102.

Chapter 2

To Church or to Prison

On the ceiling in the Banqueting House of Whitehall Palace in London are affixed nine paintings celebrating the rule of James I. Four years after James died, his son Charles I, king of England, commissioned the Flemish artist Peter Paul Rubens to honor his deceased father by painting a mural for the ceiling panels. The result was a breathtaking portrayal of monarchial propaganda.[1] The center panel depicts "The Apotheosis of James I," portraying the king, surrounded by cherubim, being taken to heaven. The location of the paintings makes for difficult viewing, forcing spectators to strain their necks to see the larger-than-life portrayal of James in all of his grandeur. Yet one can only imagine that James would have approved not only the message of the paintings but also their location. After all, he believed that he was God's chosen man for England and that his subjects should be forced to look up to God's "anointed."

James I Chooses the Church of England

When James I became king of England in 1603 after the death of Elizabeth, religious groups in England hoped to win the king's favor. James's support of Presbyterianism in Scotland encouraged Puritans. Roman Catholics took heart in that James's wife and his mother were Catholic. Anglicans believed that the king would favor the Church of England because

---

[1] For a view of the entire ceiling, see http://www.24hourmuseum.org.uk/nwh/ART25571.html, (accessed 3 May 2005). For close-ups of the three main panels, see the following: for "The Apotheosis of James I," http://www.hermitagemuseum.org/html_En/04/b2003/hm4_2_043_1.html (accessed 3 May 2005); and for "The Union of the Crowns" and "The Peaceful Reign of James I," see Simon Schama, *A History of Britain: The Wars of the British, 1603–1776*, 3 vols. (New York: Hyperion, 2001) 2:34–35.

its bishops advanced the concept dear to every monarch's heart—the divine right to rule.[2]

However, in James's opinion, and in the opinion of the Anglican Church, too many individuals were reading the scriptures for themselves, spending time focusing on self-reflection, and worshiping at home. Such activities divided both church and state. Therefore, James determined to unify the Church of England. Puritans regarded James's desire to unify the established church as "amoral spinelessness." God himself, the Puritans taught, had divided humanity into two groups, the saved and the damned, so the king should forgo his "big-tent Church" policy of trying to unite loyal Puritans and loyal Catholics into the Church of England. Puritans wanted James to clean his ecclesiastical house, ridding it of all vestiges of Catholicism and promoting true preaching and teaching.[3]

To discuss the religious situation in England, James held a conference in January 1604 between Anglican bishops and Puritan representatives at Hampton Court Palace, near London. On the second day of the conference when John Reynolds, a Puritan representative, mentioned a "presbytery," James became "somewhat stirred" because a presbytery, he declared, agreed "with a monarchy, as God, and the Devil." James believed that as the bishops go, so goes the king, or as he put it, "No bishop, no king." Rising from his chair to leave the room, the king uttered this warning to those who might object to his religious policies: "I shall make them conform themselves, or I will harry them out of the land, or do worse."[4] Such words thrilled the bishops, for if James knew that "no bishop, no king," the bishops also knew that "no king, no bishop."[5]

---

[2] H. Leon McBeth, *The Baptist Heritage: Four Centuries of Baptist Witness* (Nashville: Broadman Press, 1987) 100.

[3] Schama, *A History of Britain*, 2:41.

[4] Quoted in Edward P. Cheyney, ed., *Readings in English History Drawn from the Original Sources* (New York: Ginn and Company, 1922) 431.

[5] Charles Howard McIlwain, introduction to *The Political Works of James I*, ed. Charles Howard McIlwain (London: n.p., 1616; repr., Cambridge MA: Harvard University Press, 1918) http://www.perseus.tufts.edu/cgi-bin/ptext?doc=Perseus %3Atext%3A1999.03.0071&query=head%3D%233 (accessed 13 July 2007).

Thomas Helwys Challenges the King's Authority in Religious Matters

Thomas Helwys was one of James's subjects whom the king "harried out of England." Having overcome their "fear of men" by God's grace, Helwys and his church returned to England from Holland in 1611, settling at Spitalfields, outside the city walls of London, to "declare to prince and people plainly their transgressions, that all might hear and see their fearful estate and standing, and repent and turn to the Lord."[6] Part of Helwys's declaration consisted in sending his book *A Short Declaration of the Mystery of Iniquity* to James, perhaps even personally delivering it to him.[7] On the flyleaf of the book Helwys wrote a personal note to the king: "Men's religion to God is between God and themselves. The king shall not answer for it. Neither may the king be judge between God and man. Let them be heretics, Turks, Jews or whatsoever, it appertains not to the earthly power to punish them in the least measure."[8]

To characterize Helwys's statements as bold would be an understatement. One could argue that they were suicidal, for James, like other monarchs before and after him, claimed to have a unique relationship with God and with his subjects. According to James: "The state of monarchy is the supremest thing upon earth" because "kings...are...God's lieutenants" who sit on "God's throne" and are called "by God himself...gods.... In the scriptures kings are called gods, and so their power after a certain relation compared to the divine power."[9] "Kings" are also the Lord's "anointed...the breathing images of God upon earth."[10]

---

[6] Thomas Helwys, *A Short Declaration of the Mystery of Iniquity (1611/1612)*, Classics of Religious Liberty 1, ed. Richard Groves (Macon GA: Mercer University Press, 1998) 1.

[7] W. T. Whitley, "Thomas Helwys of Gray's Inn and of Broxtowe Hall, Nottingham," *Baptist Quarterly* 7/6 (April 1935): 250–52.

[8] Helwys, *A Short Declaration of the Mystery of Iniquity*, 53.

[9] James I, "A Speech to the Lords and Commons of the Parliament at White-Hall, on Wednesday the 21st of March. Anno 1609," in *King James VI and I: Selected Writings*, ed. Neil Rhodes, Jennifer Richards, and Joseph Marshall (Aldershot, Hants England: Ashgate Publishing Company, 2003) 327. Psalm 82:6 says, "I [God] say, 'You are gods.'" Even Helwys granted that such a lofty title belonged to the king (*A Short Declaration of the Mystery of Iniquity*, 45).

[10] James I, "A Remonstrance for the Right of Kings, and the Independence of Their Crownes, Against an Oration or the Most Illustrious Card. Of Perron,

When James I claimed that God put him on the throne, he meant it and made sure that, although God in heaven might forgive dissenters for their transgressions toward the godly monarch, they would have hell to pay on earth. James declared that to dispute what God does is blasphemous and that to dispute what the king "may do in the height of his power" is seditious: "I will not be content that my power be disputed."[11] To question the king's authority by delving into "the mystery of the king's power," James claimed, was "to wade into the weakness of princes, and to take away the mystical reverence that belongs to those who sit in the throne of God."[12]

James's special relationship with God had ramifications for his people. James contended that as the "over-lord of the whole land," the king is the "master over every person that inhabits the same, having power over the life and death of every one of them."[13] Because of their God-like powers, kings could, like God,

> make and unmake their subjects: they have power of raising and casting down: of life, and of death.... They have power to exalt low things, and abase high things, and make of their subjects like men at the [game of] chess: a pawn to take a bishop or a knight, and to cry up or down any of their subjects, as they do their money.... For to emperors, or kings who are monarchs, their subjects' bodies and goods are due for their defense and maintenance.... Now a father may dispose of his inheritance to his children, at his pleasure: yes, even disinherit the eldest upon just occasions and prefer the youngest, according to his liking; [he may] make them beggars or rich at his pleasure; restrain or banish out of his presence, as he

---

Pronounced in the Chamber of the Third Estate. Jan. 15. 1615," in McIlwain, *The Political Works of James I*, http://www.perseus.tufts.edu/cgi-bin/ptext?doc=Perseus: text:1999.03.0071&query=page%3D%23271 (accessed 13 July 2007).

[11] James I, "A Speech to the Lords and Commons of the Parliament at White-Hall," 330.

[12] James I, "A Speech in the Starre-Chamber, the 20th of June. Anno 1616," in McIlwain, *The Political Works of James I*, http://www.perseus.tufts.edu/cgi-bin/ptext?doc=Perseus%3Atext%3A1999.03.0071;query=page%3D%23426;layout=;loc=(accessed 13 July 2007).

[13] James VI, "The Trew Law of Free Monarchies," in Rhodes, Richards, and Marshall, *King James VI and I: Selected Writings*, 271.

finds them give cause of offence, or restore them in favor again with
the penitent sinner: So may the king deal with his subjects.[14]

As the "Supreme Governor" of his subjects, James maintained that part
of his duty was "to maintain the religion...professed within their
country...and to punish all those that should press to alter or disturb the
profession thereof."[15] Although the king had no authority to develop new
articles of faith, he did have the authority to defend the faith already
articulated "by reforming...religion according to his prescribed will, by
assisting the spiritual power with the temporal sword, by reforming of
corruption, by procuring due obedience to the church, by judging, and
cutting off all frivolous questions and schisms, as Constantine did."[16]

Despite demanding absolute loyalty from his subjects, James still
maintained that a Christian's first duty was to God and that no one should
be forced to violate his or her conscience.[17] Yet James's understanding of the
Crown's role in religion obviously caused problems because religious
dissenters believed that they could discern God's will for themselves without
the aid of civil or ecclesiastical power. In James's opinion, non-conformists
were free to follow their consciences as long as they were led to the true
church, the Church of England.

Despite his God-given authority to wield the sword in the name of the
Lord, James did not think that the physical coercion of dissenters would
ultimately be successful. Above all, he professed that people needed "inward
grace" if they were to abandon their heresies, and the best way for them to
change was by the persuasive doctrines and examples of ministers. If,
however, such persuasion failed, "the magistrate must compel and...leave

---

[14] James I, "A Speech to the Lords and Commons of the Parliament at White-
Hall," 327–28.

[15] James VI, "The Trew Law of Free Monarchies," 261.

[16] James I, "*Triplici Nodo, Triplex Cuneus*. Or An Apologie for the Oath of
Allegiance. Against the Two Breves of Pope Paulus Qunitus, and the Late Letter of
Cardinall Bellarmine to G. Blackwel the Arch-Priest," in McIlwain, *The Political
Works of James I*, http://www.perseus.tufts.edu/cgi-bin/ptext?doc=Perseus%
3Atext%3A1999.03.0071;query=head%3D%2324;layout=;loc= (accessed 13 July
2007).

[17] W. K. Jordan, *The Development of Religious Toleration in England: From the
Accession of James I to the Convention of the Long Parliament (1603–1640)*, 4 vols.
(Cambridge MA: Harvard University Press, 1936) 2:30.

the success to God, for it is not good to trust to a good cause and let it go alone."[18] James believed that people who disagreed with a law should express their opinions peacefully and not cause rebellion or divisions. Nevertheless, if persuasion and reason failed to bring dissenters to the true faith, the king could then resort to compulsion.

Before becoming king of England in 1603, James had claimed that religious persecution was a mark of a false church, and during the last years of Elizabeth's reign, he had proclaimed himself to be a proponent of religious liberty and had even intervened on behalf of some prisoners of conscience.[19] However, in 1612, James ordered the execution of two heretics, Bartholomew Legate and Edward Wightman, both of whom were burned at the stake. These men were not executed for the sake of conscience but, the king maintained, for the sake of national security. In 1616, for example, James asserted "That no man, either in my time, or in the late Queen's, ever died here for his conscience." People are in no danger for what they believe unless they commit "some outward act expressly against the words of the law or plot...some unlawful or dangerous practice or attempt."[20] Thus, the Crown considered Legate and Wightman to be schismatics who, by propagating their beliefs, threatened the unity of the kingdom and were therefore the enemies of both church and state. After the executions, the public had had enough of the torching of dissenters, and Wightman apparently holds the unfortunate distinction of being the last person in England to be burned at the stake for heresy. Thus, dissenters like Helwys would be spared a martyr's death (or a heretic's death depending on who was asked) by being burned at the stake, though nothing prevented them from being cast into prison to rot.

Whether James ever read Helwys's *Short Declaration of the Mystery of Iniquity* remains a mystery, but the essence of the Baptist leader's message to "God's lieutenant," "the Lord's anointed," the "breathing image of God on earth," could be summarized this way:

---

[18] Quoted ibid., 2:31, n. 1.

[19] Ibid., 2:32–33.

[20] James I, "A Premonition to All Most Mightie Monarches, Kings, Free Princes, and State of Christendome," in McIlwain, *The Political Works of James I*, http://www.perseus.tufts.edu/cgi-bin/ptext?doc=Perseus%3Atext%3A1999.03.0071 ;query=page%3D%23210;layout=;loc= (accessed 13 July 2007)

Since you liken life to a game of chess, you need to remember that, like the pawns, the king is merely a piece on the game board, not the Master Player. You may rule my body, which I concede, but you may not rule my conscience. Read my book so that you will understand that one day you will give an account of the way you deal with "heretics," and after you finish it, you will stop letting the Anglican bishops manipulate you, you will disestablish the Anglican Church, and you will allow people to worship or not worship God according to the dictates of their consciences. If you heed my advice, you will then become the godly magistrate that you wrongly think that you are now.

But as Helwys was one of James's chess pieces in the game between monarch and subjects, His Highness moved Helwys from Spitalfields to London's Newgate Prison, which for Helwys meant being checkmated.

Built sometime in the twelfth century, Newgate was infamous for its wretched conditions.[21] In 1612, an anonymous author, perhaps a former inmate, described the prison's deplorable conditions in his pamphlet *The Discovery of a London Monster Called, the Black Dog of Newgate*, which was sold at the gate of Gray's Inn, located a half mile from the prison. Like a modern scientist describing a black hole, the author depicted his cell as an

> …irksome den,
> > Where was no day, for there was ever night:
> Woes me, thought I, the object of all men,
> > Clouded in care, quite banished from light:
> Rob'd of the Skie, the Stars, the Day, the Sun,
> This Dog, this Devill, hath all my joyes undone.[22]

Newgate was a hell-hole filled with hopelessness and terror, and if there is to be an eternal hell, the author claimed, the prison would have to be rent in half to provide a place for the damned:

---

[21] See Charles Gordon, *The Old Bailey and Newgate* (New York: James Pott & Company, 1902) and Arthur Griffiths, *The Chronicles of Newgate* (London: Chapman and Hall, 1884).

[22] Quoted in Gordon, *The Old Bailey and Newgate*, 49.

See, in yon Hall are divers sorts of men,
    Some weepe, some waile, some mourne, some wring their hands,
Some curse, some sweare, and some blaspheming then,
    My heart did faint, my head's haire upright stands.
O Lord, thought I, this house will rend in sunder,
Or else there can be no hell, this hell under."[23]

But even such a pit of despair could not prevent God's word from being spread:

Thus, wondring I on suddaine did espie,
    One all in black came stamping up the staires:
Whose yon, I askt, and thus he made reply,
    Yon is the man doth mitigate our cares.
He preacheth Christ, and doth God's word deliver,
To all distrest, to comfort men for ever.[24]

Eager for a word of hope, many prisoners flocked to the messenger of the gospel:

Then drew I neere to see what might betide,
    Or what was the sequel was of that I saw:
Expecting good would follow such a guide
    As preached Christ, and taught a God to know.
A hundred clustering came the pulpit neare,
As if they long'd the Gospell for to heare.[25]

If the king did not want to listen to Helwys's message, many of the Newgate's residents apparently would have.[26]

---

[23] Quoted ibid., 51, and in Whitley, "Thomas Helwys of Gray's Inn," 252.

[24] Quoted in Gordon, *The Old Bailey and Newgate*, 51, and in Whitley, "Thomas Helwys of Gray's Inn," 252.

[25] Quoted in Gordon, *The Old Bailey and Newgate*, 52, and in Whitley, "Thomas Helwys of Gray's Inn," 252.

[26] Not all prisoners appreciated prison worship services. In 1638, for example, Francis Tucker wrote to Archbishop William Laud, complaining that Samuel Eaton, "a schismatical and dangerous fellow," was permitted to preach to as many as sixty

Helwys's literary activity while he was in prison is unknown. Nothing survives that bears his name. However, Champlin Burrage suggested that a handwritten petition dated c. 1614 "may be that of Thomas Helwys."[27] The petition contained several themes that appear in many Baptist prison writings. The petitioners began by professing their unfeigned loyalty to the king, stating that they were "the king's majesty's loyal subjects ready to testify it by the Oath of Allegiance in all sincerity."[28]

Yet if the prisoners were truly the king's "faithful subjects," as they professed to be, why were they in jail? "Only," they claimed, "for conscience towards God." When taken before "the reverend judges and justices," many prisoners gain their freedom. However, "when we fall under the hands of the bishops, we can have no benefit by the said oath, for they say it belongs only to popish recusants, and not to others." Thus, the bishops had kept the petitioners "many years in lingering imprisonments" as innocent prisoners "whose grievances are lamentable, only for cause of conscience." Appealing to the mercy of the House of Commons, the prisoners emphasized that they had been "divided from wives, children, servants and callings" to the detriment of their families.[29] They pled with the officials to commiserate with their and their families' "distressed estate" and to allow them to take the oath and be freed. A handwritten note on the petition reveals that the prisoners' moving plea for mercy and freedom moved no one: "rejected by the committee."[30]

---

prisoners at a time. See Griffiths, *The Chronicles of Newgate*, 120–21; Champlin Burrage, *The Early English Dissenters in the Light of Recent Research: Illustrative Documents*, 2 vols. (Cambridge: University Press, 1912) 2:325–26; and B. R. White, "Samuel Eaton (d. 1639): A Particular Baptist Pioneer," *Baptist Quarterly* 24/1 (January 1971): 10–21.

[27] Champlin Burrage, *The Early English Dissenters*, 1:255.

[28] "A petition from prisoners in Newgate Prison, c. 1614," in *The Early English Dissenters in Light of Recent Research*, 2:215. Enacted in 1606 after some Catholics plotted the previous year to assassinate James and members of Parliament, the Oath of Allegiance required Catholics to swear that the king, not the pope, held supreme political authority in England. The plot is known as "The Gunpowder Plot" because the would-be-assassins planned to ignite thirty-six barrels of gunpowder in the cellar of the House of Lords.

[29] "A petition from prisoners in Newgate Prison, c. 1614," 2:215.

[30] Ibid., 2:216.

Instead of signing their names to the petition, the prisoners took the opportunity to reject the name with which their opponents had branded them—that of Anabaptists ("re-baptizers"), "the ever present bogey-man of the Reformation."[31] Most members of state churches loathed and feared Anabaptists because of their anti-government stance and their teaching that Christians could not hold the secular office of magistrate. The name also stirred up memories of the acts of radical Anabaptists at Münster, Germany, in 1535. In what has been called the Münster Rebellion, Anabaptist rebels seized the town and instigated social and religious changes in order to establish a "New Jerusalem."[32] Eventually, forces led by the ousted bishop of Münster put a violent end to the rebellion. With the ominous shadow of Münster and the anti-government sentiments of Anabaptists hanging over them, Baptists took every opportunity to reject the Anabaptist label and to affirm repeatedly their loyalty to the Crown.

On a more practical level, early Baptists claimed that they did not re-baptize anyone, which was what the term "Anabaptist" implied. Instead, Baptists contended that infant baptism was no baptism at all.[33] Moreover, they did not even refer to themselves as Baptists, a term too close to Anabaptists, but one that eventually was given to them in the 1650s. Rather, early Baptists preferred names such as "the church of Christ," "baptized churches," "baptized Christians," "baptized congregation," or "baptized believers."[34]

The fate of the petitioners remains unknown. Yet in returning to England and "coming...boldly uncalled into the king's presence," Helwys

---

[31] Perry Miller, *Orthodoxy in Massachusetts, 1630–1650: A Genetic Study* (Cambridge MA: Harvard University Press, 1933) 28.

[32] See Justo L. González, *A History of Christian Thought: From the Protestant Reformation to the Twentieth Century*, 3 vols. (Nashville: Abingdon Press, 1979) 3:85–86; Justo L. González, *The Story of Christianity: The Reformation to the Present Day*, 2 vols. (San Francisco: HarperSanFrancisco, 1985) 2:58–59, 95; and Nigel G. Wright, "The 'Sword': An Example of Anabaptist Diversity," *Baptist Quarterly* 36/6 (April 1996): 268.

[33] William G. McLoughlin and Martha Whiting Davidson, eds., "The Baptist Debate of April 14–15, 1668," in *Colonial Baptists: Massachusetts and Rhode Island*, The Baptist Tradition (Massachusetts Historical Society *Proceedings*, 1964; repr., New York: Arno Press, 1980) 100.

[34] See Robert B. Hannen, "Historical Notes on the Name 'Baptist,'" *Foundations* 8/1 (January 1965): 62–71.

and his fellow church members had chosen "to lay down our lives at the feet of our lord the king in presenting the cause into the king's presence, saying with Esther, 'If we perish, we perish'" [Esther 4:16], hoping and expecting "that through the gracious work of the Lord the king will hold forth his golden rod that we may live."[35] The king, however, withheld his rod, and Helwys apparently perished in Newgate. The exact date of his death is unknown, but in 1616 Geoffrey Helwys, Thomas Helwys's uncle, died, leaving a sum of money to Joan Helwys, Thomas's wife. With the death of Helwys, the leadership of his church fell to John Murton.

John Murton Argues for Religious Liberty

Born in Gainsborough in 1583 and married to Jane Hodgkin in 1608, Murton accompanied John Smyth and Thomas Helwys to Holland, where he worked as a furrier.[36] When the church split in 1610, Murton sided with Helwys, became his assistant, and, along with Jane, returned to England the following year. Although Murton lacked a formal education, William Estep contended that Murton's writings reveal "a man of intelligence and conviction."[37] John Robinson, a contemporary of Murton in England and then in Holland, held a radically different opinion, claiming that Murton's intellectual abilities were better suited for wielding a shovel and a pick rather than for discussing theology.[38] After reading Murton's writings, however, one can only conclude that he was quite able to hold more than shovel and pick.

---

[35] Helwys, *A Short Declaration of the Mystery of Iniquity*, 60–61.

[36] For biographical information on Murton, see Walter H. Burgess, *John Smith the Se-Baptist, Thomas Helwys and the First Baptist Church in England, with Fresh Light upon the Pilgrim Fathers' Church* (London: James Clarke & Co., 1913) 297–99.

[37] William R. Estep, "The English Baptist Legacy of Freedom and the American Experience," in *Pilgrim Pathways: Essays in Baptist History in Honour of B. R. White*, ed. William H. Brackney and Paul S. Fiddes (Macon GA: Mercer University Press, 1999) 269.

[38] John Robinson, *A Defence of the Doctrine Propounded by the Synod at Dort, Against John Murton and His Associates* (n.p., 1624), in *The Works of John Robinson, Pastor of the Pilgrim Fathers, with a Memoir and Annotations*, 3 vols., ed. Robert Ashton (London: John Snow, 1851) 1:293. Available online at http://oll.libertyfund.org/ToC/0064.php.

By 1613 Murton, like Helwys, resided in Newgate Prison, where he spent much of the next thirteen years.[39] During his incarceration, he apparently authored at least two anonymous works, *Objections Answered* (1615) and *A Most Humble Supplication* (1620).[40] In *Objections Answered* Murton created a dialogue between Antichristian and Christian, in which Christian responded to Antichristian's support of persecution and to John Robinson's *Of Religious Communion* (1614), which might partially account for Robinson's disdain for Murton. In his work Robinson attempted to refute what he considered to be Helwys's "unreasonable provocation," "his rash and ungodly censures," and his laboring with "the common disease of all ignorant men" in chastising Robinson for fleeing persecution, for advocating infant baptism, and for teaching that magistrates could use force to promote the Christian faith.[41] Murton wrote *A Most Humble Supplication* to prove to

---

[39] See John Wilkinson, *The Sealed Fountaine Opened to the Faithfull, and their Seed. Or, A Short Treatise, Shewing, that Some Infants Are in the State of Grace, and Capable of the Seales, and Others Not. Being the Chief Point, wherein the Separatists Doe Blame the Anabaptists. By John Wilkinson, Prisoner at Colchester, against John Morton Prisoner at London* (London: n.p., 1646) [1]. William Arthurbury reprinted Wilkinson's pamphlet in 1646. The title page (see Wilkinson, *The Sealed Fountaine Opened to the Faithfull, and their Seed.*) of the original pamphlet read: *A Reproof of Some Things Written by John Morton, and Others of His Company and Followers, to Prove That infants Are Not in the State of Condemnation, And That Therefore They Are Not to Be Baptized.* By John Wilkinson, a Prisoner at Colchester for the Patience and Faith of the Saints, 1613.

[40] Both of these works are included in Edward Bean Underhill, ed., *Tracts on Liberty of Conscience and Persecution, 1614–1661*, Elibron Classics Series (London: J. Haddon, 1846; repr., [Chestnut Hill MA]: Adamant Media Corporation, 2003): [John Murton], *Objections Answered by Way of Dialogue, wherein Is Proved...That No Man Ought to Be Persecuted for his Religion...*(n.p., 1615) 85–180 (hereafter cited as *OA*); and [John Murton], *A Most Humble Supplication of Many of the King's Majesty's Loyal Subjects, Ready to Testify All Civil Obedience, by the Oath of Allegiance, or Otherwise, and That of Conscience; Who Are Persecuted (only for Differing in Religion), Contrary to Divine and Human Testimonies* (n.p., 1620) 183–231 (hereafter cited as *MHS*). It is possible that Helwys authored *OA* or that he, Murton, and others co-authored this work. *OA* was reprinted in 1662 under the title *Persecution Judg'd and Condemn'd: In a Discourse, between Antichristian and a Christian.*

[41] *OA*, 180; John Robinson *Of Religious Communion, Private and Public* (n.p., 1614), in *The Works of John Robinson*, 3:155, 164, 277. For Helwys's condemnation of

the king that Baptists were loyal subjects and that religious liberty threatened neither the state nor the Church of England. The writing of this work has an interesting, if not apocryphal, history. Roger Williams, a seventeenth-century American advocate for religious liberty, claimed that he had been told that the author of the *Supplication* had been a "close prisoner in Newgate." Lacking pen and ink, the author wrote the manuscript with milk on paper that was used as a stopper for his milk bottle. The paper would then be taken to a friend who would read it by fire and transcribe it.[42]

Because both works address similar topics, they will be treated together. In the dialogue between Antichristian and Christian, Antichristian summed up the attitude of the Crown and the Church of England toward Baptists and all dissenters with these words: "Well, all your pleading will not serve you turn, either you must come to church, or else go to prison."[43] But for Murton, the kind of church that people attended, the stimulus for getting people to attend church, and the purpose of their attendance were crucial. A true church, Murton argued, consisted only of baptized believers who had publicly confessed their faith in Christ.[44] He contended that people should be baptized only after they have repented of their sins, not before. No church can claim to be true if it consists of "unbaptized persons."[45] Infants should not be baptized because "they are innocents, as Christ teaches" and because "God does not speak to them, requiring anything at their hands and therefore they have not sinned, seeing sin is the breach of

---

Robinson, see book 4 and the appendix of *A Short Declaration of the Mystery of Iniquity*.

[42] Roger Williams, *The Bloudy Tenent of Persecution, for Cause of Conscience*, Classics of Religious Liberty 2, ed. Richard Groves (Macon GA: Mercer University Press, 2001) 32. Williams quoted chapters 6–9 of *MHS* near the beginning of *The Bloudy Tenent* (11–18). Several pages later he referred to "the author of these arguments" (32), thereby connecting the quoted material from *MHS* to the unusual circumstances of the document's production. See also McBeth, *The Baptist Heritage*, 106, and Edwin S. Gaustad, *Liberty of Conscience: Roger Williams in America*, Library of Religious Biography (Grand Rapids MI: William B. Eerdmans Publishing Company, 1991) 72.

[43] *OA*, 134. See also 106.

[44] Ibid., 166. See also Barrie White, "Early Baptist Arguments for Religious Freedom: Their Overlooked Agenda," *Baptist History and Heritage* 24/4 (October 1989): 9.

[45] *OA*, 158.

God's law."[46] Therefore, neither the baptism of the Catholic Church nor that of the Church of England is "Christ's baptism."[47]

According to Murton, a true church also recognized that the Holy Spirit is not the possession of a select minority of educated ministers. However, the Crown and the Church of England contended that lay men and women, as the Anglican Richard Hutchinson observed in 1552, needed spiritual masters to guide them through the burdensome process of interpreting what they heard in church and read in their Bibles. According to Hutchinson, "To the unlearned and laity, the publishing" of the scriptures

> without interpretation is like a matter as if a man would give to young children whole nuts; which, when they have tumbled long up and down in their mouths, and licked the hard shell, being not able to come to their sweetness, at last they spit out, and cast away both the shell and the kernel. The eternal God, to help the infirmity of man's capacity and understanding herein, has ordained two honorable and most necessary offices in his church; the office of preaching, and the office of reading and interpreting.[48]

Neither the Crown nor the Church of England could afford to allow the laity too much freedom in ecclesiastical matters. Controlling how people worshiped and how they interpreted the Bible were just two ways by which both the church and the state worked together to ensure that the business of the temporal and spiritual kingdoms ran smoothly.

In contrast, Murton contended that the most biblically educated people were not necessarily the most academically trained, for "'the Spirit bloweth were it listeth' (John 3:8), and is not tied to the learned."[49] Every Christian receives the Holy Spirit in order to understand and interpret the Bible, and to preach the gospel, for the Spirit is a public, not a private, gift:

---

[46] Ibid., 170.

[47] Ibid., 159–60.

[48] Quoted in Edward Bean Underhill, "An Historical Introduction," in Underhill, *Tracts on Liberty of Conscience and Persecution, 1614–1661*, cxxv. See also Antichristian's questions in *OA*, 106.

[49] *MHS*, 201.

Hence it is most plain to whom the Spirit of God is given, even to every particular saint of God. And it is no private spirit, but even the public Spirit of God which is in him, which enables him to understand, and so to declare the things given him of God. That is a private spirit that is not of God, though it be in multitudes; but the Spirit of God, though but in one saint, is not private. God's Spirit is not private, for it is not comprehended only within one place, person, or time, as man's is, but it is universal and eternal; so is not man's: therefore man's is private, though they be many; God's is public, though but in one person.[50]

Another issue important to Murton was the stimulus for getting people to attend church. Antichristian's ultimatum of choosing either church or prison raised the question of the coercion of people's consciences. According to Murton, the education of Anglican ministers had turned them into biblically ignorant persecutors and hypocrites. "You abhor" the Catholic practice of forcing people to believe what the Catholic Church teaches and of preventing people from reading the Bible, Murton scolded the Anglican bishops, but

you do that which is worse, letting us read the scriptures, whereby we may know the will of our heavenly Master, and have our consciences enlightened and convinced, but not suffer us to practice what we learn and know.... And not only so, but will you constrain us to captivate our consciences and [to] practice in that which in our souls we know to be evil and contrary to the manifest law of the Lord, and that only because the learned have so decreed—whom you acknowledge are subject to err as well as others—or else lie in perpetual imprisonment, and be otherwise grievously persecuted?[51]

Murton argued that people should not "be persecuted for" their "religion, be it true or false," as long as they are loyal to the king.[52] Forcing people "by cruel persecution" to attend worship services not of their choosing was "heinous...in the sight of the Lord." Civil and ecclesiastical authorities could "force men and women...to bring their bodies

---

[50] Ibid., 200.
[51] Ibid., 209.
[52] *OA*, 95. See also *MHS*, 210–11.

to…worship," but they could not force them to "bring their spirits."[53] Murton implored all civil and ecclesiastical leaders to search the Bible, by which one day they would be judged, before they plot to compel people "against their souls and consciences to dissemble to believe as they believe, or as the king and state believe." If only the authorities would study the scriptures, he asserted, "they would withdraw their hands and hearts therefrom, and never do as they have done, partly through inconsideration, and partly to please lord bishops being in favor with the king."[54]

Unfortunately, Murton lamented, the "cursed" Anglican persecutors had ignored the plain teachings of the Bible, and, lacking the spiritual weapons necessary to build Christ's church, had resorted to planting their "church by violence and bloodshed, forcing many thousands against their consciences to be of your church and to receive your sacraments." However, people "who fear God more than men and dare not yield" to threats and force had been cast "into noisome prisons, amongst [the] most wicked blasphemers of God, to the wounding of their souls," causing them and their families horrendous hardships.[55]

Motives for attending church were also crucial, Murton argued, because God requires that true worshipers "worship him with our souls and spirits, and…according to the truth of his word," not according to Antichristian's "book-worship." Forcing people to sit in a building in which they do not want to be, to listen to sermons they do not want to hear, to say "Amen" to prayers monotonously read from a book, and to violate their consciences was nothing but a sham. Murton concluded, "If I cannot offer it [worship] up with my spirit, it is not acceptable to God, but most abominable."[56] Rather than forcing people to worship, Murton challenged Antichristian to try convincing them "with meekness and patience" and satisfying their "conscience by the word of truth." With such tolerance, Murton asserted that he himself might "come with a willing mind," and then "shall I be accepted [by God]." Using force, however, would only "cause me to bring my body and not my spirit or soul: so shall I come near to the Lord

---

[53] *OA*, 95.
[54] Ibid., 97. See also 135.
[55] Ibid., 141–42.
[56] Ibid., 103.

with my lips, when my heart shall be far from him."[57] When "you [compel] me by tyranny to bring my body whereunto my spirit cannot be brought, you compel me to hypocrisy with God and man."[58] And when you force me to worship against my conscience, you do what no human can do, for "no mortal man, whoever he is, can compel any man to offer the sacrifices of the New Testament, which are spiritual, and purge the conscience, except he can beget faith in him, and convert his soul."[59]

Like Antichristian, those who opposed religious liberty had, from the time of Augustine, supported their persecution of heretics by citing the Bible, particularly the Old Testament. Yet Murton maintained that the kingdom of Israel was a "carnal type" of the spiritual kingdom of Christ, who fulfilled the Jewish law and who now reigns as king of Israel.[60] Opponents of religious liberty also used the New Testament to justify their persecution of people who were considered to be heretics. Murton, however, explained that such examples were all cases in which God, not humans, acted.[61]

As for Antichristian's claim that Christ commanded his disciples to compel unbelievers to attend church (see Luke 14:23), Murton countered that Christ "has no carnal weapons"; he compelled people with "his word, which is his two-edged sword" (Heb 4:12), and with the "breath of his lips" (see Rev 2:12; Isa 11:4). Christ never taught his disciples to drag unbelievers "out of their houses and put them in prison, to the undoing of them, their wives, and [their] children. This was Saul's course when he was a blasphemer and persecutor, etc. Christ taught his disciples 'to wait if at any time God would give the contrary-minded repentance' [see 2 Tim 2:25], and not to prevent their repentance by seeking their blood."[62] Jesus had all the power in the universe, but he never forced anyone to obey him.[63] "Persecution for the cause of conscience," even of those who adhered to a "false religion" and rejected Christ, violated the teachings of Jesus Christ.[64] "The whole New

---

[57] Ibid. 104.

[58] Ibid., 139.

[59] Ibid., 125.

[60] Ibid., 122–26.

[61] Ibid., 111–12. See Acts 5:1–11; 13:11, 1 Timothy 1:20, and 1 Corinthians 5:5.

[62] *OA*, 112. See also 128–29. Saul was the apostle Paul's Hebrew name.

[63] Ibid., 132–33.

[64] *MHS*, 214–15.

Testament throughout," Murton concluded, "in all the doctrines and practices of Christ and his disciples, teach no such thing as compelling men by persecutions and afflictions to obey the gospel, but the direct contrary, viz. to suffer at the hands of the wicked; when they were persecuted for righteousness' sake, to suffer it; when the unbelievers and wicked curse them, to bless and pray for their repentance, and that God would forgive them and never lay these sins to their charge."[65]

However, what was so biblical, so Christian, so right, and so godly to Murton was so Satanic, so dangerous, and so seditious to Antichristian. "If it were as you would have it, that all religions should be suffered," Antichristian exclaimed, "how dangerous would it be to the king's person and state. What treacheries and treasons would be plotted!"[66]

Murton claimed just the opposite; religious liberty would benefit both the king and his kingdom. Murton rejected the Anabaptist label and the argument that Baptists were seditious. Rather, he said, Baptists were "Christ's unworthy witnesses, [and] His Majesty's faithful subjects"[67] who prayed daily for the king and others in authority.[68] They neither plotted rebellion nor threatened the king's person. Far from being disloyal, they were the king's most loyal subjects, professing that James "is supreme head and governor over all his subjects' bodies and goods within his dominion," and detesting and abhorring "all foreign powers."[69] Baptists "unfeignedly acknowledge the authority of earthly magistrates, God's blessed ordinance, and that all earthly authority and command appertains to them; let them command what they will, we must obey, either to do or suffer upon pain of God's displeasure, besides their punishment."[70] In good conscience, Baptists "give to Caesar the things which are his: which is, to be lord and lawgiver to the bodies of his subjects, and all belonging to their outward man, for the preservation of himself, and his good subjects, and for the punishment of evil. In which preservation, the church of Christ has a special part, when their outward peace is thereby preserved from the fury of all adversaries; in

---

[65] *OA*, 120.
[66] Ibid., 113. See also 129.
[67] Ibid., 101. See also 24, 179–80 and *MHS*, 231.
[68] *MHS*, 189.
[69] *OA*, 110.
[70] Ibid., 100.

which respect princes are called nursing fathers, as many are at this day; blessed be the Lord."[71] Baptists follow Christ,

> who is that "Prince of peace" (Isa. 9:6), not of sedition, [and who] has taught that he "came not to send peace on the earth, but debate; to divide five in one house, two against three, and three against two; the father against the son, etc. And a man's enemies shall be those of his own household" (Matt. 19:34–36; Luke 12:51–52). And his desire is that the fire of such sedition should be kindled.... This Prince of peace puts difference in religion by preaching his gospel, which some receive as the savor of life to them; others refuse it, and so become enemies to the truth, and witnesses thereof.[72]

As for kings fearing the loss of "their power by permitting of freedom of religion," Murton advised them to fear not permitting it. "By using compulsion to the contrary-minded," he warned, kings "do sin grievously in causing them to sin for want of faith."[73] Also, if kings granted their people "freedom in their religion," and if people swore "their faithful allegiance to the king, the fear of the king's laws, and their own prosperity and peace, would make them live more inoffensively in that respect."[74] Moreover, "behold the nations where freedom of religion is permitted, and you may see there are not more flourishing and prosperous nations under the heavens than they are."[75] Thus, according to Murton, religious liberty produced loyal, law-abiding citizens as well as national peace and prosperity. The king had nothing to fear from Baptists. They were not demanding the liberty to break temporal laws necessary to the well being of the king and state; they were merely demanding the freedom to worship in the manner that they believed God had required.[76]

Nevertheless, Murton followed his professions of loyalty and obedience to the king in temporal matters with what many would have considered to be a heretical and seditious conjunction, "but": "but all men must let God alone with his right, which is to be Lord and Lawgiver to the soul, and not

---

[71] *MHS*, 230.

[72] *OA*, 129–30.

[73] *MHS*, 229–30.

[74] *OA*, 114.

[75] Ibid., 130. See also 114 and *MHS*, 224–25.

[76] *MHS*, 192.

command obedience for God where he commands none. And this is only that which we dare not but maintain upon the peril of our souls, which is greater than bodily affliction."[77] The king's "power and authority...is earthly," and I submit to it, Murton declared, "but my soul, with which I am to worship God,...belongs to another King 'whose kingdom is not of this world' (John 18:36), whose people must come willingly, whose weapons 'are not carnal, but spiritual' (Ps. 110:3; 2 Cor. 10:4)."[78] Therefore, Murton continued, if the king "cannot compel my soul, he cannot compel me to worship God, for God cannot be worshipped without the soul." If anyone contends that the king "may compel me to offer up a worship only with my body, for the spirit," everyone acknowledges, "he cannot compel, to whom is that worship? Not to God."[79]

To prove the evilness of religious persecution and the justice of religious liberty, Murton quoted freely and extensively from the Bible, for he believed that no church or mortals "may be the judge, rule, or umpire, in matters of faith, but only the holy scriptures."[80] Yet he did not rely solely on the scriptures to prove his points. He also quoted King James himself as well as numerous historical and patristic writers to prove the wickedness of religious persecution.[81] If James was "no blood-thirsty man,"[82] Murton wondered why he and his comrades had to rot in filthy prisons, separated from families and jobs, which had caused many of them to prefer death than to continue living in prison. Our only "crime," he said, had been to refuse to worship in a manner that we believed sinned against God.[83] Does anyone really think that such cruelty will change our hearts, Murton asked? James knows that it will not, for he admitted that only "the work of God" could change a person's mind.[84] And did not the king himself confess that experience had taught him

---

[77] *OA*, 100.

[78] Ibid., 107–108. See also 134.

[79] Ibid., 108. See also 139.

[80] *MHS*, 196. *OA* contains at least 250 scripture references; *MHS*, at least 150.

[81] For the historical and patristic examples, see *MHS*, 216–24.

[82] *OA*, 97. See also 117.

[83] *MHS*, 190.

[84] James I, "A Speech to the Lords and Commons of the Parliament at White-Hall," 344. See also *OA*, 97n3.

that blood and too much severity [never] did good in matters of religion, for, besides that it is a sure rule in divinity that God never loves to plant his church by violence and bloodshed; natural reason may even persuade us, and daily experience proves it true, that when men are severely persecuted for religion, the gallantness of many men's spirits, and the willfulness of their humors, rather than the justness of the cause, makes them to take a pride boldly to endure any torments, or death itself, to gain thereby the reputation of martyrdom, though but in a false shadow.[85]

And did not the king also write, "It is a good and sure rule in theology, in matter[s] of [the] worship of God,...according to Saint Paul (Rom. 14:5), 'Let every man be fully persuaded in his own mind'"?[86] Therefore, Murton concluded, "The vileness of persecuting the body of any man, only for the cause of conscience," not only violates "the word of God and the law of Christ"; it violates "the profession of Your Majesty."[87]

Although Murton sought to bolster his arguments for religious liberty with numerous historical examples, much of his use of quotations appear to be mere proof-texting, for, according to Leon McBeth, his citations of "historical and patristic allusions are ill-chosen, out of context, and made to support a position foreign to their original intent."[88] For example, Murton cited Martin Luther as a proponent of religious liberty. Indeed, Luther wrote many things with which Murton would have agreed; for example, "The laws of the civil government extend no further than over the body or goods, and to that which is external: for, over the soul God will not suffer any man to rule, only he himself will rule there; therefore, wherever the civil magistrate does undertake to give laws to the soul and conscience of men, he usurps that government to himself, which appertains to God."[89] Elsewhere

---

[85] James I, "A Speech to the Lords and Commons of the Parliament at White-Hall," 344. See *OA*, 100.

[86] James I, "A Meditation upon the Lords Prayer," *The Workes of the Most High and Mightie Prince, James*, by James I (London: printed by Robert Barker and John Bill, 1620) 581. See also *MHS*, 190.

[87] *MHS*, 192.

[88] Harry Leon McBeth, *English Baptist Literature on Religious Liberty to 1689* (Ph.D. diss., Southwestern Baptist Theological Seminary, 1961; repr., New York: Arno Press, 1980) 56.

[89] Quoted in *MHS*, 220–21.

Luther stated, "In the building of the temple there was no sound of iron heard, to signify that Christ will have in his church a free and willing people, not compelled and constrained by laws and statutes."[90] Such lofty words supported Murton's position nicely. However, Luther also claimed that blasphemers should be condemned without a trial,[91] and in his exposition of Psalm 101, he broadened his understanding of blasphemy to include Anabaptists. Although in 1530 the German reformer did not contend that Anabaptists should be executed, by 1532, he had changed his mind.[92] In other words, Luther had no use for people like Murton, and he probably would have vehemently rejected Murton's using his writings to support religious liberty for all people.

---

[90] Quoted ibid., 221. To these quotations from Luther could be added the following: "We should overcome heretics with books, not with fire, as the ancient fathers did. If it were wisdom to vanquish heretics with fire, then the public hangmen would be the most learned scholars on earth. We would no longer need to study books, for he who overcomes another by force would have the right to burn him at the stake" (Martin Luther, "To the Christian Nobility of the German Nation Concerning the Reform of the Christian Estate [1520]," in *Luther's Works: The Christian in Society*, ed. James Atkinson, 55 vols. [Philadelphia: Fortress Press, 1966] 196–97). "Faith is a free act to which no one can be forced. Indeed, it is a work of God in the spirit, not something which outward authority should compel or create"; and "Heresy can never be restrained by force. One will have to tackle the problem in some other way, for heresy must be opposed and dealt with otherwise than with the sword. Here God's word must do the fighting. If it does not succeed, certainly the temporal power will not succeed either, even if it were to drench the world in blood. Heresy is a spiritual matter which you cannot hack to pieces with iron, consume with fire, or drown in water. God's word prevails here" (Martin Luther, "Temporal Authority: To What Extent It Should Be Obeyed," in *Luther's Works: The Christian in Society*, ed. Walther I. Brandt, 55. vols. [Philadelphia: Muhlenberg Press, 1962] 45:108, 114).

[91] William A. Mueller, *Church and State in Luther and Calvin: A Comparative Study* (Nashville: Broadman Press, 1954) 64.

[92] W. D. J. Cargill Thompson, *The Political Thought of Martin Luther*, ed. Philip Broadhead (Sussex: Harvester Press, 1984) 161–62. According to Thompson, "Although Luther's early pronouncements appear to suggest a total opposition to all compulsion in matters of faith, it is important to emphasize that at no time in his life did Luther believe in, much less advocate complete freedom of belief. On the contrary, Luther's whole concept of the faith was entirely opposed to such an idea" (155).

Murton's use of James's writings is another example of his proof-texting. Murton continually portrayed the king as a defender of conscience, attributing any intolerant act by James to the deviousness of Anglican bishops, who feared losing power.[93] In other words, Murton believed that the bishops often duped James to act contrary to his own beliefs. Indeed, James often wrote about acting tolerantly towards dissenters. In his "Meditation upon the Lords Prayer," for example, the king said that if a person had not been raised in the church, "he must trust to his own conscience to bear him witness, what church does truly preach the word of salvation, according to the revealed will of God, and does not mix and contradict the points of salvation contained in the scripture, with their own traditions."[94] Thus, like Luther, James spoke and wrote many inspirational words about religious liberty, but the king was unwilling to grant complete religious freedom. For example, that person who was to "trust to his own conscience" about which church was the true church had limited options available to him because, James declared, "as soon as he has thus made his choice what church to live and die in,…as Christ commands," that person's "conscience…must only serve him for a guide to the right church, but not to judge her, but to be judged by her. For he who will have God to be his Father, must also have the true church to be his Mother."[95]

Furthermore, James warned his subjects "not be carried away with the wind of every doctrine, nor trust not to that private spirit or holy ghost which our Puritans glory in, for then" they will slide from one heresy "to some one sect or other of Anabaptist, and from one of these to" even worse heresies. "Thus you see," James continued, "how that letting slip the hold of the true church, and once trusting the private spirit of Reformation, according to our Puritans' doctrine, it is easy to fall and slide by degrees into chaos, filthy sink and farrago of all horrible heresies, whereof hell is the just reward. And now I turn to my purpose, craving pardon for this digression, for the zeal I have to preserve the church from these foxes, and little foxes, heretics and sectaries."[96] When James uttered the words "no bishop, no

---

[93] See *OA*, 117, 121, 131, 139–40.
[94] James I, "A Meditation upon the Lords Prayer," 577.
[95] Ibid.
[96] Ibid.

king" at the Hampton Court Conference in 1604, no bishop put a sword to his neck; he did so willingly; he was no friend of religious liberty.

Perhaps Murton knew that he used James's own words out of context; perhaps he hoped that by showing James to be a hypocrite, the king might change his persecuting ways. Murton begged the king to re-think his persecution of dissenters. You persecute us, Murton lectured James, even though we give you your due and simply claim that God "is to be Lord and Lawgiver to the soul in that spiritual worship and service which he requires. If you will take away this from God, what is it that is God's? Far be it from you to desire to sit in the consciences of men, to be lawgiver and judge therein. This is antichrist's practice, persuading the kings of the earth to give him their power to compel all hereunto, but whosoever submits shall drink of God's fierce wrath."[97]

Not content merely to prophecy doom for all persecutors, Murton bluntly and boldly informed the king of what he could and could not do:

> You may make and mend your own laws, and be judge and punisher of the transgressors thereof, but you cannot make or mend God's laws; they are perfect already; you may not add nor diminish, nor be judge nor monarch of his church; that is Christ's. He left neither you nor any mortal man his deputy, but only the Holy Ghost, as Your Highness acknowledges. And whosoever errors from the truth, his judgment is set down, and the time thereof.[98]
>
> It is not in your power to compel the heart; you may compel men to be hypocrites, as a great many are, who are false-hearted both towards God and the state, which is sin both in you and in them.[99]

No amount of professing loyalty to the king could overcome such statements, for, in James's opinion, such talk was "presumption and high contempt in a subject to dispute what a king can do, or say that a king

---

[97] *MHS*, 230.
[98] Ibid., 230–31.
[99] Ibid., 192.

cannot do this or that, but rest in that which is the king's revealed will in his law."[100]

In March 1625, James died and his son Charles succeeded him. Murton died probably in 1626, for in that year his wife returned to Amsterdam, where she joined a Mennonite church.[101] Given the choice either to go to the worship services of the Church of England or go to prison, Murton, like Helwys, chose prison. They apparently considered such a choice really no choice at all, for their consciences would not have permitted them to do otherwise. History, however, Murton confidently predicted, would judge whether the persecutors or the persecuted were right: "Will not succeeding ages cry out against the cruelty of the learned Protestants herein, as well as they cry out against the cruelty of the learned Jews and papists? Yes, we are assured they will, as many millions do in other nations this day."[102]

---

[100] James I, "A Speech in the Starre-Chamber."

[101] William R. Estep, *The Anabaptist Story* (Grand Rapids MI: William B. Eerdmans Publishing Company, 1975) 226.

[102] *MHS*, 211.

Chapter 3

Soldiers for Christ and for Parliament

In 1599 King James VI of Scotland, who later became king of England in 1603, published an instruction manual for Henry, his eldest son and heir to the throne, on how the future king should perform his royal duties. Love God first, James advised his son, because "he made you a little god to sit on his throne and rule over other men."[1] Henry did not live long enough to become, like his father, "a little god," for he died in 1612. Thus, when James died in 1625, his son Charles became king of England.

King Charles I and Archbishop William Laud

During Charles I's reign (r. 1625–1649), England experienced a growth of the "gentry" class, a group of untitled landowners who existed on the social scale between the nobility and peasants. Members of this class longed for a monarch and a Parliament that listened to them. While the gentry class was growing, the middle class was also growing. These two classes shared little in common except for their disdain of the nobles and of the Crown, both of which scorned those whom they considered beneath them. Along with these socioeconomic changes, a volatile religious environment existed in which Protestants argued with Catholics, who comprised approximately a quarter of the population, and when Protestants tired of quarrelling with the hated "papists," they fought among themselves.[2] These and other problems

---

[1] James I, "*Basilikon Doron*: Or His Majesties Instructions to His Dearest Sonne, Henry the Prince," in *The Political Works of James I*, ed. Charles Howard McIlwain (London: n.p., 1616; repr., Cambridge MA: Harvard University Press, 1918), http://www.perseus.tufts.edu/cgi-bin/ptext?doc=Perseus%3Atext%3A1999.03.0071;query=head%3D%2311;layout=;lo c= (accessed 13 July 2007). *Basilikon doron* is Greek for "royal gift."

[2] See Will Durant and Ariel Durant, *The Story of Civilization*, part 7, *The Age of Reason Begins: A History of European Civilization in the Period of Shakespeare, Bacon,*

proved to be a recipe for disaster for King Charles, whom one modern historian described as "much stupider than his father or his eldest son"[3] and whom another historian described as "a tidy-minded man who craved order. In Charles's mental world, kings ruled and subjects obeyed."[4] Unfortunately for England, Charles's attempts to mold the real world into the image of his mental world proved to be deadly.

Charles continued his father's policy of ruling both the state and the church. Vain, uncompromising, and blatantly dishonest,[5] Charles found it difficult to rule a people who craved freedom for themselves, if not for others. Like his father, he wrongly believed that political stability required religious uniformity and that religion needed the support of the state. "As the church can never flourish without the protection of the crown," Charles declared, "so the dependency of the church upon the crown is the chiefest support of royal authority."[6] The king loathed the nonconformist emphasis on preaching and the reading of scripture by individuals, and he believed that squabbling over who was part of God's elect and who was part of the damned threatened the unity of the Anglican Church. Thus, as the "Defender of the Faith, and Supreme Governor of the Church," Charles committed himself to keeping the peace of England, which meant, in part, that he would promote the unity of the state church by suppressing religious dissent.[7] Getting people back into the worship services of the Church of England and having them quietly reflect on what God and their "little god" wanted them to do, was, in Charles's mind, essential for the peace of England.

Montaigne, Rembrandt, Galileo, and Descartes: 1558–1648 (New York: Simon and Schuster, 1961) 184–92.

[3] Christopher Hill, *The Century of Revolution, 1603–1714*, The Norton Library History of England (New York: W. W. Norton & Company, Inc., 1961) 73.

[4] John Miller, *The Stuarts* (London: Hambledon and London, 2004) 69.

[5] Hill, *The Century of Revolution*, 74.

[6] Quoted ibid., 77.

[7] "The King's Declaration prefixed to the Articles of Religion," in *The Constitutional Documents of the Puritan Revolution 1625–1660*, 3rd ed., rev. ed., ed. Samuel Rawson Gardiner (Oxford: Oxford University Press, 1906), http://www.constitution.org/eng/conpur013.htm (accessed 22 June 2005).

During Charles's reign, a second group of Baptists came into existence: the Particular Baptists.[8] Theologically Calvinist, these Baptists emerged from an Independent London congregation that sought to maintain its autonomy without radically breaking with the Church of England. This congregation, founded in 1616, is often called the "JLJ Church" because of the initials of its first three pastors: Henry Jacob, John Lathrop, and Henry Jessey.

In 1633 several members withdrew from the JLJ church to "receive further baptism" and to form another church. The exact meaning of "further baptism" is unknown. It may have meant baptism by immersion or just believer's baptism. In 1638 other members withdrew from the JLJ congregation to join the 1633 group, and by 1640 two Particular Baptist churches existed in London, both teaching that believers should be baptized by immersion.[9] Daniel Featley, an Anglican minister and a vitriolic

---

[8] For the origin of Particular Baptists, see Robert G. Torbet, *A History of the Baptists*, 3rd ed. (Valley Forge PA: Judson Press, 1963) 40–43; Leon McBeth, "Baptist Origins," *Baptist History and Heritage* 15/4 (October 1980): 38–39; Leon McBeth, *The Baptist Heritage: Four Centuries of Baptist Witness* (Nashville: Broadman Press, 1987) 39–44; Bill J. Leonard, *Baptist Ways: A History* (Valley Forge PA: Judson Press, 2003) 28–30; and B. R. White, *The English Baptists of the Seventeenth Century*, A History of the English Baptists 1 (London: The Baptist Historical Society, 1983) 58–61.

[9] Particular Baptists are usually credited with introducing baptism by immersion to England. However, ministers often associated with General Baptists *might* have been immersing believers prior to Particular Baptists. See the two-part article by Stephen Wright, "Baptist Alignments and the Restoration of Immersion, 1638–44," *Baptist Quarterly* 40/5 (January 2004): 261–82, and 40/6 (April 2004): 346–68. Walter H. Burgess, *John Smith the Se-Baptist, Thomas Helwys and the First Baptist Church in England, with Fresh Light upon the Pilgrim Fathers' Church* (London: James Clarke & Co., 1913) 326–27, and Champlin Burrage, *The Early English Dissenters in Light of Recent Research: History and Criticism (1550–1641)*, 2 vols. (Cambridge: University Press, 1912) 1:378–79, also cite unnamed Baptists who might have immersed believers prior to Particular Baptists. See also Henry C. Vedder's cautionary comment (*A Short History of the Baptists*, rev. ed. [Philadelphia: American Baptist Publication Society, 1897] 144) concerning Leonard Busher's statement regarding baptism. Busher, perhaps one of the first General Baptists, wrote: "And such as shall willingly and gladly receive it [the gospel], he [Christ] has commanded to be baptized in the water; that is, dipped for dead in the water" (Leonard Busher, *Religions Peace: or A Plea for Liberty of Conscience* [n.p, 1614; repr., London: printed for John Sweeting, 1646] in Edward Bean Underhill, ed., *Tracts on Liberty of Conscience and*

opponent of Baptists, condemned them because they "cry down paedobabtism and cry up Anabaptism, not only in the pulpit, but also from the press, to the great offence of godly minds and the scandal of the church."[10] These heretics "flock in great multitudes to their Jordans, and both sexes enter into the river and are dipped after their manner with a kind of spell containing the heads of their erroneous tenets.... They defile our rivers with their impure washings and our pulpits with their false prophecies and fanatical enthusiasms, so the presses sweat and groan under the load of their prophecies," spreading the "most damnable doctrines" and "tending to carnal liberty."[11]

The year 1633 also proved to be important for the Anglican Church because Charles appointed William Laud (1573–1645), whom A. C. Underwood described as "a pious man with a narrow mind of a martinet," to be archbishop of Canterbury.[12] In a sermon before Parliament several years prior to becoming the head of the Anglican Church, Laud revealed that he was truly a man after any monarch's own heart. He stressed the significance of a unified church for the well being of both the church and the state. A divided church, he warned, "invited malice, which is ready to do hurt without any invitation, and it ever lies with an open side to the devil and all his batteries. So both state and church [are] then happy, and never till then, when they are both at unity in themselves and one with another."[13] If you

---

Persecution, 1614–1661, Elibron Classics Series [London: J. Haddon, 1846; repr., (Chestnut Hill MA): Adamant Media Corporation, 2003] 59). As with the origin of General Baptists, the Anabaptist influence on Particular Baptists is a matter of debate. See Glen H. Stassen, "Anabaptist Influence in the Origin of Particular Baptists," *Mennonite Quarterly Review* 36/4 (October 1962): 322–48, and a response to Stassen's position by James M. Renihan, "An Examination of the Possible Influence of Menno Simons' *Foundation Book* upon the Particular Baptist Confession of 1644," *American Baptist Quarterly* 15/3 (October 1996): 190–207.

[10] Daniel Featley, *The Dippers Dipt. Or, The Anabaptists Duck'd and Plung'd over Head and Eares, at a Disputation in Southwark*, 4th ed. (London: printed for Nicholas Bourn and Richard Royston, 1646) B2.

[11] Ibid., A5.

[12] A. C. Underwood, *A History of the English Baptists* (London: The Carey Kingsgate Press Limited, 1947) 56.

[13] William Laud, *A Sermon Preached on Munday, the sixt of February, At Westminster: At the Opening of Parliament* (London: printed by Bonham Norton and

want to maintain a united state, Laud informed members of Parliament, "take heed of breaking the peace of the church. The peace of the state depends much upon it. For divide Christ in the minds of men, or divide the minds of men about their hope of salvation in Christ, and tell me what unity there will be. This so far as the church is an ingredient into the unity of the state."[14] Because the state cannot exist without a unified church, "the wise ordering of the people in concord and unity is simply the strongest wall of a state: but break unity once, and farewell strength."[15]

Laud was not merely a man of words; he was a man of action. He stressed ceremony and sacrament in order to create spiritual harmony and to bring prodigals back into the true church. Rather than bore and alienate people with fiery sermons, the archbishop sought "to feast the eye rather than tire the ear" by "appealing to all those whom the Calvinists had told were either damned or saved, a way of giving hope to sinners that they might yet be among the flock of those who would see salvation."[16]

Because of his love for "spectacle and mystery," Laud believed that Anglican priests should have an aura of holiness, or separateness, about them. To create this holy ambiance, Laud set out to beautify churches, and he ordered Communion tables to be placed behind railings, thereby giving a visual as well as a physical display of the separateness of priests. This order horrified Puritans but delighted Catholics. Rome was so impressed with Laud's policies that it offered him a cardinal's hat, which he declined.[17] For Puritans, however, his actions and Rome's offer could mean only one thing: the archbishop was a papist in Protestant clothing; perhaps he was even the forerunner of the antichrist.

If unity was Laud's goal, uniformity was his means. He believed that emphasizing ceremony rather than preaching would have a tranquilizing effect on parishioners. A diverse people sitting quietly in churches, reciting the same prayers, and listening to priests mouth the same words would eventually be formed into one people united in one faith, obedient to one

---

John Bill, 1625), in William Laud, *The Works of the Most Reverend Father in God, William Laud, D.D.: Sermons*, 7 vols. (Oxford: John Henry Parker, 1847) 1:70.

[14] Ibid., 1:71.

[15] Ibid., 1:66.

[16] Simon Schama, *A History of Britain: The Wars of the British, 1603–1776*, 3 vols. (New York: Hyperion, 2001) 2:84–85.

[17] Durant and Durant, *The Age of Reason Begins*, 189.

king, and, ultimately, accountable to one God. Many people, however, preferred to hear their own ministers preach fire-and-brimstone sermons than to hear Laud's priests mindlessly mumble the written prayers in the Prayer Book.

Laud understood that not everyone was willing to accept his vision of the church. Writing to Charles in 1639, he expressed his exasperation concerning the religious situation in his own diocese: "The great thing which is amiss there, and beyond my power to remedy, is the stiffness of numerous Anabaptists and Separatists from the Church of England.... And I do not find, either by my own experience, or by any advice from my officers, that this is likely to be remedied, unless the statute concerning abjuration of your kingdom, or some other way by the power of the temporal law or state be thought upon."[18]

People dedicated to their "stiffness" had to be dealt with, and even though Laud realized that coercing people to attend church could not ultimately produce spiritual unity, nonconformists could at least be forced to embrace an external, formal uniformity.[19] Thus, even if they did not believe the tenets of the Church of England, nonconformists could at least behave as if they believed them and thereby submit themselves to King Charles's authority. In a biting commentary on Laud's dogged efforts to produce a forced uniformity, W. K. Jordan observed that the archbishop's "loyalty to this principle, which shows amazing ignorance of the true roots of religious belief, was pathetically constant."[20] Such loyalty would also one day prove to be deadly.

To punish people committed to their heresies and to coerce people into attending the services of the Church of England, Laud had the Court of High Commission at his disposal. Those who were determined to defy the king and the archbishop had to remain vigilant, for numerous spies were willing to provide authorities with information concerning nonconformists.

---

[18] William Laud, *Arch-Bishop Laud's Annual Accounts of His Province, Presented to the King* (London: printed for Ri. Chilwell, 1695), inWilliam Laud, *The Works of the Most Reverend Father in God, William Laud, D.D.: Accounts of Provinces, etc.* (Oxford: John Henry Parker, 1853) 5:361. By "abjuration" Laud meant banishment.

[19] W. K. Jordan, *The Development of Religious Toleration in England: From the Accession of James I to the Convention of the Long Parliament (1603–1640)*, 4 vols. (Cambridge MA: Harvard University Press, 1936) 2:132.

[20] Ibid., 2:134.

For example, a 1636 search warrant issued by the commission to John Wragg contained "credible information" that "in or near the city of London or suburbs thereof, and in many other parts within this kingdom of England, many sorts of Separatists and sectaries," including "Anabaptists," had refused to attend their parish churches. Rather than participating with their "parochial congregation in divine service sacraments and hearing of God's word preached," these peddlers of heresy and anarchy "meet together, in great numbers" to "keep and maintain private conventicles and exercises of religion by the laws of this realm prohibited,...[thereby] corrupting and perverting...many" English citizens, flaunting their contempt of the king's laws, and disturbing "the peace of the church." The warrant gave Wragg, and whomever he chose, the authority to

> enter into any house or place where you shall have intelligence, or probably suspect that any such private conventicles or meetings are held, kept, and frequented by any such sectaries or schismatics, and therein and every room thereof you do make diligent search for them as also for all unlawful and unlicensed books, and seditious and unlawful writings and papers. And all and every such person's writings, papers, and books so found, to seize, apprehend, and attach, or cause to be seized, apprehended, and attached, wherever they may be found, as well in places exempt as not exempt and that thereupon you detain them in safe custody, and bring them forthwith before us, or...our colleagues, His Majesty's commissioners in that behalf appointed, to be examined, dealt with and disposed of.[21]

This warrant, and others like it, gave local magistrates sweeping powers. Practically no one was secure in their own home because all magistrates needed to raid it was the mere suspicion that the occupants might be a threat to the peace of the church or the state. Such a condition, if it can be called that, was broad enough to include anything.

When prisoners appeared before the commission, they were at the mercy of merciless commissioners. The following account comes from a 1632 interrogation of Samuel Eaton and Sarah Jones, members of John

---

[21] The entire warrant is reprinted in "Baptists in the State Papers," *Transactions of the Baptist Historical Society* 5/3 (April 1917): 150–52.

Lathrop's church.[22] The commissioners demanded that Eaton and Jones explain why they worshiped at conventicles while other people were at church:

> Eaton: We were not assembled in contempt of the magistrate.
>
> London [William Laud, bishop of London]: No, it was in contempt of the Church of England.
>
> Eaton: It was in conscience to God...and we were kept from church, for we were confined in the house together by those who beset the house, [or] else many would have gone to church and many came in after the sermons were done....
>
> Canterbury [George Abbot, archbishop of Canterbury]: Where were you in the morning before you came here to this house?
>
> Eaton: We were in our own family.
>
> Canterbury: What did you do?
>
> Eaton: We read the scriptures and catechized our families, and, may it please this honorable court to hear us speak the truth, we will show you what was done [so that you might] free us from the contempt of authority, [for] we did nothing but what you will allow us to do.
>
> London: Who can free you? These are dangerous men; they are a scattered company sown in all the city.... Hold them the book.
>
> Eaton: I dare not swear nor take this oath,[23] though I will not refuse it, I will consider it....
>
> Canterbury: What do you say, woman?
>
> Jones: I dare not worship God in vain.
>
> London: Will you not swear and take an oath when you are called to it by the magistrate?
>
> Jones: Yes, I will answer upon my oath to end a controversy before a lawful magistrate.

---

[22] See Ibid., 145–47; Champlin Burrage, *The Early English Dissenters in the Light of Recent Research: Illustrative Documents*, 2 vols. (Cambridge: University Press, 1912) 2:313–15; and B. R. White, "Samuel Eaton (d. 1639): A Particular Baptist Pioneer," *Baptist Quarterly* 24/1 (January 1971): 10–12.

[23] This was the *ex officio* oath requiring prisoners to testify against themselves and others.

Earl of Dorsett [Edward Sackville]: What! do you think, woman, [that] these grave fathers of the church...here are not lawful magistrates?

Jones: I would do anything that is according to God's word.

Archbishop of York [Samuel Harsnett]: Would you? Then you must take your oath. Now you are required by your governors. You must swear in truth, in judgment, in righteousness.

Neither Eaton nor Jones wavered in their belief that they had to follow their consciences rather than succumb to the intimidation of their oppressors. At the conclusion of the interrogation, the commissioners returned the prisoners to Gatehouse Prison.[24]

While Laud struggled to force people to conform to the theology of the Anglican Church, Charles attempted to rule the affairs of the state. Like his father before him, Charles deplored parliaments, except when he needed money from them. Frustrated by Parliament's refusal to grant him all the money he demanded, the king attempted to raise funds by forcing port towns to pay for the navy and by requiring taxpayers to "lend" money to the Crown. Citizens had to pay 1 percent of the value of their land and 5 percent of the worth of their personal property. The Crown imprisoned wealthy citizens who opposed these measures; the poor who opposed them did not receive such mercy—they were forced to serve in the army or the navy. Despite these and other money-making schemes, Charles continued to be strapped for money. Therefore, in March 1628 he summoned Parliament and demanded that it give him the money he wanted. Charles revealed his contempt for members of Parliament when he told them that he was not threatening them, for he only threatened his equals.[25] Instead of issuing the funds the king had demanded, however, in May Parliament issued the Petition of Right, a document that limited the monarch's power, and demanded that Charles accept the document if he wanted money. The king

---

[24] For more on Sarah Jones, see Stephen Wright, "Sarah Jones and the Jacob-Jessey Church: *The Relation of a Gentlewoman*," *Electronic British Library Journal* (2004) art. 2, pp. 1–9, http://www.bl.uk/collections/eblj/2004/article2.html (accessed 27 September 2005).

[25] Durant and Durant, *The Age of Reason Begins*, 202.

dismissed both the petition and Parliament, which would not meet again until 1640.

In 1637 Charles decided that he would impose Anglican reforms on the staunchly Presbyterian Scots, who were quite willing to defend their state church. Failing twice to defeat them militarily in 1639 and 1640, and desperately needing funds to wage another military campaign against his stubborn subjects to the north, Charles summoned Parliament again in November 1640. He wanted to discuss money, but Parliament preferred to discuss the issues contained in the Petition of Right. Tired of the king's bullying and of Laud's strong-armed ecclesiastical policies, the House of Commons impeached and then jailed the archbishop in December for treason. Exasperated by Parliament's stubborn refusal to bow to his every command, and failing to learn the lesson of Laud's imprisonment, Charles attempted unsuccessfully in January 1642 to have five members of Parliament arrested. Despite these heavy-handed tactics, Parliament refused to disband and continued passing laws undermining the king's authority.

In 1642 the conflict between the Crown and Parliament finally transitioned from words to weapons when the first of the English civil wars began. That war lasted until 1646, when Royalist forces lost two decisive battles, which forced Charles to seek protection from his former enemies, the Scottish forces encamped in northern England.

After being ransomed by Parliament, then being kidnapped by some parliament troops, and eventually escaping to the Isle of Wight, Charles convinced the Scots to fight with him, leading to another civil war in 1648. The Royalist and Scottish forces proved to be no match for the Parliamentary Army, led by Oliver Cromwell, and were soon defeated. Because Parliament continued negotiating with the king as if he still ruled England and because soldiers were angered about not being paid, the army took over Parliament and tried Charles for treason.

During the civil wars, many Baptists joined the fight against Charles. One Baptist, Lieutenant-Colonel William Packer, so distinguished himself that when an officer dismissed him from the army because of his religious affiliation, Cromwell immediately reinstated him. Other Baptists wrote several drill-books for the cavalry and infantry, and many garrison towns had Baptist officers who were also preachers. As the army moved about England, several Baptist churches sprang up where regiments were quartered or where they laid siege. Several Baptists became commanders, and others served as chaplains.[26]

The Presbyterian Parliament

While many English citizens were preoccupied with killing each other for political reasons during the civil wars, nonconformists thrived. Many supporters of Parliament "were appalled by the Pandora's box which they unwittingly opened. They did not intend the 'anarchy of private conscience' that they let loose: the multitude of sects and heresies, the 'rude mechanick preachers,' the mystical enthusiasisms, the capricious and ignorant interpretations of scripture, and the attacks on tithes and infant baptism."[27] Yet, according to one anonymous author, more than Pandora's box had been opened: all hell had broken loose, spewing forth its errors, heresies, and blasphemies throughout England.[28]

To stem the spread of heresy, Parliament called the Westminster Assembly of Divines in 1643, which replaced the Anglican Church with the Presbyterian Church. The divines issued a confession of faith, stating that magistrates must fulfill their duty to preserve "unity and peace...in the church, that the truth of God be kept pure and entire, that all blasphemies and heresies be suppressed, all corruptions and abuses in worship and discipline prevented and reformed, and all ordinances of God duly settled, administered, and observed."[29] For too long, the divines reasoned, England had been in the clutches of ungodly, intolerant Anglican priests and bishops.

---

[26] W. T. Whitley, *A History of British Baptists* (London: Charles Griffin & Company, Limited, 1923) 73–75. See also H. Wheeler Robinson, *The Life and Faith of the Baptists*, rev. ed., in *British Baptists*, The Baptist Tradition (London: The Kingsgate Press, 1946; repr., New York: Arno Press, 1980) 32–36, 127–28, and B. R. White, "The English General Baptists and the Great Rebellion 1640–1660," *Baptist History and Heritage* 8/1 (January 1973): 17.

[27] Mark Goldie, "The Search for Religious Liberty, 1640–1690," in *The Oxford Illustrated History of Tudor & Stuart Britain*, ed. John Morrill (Oxford: Oxford University Press, 1996) 295.

[28] See *Hell Broke Loose: or, A Catalogue of the Spreading Errors, Heresies and Blasphemies of These Times, for Which We Are to Be Humbled* (London: printed for Tho. Underhill, 1646).

[29] "The Westminster Confession of Faith, 1643," in *Documents of the Christian Church*, 2nd ed., ed. Henry Bettenson (London: Oxford University Press, 1963) 247.

Now, with the blessing of Parliament, Presbyterians could show the world what a godly intolerance looked like.

Apparently, however, many preachers and authors did not think that Parliament was doing enough to suppress heretics. Preachers tried to light a fire under Parliament so that it would light fires under heretics. In a sermon on 22 October 1644, Edmund Calamy, a Presbyterian preacher, warned members of Parliament, "If you do not labor according to your duty and power to suppress the errors and heresies that are spread in the kingdom, all these errors are your errors, and these heresies are your heresies; they are your sins, and God calls for a parliamentary repentance from you for them this day. You are the Anabaptists, you are the Antinomians, and it is you who hold all religions to be tolerated."[30]

On 30 April 1645, John Burgess, a Presbyterian minister, presented Parliament with a biblical justification of persecution. In words that illustrate all too well Shakespeare's dictum, "In religion/ What damned error, but some sober brow/ Will bless it and approve it with a text!" Burgess thundered:

> Is it persecution and antichristian to engage all to unity and uniformity? Does Paul bid the Philippians "beware of the circumcision"? Does he beseech the Romans to "mark those which cause divisions and offences contrary to the doctrines they have received, and avoid them"? Does he in writing to the Galatians wish, "I would they were even cut off that trouble you"? And is it such a heinous offence now for the faithful servants of Christ to advise you to the same course? Good heavens![31]

Authors also took the opportunity to demonize religious liberty. According to the anonymous author of *Against Universall Libertie of Conscience*, "A universal liberty of conscience is a universal liberty to sin, to maintain heresy, to practice idolatry, to vent blasphemy; in a word, a

---

[30] Quoted in Henry Vedder, "Baptists and Liberty of Conscience: The Opposition of Presbyterians and Independents," *Baptist Quarterly Review* 6/23 (July–September 1884): 360.

[31] Quoted in Joseph Ivimey, *A History of the English Baptists*, 4 vols. (London: privately printed, 1811) 1:168. The verses Burgess quoted were Philippians 3:2, Romans 16:17, and Galatians 5:12. The quotation from Shakespeare comes from the *Merchant of Venice*, 3.2.77–79.

universal liberty to dishonor God, under the pretense of serving him and to damn one's own soul irrecoverably (unless everyone may be saved by his own religion, though never so false) and to hazard (as much as men can) the damnation of multitudes of others, who may be infected by such poisonfull doctrines."[32] Thomas Edwards, a Presbyterian minister, declared "toleration" to be "the grand design of the devil," containing "all evils" and violating every tenet of the Bible. The devil, Edwards continued, followed toleration "night and day, working mightily in many by writing books for it, and other ways, all the devils in hell and their instruments being at work to promote a toleration." After laying low for thousands of years, "The devil then bestirred himself and set pretended liberty of conscience on foot...as the most powerful and likely means to recover and strengthen his kingdom." Therefore, Edwards hoped that "the Parliaments, assembly, ministers, city, and the whole kingdom considering the evil of a toleration will cry it down and abominate the very thought of it."[33]

Many people predicted that the havoc created by religious liberty in the church would also be detrimental to the state. According to a group of London ministers, England "will be woefully weakened by scandals and divisions so that enemies of it both domestic and foreign will be encouraged to plot and practice against it."[34]

To counteract the numerous heresies being spread in England and to save the country from falling into the hands of Satan and his minions, Parliament acted in 1648 by passing an ordinance "for the preventing of the growth and spreading of heresy and blasphemy."[35] Among the crimes punishable by incarceration was the teaching "that the baptizing of infants is unlawful, or such baptism is void, and that such persons ought to be baptized again, and in pursuance thereof, shall baptize any person formerly

---

[32] *Against Universall Libertie of Conscience, Being Animadversions upon Two Letters Written to a Friend Pleading for It* (London: printed for Thomas Underhill, 1644) 2.

[33] Thomas Edwards, *Gangraena*, 3 vols. (London: printed by T. R. and E. M. for Ralph Smith, 1645) 1:122–23.

[34] *A Letter of the Ministers of the City of London...against Toleration* (London: printed for Samuel Gellibrand, 1645) 5.

[35] *An Ordinance of the Lords and Commons Assembled in Parliament, for Punishing Blasphemies and Heresies* (London: printed for Edw. Husband, 1648), in Thomas Crosby, *The History of the English Baptists from the Reformation to the Beginning of the Reign of King George I*, 4 vols. (London: privately printed, 1738) 1:199.

baptized."[36] This part of the ordinance directly attacked Baptists, who, in minds of many, were the "fount of all heresy."[37]

Edward Barber: A "Prisoner in Newgate for the Cause of Christ"[38]

One prominent General Baptist pastor who ran afoul of the law long before Parliament's 1648 ordinance was Edward Barber (d. 1663? or 1674?), who humbly described himself as merely a "citizen and merchant-tailor of London."[39] Contrary to the early Baptist historian Thomas Crosby, Barber probably had not been a minister in the Church of England before becoming a Baptist.[40] The exact date of Barber's acceptance of Baptist teachings is unknown, but in 1637 the church where he and his wife, Mary, worshiped excommunicated them for holding Baptist beliefs.[41]

In June 1639 the High Commission summoned Barber for denying that God had ordained "the sprinkling of infants" and the paying of mandatory tithes to support ministers.[42] Before the court, Barber refused to take the *ex officio* oath, which required defendants to testify against themselves and others. For his heresy and obstinacy, he spent eleven months in Newgate Prison.[43]

During his incarceration, Barber authored a petition titled *To the Kings Most Excellent Majesty, and the Honourable Court of Parliament* in which he argued for the religious liberty of every person. When magistrates "set laws

---

[36] Ibid., 1:203.

[37] See J. F. McGregor, "The Baptists: Fount of All Heresy," in *Radical Religion in the English Revolution*, ed. J. F. McGregor and B. Reay (Oxford: Oxford University Press, 1984) 23–63.

[38] Edward Barber, *To the Kings most Excellent Majesty, and the Honourable Court of Parliament* ([London:] n.p., 1641). Barber described himself with these words at the end of his petition. Because the petition is printed in two columns on one page, I have used lc (left column) and rc (right column) instead of page numbers. The quoted material here is centered at the bottom of the text.

[39] Edward Barber, *A Small Treatise of Baptisme, or Dipping* (n.p: 1641) [vi].

[40] "Baptists in Literature till 1688," *Transactions of the Baptist Historical Society* 1/2 (April 1909): 119.

[41] P. R. S. Baker, "Barber, Edward (d. 1663)," *Oxford Dictionary of National Biography* (Oxford: Oxford University Press, 2004), http://www.oxforddnb.com./view/article/1328 (accessed 16 July 2005).

[42] Barber, *A Small Treatise of Baptisme*, [vi].

[43] Baker, "Barber, Edward (d. 1663)."

for the souls and consciences of men," Barber contended, they usurp "that government and authority to...which appertains only to God."[44] On behalf of himself and other Newgate prisoners, whom he described as the king's "loyal and faithful subjects," Barber maintained that they had done nothing to deserve their imprisonment and that if their actions were to be judged solely by the Bible, they would be found innocent of all charges. Nevertheless, even if they had taught errors, he argued, that would still not be grounds for persecuting them because persecution violated the teachings of Jesus. In his parable of the tares and wheat (Matt 13:24–30, 36–43), Jesus taught that the tares, whom Barber identified as adherents of false religion, would receive their punishment on Judgment Day and should "should be left alone" until then (Matt 15:14). Moreover, when his own disciples asked if he wanted them to ask God to destroy his opponents, Jesus rebuked them (Luke 9:54–56), which Barber interpreted to mean "that Christ would have no man hurt for religion." When Jesus sent the disciples to preach, he told them that if people refused to listen to them, they were to shake the dust off their feet and move on (Matt 10:14–15). The apostle Paul also advocated for religious liberty because repentance was a gift of God, not something that could be produced by violence (2 Cor 10:4–5; 2 Tim 2:24–26; Eph 2:5).[45] Therefore, Barber declared that the "gospel way" of turning people who live in darkness to God's light is by exhortation and persuasion, never by coercion.

Barber used numerous passages of scripture and non-biblical examples to defend his understanding of religious liberty. At times, however, his use of the Bible can only be described as bizarre. For example, he cited two verses (Deut 27:5; Josh 8:31) describing the building of an altar (which he incorrectly called the Temple), making much of the fact that because "there was no sound of iron heard...Christ will have in his church a free consent, not compelled nor constrained by laws and statutes."[46] Perhaps Barber was trying to contrast the sound of prison irons with the lack of iron in the altar. His use of historical examples did not fare much better, for, like John Murton before him, Barber incorrectly quoted King James and Martin Luther to support his advocacy of religious liberty.

---

[44] Barber, *To the Kings most Excellent Majesty*, rc.

[45] Ibid., lc.

[46] Ibid., rc.

For people who used force in matters of religion, Barber had harsh words. Such people were "not gospel teachers" but rapists of souls. Just as a man can rape a woman, so a man can rape another's conscience, and a rapist of any stripe, Barber warned, is worthy of death.[47] The Crown and the Anglican Church could force people into church, but in so doing, they could only "make hypocrites, but not true Christians."[48]

After being released from prison, Barber continued his preaching and writing ministry. His book *A Small Treatise of Baptisme, or Dipping* perhaps "was the first work in England during the seventeenth century that favored immersion as a form of baptism."[49] Barber's church in London was most likely the first Baptist church to lay hands on baptized believers, a practice that probably began in 1646.[50] The circumstances and date of Barber's death are unknown.

Henry Denne: "A Man of Decision and Zeal"[51]

While many Baptists fought in the Parliamentary Army, others fought in court. Henry Denne (c. 1605–1666), however, fought in both war zones and spent time in prison during the first English civil war before spending time in the army. Twice a graduate of Oxford, Denne served as an Anglican minister for ten years after being ordained in 1630. In a scathing sermon

---

[47] Ibid., rc. Barber cited Deuteronomy 22:25: "But if the man meets the engaged woman in the open country, and the man seizes her and lies with her, then only the man who lay with her shall die." See also Henry Adis, "An After-Writing to the King," in *A Fannaticks Mite Cast into the Kings Treasury: Being A Sermon Printed to the King Because not Preached before the King*, by Henry Adis, 2nd ed. (London: printed by S. Dover for the author, 1660) [vi], and Busher, *Religions Peace*, 34: "Thirteenthly—Because persecution for religion is to force the conscience; and to force and constrain men and women's consciences to a religion against their will, is to tyrannize over the soul, as well as over the body. And herein the bishops commit a greater sin, than if they force the bodies of women and maids against their wills."

[48] Ibid., rc.

[49] Baker, "Barber, Edward (d. 1663)."

[50] Thompson Cooper, "Barber, Edward (d. 1674?)," *Dictionary of National Biography*, ed. Leslie Stephen and Sidney Lee, 63 vols. (London: Smith, Elder, & Co., 1885) 3:146; Baker, "Barber, Edward (d. 1663)."

[51] Adam Taylor, *The History of the English General Baptists: The English General Baptists of the Seventeenth Century*, 2 vols. (London: printed for the author, 1818) 1:101

preached in 1641, Denne criticized his fellow Anglican ministers for their pride, greed, and laziness.[52] Realizing that his days in the Church of England were over, he then left the established church.

By 1643 Denne had become a Baptist and a member of Thomas Lamb's General Baptist church in London. This church sent him out to be a traveling evangelist and church planter.[53] His success earned him the scorn of Thomas Edwards, who called him "an Anabaptist...a great Antinomian, [and] a desperate Arminian." Edwards claimed that Denne had been "re-baptized by a mechanic" and then traveled about, preaching "universal grace," re-baptizing many people, and doing "much mischief."[54]

Despite being "an avowed Baptist," Denne pastored a parish church at Eltisley, near Cambridge, probably in 1643.[55] The following year he preached against infant baptism, which resulted in his being arrested and then jailed at Cambridge, where he spent several weeks before being sent to London to be imprisoned in Peterhouse Prison on Aldersgate Street. After his release in 1645, he continued to preach and was again arrested in 1646 at Spalding for baptizing four converts in a river. Denne confessed to preaching four sermons there, but not to baptizing anyone.[56]

Out of jail, but also out of work and money, Denne joined the Parliamentary Army in 1647 and was a captain in a cavalry regiment. In 1649 he participated in a Leveller-led mutiny. The Levellers were so-named because their opponents claimed that the group wanted to reduce everyone to the same socioeconomic level. The mutiny failed, and Denne and three others were sentenced to be executed. Denne, however, recanted and was pardoned; the other condemned mutineers were shot. Of his good fortune, he confessed, "I am not worthy of such a mercy; I am more ashamed to live, than afraid to die."[57] Most Levellers would have agreed with Denne's self-

---

[52] For the introduction to Denne's sermon, see Crosby, *The History of the English Baptists*, 1:298–300.

[53] T. L. Underwood, "Denne, Henry (1605/6?–1666)," *Oxford Dictionary of National Biography*, http://www.oxforddnb.com./view/article/7497 (accessed 22 July 2005).

[54] Edwards, *Gangraena*, 1:76.

[55] Taylor, *The History of the English General Baptists*, 1:103.

[56] Underwood, "Denne, Henry (1605/1606?–1666)."

[57] Quoted in W. Harvey Smith, "Some Seventeenth Century Baptists: Denne—Keach—Bunyan; and Others," in *The English Baptists: Who They Are, and What They*

assessment, for his capitulation earned him the scorn of one imprisoned Leveller leader who branded him as "that accursed English Judas."[58] After leaving the army, Denne returned to the pastoral ministry.

Before his death in 1666, Denne authored at least five books. Although his writings reveal a confrontational spirit, his preaching "was persuasive and affectionate."[59] His epitaph, allegedly written by an Anglican minister, highlighted Denne's character: "To tell his wisdom, learning, goodness unto men,/ I need to say no more, but—here lies Henry Denne."[60]

Denne left behind one document that he perhaps wrote in prison, or at least one he began in prison. Upon entering the London's Peterhouse Prison in 1645, he received a copy of Daniel Featley's *The Dippers Dipt*. After reading the book, Denne felt compelled "to defend the truth against the adversary."[61] He publicly debated Featley, a fellow inmate in Peterhouse who had been accused of being a Royalist spy. After the two debated a few topics, Featley refused to continue. He then sent word to Denne, asking him to write what he believed and then Featley would respond. Denne accepted the challenge and, "from prison in the Lord," hurriedly wrote *Antichrist Unmasked*, which also included a response to a book by Stephen Marshall, an Anglican minister.[62]

In his book Denne reminded his readers that they lived in a day when "many adversaries…bestir themselves, with policy and force, to keep us (if it were possible) in perpetual darkness and to hinder the rising of the sun in our hearts."[63] Nevertheless, "The Lord has been pleased at this day, to put into the hearts and tongues of some, to stand up in the defense of his truth" concerning believer's baptism. Many, however, were prepared to respond to

---

Have Done, ed. John Clifford (London: E. Marlborough & Co., 1881) 79. For Denne's account of the mutiny, see *The Levellers Designe Discovered* (London: n.p., 1649), available online at http://baptistlibraryonline.com/blo/ content/view/33/25.

[58] Richard Overton, *Overton's Defyance of the Act of Pardon* (London: n.p., 1649) 5. See also Cecil M. Roper, "Henry Denne and the Fenstanton Baptists in England," *Baptist History and Heritage* 16/4 (October 1981): 29.

[59] Taylor, *The History of the English General Baptists*, 1:102.

[60] Quoted in Roper, "Henry Denne and the Fenstanton Baptists in England," 30.

[61] Henry Denne, *Antichrist Unmasked in Two Treatises. The First, An Answer unto Two Paedobaptists, Dan. Featly, D.D. and Stephen Marshall, B.D.…* (n.p., 1645) A2.

[62] Ibid., [A3].

[63] Ibid., 2.

this truth "with reviling and railing accusations," and if these responses proved to be futile, defenders of infant baptism stood ready to imprison or banish "those who shall dare to uphold or maintain that which in conscience they are persuaded to be the truth."[64] Denne then addressed ten arguments, in an argument-response format, that paedobaptists used to support infant baptism. What follows is a brief summary of those arguments accompanied by selections of Denne's responses. These critically important arguments against infant baptism reveal precise reasons why many Baptists were imprisoned in the 1600s.

Argument 1: Christ commanded his disciples to preach, baptize, and disciple people in all nations (Matt 28:19). Therefore, because children comprise a large percentage of a nation's population, they too should be baptized.

Response: Such an argument is deceptive and false, "for something may extend to all nations, which does not belong to every particular person in the nation, nor yet to every condition of men in the nation."[65] For example, Abraham's seed is a blessing to all nations (Gen 22:18), yet the only people in those nations who are blessed are those who accept Christ (see Rom 4:11; Gal 3:9). Moreover, preaching extends to all nations, but even Featley admitted "that it does not extend itself to little children in the cradle."[66] Therefore, Denne concluded, children cannot be made disciples (see Luke 14:27).[67]

Argument 2: No one should exclude children from the kingdom of heaven, which denying them baptism does.

Response: If by "kingdom of heaven" paedobaptists meant the visible church on earth, Denne maintained that children should be excluded because they are "incapable of membership in a visible church" because they are "incapable of hearing, with understanding, the sound of the gospel."[68] If paedobaptists equated the kingdom with God's revelation to a person's soul (see Rom 14:17; Luke 17:21), then infants are again excluded from the kingdom, for they are "incapable of discerning either good or evil, and of

---

[64] Ibid., 2–3.
[65] Ibid, 6.
[66] Ibid., 7.
[67] Ibid., 10.
[68] Ibid., 14–15.

receiving the manifestations and apprehensions of God in the soul."[69] If, however, paedobaptists interpreted the kingdom as God's grace, mercy, and favor as revealed in Christ (which, according to Denne, they did), then denying baptism to infants does not exclude them from the kingdom because "children are as free from sin, as fully in the favor and grace of God before baptism, as after."[70]

Argument 3: Christ's apostles baptized whole families, which included infants (see Acts 10:2, 11:14, 16:33).

Response: No one can prove that these families included children. Those baptized heard the word of God, believed, and rejoiced; therefore, "how any such should be a child in a cradle, not able to discern good and evil, we are (as yet) not able to understand."[71]

Argument 4: Like Jewish parents who circumcise their children as a seal of God's covenant, Christian parents must now baptize their children, for baptism has replaced circumcision as the seal (see Col 2:8–12).

Response: God commanded that all Jewish male children be circumcised. Yet John the Baptist claimed that only repentant people should be baptized (see Matt 3:1–12). John's message, Denne asserted, was this: "Until now you [Jews] have lived under a national church, under carnal ordinances, wherein the chaff and the wheat have been mingled together, without separation, and have seemed to enjoy the same privileges and prerogatives under the carnal commandment. But now comes one, 'whose fanne is in his hand, and hee will thoroughly purge His Floure, and gather the Wheat into his Garner, but the Chaffe will Hee burne with unquenchable fire'" (Matt 3:12).[72] Thus, the gospel places higher requirements for baptism than the law did for circumcision. Moreover, since only male Jewish children are circumcised, Denne wondered, why then do paedobaptists baptize female infants?

Argument 5: Those who lived in the covenant community were not prohibited from receiving the seal of the covenant through circumcision; therefore, they had to receive it. Now, because children live in the covenant

---

[69] Ibid., 15.
[70] Ibid.
[71] Ibid., 23.
[72] Ibid., 27.

of faith and because baptism has superseded circumcision as the seal of the covenant, children must be baptized.

Response: Male children were part of the Jewish covenant community "before they were eight days old because God had set the eighth day [as] an expressed time for circumcision. And so has God [now] set an expressed time for baptism: *viz. The time of believing.*"[73]

Argument 6: Those who were baptized under the law, as the crossing of the Red Sea symbolized, are capable of being baptized under the gospel. The throng that passed through the sea included children; therefore, children can now be baptized.

Response: The passing through the Red Sea was in no way a symbol or type of Christian baptism. Moreover, though children did pass through the sea, so did non-Israelites and cattle. Should they be baptized too?[74]

Argument 7: Every member of Christ's kingdom should be baptized, and since Christ taught that children belong to his kingdom (Mk 10:14–15), no one should deny them entrance into the kingdom through baptism.

Response: People belong to Christ's kingdom in two ways: first, by election, which is secret; and second, by calling, which is visible. Baptism belongs to calling. Jesus, "by his divine knowledge," did say that the children mentioned in Mark 10:14–15 belonged to his kingdom, "yet...he neither baptized them, nor...commanded them to be baptized, although (I say) he knew they belonged to his kingdom." How "dare you baptize infants," Denne reproached his opponents, "when you do not know whether they belong to the kingdom of God or not."[75]

Argument 8: Because children can receive inward grace, they should not be prevented from receiving the outward sign (baptism) of that grace. No one, the apostle Peter declared, can deny baptism to anyone who has received the gift of the Holy Spirit (Acts 10:47).

Response: Such is the "deceitful, and puddled, and confounded" argument of men who "have yet to receive the gift of which Peter" spoke. Only those persons who can understand God's grace and mercy, and who, in good conscience, can lead the life of faith should be baptized.[76] Children

---

73 Ibid., 37–38.
74 Ibid., 45.
75 Ibid., 46.
76 Ibid., 48.

have neither understanding of nor the ability to live the Christian faith; therefore, they cannot be baptized.

Argument 9: According to Featley, "The baptism of children is an apostolic tradition" that the church should continue, and Marshall wrote, "Origin says, the church received the traditions of baptizing infants from the" written and unwritten traditions of the apostles.[77]

Response: Featley and Marshall quoted the Bible and the early church fathers out of context to prove their positions. Fealtey "himself confessed to me," Denne alleged, that he did so intentionally. "With great fraud" Featly did this. "Judge I pray you," Denne challenged his readers, whether such conduct was "Christian or not."[78] In Denne's opinion, it was "not."

Argument 10: All members of the Protestant Reformed Churches should adhere to the teaching of the Protestant confessions, which advocate infant baptism; therefore, "let the Anabaptists" either "disclaim the name of Protestants" or accept infant baptism.

Response: "O man full of subtlety! How long will you labor to deceive?" Denne exclaimed. When the teachings of the confessions are biblically grounded, Baptists accept them. When they are not, Baptists reject them. Denne agreed that the confessions endorsed infant baptism, "but that these confessions are in this point grounded upon scripture is the thing we deny," and where "they have swerved from the line, their example must not be our precedent: for 'wee have a more sure word of prophesie, whereunto yee do well, that yee take heed as unto a light shining in a darke place, untill the day dawne, and the day-starre appeare in you hearts' (2 Pet. 1:19)."[79]

As the title suggests, *Antichrist Unmasked* was not a friendly dialogue between Christians who differed on some minor points of theology. In the book Denne repeatedly emphasized the position Baptists held in the 1640s, a position for which they often paid a heavy price: Only believers can be baptized; infants cannot believe; therefore, ministers cannot baptize infants. In light of the passion with which he wrote and the utter disdain in which he held paedobaptists, that Denne did not spend the rest of his life languishing in prison is amazing.

---

[77] Ibid., 49.
[78] Ibid., 50.
[79] Ibid., 52.

Lawrence Clarkson: A "Dipper" Turned from Dipping

Throughout their prison experiences, men like Thomas Helwys, John Murton, Edward Barber, and Henry Denne remained Baptists. However, not everyone who entered prison a Baptist came out a Baptist. Lawrence Clarkson (1615–1667) grew up in an Anglican home, but, defying his father's wishes, he often snuck out to listen to "godly ministers." He left the Anglican Church to become a Presbyterian, but he later became an Independent. Clarkson pastored a church for a while, but he was fired because, he said, jealous ministers accused him of stealing their members. He continued to preach in the areas around Suffolk and Norfolk, northeast of London, but he then met John Taylor, a Baptist, who took him to London, where, on 6 November 1644, Clarkson "was buried under the water."[80]

After his baptism, Clarkson returned to the Suffolk area, preaching and baptizing eleven people, for which he was eventually arrested and imprisoned in January 1645. Clarkson tried but failed to get released. After a visit by a couple of Seekers who convinced him that baptism had ended with the apostles, Clarkson recanted his Baptist beliefs. In July he petitioned the authorities to release him, stating: "Whereas your petitioner has been about six months in bonds for dipping: in which time he has taken great pains, both by dispute and searching the scriptures, in which he does find, and is convinced, that he ought not to dip any more, neither after the day of his convincement, being the 10th of July, will your petitioner either dip, or teach for the same, but only wait upon God for a further manifestation of his truth: so expecting your worships answer, [I] shall daily pray."[81]

On 15 July 1645 Clarkson testified before a committee overseeing his case. He admitted to having been an "Anabaptist" and to "dipping" people; however, despite his previous proclamation that

> he would not leave his dipping if he might gain all the committee's estates by it, now he says that he, by the holy scriptures, is

---

[80] Edwards, *Gangraena*, 1:72; A. L. Morton, "Clarkson (or Claxton), Lawrence (1615–1667)," in *Biographical Dictionary of British Radicals in the Seventeenth Century*, ed. Richard L. Greaves and Robert Zaller, 3 vols. (Brighton England: Harvester Press, 1982) 1:149.

[81] Reprinted in Edwards, *Gangraena*, 1:72.

convinced that his said opinions were erroneous, and that he will not, nor dare not practice it again if he might gain all the committee's estates by doing it; and that he makes his recantation, not for fear or to gain his liberty, but merely out of a sense of his errors, wherein he will endeavor to reform others.[82]

Having convinced the committee that he had repented of his errors, Clarkson gained his freedom and, according to Edwards, "turned from Anabaptist and dipper to be a Seeker, and [ultimately] to deny the scriptures to be the rule of a Christian."[83]

The Decapitations of the Archbishop and the King

The tumultuous decade of the 1640s saw drastic religious and political changes. England had a new state church, yet the numerous dissenting sects felt emboldened to spread their beliefs. The events that symbolized these changes occurred when the heads of both church and state literally lost their heads. Archbishop Laud had vehemently denied ever persecuting people for their religious beliefs. "God forbid," he wrote to King Charles in 1639, that "I should ever offer to persuade a persecution in any kind, or practice it in the least…. But, on the other side, God forbid, too, that Your Majesty should let both laws and discipline sleep for fear of the name of persecution."[84] That "but" was partly what got Laud impeached and imprisoned. Commenting on one of the charges against him, he declared in his diary: "I have neither by myself, nor by command to my officers, silenced, suspended, deprived, degraded, or excommunicated any learned, pious, and orthodox preachers, nor any other but upon just cause proved in court, according to law. And I think it will appear that as few (be the cause never so just) have been suspended or deprived in my diocese, as in any

---

[82] Reprinted ibid., 1:73.

[83] Ibid.

[84] William Laud, epistle dedicatory to *A Relation of the Conference between William Laud, Late Lord Archbishop of Canterbury, by the Command of King James, of ever Blessed Memory…*, 6th ed. (Oxford: John Henry Parker, 1849) x. Available online at http://justus.anglican.org/resources/pc/lact/laud/v2/dedicatory.html (accessed 14 March 2005).

diocese in England. Nor have I by these suspensions hindered the preaching of God's word, but of schism and sedition."[85]

On the first day of his trial before the House of Lords in 1644, Laud stood firm in his belief that uniformity in faith and practice was the key to spiritual unity. He told his accusers, "Ever since I came in place, I labored nothing more than that the external worship of God (too much slighted in most parts of this kingdom) might be preserved, and that with as much decency, and uniformity as might be; being still of the opinion that unity cannot long continue in the church, where uniformity is shut out the door."[86] At the end of the twenty-day trial, which was stretched over nine months, the Lords adjourned without voting on the archbishop's guilt or innocence. Sensing that the Lords would not vote to condemn Laud, the House of Commons substituted its impeachment with a bill of attainder, which allowed the Lords to punish Laud without a trial. With only nineteen members present, the Lords passed the bill and had Laud beheaded on 10 January 1645.

On 30 January 1649 Laud's king, who had been found guilty of treason, also lost his head. On the cold morning of his execution, Charles put on two shirts to keep him from shivering and appearing to be afraid. As he walked to his execution, he passed through the Banqueting Hall in Whitehall Palace, where Rubens's paintings symbolizing the divine right of kings adorned the ceiling, though covered with boards. The British historian John Miller described Charles's execution this way: "When he was led to the scaffold, he made a short speech. He declared that he was going from a corruptible to an incorruptible crown and that 'a subject and a sovereign are clear different things.' A single blow of the axe severed his head from his

---

[85] William Laud, *The History of the Troubles and Tryal of the Most Reverend Father in God, William Laud* (London: printed for Ri. Chilwell, 1694), in William Laud, *The Works of the Most Reverend Father in God, William Laud, D.D.: Devotions, Diary, and History*, 7 vols. (Oxford: John Henry Parker, 1847) 3:420. For examples of some of the men whom Laud helped to be imprisoned, beaten, and mutilated, see Durant and Durant, *The Age of Reason Begins*, 189–90.

[86] William Laud, *The History of the Troubles and Trial of Archbishop Laud*, in *The Works of the Most Reverend Father in God, William Laud, D.D.: History of the Troubles and Trial, etc.*, 7 vols. (Oxford: John Henry Parker, 1854) 4:60.

body. When the executioner held up his head, the cheers of the soldiers were drowned by a great collective groan."[87]

"'You are gods,'" said God, according to a psalmist (Ps 82:6). Monarchs loved to quote this part of the verse to remind their subjects that "a subject and a sovereign are clear different things." Yet the executioner's axe should have reminded everyone, including monarchs, that the rest of the verse was equally applicable: "Nevertheless, you shall die like mortals, and fall like any prince." When the heads of Laud and Charles fell, so did the Church of England and the monarchy. Unlike the archbishop and the king, however, the Church of England and the Crown would rise again in England, and they would continue imprisoning Baptists. The question that faced England in the meantime was, who would fill the power vacuum left by the decapitations of Laud and Charles I?

---

[87] Miller, *The Stuarts*, 111.

Chapter 4

Birds in a Cage

When two fellow members of Parliament asked Oliver Cromwell what he would put in the place of the Church of England, he responded, "I can tell you, sirs, what I would not have, though I cannot, what I would."[1] That answer could also have been given to a question concerning the monarchy. Many English men and women knew that they did not want a tyrant for a king, but they were at a loss as to who should replace him. Parliament eventually chose Presbyterianism as the state religion, and eventually Cromwell, a mediocre member of Parliament who turned out to be an exceptional military leader, replaced the king.

The Interregnum (1649–1660)

The Interregnum, the time between reigns of Charles I and his son Charles II, was chaotic. With the king dead, England needed a strong leader to guide it through perilous waters, and Cromwell filled that leadership void. He had proven himself during the civil wars, which, in the eyes of many, made him the logical choice to lead England. That Cromwell headed the most powerful military force in England did not hurt his chances either.

During the years that Cromwell governed England, Baptists, like other dissenting groups, experienced a respite from the previous decades of persecution. The religious toleration that England experienced was, nevertheless, always a tenuous one. Legally, Baptists could still be punished for their faith, and they did not have anything resembling civil or political rights. Thus, the toleration during the Interregnum was the offspring of the

---

[1] Quoted in Christopher Hill, *The Century of Revolution, 1603–1714*, The Norton Library History of England (New York: W. W. Norton & Company, Inc., 1961) 106.

political necessity to unite diverse groups to remove Charles I.[2] Yet Cromwell was noted for his religious toleration. He permitted Jews, who as a group had been banished from England in 1290, to return, and Catholics and Anglicans could worship freely, provided that they did so quietly.[3] However, Cromwell withheld such leniency from Quakers. Because of his inclination toward toleration, Baptists generally welcomed his leadership.[4]

The freedom enjoyed by most nonconformist groups, however, had its limits. Parishes could choose their own ministers, but to ensure that only godly men held pastoral positions, Cromwell established the Committee of Triers in 1654. Consisting mainly of Independents, Presbyterians, and Baptists, triers interviewed ministers to determine their attitudes toward the government and their commitment to Puritan ideals. The government also appointed ejectors commissioned to evict ministers who did not satisfy the triers. Apparently some Baptists, now free from being persecuted for their beliefs, saw an opportunity to rid the country of ministers they deemed inferior. Writing near the end of the nineteenth century, Henry Vedder, a Baptist historian, offered the following rebuke of Baptist triers and of Baptist ministers who received their income from the government: "Several Baptists served as triers, and many others received benefices during this time—a very inconsistent course for Baptists to take, and one that it is not easy to pardon, for they sinned against the light."[5]

---

[2] Henry Vedder, "Baptists and Liberty of Conscience: The English Baptists, 1644–1689," *Baptist Quarterly Review* 6/22 (April–June 1884): 224.

[3] For a discussion of Cromwell's attitude toward the Jews, see Simon Schama, *A History of Britain: The Wars of the British, 1603–1776*, 3 vols. (New York: Hyperion, 2001) 2:233–35.

[4] For two differing Baptist attitudes toward Cromwell, see Edward Bean Underhill's introductory notices to *The Necessity of Toleration in Matters of Religion*, by Samuel Richardson (London: n.p., 1647), and to *A Plea for Toleration of Opinions and Persuasions in Matter of Religion*, by John Sturgion (London: printed by S. Dover, 1661), in *Tracts on Liberty of Conscience and Persecution, 1614–1661*, ed. Edward Bean Underhill, Elibron Classics Series (London: J. Haddon, 1846; repr., [Chestnut Hill MA]: Adamant Media Corporation, 2003) 238–43 and 318–21, respectively. *Tracts on Liberty of Conscience and Persecution* is cited hereafter as *TLCP*.

[5] Henry C. Vedder, *A Short History of the Baptists*, rev. ed. (Philadelphia: American Baptist Publication Society, 1897) 150–51. Available online at http://www.reformedreader.org/history/vedder/preface.htm (accessed 28 October 2005).

Despite his toleration in religious matters, Cromwell often ruled with a heavy hand. For example, he crushed the Leveller movement, which advocated a more democratic form of government.[6] And when he became dissatisfied with Parliament, Cromwell, backed by a company of soldiers, dismissed it on 20 April 1653, which one modern historian described "as a text-book *coup d'état*: the bludgeoning of a representative assembly by armed coercion."[7] Later that year when Cromwell accepted the title of Lord Protector, many people wondered what the two civil wars had really accomplished. Cromwell's ruthless actions toward political opponents proved to many that, although the tyrant Charles I was dead, his spirit lived on in the Lord Protector.[8]

Before he died on 3 September 1658, Cromwell named Richard, his son, to succeed him. The best that could be said about Richard "was that no one could think of any reason to dislike him." He lacked his father's iron will and leadership skills, making him "politically defenseless as well as clueless."[9] Presented with a petition signed by 20,000 people demanding that he recall the Parliament that his father had dismissed in 1653 or else face a military insurrection, Richard abdicated and fled to France. For many English men and women, Richard's obvious replacement was Charles I's eldest living son and heir to the throne, Charles II.

---

[6] For a description of the Leveller movement, see Schama, *A History of Britain*, 2:181–89; Joseph Frank, *The Levellers: A History of the Writings of Three Seventeenth-Century Social Democrats: John Lilburne, Richard Overton, William Walwyn* (Cambridge MA: Harvard University Press, 1955); D. Mervin Himbury, "The Religious Beliefs of the Levellers," *Baptist Quarterly* 15/6 (April 1954): 269–76; Brian Manning, "The Levellers and Religion," in *Radical Religion in the English Revolution*, ed. J. F. McGregor and B. Reay (Oxford: Oxford University Press, 1984) 65–90; Michael R. Watts, *The Dissenters: From the Reformation to the French Revolution*, 2 vols. (Oxford: Clarendon Press, 1978) 1:117–29; and Carl Watner, "'Come What, Come Will!': Richard Overton, Libertarian Leveller," *Journal of Libertarian Studies* 4/4 (Fall 1980): 405–10. Watner's article is available at http://64.233.161.104/search?q=cache:_ 9isBTSYcz4J:www.mises.org/journals/jls/4_4/4_4_7.pdf+%22Come+what,+come+wi ll!%22&hl=en (accessed 17 August 2005).

[7] Schama, *A History of Britain*, 2:226.

[8] For a discussion concerning Cromwell's role as a dictator, see Augustine J. D. Farrer, "Cromwell as Dictator," *Baptist Quarterly* 7/5 (January 1935): 193–201.

[9] Schama, *A History of Britain*, 2:246.

The Resurrections of the Monarchy and the Church of England

Having fled England during the civil wars, Charles II (r. 1660–1685) spent a little more than eight and a half years on the European Continent, trying to recoup what he believed to be his divinely ordained crown. Finally, on 8 May 1660 Parliament proclaimed Charles as king. Seventeen days later, the new king landed at Dover, and on 29 May 1660, with an ecstatic crowd of 120,000 cheering him on, Charles triumphantly entered London. The monarchy had risen from the dead.

In the month prior to Parliament's proclaiming him king, Charles issued a declaration from the Dutch town of Breda. Part of the declaration addressed the religious situation in England:

> And because the passion and uncharitableness of the times have produced several opinions in religion, by which men are engaged in parties and animosities against each other (which, when they shall hereafter unite in a freedom of conversation, will be composed or better understood), we do declare a liberty to tender consciences, and that no man shall be disquieted or called in question for differences of opinion in matter of religion, which do not disturb the peace of the kingdom; and that we shall be ready to consent to such an act of Parliament, as, upon mature deliberation, shall be offered to us, for the full granting that indulgence.[10]

The number of ecstatic dissenters who stopped reading after the king's promise of "liberty to tender consciences" is unknown. Those who read, and understood, the meaning of the phrase "which do not disturb the peace of the kingdom" and of the clause "we shall be ready to consent to such an act of Parliament...for the full granting that indulgence" knew that trouble lay ahead for "tender consciences." Parliament had no intention of coddling nonconformists because their very existence threatened the kingdom, and from 1661 on it determined what disturbed "the peace of the kingdom." Filled with Royalists and pro-Anglican members, Parliament resurrected the Church of England, restoring it as the state church.

---

[10] "The Declaration of Breda," in *Documents Illustrative of English Church History*, ed. Henry Gee and William John Hardy (London, Macmillan and Co., Ltd., 1914) 587. Available at http://www.constitution.org/eng/conpur105.htm (accessed 19 June 2004).

On 6 January 1661 an event occurred that even most nonconformists would have equated with disturbing "the peace of the kingdom." On that day approximately fifty-one Fifth Monarchists led by Thomas Venner terrorized London for three days in an attempt to overthrow Charles II. Adherents of this movement believed that Christ would soon return in glory to establish the fifth and final monarchy.[11] Venner's group believed that its actions would instigate Christ's return. When soldiers finally quashed the rebellion, thirteen of the rebels, including Venner, were executed. The day after Venner's arrest, the government prohibited dissenters from meeting at "unusual hours" or in large numbers, which meant that they could not worship in their own way. Baptists quickly distanced themselves from Venner, stating that most of his supporters were paedobaptists who had previously denounced Baptist teachings.[12] Nevertheless, many people associated the rebellion with Baptists. Consequently, in the eighteen weeks following the insurrection, authorities jailed approximately 400 Baptists in Newgate Prison and many more in other jails.[13]

To solidify the Anglican Church's power once again, from 1661 to 1665 Parliament passed a series of statutes called the Clarendon Code.[14] The first statute, the Corporation Act (1661), required anyone holding a municipal office to take the Oaths of Allegiance and Supremacy, which prevented Baptists from holding office; to swear to the illegality of any armed revolt against the king; and to renounce any ties with Presbyterianism. The act also required that public officials receive, within one year, the Lord's Supper according to the practice of the Church of England.[15]

---

[11] The first four monarchies being Egypt, Persia, Greece, and Rome.

[12] B. R. White, *The English Baptists of the Seventeenth Century*, A History of the English Baptists 1 (London: The Baptist Historical Society, 1983) 97.

[13] Underhill, introductory notice to *A Plea for Toleration of Opinions and Persuasions in Matters of Religion*, 317–18. See also Watts, *The Dissenters*, 1:223.

[14] The code was named after Charles's advisor Edward Hyde, First Earl of Clarendon. For a description of all of the acts in the code, see Henry Bettenson, ed., *Documents of the Christian Church*, 2nd ed. (London: Oxford University Press, 1963) 293–98; Roger Hayden, ed., *The Records of a Church of Christ in Bristol, 1640–1687* (Bristol: Bristol Record Society, 1974) 57–69; and H. Leon McBeth, *The Baptist Heritage: Four Centuries of Baptist Witness* (Nashville: Broadman Press, 1987) 115–16.

[15] White, *The English Baptists of the Seventeenth Century*, 98–99.

In 1662 Parliament designed and passed the Act of Uniformity in order to purge the Church of England of Puritans. This statute established ministerial requirements, including the following: wearing surplices, kneeling to receive the sacrament, receiving Anglican ordination, and rejecting Presbyterianism.[16] Approximately 2,000 ministers, including twenty-six Baptist ministers, lost their livelihoods because of the act.[17]

A third statute, the Conventicle Act (1664), prohibited meetings of more than five people over sixteen years old who were not members of the family in whose house the meetings were held. The act also required citizens to attend their parish church. The final act of the Clarendon Code, the Five Mile Act (1665), prohibited ejected ministers from coming within five miles of the towns where they were formerly employed.

Each act of the Clarendon Code contained punishments of fines, imprisonments, and even banishment, depending on the number of times an offender violated an act. The code was anything but a balm for "tender consciences."

Charles, who was a Catholic at heart, opposed most aspects of the Clarendon Code. In an attempt to relieve the burden Parliament had placed on nonconformists, particularly Catholics, he published his Declaration of Indulgence in 1672. He informed his subjects that he was determined to use his "supreme power in ecclesiastical matters" to stop compelling people to conform to the Anglican Church because "the sad experience of twelve years" had proved "that there is very little fruit" in using such force. Therefore, the king suspended all laws designed to punish nonconformists.[18] Nonconformists could worship publicly and Catholics privately, provided that their ministers and places of worship obtain a license.

The Declaration of Indulgence turned out to be a two-edged sword. It provided nonconformists with a respite in the storm of persecution, which

---

[16] Mark Goldie, "The Search for Religious Liberty, 1640–1690," in *The Oxford Illustrated History of Tudor & Stuart Britain*, ed. John Morrill (Oxford: Oxford University Press, 1996) 299–300.

[17] A. C. Underwood, *A History of the English Baptists* (London: The Carey Kingsgate Press Limited, 1947) 96; White, *The English Baptists of the Seventeenth Century*, 102.

[18] "The Declaration of Indulgence, 1672," http://www.swan.ac.uk/history/teaching/teaching%20resources/Revolutionary%20England/Indulgence.htm (accessed 8 September 2004).

nurtured in them "the consciousness that they could defy their persecutors."[19] However, because the applications for licenses required the names of ministers and the locations of meeting places, these documents later proved to be useful when Parliament, infuriated by the king's declaration, forced Charles to rescind his indulgence in March 1673. Persecutors now had the names of ministers and addresses of meeting places, thereby making arrests and raids much easier.

Despite the tolerant attitudes of Cromwell and of Charles, many dissenters found their way into prison in the years 1649 to 1685. Yet whether they were imprisoned for their politics during Cromwell's rule, or whether they were punished for violating the acts of the Clarendon Code, imprisoned Baptists did not remain silent. Like Shakespeare's King Lear, who encouraged his wife to "Come, let's away to prison,/ We...will sing like birds in the cage,"[20] many Baptists were led away to prison, and there, like birds in a cage, sang about the liberty that they had received from God.

Richard Overton: "A Vigorous, Fearless, and Refreshing Thinker"[21]

Like Thomas Helwys, John Murton, and many others, Richard Overton (fl. 1640–1663) was a Baptist who graced Newgate with his presence. Overton's ties to Baptists are ambiguous, and he is best known for his work with the Levellers, which B. J. Gibbons described as a group that "clearly owed much to the Baptists, both in personnel and in organization; so much so that it might be regarded as the political wing of the Baptist movement."[22] Scholars posit two accounts of Overton's early life, both of which are speculative. One account has Overton being born in England sometime in the late sixteenth century and being baptized in Holland around 1615.[23] After returning to England sometime prior to 1640, he

---

[19] W. T. Whitley, introduction to the *Minutes of the General Assembly of the General Baptist Churches in England* (London: The Kingsgate Press, 1908) 1:xvii.

[20] Shakespeare, *King Lear*, 24.8–9.

[21] W. K. Jordan, *The Development of Religious Toleration in England: Attainment of the Theory and Accommodation in Thought and Institutions (1640–1660)*, 4 vols. (Cambridge MA: Harvard University Press, 1940) 4:190, n. 2.

[22] B. J. Gibbons, "Richard Overton and the Secularism of the Interregnum Radicals," *Seventeenth Century* 10/1 (Spring 1995): 69.

[23] See Benjamin Evans, *The Early English Baptists*, 2 vols. (London: J. Heaton & Son, 1862) 1:254–56 for Overton's pre-baptismal confession of faith, the date of

earned a living as a printer.[24] If he died in jail sometime in or shortly after 1663, he would have been nearly seventy years old. According to Gibbons, such an account "of Overton's early life is doubtful." Instead, Gibbons suggested that Overton was born around 1614, received a good education, became a prolific writer, and made his profession of faith perhaps around 1643.[25] Sometime in the early 1640s, Overton married a woman named Mary, with whom he had at least four children.[26]

Overton joined the Levellers sometime in the 1640s, during which he also participated in theological debates. In his book *Mans Mortalitie* (1644), Overton contended that Adam was created immortal but that his body and soul became mortal after the Fall. At the last judgment, however, God would restore every person's body and soul to immortality.[27] In 1646 Overton

---

which is unknown. According to Henry Martyn Dexter, John Smyth baptized someone named "Overton." Henry Martyn Dexter, *The True Story of John Smyth, the Se-Baptist as Told by Himself and His Contemporaries* (Boston: Lee and Shepard, 1881) 30. Whether this person was Richard Overton is unknown.

[24] See Frank, *The Levellers*, 39–40; Glen H. Stassen, *Just Peacemaking: Transforming Initiatives for Justice and Peace* (Louisville KY: Westminster/John Knox Press, 1992) 141–43; Charles Harding Firth, "Overton, Richard (fl. 1646)," *Dictionary of National Biography*, ed. Leslie Stephen and Sidney Lee, 63 vols. (London: Smith, Elder, & Co., 1895) 42:385; and M. Gimelfarb-Brack, "Overton, Richard, (fl. 1631–1664)," *Biographical Dictionary of British Radicals in the Seventeenth Century*, ed. Richard L. Greaves and Robert Zaller, 3 vols. (Brighton England: Harvester Press, 1983) 2:276.

[25] Over 150 pamphlets have been attributed to Overton. For a summary of several of Overton's pamphlets, see Frank, *The Levellers*; Stassen, *Just Peacemaking*, 143–55; B. J. Gibbons, "Overton, Richard (fl. 1640–1663)," *Oxford Dictionary of National Biography* (Oxford: Oxford University Press, 2004), http://www.oxforddnb.com./view/article/20974 (accessed 20 May 2005); Don M. Wolfe, "Unsigned Pamphlets of Richard Overton: 1641–1649," *Huntington Library Quarterly* 21/1–4 (1957/1958): 167–201; and Watner, "'Come What, Come Will!'" 410–29.

[26] Gibbons, "Overton, Richard (fl. 1640–1663)"; Gibbons, "Richard Overton and the Secularism of the Interregnum Radicals," 64–65.

[27] Gibbons, "Overton, Richard (fl. 1640–1663)"; Gibbons, "Richard Overton and the Secularism of the Interregnum Radicals," 65–68. *Mans Mortalitie* was considered heretical to some commentators. See Thomas Edwards, *Gangraena*, 3 vols. (London: printed by T. R. and E. M. for Ralph Smith, 1645) 1:126–27, and *Hell Broke Loose: or, a Catalogue of the Spreading Errors, Heresies and Blasphemies of These Times, for which We Are to Be humbled* (London: printed for Tho. Underhill, 1646) 4.

moderated a debate "about the immortality of the soul by some Anabaptists" at Thomas Lamb's General Baptist church in London, where Overton might have been a member. When two marshals sent by the mayor arrived to break up the meeting, Overton asked Lamb, "Brother Lamb, had Paul done well if he had desisted from preaching in the name of Jesus if he had been commanded by the high priest to forbear? Had he done well or not?" "No," Lamb answered. Then, Overton replied, "Nor ought we to obey master mayor."[28] After spending an hour debating the legitimate scope of the mayor's authority, the participants moved on to debating the soul's immortality.

The attitude Overton displayed toward the marshals partly explains why he spent at least two stints in prison. His first arrest occurred early in the morning of 11 August 1646, when several men broke into his house to arrest him for writing a pamphlet critical of the House of Lords. These men, according to Overton, dragged him "in warlike manner" before a committee of Lords, where he refused to answer questions, declaring instead that defendants should not be forced to testify against themselves.[29] The committee then sent Overton to Newgate.

On 3 November 1646 Overton appealed his arrest to a committee of the House of Commons. Despite agreeing with him that his detention had been illegal, the committee sent Overton back to Newgate. However, he did not return willingly to that "stinking, lousy, barbarous jail."[30] Overton told his jailors that if the House of Lords issued warrants to arrest him, "so should their lordships find legs to obey them, for I was resolved [that] mine should not be enslaved to...their usurpation to do their arbitrary drudgery, [and that] I would rather loose my life than...to do them that vassalage. My

---

[28] Quoted in Edwards, *Gangraena*, 2:17–18. See also Gibbons, "Overton, Richard (fl. 1640–1663)."

[29] Richard Overton, *An Appeale from the Degenerate Representative Body the Commons of England Assembled at Westminster* (London: n.p. 1647), in *Leveller Manifestoes of the Puritan Revolution*, ed. Don M. Wolfe (New York: Thomas Nelson and Sons, 1944) 163. *See also* Frank, *The Levellers*, 87.

[30] Richard Overton, *The Commoners Complaint* (London: n.p., 1646), in *Tracts on Liberty in the Puritan Revolution, 1638–1647*, ed. William Haller (New York: Octagon Books, Inc., 1965) 377 [3]. The 377 refers to the page in Haller; the [3] to the original. Note also that, according to the new style (Gregorian) calendar, the publication date was 1647.

legs were born as free as the rest of my body, and therefore I scorn that legs, or arms, or hands of mine should do them any villainess service, for as I am a freeman by birth, so I am resolved to live and die."[31] After being dragged back to prison, Overton spent the next ten months there, where he authored several pamphlets.[32]

Overton was not the only member of his family to experience the wrath of the House of Lords. On 6 January 1647 officers raided Overton's home in London and arrested his wife, Mary, and his brother Thomas, who were taken, along with Overton's six-month-old child, to Maiden Lane Prison.[33]

With a flare for the dramatic, Overton described Mary's transfer from Maiden Lane to Bridewell Prison, "the common center and receptacle of bauds, whores, and strumpets."[34] When officers arrived to take her to Bridewell, Mary refused to go. The city marshal came with more officers and broke down the door of her cell. Strutting "towards her like a crow in a gutter and with his valiant looks like a man of mettle," the marshal tried unsuccessfully to wrench Mary's infant from her arms. Yet Mary, a "poor, little, harmless, innocent woman" with a "tender babe on her breast," still refused to leave, so the thugs "laid violent hands upon her and dragged her down the stairs, and in that infamous barbarous manner, drew her headlong upon stones in all the dirt and mire of the streets, with the poor infant still crying and mourning in her arms,...and all the way as they went, utterly to defame and render her infamous in the streets,...calling her 'strumpet' and 'wild whore.'"[35]

---

[31] Ibid., 381–82 [9–10]. *See also Overton,* An Appeale, *164.*

[32] See Gibbons, "Overton, Richard (fl. 1640–1663)." In Newgate, Overton wrote or co-authored the following (all dates are according to the Gregorian calendar): *A Defiance against All Arbitrary Usurpations* (1646); *An Arrow against All Tyrants and Tyranny, Shot from the Prison of New-gate into the Prerogative Bowels of the Arbitrary House of Lords and All Other Usurpers and Tyrants Whatsoever* (1646); *An Unhappy Game of Scotch and English* (1646); (perhaps a co-author) *Vox plebis* (1647); *Regall Tyrannie Discovered* (1647); *Liberty Vindicated against Slavery* (1647); The *Commoners* Complaint (1647); (co-author) *The Out-cryes of Oppressed Commons* (1647); (perhaps the author) *The Humble Appeale and Petition of Mary Overton* (1647); *A New Found Stratagem* (1647); and *An Appeale from the Degenerate Representative Body the Commons of England Assembled at Westminster* (1647).

[33] Overton's sister cared for his three older children.

[34] Overton, *The Commoners Complaint,* 389 [17].

[35] Ibid., 390–91 [18–19].

The date of Mary's release from prison is unknown, but the authorities finally released Overton unconditionally on 16 September 1647. He remained free until 28 March 1649 when he and three other Leveller leaders, John Lilburne, William Walwyn, and Thomas Prince, were arrested and then imprisoned in the Tower of London for writing *The Second Part of Englands New-Chaines Discovered*, a treatise critical of Parliament and Cromwell.[36] Overton also wrote several pamphlets during his second imprisonment.[37]

Overton's prison writings reveal him to be a man possessed with a social conscience. His Christian faith would not permit him to sit idly by while England exchanged a monarchial tyranny for a parliamentary one, or even a dictatorship, in which the rights and liberties of free people were trampled and the poor oppressed.[38] Following are some of the themes central to the cause that Overton described as "the life of my life; without it I am nothing, with it I live."[39]

One theme Overton repeatedly addressed was the origin of political power and authority. He contended that such power and authority ultimately resided with the citizens of England, not with the king or with Parliament. Because God creates every person as a "king, priest, and prophet," no one could govern another person except "by deputation, commission, and free consent from him whose natural right and freedom it

---

[36] Overton recounted his arrest and his appearance before the Council of State (a group of fifteen to twenty men who directed domestic and foreign policy) in John Lilburne, Thomas Prince, and Richard Overton, *The Picture of the Councell of State, Held forth to the Free People of England* ([London:] n.p., 1649), in *The Leveller Tracts, 1647–1653*, ed., William Haller and Godfrey Davies (Gloucester MA: Peter Smith, 1964) 214–27.

[37] In the Tower, Overton penned or co-authored several pamphlets (all dates are according to the Gregorian calendar): (co-author) *A Manifestation from Lieutenant Col. John Lilburn, Mr. William Walwyn, Mr. Thomas Prince, and Mr. Richard Overton* (1649); *Agreement of the Free People of England* (1649); *Overton's Defyance of the Act of Pardon* (1649); *The Baiting of the Great Bull of Bashan Unfolded* (1649); and (co-author) *The Picture of the Councell of State* (1649).

[38] When Overton wrote about "free" English men and women, he meant people who could freely dispose of their labor and not people like servants, apprentices, and paupers.

[39] Richard Overton, *The Baiting of the Great Bull of Bashan Unfolded* (London: n.p., 1649) [7].

is." Human power flows "not immediately from God (as kings usually plead their prerogative) but mediately by the hand of nature, as from the represented to the representers."[40] Therefore, as a "representer," the king exists "for the kingdom, not the kingdom for the king, and...the kingdom is no more his own than the people are his own."[41] Also, members of Parliament, as "representers," hold legitimate political power and authority only in "the discharging of their trust in moving and acting only for the weal and safety of the people" who have empowered them and entrusted their welfare to them.[42] No person, Overton argued, is entitled to be a member of Parliament or to be a government official, such as mayor, sheriff, or justice of the peace. Instead, people must choose their representatives and public officers through free elections.[43]

All government officials, including monarchs, are trustees of the people's welfare and have been empowered by the people to work toward that end. If, however, trustees violate the people's trust by acting contrary to their well being, those officials lose their authority to govern and should not be obeyed.[44] No person or legislative body, Overton argued, may "turn oppressors and tyrants at pleasure."[45] If this happens, and he believed that it had indeed happened, these persons or legislative bodies should "be abhorred, condemned, and resisted by all possible ways and means whatsoever."[46] Overton maintained that it was foolish for "members in

---

[40] Richard Overton, *An Arrow against All Tyrants and Tyranny, Shot from the Prison of New-gate into the Prerogative Bowels of the Arbitrary House of Lords and All Other Usurpers and Tyrants Whatsoever* ([London:] n.p., 1646), in *The English Levellers*, Cambridge Texts in the History of Political Thought, ed. Andrew Sharp (Cambridge: University Press, 1998) 55, 62–63. Also available online http://www.constitution.org/lev/eng_lev_05.htm (accessed 1 September 2005). See also Overton, *An Appeale, 162*, and Overton, *An Arrow*, 62–63.

[41] Overton, *An Appeale*, 175–76.

[42] Ibid., *168*.

[43] Ibid., 189–91; *John* Lilburne, William Walwyn, Thomas Prince, and Richard Overton, *An Agreement of the Free People of England* ([London:] n.p., 1649), in Wolfe, *Leveller Manifestoes of the Puritan Revolution*, 408, art. 27.

[44] Overton, An Appeale, 163, 174; Frank, *The Levellers*, 107; and John Lilburne and Richard Overton, *The Out-cryes of Oppressed Commons*, 2nd ed. ([London:] n.p., 1646) 16.

[45] Overton, *An Appeale*, 175. See also 160, 173, 176, 182.

[46] Ibid., 178. See also 181–82.

Parliament to think that we will justify or tolerate the same among them, which we would not endure in the king, to pluck off the garments of royalty from oppression and tyranny, to dress up the same in Parliament robes."[47]

Because they had become tyrants, members of the House of Lords, which, according to Overton, was one of the two "most insufferable evils" in England, were unfit to govern.[48] Never one to couch his opinions in diplomatic language, Overton declared that "halters and gallows" were "more fit for the Lords than were seats in Parliament."[49] These "unnatural tyrants and usurpers" were "delinquents and traitors"; they were "putrified and incurable members" who should "be cut off for the safety of the whole."[50]

Even while expressing his contempt for the House of Lords, Overton could not understand why members refused to listen to him, which was just one sin among many that rendered them tyrannical. One way for government officials to wield their entrusted power, Overton maintained, was for them to listen to the grievances of the people. In his opinion, Parliament existed for "bearing the cries and groans of the people, [and for] redressing and easing their grievances." However, instead of liberating people from oppression, Parliament oppressed them. Moreover, Parliament silenced "the mouths of the oppressed" by not allowing the people to complain, and if the people did complain, Parliament punished them for complaining. Such action Overton characterized as "the highest kind of tyranny in the world." The Lords "shut their doors and ears against the cry of the people...though the burdens of the oppressed are so great that multitudes have attended the House daily with petitions for no other thing than for the removal of oppression and recovery of freedom."[51]

If the House of Lords was but one of the "two most insufferable evils" in England, "the barbarous, inhuman, blood-thirsty desires and endeavors of the Presbyterian clergy" comprised the other.[52] Overton claimed that, after Presbyterians came into power in Parliament, they looked upon their fellow

---

[47] Ibid., 176–77.

[48] Overton, *An Arrow*, 57.

[49] *Overton*, An Appeale, *172*.

[50] Ibid., 173, 176.

[51] Ibid., 170. See also 195, and Lilburne and Overton, *The Out-cryes of Oppressed Commons*, 13.

[52] Overton, *An Arrow*, 57.

citizens with "wolfish, cannibal, inhuman intents." Like "ravening wolves, even as roaring lions wanting their prey," they searched for whomever "they may devour."[53] Those "bloody-minded men...of the black presbytery" showed "little love, patience, meekness, longsuffering and forbearance" toward those who did not share their beliefs.[54]

Another theme Overton addressed was the role magistrates should play in religion. Believing Jesus' maxim to give to God what is God's and to Caesar what is Caesar's (Matt 22:21; Luke 20:25), Overton claimed that civil magistrates had no authority in spiritual matters. Only God could govern the spiritual lives of people, and such governance could only be waged "by the word, not by the sword, for the sword pierces but the flesh," touching only "the outward" person, not "the inward."[55] Therefore, because nothing had "caused more distractions and heart burnings in all ages than persecution and molestation for matters of conscience in and about religion," magistrates had no authority to force "any person to [do] anything in or about matters of faith, religion, or God's worship, or to restrain any person from the profession of his faith, or exercise of religion according to his conscience."[56] Nor could magistrates bar anyone from holding "any office in the commonwealth, for any opinion or practice in religion excepting such as maintain the pope's (or other foreign) supremacy."[57]

Because churches should not rely on the state to support them, Overton called for the end of mandatory tithes for the support of clergy, suggesting instead "the more easy and evangelical practice of contribution."[58] Members of individual churches should also have the "free liberty...to choose" their own ministers "upon such terms and for such reward as" they would "be willing to contribute or...contract for."[59]

Overton's emphasis on a representative form of government, his hatred of tyranny, and his demand for the disestablishment of religion flowed

---

[53] Ibid., 64. The reference to "ravening wolves" can be found in Matthew 7:15.

[54] Ibid., 66.

[55] Overton, *An Appeale*, 181.

[56] Lilburne, Walwyn, Prince, and Overton, *An Agreement*, 405, art. 10.

[57] Ibid., 408, art. 26.

[58] Overton, *An Appeale*, 192–94. For the elimination of mandatory tithes, see Lilburne, Walwyn, Prince, and Overton, *An Agreement*, 408, art. 23.

[59] Lilburne, Walwyn, Prince, and Overton, *An Agreement of the Free People of England*, 408, art. 24.

directly from his passion for liberty, a theme that runs throughout his writings. Because liberty was "more precious" to a person than anything else, its loss was to be feared even more than death.[60] The universal yearning for liberty, Overton argued, was "a firm law and radical principle in nature engraved in the tables of the heart by the finger of God in creation for every living moving thing." As long as people can breathe, they will either defend themselves against tyranny or seek to liberate themselves from the stranglehold of tyrants. To deny this truth, Overton claimed, was irrational, unnatural, and irreligious.[61]

The preciousness of liberty that God creates in the being of every person should govern how both the government and the judicial system did business. Overton demanded that the state write its laws in English (not in Latin or French) and without legalese so that even the least educated people could understand their own legal proceedings.[62] Nor should the state force people to take oaths or to incriminate themselves. Such acts were, according to Overton, "illegal and contrary to the natural rights, freedoms, and properties of the" English people.[63] He also argued that, instead of allowing defendants to languish in prison for months or even years, they had the right to a "speedy trial."[64] Then, once at trial, defendants had the right to call witnesses in their favor.[65] Finally, Overton contended that no one, neither monarchs nor Parliaments, could imprison someone until that person had been tried and found guilty by a jury of his or her peers.[66] Overton's judicial reforms, of course, would have hampered the ease with which authorities dealt with persons deemed a threat to both church and state. After all, the government had an effective system in place and saw no need to yield its powers to commoners.

Overton's concern for defendants did not end in the courtroom; it extended even into the prisons, for he maintained that the state had to treat its prisoners humanely. The government must prevent jailors and their

---

[60] Overton, *An Arrow*, 58; Overton, *An Appeale*, 177–78.

[61] Overton, *An Appeale*, 159–60. *See also 162.*

[62] *Ibid.*, 192.

[63] Overton, *An Arrow*, 69. See also Overton, *An Appeale*, 192, and Lilburne, Walwyn, Prince, and Overton, *An Agreement* 406, art. 16.

[64] Overton, *An Appeale*, 166, 190.

[65] Lilburne, Walwyn, Prince, and Overton, *An Agreement*, 407–408, art. 16.

[66] Overton, *An Arrow*, 58.

assistants from committing "extortions and cruelties now frequent in all jails of the land." Another frequent abuse Overton sought to end was the continued imprisonment of inmates who had been legally discharged. He demanded that severe penalties be imposed on jailors who committed such an act. He also proposed that the state, not the inmates themselves, pay for the incarceration of prisoners.[67]

Throughout his prison writings, Overton attempted to call the English people to action—to stand up for their rights, to be jailed for demanding those rights, and, if necessary, to die for those rights. His call sometimes took the form of encouragement: "Oh...rouse up your spirits, resume and take up your strength and authority into your own hands; disown and disclaim those desperate tyrants and traitors, and cast them forth from your trust as dirt and dung, or salt that has lost its savor.... What, will you be more fearful of them to bring them to justice than they were to burn your laws and your liberties?"[68]

At other times Overton tried to shame his readers to action: "rub up your wits.... Your time had not better been spent in considering some way wherein you might equally discharge your duties with us who are so close immured in the Tower."[69] We rot in prison, he scolded his readers, "while you stretch yourselves upon your beds and take your ease.... My friends, the cause is as much yours as ours and your duties with ours are of equal extent, but how comes your practice so short, so dull, and remiss.... I cannot see but that a prison, the gallows, or halters would become the best of you as well as any of us.... But you spit in our mouths and clap us on the backs like dogs.... You shrink and skulk into your holes."[70]

Overton could also be condescending. People might call him a madman or a fool, he admitted, but could not his readers, who willingly submit like "contented slaves," be classified as such too? Like a father lecturing his naughty children, Overton chastised his readers: "Come, come, now is no time to sit thrumming of caps. If they will not give us leave to use

---

[67] Overton, *An Appeale*, 191–92. See ibid., 166, for the expenses Overton incurred for his wife's, his brother's, and his own incarcerations.

[68] Ibid., *172–73*.

[69] The "us" refers to Overton, Lilburne, Walwyn, and Prince.

[70] Richard Overton, *Overton's Defyance of the Act of Pardon* (London: n.p., 1649) 5–6.

our tongues and our pens to present and make known our grievances, we must take leave to make use of our hands and swords for the defense and redemption of our lives, our laws, and our liberties from the hand of the destroyer, for our safety must be maintained."[71]

Like the beaten man in Jesus' parable of the good Samaritan (Luke 10:25–37), Overton believed that England had "fallen amongst a crew of thieves" and had been "stripped of its precious raiment of freedom and safety, wounded and left groveling in its blood, even half dead." England awaited good Samaritans who would defend and preserve the liberties of the people, and who would exhibit love, mercy, and compassion to the "helpless and destitute."[72] Overton's message was clear: Did his readers want to be like the priest and Levite and pass England by while it was raked, raped, and ruled by tyrants, thugs, and an unlordly Lord Protector? Or did they want to be good Samaritans and heroes, like Overton and his fellow inmates, who made sacrifices for England's honor? If the latter, Overton seemed to say, "Go and do likewise."

In his discussion of human rights and liberties, Overton often emphasized the importance of the individual. According to Gibbons, Overton taught a doctrine of "possessive individualism," arguing "that everyone possesses a 'self-property' or right of property in their own person. This self-property was inalienable and formed the basis of all other political rights."[73] Such a doctrine for Overton meant that no person could violate another person's rights. These rights and the dignity of each person were rooted in creation by God, who "by nature has made" everyone free.[74]

Despite his emphasis on the individual and the universality of human rights, Overton was no atomistic individualist, for he possessed a social conscience.[75] Thus, he preached not only the rights and liberties of

---

[71] Overton, *An Appeale*, 173.

[72] Ibid., *179*. See also Overton, *Overton's Defyance*, 3–4.

[73] Gibbons, "Overton, Richard (fl. 1640–1663)." See also Frank, *The Levellers*, 96.

[74] Overton, *An Arrow*, 55. See also Overton, *An Appeale*, 163.

[75] According to Stassen (*Just Peacemaking*, 138–39), "Many think the idea" of human rights "came from the rationalism of the Enlightenment, and thus human rights are seen as a product only of rationalistic and individualistic reasoning.... The concept and the term 'human rights' originated more than a half-century prior to the Enlightenment and the French Revolution, among the free churches at the time of

individuals but also the responsibility of individuals to care for others. Believing that "justice is no respecter of persons"[76] and that Jesus really meant that people should treat others as they themselves wanted to be treated (see Matt 7:12), Overton proclaimed that individuals and society were responsible for helping the poor, for "no man is born for himself only, but [is] obliged by the laws of nature (which reaches all), of Christianity (which engages us as Christians), [and] of public society and government to employ our endeavors for the advancement of a communitive happiness, [and] of equal concernment to others as ourselves."[77]

In his multi-faceted defense of the rights of the destitute and the oppressed, Overton echoed common Leveller positions, such as the elimination of debtors' prisons, yet he advocated three proposals that were even unique among Levellers: he proposed that the state provide free public education; establish hospitals to care for "poor orphans, widows, [the] aged, and impotent persons"; and open enclosed lands for common use and for the poor.[78]

Overton based his defense of human rights and liberty, and his position on the origin of political power and authority on his understanding of reason. Yet he was no secularist.[79] Although he did believe that "all forms of laws and governments may fall and pass away, but right reason (the fountain of all justice and mercy to the creature) shall endure forever," and that "nothing which is against reason is lawful, reason being the very life of the law of our land,"[80] he also maintained that "God is not a God of irrationality and madness, or tyranny; therefore, all his communications are reasonable

---

the Puritan Revolution, as an affirmation of the religious liberty of all persons." The italics are Stassen's.

[76] Overton, *An Appeale*, 161.

[77] John Lilburne, William Walwyn, Thomas Prince, and Richard Overton, *A Manifestation from Lieutenant Col. John Lilburn, Mr. William Walwyn, Mr. Thomas Prince, and Mr. Richard Overton* ([London:] n.p., 1649), in Wolfe, *Leveller Manifestoes*, 388. See also Overton, *An Appeale*, 182, and Frank, *The Levellers*, 88.

[78] Overton, *An Appeale*, 194.

[79] Contra Frank, *The Levellers*, 44, and Jordan, *The Development of Religious Toleration in England*, 4:190. See Lilburne, Walwyn, Prince, and Overton, *A Manifestation*, 393, and Gibbons, "Richard Overton and the Secularism of the Interregnum Radicals," 64–75.

[80] Overton, *An Appeale*, 158–59.

and just, and what is so, is of God."[81] Thus, according to Gibbons, "Like...other General Baptists," Overton identified reason "with the spirit of God working in the human soul."[82]

Much of what Overton attributed to reason is common sense. For example, would people rather be ruled by tyrants, or would they prefer to be governed by freely elected representatives? Would people rather live in the fear of having their doors kicked in by agents of the government, or would they choose to live securely in their own homes? Would people rather have their grievances ignored by the government, or would they demand to be heard? Would people rather be forced to testify against themselves when arrested, or would they rather remain silent? In Overton's mind, a reasonable person, or a person with God-given common sense, would affirm the second part of each question.

Overton ended his prison literary career when he and his fellow Levellers were released from the Tower on 8 November 1649 after a jury acquitted Lilburne of treason. In 1653 and 1654, Overton earned some income by acting as a double agent, ironically spying for Cromwell's government while simultaneously plotting to overthrow it. Following his participation in this failed plot, in February 1655 Overton fled to Amsterdam, where he again conspired unsuccessfully with other English exiles to overthrow Cromwell.[83] Later, after returning to England, Overton was arrested in 1659 for an unknown reason but was soon released. A warrant issued on 22 October 1663 for his arrest, perhaps for publishing a pamphlet criticizing Charles II, contains the last known reference to the passionate Leveller leader.

Like all religious reformers, and many social reformers, Overton believed that God had called him to invest himself in a "righteous cause."[84] To describe him as a man ahead of his time would be a gross understatement. Many of his social, political, and religious reforms and many of his demands bear striking similarities to the United States Constitution. Compare his demand for the elimination of religious

---

[81] Ibid., 158.

[82] Gibbons, "Overton, Richard (fl. 1640–1663)."

[83] Ibid.; Gibbons, "Richard Overton and the Secularism of the Interregnum Radicals," 68.

[84] Overton, *Overton's Defyance*, 3–4.

requirements for public officials with "no religious test shall ever be required as a qualification to any office or public trust under the United States"[85]; his emphasis on religious voluntarism and his passion for the right to petition the government with "Congress shall make no law respecting an establishment of religion, or prohibiting the free exercise thereof; or abridging…the right…to petition the Government for the redress of grievances"[86]; his protest against unwarranted intrusions of his home with "the right of the people to be secure in their person, houses, papers, and effects, against unreasonable searches and seizures, shall not be violated, and no warrants shall issue, but upon probable cause, supported by oath or affirmation, and particularly describing the place to be searched, and the person or things to be seized"[87]; his objection to self-incrimination with "no person…shall be compelled in any criminal case to be a witness against himself, nor be deprived of life, liberty, or property, without the due process of law"[88]; and his demand for a speedy trial and for the calling of favorable witnesses with "in all criminal prosecutions, the accused shall enjoy the right to a speedy and public trial, by an impartial jury…; to be confronted with the witnesses against him; [and] to have compulsory process for obtaining witnesses in his favor."[89]

That Overton was a man ahead of this time explains his imprisonments for writing about his "righteous cause." The title of his *An Arrow…Shot from the Prison of Newgate* typifies the nature of his writings, for he wanted his words to pierce the consciences of every Christian as well as those in powerful government and ecclesiastical positions. Many of his phrases and narrations of events are jewels, though they are often buried in the many sentences running well over 180 words. His writings are simultaneously comforting and caustic, straightforward and dramatic, encouraging and afflicting, humorous and sad, spiritual and vulgar. For example, his

---

[85] US Constitution, art. 6, cl. 3. However, some Levellers seemed to have approved of having an established church, provided that the state not force anyone to attend or support that church. See Manning, "The Levellers and Religion," 81.

[86] US Constitution, amend. 1.

[87] Ibid., amend. 4.

[88] Ibid., amend. 5.

[89] Ibid., amend. 6.

description about grabbing the genitals of the bull of Bashan (Cromwell)[90] offended many people, even some Levellers, who told him that his "uncivil language" disgraced "the gospel of Christ."[91] Even Overton understood that his language was at times "a little too sharp," but he asked his readers to attribute such language "to the heat of my zeal and ardent affections to the promotion of that cause" of human rights and freedom.[92] To that cause Overton vowed to fight "to the last gasp of vital breath; and I will not beg" anyone's "favor, nor lie at their feet for mercy; let me have justice, or let me perish. I'll not sell my birthright for a mess of pottage, for justice is my natural right, my heirdom, my inheritance by lineal descent from the loins of Adam, and so to all the sons of men as their proper right without respect of persons."[93]

A Letter and Petitions from Prison

Whereas Overton's prison writings dealt with a broad range of themes that can be loosely described as "social" issues, most imprisoned Baptist writers focused on "spiritual" issues. For example, six Baptists incarcerated in Reading Prison for refusing to take the Oaths of Allegiance and Supremacy described in their letter of 16 July 1660 four spiritual lessons they had learned in jail: (1) they rejoiced knowing that they took more comfort in losing their worldly possessions than "the enemy will do in the spending of them"; (2) they learned to be content despite their imprisonment; (3) they were willing to lose everything for the Lord; and (4) they had experienced "a greater sweetness in the promises of the Lord than formerly" and were now committed to having "a more watchful frame over our hearts, thoughts, and actions, by these trials than formerly."[94]

---

[90] See Overton, *Overton's Defyance*, 6, and Overton, *The Baiting of the Great Bull of Bashan unfolded*, [2]. For the biblical reference to the bulls of Bashan, see Psalm 22:12–13.

[91] Ibid., [1].

[92] Ibid., [7].

[93] Quoted in Watner, "'Come What, Come Will!'" 415. See also Overton, *The Commoners Complaint*, 395 [2].

[94] John Jones et al., "Letter from Reading Prison, 16 July 1660," in *The Lord's Loud Call to England*, by Henry Jessey (London: printed for Francis Smith, 1660) 24–25.

Like the Baptists in Reading Prison, Baptist prisoners in the county of Kent also took up their pens. In that county, according to Adam Taylor, "The General Baptists were numerous and flourishing...at the period of the Restoration, but [they] were soon called to drink deep of the cup of persecution."[95] From their jail at Maidstone, approximately thirty-one miles southeast of London, four Baptists—two elders of a Bradbourne church and two co-pastors of a church at Biddenden—wrote a petition dated 25 January 1661, acknowledging their loyalty to the king and providing reasons for the king to protect "their civil and spiritual rights."[96] They composed their *Humble Petition* "in the name of Baptists" imprisoned with them, explaining why they refused to take the Oath of Allegiance.[97]

As English citizens, the petitioners claimed that no one could deprive them of their "property and native birthright, without violating the laws of God and nature"; unfortunately, these laws had been violated by people who, without any warrants from the king or any of his ministers, broke into the petitioners' homes, stole their property, and dragged them from their homes and places of worship to jail. The petitioners appealed to the Charles's mercy, informing him that they had fed their families the past year with food bought on credit, but now that "all of us being detained from our employments, the cries of our families, who suffer hunger," have "become great."[98] Despite their suffering, the Kentish Baptists did not despair because God "has ordained government and set up magistrates to execute such

---

[95] Adam Taylor, *The History of the English General Baptists: The English General Baptists of the Seventeenth Century*, 2 vols. (London: printed for the author, 1818) 1:269.

[96] William Jeffrey et al., *The Humble Petition and Representation of the Sufferings of Several Peaceable and Innocent Subjects, Called by the Name of Anabaptists, Inhabitants of the County of Kent, and Now Prisoners in the Gaol of Maidstone, for the Testimony of a Good Conscience* (London: Printed for Thomas Smith, 1660), in *TLCP*, title page [289]. Available online at http://www.baptistlibraryonline.com/library/Jeffery/petition.pdf (accessed 13 August 2005). The two elders were William Jeffrey and John Reve; the two co-pastors, George Hammon and James Blackmore. Note also that, according to the new style (Gregorian) calendar, the publication date was 1661.

[97] Ibid., 308.

[98] Ibid., 299. For other Baptists who taught that religious persecution violated natural law, see Richardson, *The Necessity of Toleration in Matters of Religion*, 263, and Leonard Busher, *Religions Peace: or A Plea for Liberty of Conscience* (n.p., 1614; repr., London: printed for John Sweeting, 1646), in *TLCP*, 24, 37.

power as is given from himself" to unburden the oppressed, to uphold justice, and to prevent God's creation from being plunged into chaos.[99] The prisoners, therefore, wanted the king to fulfill his God-ordained role to lift their oppression, right their wrongs, and restore order to their lives.

The Maidstone prisoners also reminded Charles that the Bible clearly supported his authority to rule their actions in civil matters. However, the king had mistakenly contended that they had committed a "crime" by refusing to acknowledge that God had granted him the authority to rule "in spiritual things or causes." Charles erroneously had claimed that, as a Christian magistrate, he was "lord over our faith" and had the authority to use "outward force to impose anything in the worship of God, on our consciences." But "you have no such power," they informed the king.[100] They then politely suggested that Charles consider the ramifications of such erroneous claims by a magistrate:

1. If a Christian magistrate can make such claims, so can any magistrate. If we lived in Turkey, the petitioners argued, we would have to accept "the Koran and be a worshipper of Mahomet." If we lived in Spain, we would have to be Catholics; if in England during Henry VIII's reign, Catholics; if during Edward VI's reign, Protestants; if during Mary I's reign, Catholics again; if during Elizabeth I's reign, Protestants again. Thus, as the magistrate goes, so goes a subject's religion. All that could be said about such nonsense was, "God forbid."

2. Christ's apostles commanded Christians to obey their magistrates, yet these same apostles also refused to obey when magistrates ordered them to violate the true worship of God (see Acts 4:19; 5:29).

3. Although the authors of the New Testament commanded Christians to obey civil authorities, they never required Christians to obey pagan emperors "in matters of faith or worship, for then the Christians who lived under those emperors, must needs have denied Christ and worshipped the Roman gods, as some of the emperors commanded."

4. Therefore, "O king, that no man as he is a Christian has power to be a lord over another's faith, or by outward force to impose anything in the worship of God, is clear."[101]

---

[99] Jeffrey et al., *The Humble Petition*, 299.
[100] Ibid., 300–301.
[101] Ibid.

If the preceding arguments would not change Charles's mind, the imprisoned Baptists reminded him that neither Jesus nor his apostles used or sanctioned the use of force in spiritual matters.[102] Remember also, they urged the king, that Jesus died as a blasphemer and an enemy of Caesar (see Matt 26:65; John 19:12) and that many "faithful martyrs of Jesus" who were executed for their faith had been "accused of being pestilent fellows, movers of sedition, turners of the world upside down, enemies to Caesar, when the contrary was most true" (see Acts 6:13–14; 7:59; 17:6–7). Even today, the petitioners claimed, magistrates continue to kill "the saints of God" for their so-called heresies and blasphemies.[103]

Thus, the petitioners contended that they could not take the Oath of Allegiance because the New Testament prohibited Christians from taking any oaths (see Matt 5:33; James 5:12). They promised to live as good citizens, but if the king meddled in spiritual matters, they promised not to fight him "with any carnal or temporal weapons"; instead, they would "patiently suffer such punishment as shall be inflicted on us for our consciences."[104]

The petition probably had no effect on anyone in a position of authority. Nevertheless, all of the petitioners probably gained their freedom, and two of them co-authored a 1661 publication against religious persecution.[105]

Two other petitions in 1661 from Kentish Baptists originated in Dover. In their appeal to King Charles, the petitioners quoted or alluded to twelve passages from the Bible, which they prized "above all the world,"[106]

---

[102] Ibid., 302–303. The authors refered to the following passages to support their position: Luke 9:55–56, Matthew 20:25–26, 1 Peter 5:2–3, and Matthew 13:24–30, 36–43.

[103] Ibid., 303.

[104] Ibid., 307.

[105] See Thomas Monck et al., *Sion's Groans for Her Distressed, or Sober Endeavours to Prevent Innocent Blood* (n.p., 1661), in *TLCP*, [343]–82. Available online at http://www.baptistlibraryonline.com/library/monck/zions_groans.pdf (accessed 13 August 2005).

[106] "The Petition of James Houson et al., to Charles II, 1661," in *The History of the English Baptists from the Reformation to the Beginning of the Reign of King George I*, by Thomas Crosby, 4 vols (London: privately printed, [1738]) 2:158.

to express their differences with the Church of England and to acknowledge their sincere loyalty to the king "in all temporal things."[107]

"In conscience to God," the petitioners declared that they could not, "in faith and love," obey laws requiring them to conform to the Church of England. In due time, they warned, such laws would ruin them and their families. Instead of persecuting "tender consciences," the inmates asked Charles to alleviate the sufferings of all nonconformists by fulfilling the promises that he made in his Declaration of Breda and in his previous dealings with some General Baptists.[108] Realizing that Charles would deny them the liberty to follow "the law of God and nature," the Baptists, "in the strength of the Lord," vowed to "patiently suffer what is inflicted upon us." They ended their appeal by quoting the apostle Paul: "For the weapons of our warfare are not carnal, but spiritual and might, to the pulling down of strongholds" (2 Cor 10:4).[109] Implicit in this passage was the message: "We will follow the teachings of the New Testament and fight you with spiritual weapons while you, king, fight us with the carnal weapons of the state. Nevertheless, we, not you, will ultimately prevail."

After languishing in prison for six more weeks, the petitioners then wrote to Charles's brother James, the Duke of York. As the Duke's "harmless people and peaceable subjects to the king," they informed James that their only crime had been to worship God peacefully, which had put them and their families "into great straits." Why, they wondered, were they punished while their "friends in other places" were left unscathed for doing the same thing?[110]

The prisoners pled for mercy so that "the cries of our little ones and families" would not provoke God to wreak havoc on England. Not only could the Duke avert God's wrath by setting the prisoners free; he could reap the reward Jesus offered to anyone "who gives a cup of cold water to

---

[107] Ibid., 2:156.

[108] General Baptists presented Charles with a declaration of their beliefs in July 1660 and then with two other declarations in January and February 1661, following Venner's rebellion.

[109] "The Petition of James Houson et al., to Charles II, 1661," 2:156–58.

[110] "The Petition of James Houson et al., to the Duke of York, 17 November 1661," in Crosby, The History of the English Baptists, 2:158.

any of his suffering people" (Matt 10:42).[111] Whether they received their "cup of cold water" is unknown.

Francis Bampfield: The Lord's Free Prisoner

Francis Bampfield (1614–1684) was born at Poltimore, four miles northeast of Exeter. Wanting their son to be a minister, Bampfield's parents had him educated by pious families. He then entered Wadham College, Oxford, in 1631, where he earned two degrees. During his undergraduate years, he neglected his spiritual life and ridiculed Puritan students.[112] Despite these "void spaces," as he described those years of neglected Bible study, he eventually became an ordained deacon and priest in the Church of England.[113]

In 1639 Bampfield became rector of Rampisham, ten miles northwest of Dorchester, in southern England. While at Rampisham, he used his income to help the poor and to purchase Bibles for people. During the first civil war he supported the king and continued to use the *Book of Common Prayer*, only stopping when Parliamentary troops forced him to do so.[114]

In 1647 Bampfield became the rector of Wraxall, near Bristol, serving there for approximately six years. He then began preaching at Sherborne, thirty-five miles south of Bristol, and officially became its vicar during a service attended by 2,000 people in 1657.[115] Five years later, Bampfield had to leave his position at Sherborne because of the Act of Uniformity. Having become a nonconformist, he testified that the Lord had told him not to even "touch that unclean constitution of humanely invented worship," the *Book of Common Prayer*.[116]

---

[111] Ibid., 2:159.

[112] Francis Bampfield, *A Name, an After-one* (London: printed for John Lawrence, 1681) 2; Richard L. Greaves, "Bampfield, Francis (1614–1684)," *Oxford Dictionary of National Biography*, http://www.oxforddnb.com./view/article/1258 (accessed 28 May 2005).

[113] Don A. Sanford, *A Choosing People: The History of Seventh Day Baptists* (Nashville: Broadman Press, 1992) 70; Richard L. Greaves, *Saints and Rebels: Seven Nonconformists in Stuart England* (Macon GA: Mercer University Press, 1985) 180–81.

[114] Bampfield, *A Name, an After-one*, 2; Greaves, *Saints and Rebels*, 181; and Greaves, "Bampfield, Francis (1614–1684)."

[115] Greaves, "Bampfield, Francis (1614–1684)."

[116] Bampfield, *A Name, an After-one*, 4.

On 19 September 1662, soldiers arrested Bampfield and approximately twenty-six others as they worshiped at his home in Sherborne.[117] Contending that his meetings were not seditious, Bampfield was released on bond five days after his arrest. He continued to hold services and was arrested again on 23 July 1663 in Shaftesbury and then imprisoned in Dorchester, in the southern county of Dorset. Authorities eventually offered to free Bampfield if he promised to behave, but, despite spending eighteen months in jail, he refused, equating such a promise with an admission of guilt.[118] While in jail (c. 1665), he concluded that the Bible and nature taught that Saturday was the Sabbath for Jews and Christians, so he began holding services on that day.[119] During his nearly nine years in the Dorchester prison, Bampfield started a church and near the end of his incarceration often preached sixteen sermons per week, many to people assembled in a yard adjoining the jail.[120] Along with becoming a Sabbatarian in prison, he also accepted the teaching of believer's baptism (c. 1665). Because he could not be immersed while in prison, Bampfield delayed being baptized until he was released.[121]

After being released on 17 May 1672, Bampfield soon received the required license to preach. On 23 September 1673 he married Damaris Town, a woman who ministered to prisoners in Dorchester, and the couple moved to London, where he preached in several churches. Sometime probably in that same year, Bampfield and an unidentified person traveled from London to Salisbury, eighty miles southwest of London, where he first

---

[117] See *A Brief Narration of the Imprisonment of Mr. Francis Bampfield* (n.p., 1662) for details surrounding these events. The anonymous author of the narration claimed that an "eye and ear-witness" told him about the events. See also Greaves, *Saints and Rebels*, 186–87.

[118] Greaves, *Saints and Rebels*, 187.

[119] Bampfield defended his sabbatarian beliefs in a letter to William Benn. See Francis Bampfield to William Benn, c. 1672, in *The Judgment of Mr. Francis Bampfield, Late Minister of Sherborne in Dorsetshire for the Observation of the Jewish, or Seventh Day Sabboth*, by William Ben (London: printed by W. Godbid for Sarah Nevill, 1677) 3–8. See also Bampfield, *A Name, an After-one*, 12–14.

[120] Greaves, "Bampfield, Francis (1614–1684)"; Greaves, *Saints and Rebels*, 188.

[121] See Bampfield, *A Name, an After-one*, 14.

baptized himself "as by the hand of Christ himself" and then the other person in the Avon River.[122]

Probably as a consequence of his baptism, Bampfield spent eighteen weeks in the Salisbury jail, and during this incarceration, he defended himself in a letter titled "The Open Confessor, and the Free Prisoner," which was addressed to a group identified only as "dearly beloved."[123] In the letter he contended that he was imprisoned merely for professing openly "that Jesus Christ is the one and the only LORD over the conscience and Lawgiver to the soul, and that the scriptures of truth are the one and the only rule of faith, worship, and life."[124] Contrary to his opponents' characterization of him, Bampfield claimed that he neither sought to be persecuted, nor was he unhappy when he was out of jail. He preached when people asked him to preach, and when he preached, he did so to save people's souls. Such preaching often got him into trouble, he admitted, but the salvation of others was far more important than his physical liberty: "Souls, souls, precious souls—'watch for our souls, as one who must give account, come over and help us'; this is a sound that is loud in my ears, and I may not be deaf against it."[125]

Bampfield's call to be the Lord's open confessor took courage, yet he professed that he was nothing without the grace and power of the Holy Spirit. "If at any time I stand," he humbly confessed, "it is by faith; I may not be high-minded but must fear, with a holy fear, with the fear of Jehovah in my heart, that I may not depart from him."[126] With such a holy fear, "Who would fear a cross that believes a crown, or dread a prison, who expects a

---

[122] Ibid., 17. See also Greaves, *Saints and Rebels*, 192–93, and Sanford, *A Choosing People*, 70–71.

[123] This letter was printed in 1675 under the title *Open Confessor and the Free Prisoner* (London: n.p., 1675). The title page included the author's name, "F. B. the Lord's prisoner in Salisbury," and the purpose of publishing the letter: "If you would know the reason of Mr. Bampfield's letter being made public, it is to satisfy the desires of many who were earnest to have copies thereof and to prevent the trouble of transcribing. Some (to whom it was sent) have prevailed with the worthy author to give his assent for the publishing hereof." A copy of the *Open Confessor and the Free Prisoner* can be found at the Massachusetts Historical Society, Boston.

[124] Ibid., 1.

[125] Ibid., 2.

[126] Ibid., 4.

palace?"[127] Like a man raptured into heaven, Bampfield exhorted his readers to cling to the promises of God, who promised to love, comfort, and protect his people. If only we would keep our eyes on Christ and live in beatific vision, Bampfield proclaimed, we would sing like birds in a cage, and "how melodious would our chirps be."[128]

Despite being imprisoned, Bampfield declared that his jailors could neither control nor silence him. Like the apostle Paul, Bampfield declared, "How much louder and further does my confinement preach than my liberty could; my prison always speaks, even when the pulpit is silent (Phil. 1:12–14). The word of my God is not bound, though I am shut up; that [word] shall run, and have free course, and be glorified, though I am kept within bounds (2 Tim. 2:9; 2 Thess. [numerals unreadable]). The most watchful keeper of the jail cannot hinder the walks of my soul and the flights of my spirit." For Bampfield believed that his spirit could leap over prison walls, flee through prison bars, fly to London to weep over its sins, and be "charioted" into heaven: "How high above my prison am I then carried upon wings of faith and of love. Then could I shout and sing, and bear a part in the holy melodiousness with the glorified ones above, if Christ my Advocate will own me, and plead for me there."[129] Bampfield might have been the king's prisoner in Salisbury jail, but that could not prevent him from also being the Lord's free prisoner.

After his release from the Salisbury jail, Bampfield returned to London, where he started a church in 1674. The church eventually split, forcing him to start another church on 5 March 1676.

Bampfield managed to stay out of prison for nearly nine years. Then, on 17 February 1683, a constable, accompanied by several armed deputies, burst into the meeting hall where Bampfield's church gathered and, in the king's name, ordered Bampfield to stop preaching. He countered that he was performing his duty "in the name of the King of kings." When the constable boasted that he had a warrant from the mayor, Bampfield responded that he had "a warrant from Christ." He continued preaching

---

[127] Ibid., 5.
[128] Ibid., 6.
[129] Ibid., 7.

until a deputy pulled him down from the pulpit.[130] The authorities arrested the defiant minister and six others, taking them to the mayor, who accused them of spreading "popery," a charge that the Baptists vehemently denied. After fining some of the prisoners, the mayor released them all.[131]

A week later, the authorities arrested Bampfield again and dragged him through the streets while he clutched his Bible and shouted that he was being persecuted for the cause of Christ. When Bampfield was finally brought before some magistrates, the doorkeeper tried to prevent anyone else from entering the court. At this point, Bampfield "declared...that courts of justice ought to be open" to ensure that he got a fair hearing. When the magistrates finished questioning Bampfield, they sent him into open court, where he refused to take the Oath of Allegiance, for which he was then sent to Newgate.

Bampfield returned to court for trial on 17 March and again refused to take the oath. He informed the court that only Christ could judge him. Ignoring the rebellious preacher, Lord Chief Justice Edmund Saunders ordered the jury to find him guilty, which it did. On 28 March the judge sentenced Bampfield to life in prison or until the king pardoned him.[132] When Bampfield attempted to speak, people in the courtroom shouted for officers to take him out of the courtroom. As he was being dragged out, he raised his hands, one holding a Bible, and cried out, "The righteous Lord loves righteousness. The Lord be [the] Judge in this case."[133]

Bampfield refused to take the oath three other times, once on 18 April and twice in October.[134] On 12 October he informed the court that forcing prisoners to take the oath violated English law. He also stated that he had

---

[130] Francis Bampfield, *The Lords Free Prisoner* (London: printed for W. T., 1683) 2. Also available online at http://www.seventh-day-baptist.org.au/library/books/prisoner.htm.

[131] Ibid., 2–4.

[132] Francis Bampfield, *A Continuation of a Former Just Appeal, From Lower Courts on Earth, to the Highest Court in Heaven* ([London: n.p., 1684]) 2. See also Greaves, "Bampfield, Francis (1614–1684)."

[133] Bampfield, *A Continuation of a Former Just Appeal*, 3.

[134] Francis Bampfield, *A Just Appeal, from Lower Courts on Earth, to the Highest Court in Heaven* (London: printed for the author, 1683) 2. See also pages 3–8, for Bampfield's understanding of oaths in general, and *A Continuation of a Former Just Appeal*, 3–12, for his arguments against taking the Oath of Allegiance.

been informed previously by a judge that taking the oath was equivalent to promising to attend the worship services of the Anglican Church, to take the sacraments, to stay away from conventicles, and to obey all of the king's laws. This last requirement, Bampfield informed the court, was impossible because he did not know every English law and because many lawyers contended that a legal education, perhaps lasting four years, was necessary to understand many laws. As for the first three requirements, Bampfield stated that he had spent nearly ten years in prison for violating them, so he did not feel the need to change his mind at this point in his life. After being subjected to a lecture on the finer points of English law by the Baptist preacher, the court remanded him back to prison.

The next day, the court repeatedly ordered Bampfield to state whether he was guilty or not guilty of refusing to take the oath, but he refused to answer, protesting that his case was not that simple. Finally, the judge ordered the court clerk to register a "not guilty" answer. Then, after a "professed papist" refused to take the Oath of Supremacy, the judge, according to Bampfield, implied that all the religious prisoners, including Bampfield, "were all of one religion." At that, Bampfield exploded: "I renounce the pope and those who are popishly affected. You cannot cast me out of the protection of the King of kings and Lord of Lords. I have liberty and goods (meaning spiritual and eternal ones) which you cannot take from me."[135] The court, however, could take his worldly possessions and his freedom, and it sent him back to Newgate, where he wrote three pamphlets defending his refusal to take the oath and countering charges that he promoted Catholicism.[136] In two court appearances in January 1684, Bampfield again refused to take the oath.

Bampfield died in Newgate on 16 February 1684. According to one unsympathetic author, Bampfield "was always a person so strangely fickle and unsteady in his judgment that he was first a churchman, then a

---

[135] Ibid., 3. For Bampfield's opinion of Catholicism, see *The Lords Free Prisoner*, 2–3, and *A Just Appeal*, 8.

[136] The three pamphlets, already cited, are: *The Lords Free Prisoner* (1683); *A Just Appeal, From Lower Courts on Earth, to the Highest Court in Heaven* (1683); and *A Continuation of a Former Just Appeal, From Lower Courts on Earth, to the Highest Court in Heaven* ([1684]). In his last prison writing, *The Holy Scripture* (1684), Bampfield proposed that children should be taught Hebrew and biblically-based arts and sciences. See Greaves, *Saints and Rebels*, 207–208.

Presbyterian, afterwards an Independent, or at least a sider with them, and an Anabaptist, and at length almost a complete Jew, and what not."[137] While all that might be true, it can also be said of Bampfield that he was faithful to what he believed God had called him to do. He believed that he was participating in the sufferings of Christ. Like Christ, Bampfield contended that he was publicly humiliated and mocked,[138] had a cross to bear,[139] and was numbered among transgressors.[140] He felt honored to suffer for Christ,[141] and instead of being bitter, Bampfield maintained that during his many years of imprisonment, he had never "had one hour's trouble."[142] He would never have attributed his peace in prison to his own strength; rather, "the Holy Spirit sent from the Father in the name of his Son, does continue me in a thankful, rejoicing, glorying state, frame, and acting, to the praise of his abounding mercy, rich grace, and free love: to this all-glorious Jehovah, my Elohim, be all the glory and honor, for ever and ever."[143] Thus, in whatever prison cell he found himself, Bampfield always considered himself to be the Lord's free prisoner.

Thomas Delaune: A Martyred Champion for Religious Liberty

In November 1683 another Baptist, Thomas Delaune (d. 1685), joined Bampfield in Newgate.[144] Born into a poor, Irish Catholic family, Delaune lived on the farm of Edward Riggs, the founder of Cork Baptist Church. Riggs helped educate Delaune, who eventually became a Baptist. Delaune's decision to become a Baptist raised the ire of his Catholic neighbors, so he immigrated to England, where he married Hannah Hutchinson, the daughter of a Baptist preacher. The couple lived in London, where Delaune

---

[137] Anthony Wood, *Athenæ Oxonienses: An Exact History of all the Writers and Bishops Who Have Had Their Education in the Most Ancient and Famous University of Oxford*, 4 vols. (London: printed for Tho. Bennet, 1692) 2:571.

[138] Bampfield, *The Lords Free Prisoner*, 3.

[139] Ibid., 1; Bampfield, *A Continuation of a Former Just Appeal*, 12.

[140] Bampfield, *A Just Appeal*, 3.

[141] Ibid., 8; Bampfield, *The Lords Free Prisoner*, 1; Bampfield, *Open Confessor and the Free Prisoner*, 1; Bampfield, *A Name, an After-one*, 7.

[142] Bampfield, *A Continuation of a Former Just Appeal*, 8.

[143] Bampfield, *A Just Appeal*, 3. See also Bampfield, *Open Confessor and the Free Prisoner*, 4.

[144] Delaune's name is often spelled "de Laune" or "DeLaune."

translated literature, ran a grammar school, and published religious works. He also authored some pamphlets and became a prominent figure in London Particular Baptist circles.[145]

In 1683 Benjamin Calamy, the rector of St. Lawrence Jewry, published a sermon, *A Discourse about a Scrupulous Conscience*, in which he denounced dissenters and claimed that any objective person who studied the differences between the teachings of the Church of England and of dissenters would conclude that the established church was correct.[146] Taking up Calamy's challenge, Delaune wrote *A Plea for the Non-Conformists*, in which he lambasted the Church of England, charging that it altered the words of the Lord's Prayer; that it forced people to repeat prescribed prayers, thereby contradicting Christ's teachings; that it required women to pray, which also violated the teachings of Christ; and that it had congregants sing the Lord's Prayer, which had no scriptural warrant.[147]

Before the *Plea* was published, the authorities arrested Delaune during the evening of 29 November 1683, and soon thereafter he was sent to Newgate, where he penned *A Narrative of the Tryal and Sufferings of Thomas DeLaune*, in which he described his imprisonment, trial, and failed efforts to get Calamy's help in securing his release from prison. Before being sent to Newgate, however, Delaune spent the night in what he described as a "most

---

[145] Michael A. G. Haykin, "Delanue, Thomas (d. 1685)," *Oxford Dictionary of National Biography*, http://www.oxforddnb.com./view/article/7451 (accessed 28 May 2005); A. C. Bickley, "Delaune, Thomas (d. 1685)," *Dictionary of National Biography*, 14:315.

[146] Jim Spivey, "Calamy, Benjamin (bap. 1646, d. 1685/6)," *Oxford Dictionary of National Biography*, http://www.oxforddnb.com./view/article/4354 (accessed 30 July 2005).

[147] See Thomas Delaune, *A Narrative of the Tryal and Sufferings of Thomas DeLaune* (n.p.: printed for the author, 1683; repr., n.p., 1704), in *A Plea for the Non-Conformists*, by Thomas Delaune ([repr.]; London: n.p., 1704) 62 [60], 66–67 [64–65]. Pages 61–68 in the text are incorrectly numbered 59–66. The numbers in brackets are those that appear in the text. Several years after Delaune's death, Daniel Defoe praised the *Plea* in his preface to later editions of the book: "If any man asks what we can say [about] why the dissenters differ from the Church of England, and what they can plead for it, I can recommend no better reply than this: Let them answer, in short, Thomas Delaune, and desire the querist to read the book" (Daniel Defoe, preface to *A Plea for the Non-Conformists*, by Thomas Delaune [London: printed for John Marshall, 1720] 11–12).

wretched accommodation. I was turned in among the common-side prisoners, where a hard bench was my bed, and two bricks my pillows. And [I was] not suffered to see some of my acquaintance who were prisoners there as dissenters."[148]

The next day, Delaune's situation got worse because he was sent to Newgate. In the warrant committing him to the prison, Thomas Jenner noted that Delaune had confessed "that he is the author and pen-man of a certain pamphlet entitled *A Plea for Non-Conformists*, and has caused many hundred sheets thereof to be printed, wherein are contained several seditious and dangerous matters against the government, and for that he refused" to post bond.[149] Once in Newgate, Delaune "lodged among felons, whose horrid company made a perfect representation of that place which you describe when you mention hell. But after two days and nights, without any refreshment [and] the unusualness of that society and place having impaired my health, the constitution of which at best is very tender and crazy, I was removed and am now in the press yard, a place of some sobriety, though still a prison."[150]

A few days later after arriving at Newgate, Delaune sent a letter to Jenner, denying that he had refused to pay bail and maintaining that his pamphlet contained nothing against the government. The sole purpose of the pamphlet, Delaune stated, was to respond to Calamy's invitation, "but if the guides of the church (as Dr. Calamy calls the beneficed men of the Church of England) will make public challenges, they should receive objections without punishing the objectors, whose (supposed) crime is only for obeying them."[151] He then wrote three letters to Calamy pleading his case and asking for help.

The letters expressed Delaune's bewilderment and anger at being imprisoned for writing his *Plea*. "If you did not expect an answer," he chastised Calamy, "or thought that none (for fear of the Act of Uniformity, etc.) would make any return to your call, what can a man of reason judge, but that it was a florid declamation or a triumphant harangue, a mere mockery and ensnaring of poor 'scrupulous consciences,' when they must be

---

[148] Delaune, *A Narrative*, 56.
[149] Ibid.
[150] Ibid., 56–57.
[151] Ibid., 57.

so muzzled that they must not exhibit the causes of their doubts. Sir, you know that it is unequal to gag the respondent when the opponent's mouth is at liberty, or to manacle the assaulted when the challenger flourishes a menacing sword."[152] Delaune argued, like others before him, that the power of the secular government could only make hypocrites, not Christian converts. In reminding Calamy that persecution violated the Christian faith, he turned the name of his infamous prison into a damnable verb: "I cannot find that Christ or his disciples ever church-cursed or Newgated 'scrupulous consciences' to conformity."[153] If you want to win nonconformists to your cause, Delaune advised the Anglican minister, do so biblically "by plain demonstrative arguments, [and] meek and winning persuasions, not the syllogisms of prisons, pillories, etc."[154] Delaune's wife took the letters to Calamy, who purportedly replied that Delaune's problems were none of his business.[155]

In court on 13 December, Delaune heard his indictment read. Along with containing citations from his *Plea*, the indictment charged him with plotting to disturb the peace of England, putting "the king into the greatest hate and contempt of his subjects," scheming "sedition and rebellion," and criticizing and scandalizing the *Book of Common Prayer*. "By force and arms," the indictment continued, Delaune "unlawfully, seditiously, and maliciously did write, print, and publish…a certain false seditious and scandalous libel of and concerning…the king and the *Book of Common Prayer* aforesaid, entitled *A Plea for the Nonconformists*."[156]

At his trial four days later, Delaune pled not guilty and reiterated that he wrote the *Plea* only in response to Calamy's public challenge. Delaune told the court, "Now since public challenges are made to be answered, to punish me for obeying a guide of the church is hard, very hard…. If what I have written is true, it is no crime, unless truth is made a crime. If false, let Dr. Calamy or any of the guides of your church confute me…by good scripture and good reason, then I'll submit. If the latter method is not taken,

---

[152] Ibid., 58.

[153] Ibid.

[154] Ibid., 59.

[155] However, see Spivey, "Calamy, Benjamin (bap. 1646, d. 1685/6)," and Alexander Gordon, "Calamy, Benjamin, D.D (1642–1686)," *Dictionary of National Biography*, 8:226.

[156] Delaune, *A Narrative*, 62 [60].

I must repeat it, `tis very hard, my lord, `tis very hard."[157] The following day, to no one's surprise, the jury found Delaune guilty. Sir George Jeffries, the judge and a good friend of Calamy, sentenced Delaune to prison until he paid a fine of 100 marks, demanded security for good behavior for six months, and ordered that Delaune's books be publicly burned.[158] Unable to pay the fine, Delaune remained in prison.

Receiving no help from Calamy, Delaune bordered on calling the Anglican minister a coward for boasting in his sermon that no one would dare respond to it because Jeffreys, the lord chief justice, sided with him. Instead of hiding behind your powerful patron, Delaune challenged Calamy, treat me as a weak brother like the apostle Paul commanded (see Rom 15:1; 1 Cor 8:12–13; 1 Thess 5:14; Gal 6:1). Paul would never have offended a weak brother, nor would he have cloaked "his writings, or preachings, under the terrible patronage of" secular rulers, as you have done. I used "no force and arms against you…, but pen, ink, and a few papers. The indictment makes this a very formidable kind of artillery."[159]

Despite his pleas and arguments, Delaune never left prison. Daniel Defoe, author of the classic *Robinson Crusoe*, sadly noted that Delaune was "one of nearly 8,000 Protestant dissenters who perished in prison in the days of that merciful prince, Charles II, and that merely for dissenting from the church, in points which they could give such reasons for as" Delaune's *Plea* "assigns, and for no other cause were stifled (I had almost said murdered) in jails for their religion, in the days of those gentlemen's power who pretend[ed] to abhor persecution."[160] That dissenters like Delaune died in prison merely for printing their religious beliefs is a sad commentary on the character of those who threw them in prison. However, his persecutors permitted even more heinous crimes to occur. After Delaune had been found guilty of sedition, his wife and two small children, without anyone to support them, joined him in Newgate. The wretched prison conditions of the prison took Delaune's life in 1685, but not before they took the lives of his family.

---

157 Ibid., 63 [61].
158 Ibid., 64 [62].
159 Ibid., 64–65 [62–63].
160 Defoe, preface to *A Plea for the Non-Conformists*, 4.

Few people today would disagree with Defoe's conclusion and condemnation that "such a Christian [and] such a scholar" as Delaune "should starve in a dungeon, and the whole body of dissenters in England, whose cause he died for defending, should not raise" the money to free him was deplorable. "Such a champion of such a cause," Defoe wryly noted, "deserved better."[161] Delaune's wife and children deserved better too.

Vavasor Powell: "The Baptist Apostle of Wales"[162]

Another imprisoned preacher who died in prison was the Welsh evangelist Vavasor Powell (1616–1670).[163] Arrested numerous times during his life, Powell spent a total of eleven years (20 percent of his life) in prison. Nothing in his early years indicated that he would one day be an evangelist whose activities would be monitored by the government. Powell left his Welsh home to attend Jesus College, Oxford, but did not earn a degree. After leaving Oxford, he returned to Wales to become a schoolmaster at Clun, six miles from Knucklas, his hometown.

Though a member of the Church of England, Powell was not a deeply religious man until the late 1630s when he began listening to the preaching of Puritans and reading their works. Powell heard Walter Cradock's sermon on Mark 16:15, in which he urged the congregation to accept Christ, but warned that those who did would have to welcome the persecution that accompanied this decision. After hearing the sermon, Powell began to read

---

[161] Ibid., 11.

[162] John C. Carlisle, *The Story of the English Baptists* (London: James Clarke & Co., 1905) 128.

[163] For the position that Powell was "an independent pastor of gathered churches, having affinities with certain Baptists," but not a Baptist, see Barbara Coulton, "Vavasor Powell and His Baptist Connections," *Baptist Quarterly* 40/8 (October 2004): 477–87. For those who accept that Powell was a Baptist, see Champlin. Burrage, ed., "Early Welsh Baptist Doctrines, Set forth in a Manuscript, ascribed to Vavasor Powell," *Transactions of the Baptist Historical Society* 1/1 (November 1908): 3–4; David Davies, *Vavasor Powell: The Baptist Evangelist of Wales in the Seventeenth Century* (London: Alexander and Shepheard, 1896); J. Davis, *History of the Welsh Baptists: From the Year Sixty-Three to the Year One Thousand Seven Hundred and Seventy* (Pittsburgh: D. M. Hogan, 1835) 28–30; Alexander Gordon, "Powell, Vavasor (1617–1670)," *Dictionary of National Biography*, 46:250; and R. T. Jones, "Powell, Vavasor (1617–1670)," in *Biographical Dictionary of British Radicals in the Seventeenth Century*, 3:56.

the Bible, pray, and listen to preachers whom he considered to be godly. During the next four years, he struggled with "constant doubts and great fears, as to" his "eternal condition, being of ten times tempted by Satan to destroy" himself.[164]

After leaving the established church sometime in 1639, Powell became a popular evangelist among Independents in Wales. He often preached two or three times a day, rarely going two days without preaching, and often traveled 100 miles in a week.[165] With success, however, came the persecution about which Cradock had warned. Despite being arrested twice for preaching, Powell was not convicted of any crime.

When the first civil war began in 1642, Powell left Wales for London, where he preached freely for two years and converted many. While in London and suffering a life-threatening illness, Powell conquered his four-year struggle with doubt and fear when the "God of grace" impressed on him the Bible verse John 3:36: "He that believeth on the Son hath Everlasting Life." Powell believed and found peace.[166] After ministering in London, he settled in Dartford, Kent, where he continued to win converts.[167]

In 1646 Powell returned to Wales, and seven years later he began openly and bitterly opposing Cromwell's protectorship, denouncing the Lord Protector as a "vile person."[168] Arrested in London on 21 December 1653 for his political views, Powell took the opportunity to denounce Cromwell in a sermon to people waiting to enter the courtroom. After three days in jail, the authorities released Powell, who then returned to Wales. In

---

[164] Vavasor Powell, "Mr. Powell's Account of His Conversion and Ministry," in *The Life and Death of Mr. Vavasor Powell*, by Edward Bagshaw (London : n.p., 1671) 12; Davies, *Vavasor Powell*, 39.

[165] Thomas Crosby, *The History of the English Baptists from the Reformation to the Beginning of the Reign of King George I*, 4 vols. (London: privately printed, 1738) 1:376–77.

[166] Powell, "Mr. Powell's Account of His Conversion and Ministry," 13; Davies, *Vavasor Powell*, 40.

[167] Crosby, *The History of the English Baptists*, 1:374–75.

[168] Stephen K. Roberts, "Powell, Vavasor (1617–1670)," *Oxford Dictionary of National Biography*, http://www.oxforddnb.com./view/article/22662 (accessed 28 May 2005).

1655 he wrote a petition denouncing Cromwell, for which he was again arrested.

Not all Independents in Wales opposed the Lord Protector, which might partially explain Powell's becoming a Baptist. After a pamphlet supporting Cromwell appeared in Wales, Powell traveled to northern Wales, where he was the guest of a Baptist named Thomas Edwards, who, according to tradition, convinced him that immersion was the scriptural mode of baptism. Powell was then baptized by immersion, probably in 1655.[169] He had already denounced infant baptism as early as February 1654, but despite this denunciation, Powell was an open-communion Baptist; that is, he did not make baptism by immersion a requirement for fellowship because, he said, in a discussion about "baptism, as in many other cases, difference in persuasion and practice may well consist with brotherly love and Christian communion (see Phil 3:15; Rom 14)."[170]

As a result of his influence as a preacher and his opposition to Cromwell, the government monitored Powell's activities. For example, Secretary of State John Thurloe commented on Powell's baptism in a letter (1 January 1656) to Major-General Henry Cromwell in Ireland: "Amongst many other things which are daily sent abroad for inflaming the people, your lordship will receive herewith a paper newly exhibited to the world by Vavasor Powell (who is lately re-baptized) and several other of his party, whereupon I will make no observations though many others do."[171]

In 1658 Powell landed in jail again, this time in Cardiff. The circumstances surrounding this imprisonment are unknown. While waiting to be released, Powell rewrote his will on 21 December 1658. Along with directions concerning the disposal of his worldly goods, the Welsh preacher professed his belief in the resurrection of the dead:

> I do willingly surrender up my soul and spirit to God, who gave it being, assured that immediately after its dissolution from the body it shall, through Jesus Christ, be gathered up and carried into eternal life and glory. I leave my body to be interred in a civil Christian manner, where and how Christian friends shall judge

---

[169] Davies, *Vavasor Powell*, 96; Carlisle, *The Story of the English Baptists*, 129.

[170] Vavasor Powell, "A Confession of Faith," in Bagshaw, *The Life and Death of Mr. Vavasor Powell*, 36; Gordon, "Powell, Vavasor (1617–1670)," 46:250–51.

[171] Davies, *Vavasor Powell*, 99.

most convenient (but I desire no funeral solemnities), not doubting but by the power of Christ it shall be raised with the bodies of the just who die in the Lord, and shall be then made like unto the glorious body of Jesus Christ.[172]

The date of Powell's release from the Cardiff jail is unknown. However, he was free when Charles II returned to England in 1660, but not for long. Soon after the Restoration, Powell was the first Welshman to be imprisoned. Fearing his influence and determined to silence him, the Crown charged him with seditious preaching and had him jailed in April 1660 in Shrewsbury, west of Birmingham. He spent nine weeks there before being released by the king's order. Rearrested on 18 July for preaching, Powell refused to take the Oaths of Supremacy and Allegiance. The State Papers Domestic for 18 and 24 July 1660 contained the justification for jailing Powell. These documents described him as "a most factious and dangerous minister" who "countenanced unlawful assemblies and seditious persons." The government also accused him of concealing weapons and being part of a plot "to cut the throats of all the" Royalists in Wales.[173]

During his incarceration in Shrewsbury, Powell wrote *Common-Prayer-Book No Divine Service*, most of which he devoted to presenting numerous reasons that the *Book of Common Prayer* was deficient and offensive to good Christians.[174] In the book he also declared that forcing people to worship according the Prayer Book was "unlawful," for "no magistrate, minister, nor any other persons under heaven can produce any" biblical justification for such violence. Moreover, the Second Commandment prohibits "the ordinances, traditions, and rudiments of men," which "stinted liturgies, or common prayer books, are."[175]

Coercing people to worship according to the Prayer Book was also wrong because it forced "many Christians to sin against their consciences, or to suffer for not so sinning."[176] Uniformity of worship cannot lead to unity

---

[172] The entire will is reprinted in Davies, *Vavasor Powell*, 161–62. The material quoted here is on 161.

[173] Quoted ibid., 135.

[174] Vavasor Powell, *Common-Prayer-Book no Divine Service* (London: printed for Livewell Chapman, 1660) 18–26.

[175] Ibid., 1.

[176] Ibid., 5.

of spirit, Powell maintained, for "to yoke believers and unbelievers together in church communion and worship is contrary to the scriptures, and therefore unlawful." The result, however, of "the forming and making of such stinted liturgies, or common prayer books," is the mixing of believers and unbelievers in worship, for that "is the main end of making them."[177]

Powell also had strong words for Anglican priests. Ministers who could not pray without written prayers were "more like Jeroboam's simpletons (1 Kings 12:31), and the blemished priests under the Law (Lev. 21), and the dumb dogs which the prophet reproves (Isa. 56:10) than gospel ministers."[178] To those who argued that liturgies helped people to pray, just like crutches helped the lame to walk, Powell responded that liturgies are more of "a hindrance than help, for people would, if it were not for such forms, seek the Spirit of God, which would be given to help them. Either these [liturgies] are to help those who have no grace, or those who have grace; [they cannot be for] those who have none, for what good will crutches do to a dead man? (as every graceless or natural man is.)"[179] Of course, those who have grace need no liturgical crutches; they have the Spirit.

In rejecting the *Book of Common Prayer*, Powell was advocating spontaneous, heart-felt worship services instead of what he considered to be the Anglican Church's mechanical, spirit-suffocating liturgy. For Powell, ministers led by God's Spirit could lead God's Spirit-led people. However, graceless, Spirit-less ministers who could do little more than read a book written by other graceless, Spirit-less ministers might lead people, but they certainly would not lead anyone to the Promised Land. Do not tie worship to a fallible, lifeless Prayer Book, Powell declared. Free the Spirit in your worship services, and you yourselves will be free.

Sometime in 1661, perhaps September, the Shrewsbury authorities transferred Powell to London's Fleet Prison, where he resided until 1662. For one year, he could not leave his cell, which, along with the stench of a manure heap just outside his window, harmed his health to such an extent that he never fully recovered.

While in Fleet, Powell wrote *The Bird in the Cage*, in which he advised and encouraged the persecuted churches of Wales. He also provided his

---

[177] Ibid., 6.

[178] Ibid., 2.

[179] Ibid., 14.

interpretation of the persecution that the Welsh churches had begun to experience. God, Powell said, is omnipotent and rules the affairs of all people, both the persecuted and the persecutors. Using numerous biblical examples, he proved, at least to his satisfaction, "that God's will and hand are in all matters that are done upon earth."[180] Whatever happens, Powell insisted, happens "by the will and appointment of the Lord." God has reasons for doing what he does. But, someone might argue, could not persecutors then claim that they were doing God's will, after all, how could they go against the Almighty's decree? Absolutely not, Powell countered, because "God will turn the rage of man to his own praise." But why would God decree that people persecute others? For Powell, the answer was simple: "I may (and oh that I could with tears mention it, and that my blood were fit to write it!) answer with the same prophet: 'For the greatness of our iniquities'" (Jer 13:22).[181]

Thus, according to Powell, the Restoration, and with it the persecution that followed, was the consequence of the sins of God's people. We have the greatest preachers since the days of the apostles and a lot of preaching, Powell confessed, yet "we have been stomach-full, sick, and surfeited with the sweet and fat things of God's house.... We have trampled and trod under foot the good pastures, which God has provided for us."[182] The churches have prospered—membership is up, and so is giving—yet our "love, zeal, spiritual watchfulness, self-denial, humility, pity to and praying for others" have declined, and we have grown "bitter, sour, and selfish."[183] Therefore, the present persecutions, these "appointments and ordinances of God," are as necessary as they are profitable, Powell asserted, for they purify God's people of their sins.[184]

Not only did the sins of these Christians cause them to be punished, but their profession of faith also resulted in their being persecuted. Thus, according to Powell, Welsh Christians were persecuted for doing the wrong things and the right things; they were punished for being sinners and for

---

[180] Vavasor Powell, *The Bird in the Cage, Chirping Four Distinct Notes to His Consorts Abroad* (London: printed for L. C., 1661) 5.

[181] Ibid., 8.

[182] Ibid., 9.

[183] Ibid., 12.

[184] Ibid., 14.

being saints. "A Christian should never do anything for Christ (2 Tim. 1:11–12), but [that] he should expect to suffer for so doing," Powell reminded his readers, for how can you fight the devil and expect the devil not to fight back?[185] To help his fellow Christians persevere during their persecution, Powell offered some pastoral advice: (1) Remember that God chastises those whom he loves [Heb 12:6; Rev 3:19]; (2) Remember that God's corrections are profitable [Heb 12:1]; (3) Remember that "there is safety in no other" than God; (4) Fear God, not "poor mortals, who are but grass, worms, and thimbles full of dust"; (5) Fast, pray, and encourage each other; (6) Be wise and glorify Christ; (7) Do not flee persecution, unless God has called you do to do so; (8) Flee the temptation to sin; and (9) Be patient.[186]

In 1662 prison authorities transferred Powell again, this time to Southsea Castle, near Portsmouth, on the coast of the English Channel. After the Earl of Clarendon's death in 1667, Powell gained his release and, unrepentant and undeterred by more than nine years in prison, resumed preaching.

In fall 1668, during a evangelistic tour in Wales, Powell's preaching resulted in yet another arrest, this time at Merthyr Tydfil. Gregory Jones, the pastor of the parish church and "notorious throughout the country for drunkenness, dishonesty, licentiousness, and moreover for having put away his own wife," attended a service led by Powell. Jones informed authorities that many of the congregants were armed, and armed guards later arrested Powell and jailed him at Cardiff.[187]

During three interrogations (17 October and 8 November 1668; 13 January 1669), Powell refused to take the Oaths of Allegiance and Supremacy.[188] Hoping to have his case heard by more sympathetic magistrates, he requested and was granted a transfer from Cardiff to London. On 24 May 1669, Powell entered Fleet Prison, where he spent the remainder of his life.

---

[185] Ibid.

[186] See ibid., 31–41.

[187] Davies, *Vavasor Powell*, 147; R. Tudur Jones, "The Sufferings of Vavasor," in *Welsh Baptist Studies*, ed. Mansel John (Llandysul: The South Wales Baptist College, 1976) 84, 90, n. 36.

[188] Crosby, *The History of the English Baptists*, 2:228–29; Jones, "The Sufferings of Vavasor," 84–86.

The authorities at Fleet allowed Powell to write letters, visit occasionally with friends in London, and preach to visitors. He also probably began work on a concordance, which was finished by friends after his death.[189] Powell spent his final days preaching and singing when he could muster the strength. He died in prison on 27 October 1670.

A few months before his death, Powell received a letter from Edward Terrill, a member of a church in Bristol, requesting assistance in securing Thomas Hardcastle to become the pastor of Terrill's church. Powell informed Terrill that Hardcastle was his brother-in-law and that he would provide whatever help he could. The prisoner also took the opportunity to encourage Terrill, reminding him that "our safety is in the Lord, and in doing our duty, and [in] cleaving close to him." Nothing that we can experience on earth, Powell proclaimed, could compare with "the weight of glory and crown of righteousness, prepared and reserved for those who continue faithful to the end."[190]

In a subsequent letter to Terrill, Powell regretfully explained that the Bristol church should seek another man because insurmountable circumstances would prevent Hardcastle's moving to Bristol. Powell told Terrill that he hoped that "the great Shepherd will provide for you, he having promised to feed both the scattered and slaughtered flock (Ezek

---

[189] One famous prisoner used Powell's concordance in prison. A copy of *A New and Useful Concordance* in the Museum of the Baptist College, Bristol, contains the following words on the flyleaf: "John Bunyan his book." See Davies, *Vavasor Powell*, 155–57.

[190] Vavasor Powell to Edward Terrill, 6 June 1670, in *The Records of a Church of Christ, Meeting in Broadmead, Bristol. 1640–1687*, ed. Edward Bean Underhill (London: J. Haddon, 1847) 108–109.

34:14; Zech 11:7)."[191] In May 1671, "the great Shepherd" did provide Terrill's church with a pastor: Thomas Hardcastle.

---

[191] Vavasor Powell to Edward Terrill, 29 August 1670, in *The Records of a Church of Christ*, 116. The circumstances are discussed in the next chapter.

Chapter 5

No Armor for the Back

Typical records of churches' early histories present the mundane aspects of church life. Extraordinary records also include the dates of its persecutions, peaceful Sundays, times persecutors disturbed a church's worship, and the names of members imprisoned for their religious beliefs. Such a church is Broadmead Baptist Church of Bristol, England. Blessed with courageous pastors and members, the church prospered through two civil wars and several periods of intense persecution.[1]

The Beginnings of Broadmead Baptist Church

Broadmead Baptist Church began in 1640 as an Independent congregation when a group of five people decided to worship God according to the dictates of their consciences. No longer able to hear the *Book of Common Prayer* in good conscience, they covenanted together to attend worship services of the Church of England only after the prayers had been read and Matthew Hazzard, the vicar of their church, St. Ewins, had begun to preach. On Sunday afternoons, the small group would then meet to encourage one another.[2] Ironically, the five dissenters began meeting at

---

[1] For a discussion of the church's history during the time period discussed in this chapter, see Roger Hayden, ed., *The Records of a Church of Christ in Bristol, 1640–1687* (Bristol: Bristol Record Society, 1974) 1–70; John Swaish, *Chronicles of Broadmead Church, Bristol: 1640–1923: A Brief Narrative* (Bristol: Young & Humphrys, [1927]) 12–25; and C. E. Shipley's essays "Broadmead: 1640–1687," and "Broadmead: Persecutors and Persecuted," in *Broadmead Origins: An Account of the Rise of Puritanism in England, and of the Early Days of Broadmead Baptist Church, Bristol*, ed. Robert L. Child and C. E. Shipley (London: The Kingsgate Press, [1940]) 38–52 and 53–65.

[2] Edward Bean Underhill, ed., *The Records of a Church of Christ, Meeting in Broadmead, Bristol, 1640–1685* (London: J. Haddon, 1847) 18. Hereafter cited as *RCC*.

Hazzard's home because his wife, Dorothy, was the group's leader. According to Edward Terrill, a church elder, a schoolmaster, and a businessman who recorded much of the early history of the Broadmead church, Dorothy "was like a he-goat before the flock" and "like Deborah she arose, with strength of holy resolution in her soul from God, even a mother in Israel."[3] Thus, the first dissenting church in Bristol began in the parsonage of the Anglican vicar of St. Ewins. Two years after its formation, the church had 160 members who often had to meet clandestinely, though at other times they rented a public place for worship.[4] The congregation eventually purchased a building on the site where it has continued to worship since 1671.[5]

Robert Bacon, a Separatist minister, led the Broadmead congregation for three years (1640–1642) before another Separatist minister, a Mr. Pennill, pastored it for a short period. At the start of the first civil war in 1642, members of a church from Llanvaches, Wales, fled to Bristol. That church's minister, Walter Cradock, then pastored both congregations. When Bristol fell to Royalist forces in 1643, both congregations fled to London and worshiped at All Hallows open communion Baptist church.[6]

When the Broadmead congregation returned to Bristol in 1645 after Parliament forces had retaken the city, some members believed that the church should not observe the ordinances of baptism and the Lord's Supper; other members disagreed. After the two groups split, the group that did observe the ordinances called Nathaniel Ingello, who pastored the congregation for about five years until his worldly lifestyle upset some of the members. According to Terrill, Ingello offended many

> with his flaunting apparel, for he, being a thin, spare, slender person, did go very neat, in a costly trim, and in some time began to exceed in some garments not becoming the gospel, much less a

---

[3] Ibid., 10. For the reference to Deborah, see Judges 5:7. For more on Dorothy Hazzard, see Margaret McLaren Cook, "Dorothy Hazzard," in *Great Baptist Women by Baptist Women*, ed. A. S. Clement (London: The Carey Kingsgate Press Limited, 1955) 9–16.

[4] Swaish, *Chronicles of Broadmead Church*, 13–15.

[5] Although the congregation did not purchase a building here until 1671, I will refer to the church as Broadmead throughout the chapter.

[6] *RCC*, 28–31; Hayden, *The Records of a Church of Christ in Bristol*, 13–14.

minister of Christ; together with his being given so much to music, not only at his own house, but at houses of entertainment out of town; sometimes with some of his relations, and [sometimes with the] gentry of the city of his acquaintance, he would be at his music. Because of this, when some of the members heard, they were much troubled and offended.[7]

When Ingello told the offended members that his music was his life, the church told him to sing elsewhere and began to search for a new leader.

Thomas Ewins: A Man "Remarkable for His Meekness, Patience, and Charity"[8]

In 1651 the church called Thomas Ewins (1617–1670) as its pastor, though technically he served only as a teaching elder.[9] A tailor by trade, Ewins had been a member of the All Hallows congregation in London until 1648 when the church sent him and five others to Llanvaches to work with the congregation that had been led by Walter Cradock. When invited to serve the Broadmead church, Ewins was reluctant to accept because he did not want to leave Llanvaches. However, the Bristol city authorities finally convinced him to accept the position of city lecturer. He preached and lectured at several Bristol churches during the week and met with the Broadmead congregation on Thursdays. Ewins was not ordained and preferred to be regarded as a preacher of the gospel rather than as a pastor. He took no salary, but accepted donations.

Ewins had not been in Bristol long when, in 1652, Thomas Munday, a member of the Broadmead church, became convinced that believer's baptism by immersion was the true baptism and asked for leave of the church so that he could join another Bristol congregation that immersed believers. The following year another member, Timothy Cattle, informed the church that he too wanted to be immersed. Because Cattle often traveled to London on business, "the church gave him a letter to one Mr. Henry Jessey, a gracious, baptized minister, in London, desiring him to

---

[7] RCC, 36.

[8] Edmund Calamy, The Nonconformist's Memorial, 3 vols. (London: printed by J. Cundee, 1803) 3:175.

[9] For biographical information on Ewins, see Hayden, The Records of a Church of Christ in Bristol, 27–34.

baptize...Cattle, which...he did. After this, many others of the church were baptized, according to scripture example, in a river."[10]

After nineteen members left the church in 1654 over a dispute concerning Quakerism, the remaining sixty members fasted and prayed, seeking guidance as to why such a schism had occurred. They determined that one reason for the schism was their failure to remain true to their faith. Consequently, Ewins and Robert Purnell, a ruling elder, "were pressed in their spirits to take up the ordinance of baptism.... Thus, they being now stirred up to their duty, to glorify God in their day, in owning his commands in the gospel, and [in] laying aside the traditions of man in worship, these two...went to London...where they were...baptized by brother Mr. Henry Jessey, after which they came down and proceeded in the church and work of the Lord."[11]

The Broadmead church worshiped freely during the Interregnum (1649–1660), and in 1659 Terrill recorded that "we had peace."[12] Things changed drastically, however, after the Restoration in March 1660, for when Charles II returned from exile, "then Satan stirred up adversaries against us, and our trouble or persecution began."[13] As Roger Hayden observed, "Revenge seeking royalists, now back in power as civil leaders, sought every opportunity to harry dissenters."[14] The following December the Crown required that everyone over sixteen years old take the Oaths of Allegiance and Supremacy. Ewins refused and was dismissed from his city lectureships. The Broadmead church discussed the oaths with another Bristol congregation, and both agreed that the churches should obey the Crown, but only in civil matters. The churches then composed a document stating what they would and would not do and sent it to the mayor of Bristol, Henry Creswick, who then sent it to the king. The Crown's response was that the people had to swear to the oaths just as they were written. When Creswick informed the churches that they would not be required to swear to anything unscriptural, some members took the oaths; some did not.[15]

---

[10] *RCC*, 42.

[11] Ibid., 51.

[12] Ibid., 69.

[13] Ibid., 70.

[14] Roger Hayden, "Broadmead, Bristol in the Seventeenth Century," *Baptist Quarterly* 23/8 (October 1970): 355.

[15] *RCC*, 70–71.

Shortly after Venner's rebellion in January 1661, Creswick informed Ewins that he could no longer preach in his home. Undaunted, Ewins started preaching at a public chapel called the Friars. On 25 June 1661, Creswick had Ewins brought before him and prohibited him from preaching at the Friars. Ewins again ignored the mayor, and the next month, he was jailed for sixteen days. After his release, Ewins was confined to his home for a month and a half, after which he was free to travel as he wished. Once free, he returned to preaching openly at the Friars.[16]

On 24 June 1662, the church ordained Ewins, and he continued to lead worship openly every Sunday and hold church conferences every Thursday. Such openness got Ewins in trouble again, for he was arrested on 26 October and spent nineteen days in jail. Following his arrest, however, the church remained free from persecution for almost a year until a new mayor was elected.

Soon after Sir John Knight[17] became mayor of Bristol in 1663, he summoned Ewins to his home and demanded that he stop preaching. Ewins informed the mayor that he must obey the Lord, not the mayor, and the next day he preached at the Friars. On Sunday, 4 October 1663, Knight sent several men to arrest Ewins and Mr. Patient, a minister of "the other baptized congregation" in Bristol, for violating the Act of Uniformity (1662), requiring that all church services conform to the *Book of Common Prayer*.[18] Both were jailed in the Bristol prison called Newgate. Terrill filled in for Ewins that afternoon until word came that a warrant had been issued for his and Deacon Robert Simpson's arrest. The elders told Terrill to stop preaching and sit down. When officers arrived at the service, they did not know whom to arrest, so they left. The next day, however, the mayor had Terrill, Simpson, Ewins, and Patient brought to his home, where he

---

[16] Ibid., 71–72.

[17] *RCC* mentions three men named John Knight: (1) Sir John Knight, the elder: sheriff [1660], alderman [1662–1683], mayor [1663], and MP for Bristol [1660–1680]; (2) Mr. John Knight, cousin of Sir John Knight, the elder: sheriff [1664–1665] and mayor [1670–1671]; and (3) Sir John Knight, the younger: usually referred to as "Sheriff Knight," son of Mr. John Knight, sheriff [1681–1682], mayor [1690–1691], and MP for Bristol [1689–1695]. Fortunately, John Knight, the son of Sir John Knight, the elder, is not mentioned in the book. See Hayden, *The Records of a Church of Christ in Bristol*, 297–98.

[18] *RCC*, 74.

demanded that they post bond for good behavior. Their refusal landed them in jail. Terrill spent two weeks there, but the others spent approximately three months waiting for their trial. After they were found guilty of inciting a riot, Knight fined Ewins and Simpson £50 each, and Terrill £5.[19] The men refused to pay and were jailed. Terrill spent three months in jail before a friend paid his fine. Friends later paid the fines for Ewins and Simpson on 26 September 1664.[20]

Ewins spent part of his time in prison preaching twice a week to people assembled outside the prison walls. He also wrote at least three letters, one to his church, the others to Terrill. With their pastor imprisoned and persecution a present reality, members of the Broadmead congregation decided to meet clandestinely because many members feared banishment under the Conventicle Act (1664), which had been passed while their pastor was in prison.

The Conventicle Act emboldened Bristol authorities to crack down on nonconformist churches in the city. Terrill noted that, like animals, "we were hunted by the Nimrods" and had to abandon worshiping at the Friars.[21] One time during a weekday meeting at Thomas Ellis's home, members escaped the authorities by running into the cellar that opened out into a public street. Another time during a Sunday worship service, several men, including Sir John Knight, broke into Ellis's home to arrest the worshipers. Although many people escaped through an attic door that Ellis had concealed behind a huge cupboard, thirty-one members and visitors spent a month in prison at Bridewell.[22]

In the letter to his congregation, Ewins confessed that "the condition of the church is a greater trouble to me than all my imprisonment." He wrote that he preferred that the church continue to meet openly until some members had been arrested so that "a testimony might be borne for the Lord and the work of his patience," for they had not finished their testimony. Therefore, Ewins encouraged his members to bear witness

---

[19] No amount was recorded for Patient.

[20] *RCC*, 75–76.

[21] RCC, 77. Nimrod was "a mighty hunter before the LORD" (Gen 10:8).

[22] Ibid. Sir John Knight, the elder, was quite proud of his incarcerating prowess. He boasted that he had helped send 900 people to prison. See Swaish, *Chronicles of Broadmead Church*, 19.

against "this late unrighteous act" by getting arrested. If members did not want to pay the fine, their pastor assured them that they would be released in a week or two, after which they could then worship privately with their families.[23]

Ewins also addressed a situation that had caused ill feelings among some members: some elders either had abandoned the church or, fearing imprisonment, had had second thoughts about preaching publicly. The congregation perhaps interpreted such hesitation as weakness and encouraged the leaders to preach themselves into prison. To this situation their imprisoned pastor urged patience and understanding. Do not let your hearts burn against these men, Ewins counseled, "because they do not stick to you, as I once thought they would have done;—we must allow all men something. No man can be forced beyond his freedom. Let every man look to his own heart."[24] Ewins, who had preached himself into prison, understood what the church leaders were experiencing, yet the one who had every right to judge the wavering leaders and to demand that they stand strong, counseled the church to be understanding.

Because Terrill assumed the leadership in the church during Ewins's absence, the imprisoned pastor encouraged his friend not to let the discouragement of some people hamper his ministry during these perilous times, for following Christ meant that he would "meet with wounds in the house of" his friends. By the providence of God, Terrill had been called "to break the bread of life to the poor and hungry." Ignore those people who question your call to minister in my stead, Ewins counseled, and "go on in the fear of the Lord to feed his flock until the elder brethren, or servants, come home."[25]

Upon his release from prison on 26 September 1664, Ewins returned home and to preaching. His time in prison, unfortunately, damaged his health. He had strained his voice shouting to worshipers assembled below his cell window, and during his first sermon after being released from prison, he fainted. Ewins never completely recovered from his prison experience.[26]

---

[23] Thomas Ewins to his church, no date, in *RCC*, 80.

[24] Ibid., 81.

[25] Thomas Ewins to Edward Terrill, 23 July 1664, in *RCC*, 83.

[26] *RCC*, 76.

When Ewins died in April 1670, hundreds of mourners accompanied his body to the cemetery. Terrill commented that Bristol had never witnessed such a funeral before. He also noted that his pastor had "left so good a savor behind for faithfulness to God and humility towards man" that even Sir John Knight remarked that even he believed that Ewins had gone to heaven.[27] None of the Broadmead members, however, would have said the same about Knight.

Robert Simpson: A Detained Deacon

During his stay in Newgate, Ewins enjoyed the company of Robert Simpson (1592–1677), a deacon of the Broadmead church. While in prison, Simpson wrote a rambling, and at times incoherent, letter to Terrill, whom he called his "loving brother." Simpson asked the Bristol schoolmaster for help with the placement of Greek words in a document he was writing.

The purpose of Simpson's letter, however, was to encourage Terrill and to praise God. Terrill's friend constantly prayed for his success and encouraged him to be thankful for God's using him to be "a blessing to many."[28] Be patient, Simpson told his friend, and be open to the guidance of God's Spirit. Obey the biblical injunction to remember the promises of God. Remember that God promised that those who wait for him will be blessed. Remember that in the last days "young men shall see visions" and that God will "pour out his Spirit upon his servants and handmaidens" and "they shall prophesy" (Acts 2:17–18). Remember also to stand upon the promises set forth in Isaiah 41:17–20, in which the prophet describes God's turning a wilderness into a land teeming with life. "God is a carrying on his work," Simpson proclaimed triumphantly, and cannot be stopped.[29]

Anyone reading the Simpson's letter without knowing the circumstances in which it was written might never realize that he wrote it in prison. The letter appears to have been written by someone sitting in his study, praising God, and working on a writing project; it contains no hint of prison, no mention of persecutors, and no mention of suffering. Despite his circumstances, the detained deacon appeared to be enjoying himself.

---

[27] Ibid., 98.

[28] Robert Simpson to Edward Terrill, 27 June 1664, in *RCC*, 78.

[29] Ibid., 79.

Along with Ewins, Simpson left prison on 26 September 1664 and returned home. However, he had not seen the last of Newgate, for the eighty-three-year-old "aged disciple" and two others were sent to the hellish prison on 25 April 1675 for attending an illegal worship service. The length of Simpson's stay in prison is unknown, but he was free at least a week prior to 20 February 1677, the day on which he died.[30]

Thomas Hardcastle: "A Champion for the Lord"[31]

When Ewins died in 1670, the congregation began the process of finding another pastor. Terrill informed Vavasor Powell, the Welsh evangelist who at that time was incarcerated in London's Fleet Prison, that the Broadmead congregation was interested in having Powell's brother-in-law, Thomas Hardcastle (1636–1678), to serve as its pastor.[32] Terrill wanted to know whether Hardcastle was free from other church obligations and whether he would be a good fit for the Broadmead church.[33] Powell informed Terrill that Hardcastle would be an excellent match for the Broadmead church and that he had forwarded Terrill's letter to his brother-in-law.

In a letter to Terrill, Hardcastle expressed his willingness to go to Bristol, but two things stood in his way: he was currently serving a six months' prison sentence for violating the Second Conventicle Act (1670), and he also was "on trial for eldership" (being considered as pastor) for the Swan Alley church in London.[34] Though he was willing to pastor the Broadmead congregation, he expressed doubts that he would be able to move to Bristol.

Hardcastle's decision whether to move to Bristol was made even more difficult when John Smith, a member of the Swan Alley congregation,

---

[30] *RCC*, 237, 378.

[31] Ibid., 388.

[32] For biographical information on Hardcastle, see Roger Hayden, "Hardcastle, Thomas (bap. 1637, d. 1678)," *Oxford Dictionary of National Biography* (Oxford: Oxford University Press, 2004), http://www.oxforddnb.com./view/article/12250 (accessed 28 May 2005), and Hayden, *The Records of a Church of Christ in Bristol*, 34–42.

[33] *RCC*, 107.

[34] Thomas Hardcastle to the Church of Christ meeting in Bristol, 24 August 1670, in *RCC*, 111.

opened and read one of Hardcastle's letters to the Broadmead congregation. Following the discovery of Hardcastle's correspondence with the Bristol church, the London congregation fought hard to keep him.[35] Some members warned Hardcastle that he would be committing a sin if he pastored the Broadmead church; others predicted that he would be cursed if he went. Such threats, however, did not faze Hardcastle. He responded that refusing to accept Broadmead's offer would be a sin, and as for being cursed, he was defiant: "I told them I did not use to be frightened by great words, and that no man's conscience should be the rule of mine."[36]

Ultimately, Hardcastle went to Bristol; however, the road there had been difficult, for he was no stranger to a prison cell, having often been arrested and imprisoned for preaching.[37] When Parliament passed the Act of Uniformity (1662), Hardcastle was vicar of Bramham in Yorkshire. His refusal to obey the act resulted in his ejection from his vicarship, but he continued his ministry when the residents of Shadwell asked him to preach at the "chapel of Ease."[38] However, after he preached on Sunday, 18 June 1665, several bailiffs armed with warrants "to apprehend all persons riotously, seditiously, and impudently all assembled at any unlawful conventical or meeting" arrested Hardcastle and twenty-five others.[39] Imprisonment, however, did not dissuade him from preaching after being paroled in August 1665, for he was again jailed in January 1666 for violating parole. After being imprisoned first at York and then for more than a year in Chester Castle, Hardcastle petitioned for his release, which was granted on 20 December 1667, after friends paid £1,000. While at Chester, he met his future wife, Anne Gerard, who probably ministered to prisoners and who was also the sister of Vavasor Powell's wife, Katherine.

---

[35] The two churches exchanged several angry letters concerning Hardcastle, and the animosity between them lasted for seven years, ending only when Hardcastle died in 1678. The letters can be found in *RCC*, 117–20, 153–55, 198–205.

[36] Thomas Hardcastle to Edward Terrill, 3 July 1671, in *RCC*, 149.

[37] See Hayden, *The Records of a Church of Christ in Bristol*, 35, for a list of Hardcastle's arrests and imprisonments, although Hardcastle's first arrest occurred in June 1665, not August.

[38] "Two Hardcastles, Presbyterian and Baptist," *Transactions of the Baptist Historical Society* 4/1 (April 1914): 33.

[39] "To the reader," in *A Sermon Preached at Shadwell-Chapell in Yorkshire*, by Thomas Hardcastle (London: n.p., 1665) A3.

As was his custom upon being released from prison, Hardcastle immediately returned to preaching and was arrested along with twenty-four others on 8 January 1668, after only nineteen days of freedom. Released again on parole, Hardcastle did not enjoy that freedom for long. He went to Leeds, where he was arrested again on 21 January 1668, for a parole violation.[40] After his release, the authorities arrested Hardcastle again for preaching at Leeds on 28 May 1668. He moved to London sometime in 1669 or 1670 after being released from prison, was baptized, and became a member of "that ancient and honorable society...formerly walking with Mr. Henry Jessey" in Swan Alley.[41] Hardcastle then spent sixth months in prison, during which time he began corresponding with the Broadmead congregation.

Hoping that they could convince Hardcastle to accept their call, the Broadmead members invited the gifted preacher to visit Bristol. He suggested to his London church that it allow him to visit Bristol for a month, only to express his gratitude to the Broadmead church and to help it with a controversy raging at that time as to whether believers who had been baptized as infants should be allowed to participate in the Lord's Supper.[42] Initially, Hardcastle's church refused to let him go, but it eventually relented. At the end of his month-long visit in May 1671, the Broadmead church voted unanimously to call Hardcastle as its pastor. Terrill wrote the church's call, which was signed by all the members and presented to Hardcastle on 29 May 1671. When he entered the room in which the church was meeting, all of the members present raised their right hands to signify their desire to have him as their pastor. Moved by the show of hands,

---

[40] "Two Hardcastles, Presbyterian and Baptist," 34.

[41] Thomas Hardcastle, dedicatory to *Christian Geography and Arithmetick*, by Thomas Hardcastle (London: printed for Richard Chiswell, 1674) [iv]. See also Hayden, *The Records of a Church of Christ in Bristol*, 35, and *RCC*, 388.

[42] Thomas Hardcastle to Edward Terrill, 10 March 1671, in *RCC*, 122–23. Hardcastle advised allowing non-immersed believers to participate: "Let the brethren who are for infant baptism clearly see by your carriage that you prefer mutual love before the imposing [of] your persuasion.... I would choose the way to a man's understanding through his heart, especially seeing it is the way which the gospel so much insists on; I have always found it true, that union in hearts had more considerable effect than union in heads" (123).

Hardcastle promised that he would be their pastor if that was God's will.[43] He then returned home in order to discuss his future with his London congregation.

Almost a month after the Broadmead members called Hardcastle, the Swan Alley members also voted to call him as their pastor. Although the vote and the arguments of the London church to keep Hardcastle troubled him, he assured Terrill that "they do not turn me."[44] Thus, believing that God had called him to Bristol, Hardcastle moved there in July 1671 to begin a fruitful seven-year ministry.

The Broadmead church had experienced several periods of persecution prior to Hardcastle's pastorate, and in October 1674 Terrill recorded the beginning of the church's "eighth persecution in this city" since the Restoration in 1660. Guy Carleton, a new bishop who had been a captain in Charles I's army and had spent time with Charles II in exile, had arrived in Bristol. Carleton's goal as bishop, Terrill recorded, was to eliminate the six nonconformist churches in Bristol and force all the dissenters to attend the worship services of the Church of England.[45] Carleton, whom Terrill called "Goliath," used the Bristol mayor, Ralph Ollive, "a great drinker," to do his bidding.

Along with Carleton and Ollive, Terrill noted that the Lord raised up a third persecutor against the Broadmead church, a lawyer, tavern owner, and parish constable named John Hellier.[46] Hellier appears in the records of Broadmead church numerous times, never in a positive light. Terrill derisively described him as a "pestilent adversary," "that wicked man," "this debauched fellow," and the "troubler of our Israel."[47] According to Hayden, Hellier had a financial motive for persecuting nonconformists. An incentive under the Second Conventicle Act provided that fines on dissenters would be split three ways: a third to the king, a third to parish authorities for poor relief, and a third to the informer. Thus, by persecuting dissenters, Hellier

---

[43] *RCC*, 133–37.

[44] Thomas Hardcastle to Edward Terrill, 26 June 1671, in *RCC*, 149.

[45] *RCC*, 212–13.

[46] Ibid., 214–15.

[47] Ibid., 215, 228, 317, 345. For more on Hellier, see Child and Shipley, "Broadmead: Persecutors and Persecuted," 54–58, and *The Devouring Informers of Bristol, etc.*, (Bristol: n.p., 1682).

collected a third of the fines for his parish and a third for himself.[48] To this financial motive could also be added that Hellier apparently loved his work as an informer. He and his associates often interrupted Broadmead's morning and afternoon services, sometimes as many as six times on any given Sunday. On one occasion, after a week's break from persecuting, Hellier told Terrill that he had been "troubled in his conscience for" not harassing the congregations.[49] Therefore, to assuage his guilty conscience, Hellier resumed his persecution of Bristol's dissenting churches.

On 14 February 1675 Ollive and several other men arrested Hardcastle, who then refused to swear to the oaths required by the Corporation Act (1661).[50] For his refusal, Hardcastle spent six months in Newgate, Bristol. After his release on 6 August, he preached at his church two days later and was arrested by Hellier. This time Hardcastle was convicted for violating the Five Mile Act (1665), but the mayor had to release him because Hardcastle could not be imprisoned for his first offense under the act.[51]

Nothing, however, prevented the Bristol authorities from sending Hardcastle to prison for his second violation of the Five Mile Act. On Sunday, 15 August, twenty men led by Hellier arrested Hardcastle, who was then sent again to Newgate to serve yet another six-month prison term. During this prison term, Hardcastle wrote twenty-two weekly letters to be read during his church's Sunday afternoon services. In a letter written three days after his arrest, Hardcastle told his congregation, "Though you cannot see my face, nor hear my voice, yet I can write epistles to you, which being read among you, may, through the blessing of God, be a means to encourage, instruct, and establish you."[52] According to Hayden, these letters "contain some of the most discerning words about the meaning of 'true faith' written in the seventeenth century."[53] Following are some of the

---

[48] Hayden, "Broadmead, Bristol in the Seventeenth Century," 355–56.

[49] *RCC*, 261.

[50] Ibid., 222.

[51] Ibid., 253.

[52] Thomas Hardcastle's first letter to Broadmead Church, 18 August 1675, in *RCC*, 257. All page numbers for Hardcastle's letters to his Broadmead congregation refer to *RCC*.

[53] Hayden, *The Records of a Church of Christ in Bristol*, 42.

themes Hardcastle developed in the letters to encourage his congregation during perilous times.

Hardcastle reminded his "beloved friends" about the meaning of professing Christ: "We speak much of faith, and hope, and patience, and commend them, but care not to have occasion to make use of them ourselves.... We must follow Christ in the way that he chooses, and not in the way that we choose for ourselves."[54] The Broadmead congregation had experienced a lengthy period of peace, during which it heard sermons and celebrated the ordinances. But such freedom from harassment, Hardcastle maintained, had only served to soften the congregation, making it apathetic. In God's time, however, God sought to rouse the Broadmead members from their religious slumber. Seeing "your ministers torn from you, before your eyes, by ungodly men,...may be an awakening sermon and make you remember" what being a Christian involves.[55] Do not be ashamed of proclaiming the gospel, for we must "walk answerably to our profession."[56] We are duty-bound to be constantly on the offensive and never in retreat. "Religion is still for standing and going forward," Hardcastle declared. "There is no armor for the back."[57]

Hardcastle served as a general commanding his forces from prison to fight to the finish. Apparently, some of his troops wanted to make peace with their persecutors because Jesus said that Christians should be peacemakers (Matt 5:9). However, Hardcastle reminded his congregation, Jesus also said that he did not come to bring peace to the enemies of the gospel but a sword (Matt 10:34). Our enemies "are not able to bear the light of the gospel, which discovers their works of darkness." If you want peace, you will have to stop bearing witness to the gospel: "Take but the candle of the word out of" your persecutors' "eyes and then they will be quiet, and you shall have peace, but our Lord and Master, who is the peacemaker and is all for peace, does yet allow no such thing, but will have a war rather than such a peace." Thus, Hardcastle reminded his besieged troops, only when

---

[54] Hardcastle's first letter, 18 August 1675, 261.

[55] Ibid., 257.

[56] Ibid.

[57] Ibid., 258. See also Thomas Hardcastle's twentieth letter, 8 January 1676, 344, and his twenty-second letter, 22 January 1676, 351–52.

you are at war with sin and are bearing witness against sinners are you at peace with God.[58]

Waging spiritual warfare would be costly, particularly for ministers. Even though all Christians must be ready to exchange their liberty for prison, if that was what God willed, Hardcastle claimed that ministers had a special responsibility to accept persecution. Just like the priests who stood in the Jordan while the ark of the covenant passed into the Promised Land (Josh 3), so "ministers and watchmen must meet with the waters of affliction, and stand in them, and see to the safety of the whole," even to their own detriment (2 Cor 12:15). They must be prepared, like Jesus and Paul, to sacrifice their freedom by taking up "up the cross of imprisonment, when it directly lies in our way."[59] Preaching the gospel and being imprisoned for it are both inherent to a minister's calling. Being afraid of prison never convinced anyone to believe in Christ, and fear and unbelief belong to those who are destined for eternal darkness. For Hardcastle, the choice between faithfulness (prison) and faithlessness (freedom) was simple: "Better go to Newgate with faith, than to hell with fear."[60]

The Broadmead members had to continue worshiping publicly, even while their pastor was in prison, because, as Hardcastle had taught them, being persecuted was part of what it meant to be a Christian. Read Matthew 10:16–21, he suggested: "They will deliver you up, and scourge you." Yet how will our persecutors find us if we are hiding and therefore shirking our duty to worship publicly?[61] Do not think that retreating during persecution will protect you, and do not focus on the power of the persecutors, for "the greatest safety lies in duty and keeping close to it. He is most in danger, and runs into it, who declines duty for fear of the cross and suffering from men. It has been our great error that we have not trusted in the power of God. We have reasoned about the worst that men can do, but have not believed the best that God can do."[62] We must take up our cross and follow Christ, for that is essence of our faith. "Believing on Christ" is the greatest gift one

---

[58] Hardcastle's twentieth letter, 8 January 1676, 344.

[59] Thomas Hardcastle's third letter, 3 September 1675, 265. See also Hardcastle's first letter, 18 August 1675, 260.

[60] Thomas Hardcastle's fourth letter, 8 September 1675, 270.

[61] Ibid.

[62] Ibid.

can receive, but the second greatest, Hardcastle informed his congregation, "is suffering for Christ. A crucified Christ is the foundation of faith; the cross of Christ is the fruit of faith."[63]

Thus, according to the imprisoned pastor, he and his congregation suffered persecution because that was the will of God. "The Lord has been pleased," Hardcastle informed his congregation, "to permit the wrath of the adversary to break out so far upon us, as to separate us, and shut me up in prison again and out of the public assembly for a season. Thus divine pleasure thinks fit to deal with us."[64] All things happen according to God's will, and true believers always respond patiently by accepting whatever the Lord sends. "Thy will be done" should be our "daily pleasure." My sickness, poverty, imprisonment, loss of property is God's will, Hardcastle professed. Can a sparrow fall to the ground without God? Never (Matt 10:29). "Every little wheel of providence," Hardcastle assured his beleaguered congregation, "has its proper motion, and, how cross and contrary so ever the motion is, they all tend to bring about the great ends of God's glory and his people's good."[65]

Lest the members of the Broadmead congregation believe that they experienced persecution solely because of their acceptance of Christ, Hardcastle reminded them several times that God had sent persecution to punish them for their sins. "We have sickly souls, sickly churches, and a sickly state; sin lies at the bottom of all."[66] Therefore, "we must acknowledge ourselves guilty, guilty, and that he has punished us less than our iniquities have deserved."[67] What were some of the sins of which they were guilty? They had become distracted from doing God's will; they had been irreverent; their worship had become formal and hypocritical; they had treated the Lord's day like any other; they had forgotten, during peaceful times, those Christians who were being persecuted; and their love for each other had grown cold.[68] Not persecutors like Hellier and Carleton but "our wills have been the cause of all our woes. We have not considered the

---

[63] Thomas Hardcastle's sixth letter, 18 September 1675, 278.

[64] Hardcastle's first letter, 18 August 1675, 257.

[65] Hardcastle's sixth letter, 18 September 1675, 276.

[66] Thomas Hardcastle's fifteenth letter, 20 November 1675, 319.

[67] Hardcastle's first letter, 18 August 1675, 260. See also Thomas Hardcastle's seventeenth letter, 3 December 1675, 326.

[68] Thomas Hardcastle's second letter, no date, 262–63.

sovereignty of God, but have chosen rather to fulfill our own desires, which have been carnal and selfish, than obey the commands of the great Creator and gracious Redeemer." Be honest with yourselves, Hardcastle implored his friends. Have you deserved what you have received? Or have you deserved to be punished even more severely? Do you ever ask yourselves why you had it so easy before the recent persecutions? Are you now ready to ask God to purge you of your sin, which has been the cause of God's wrath upon you?[69] Nowhere in his letters did Hardcastle attempt to exempt himself from being punished for his sins. Like his fellow spiritual soldiers, he too was a filthy, wretched soul.

The message that Hardcastle preached through his letters was not completely negative, for he often emphasized the positive results that trials could produce. The persecution by the "profaning wretches" of Bristol could make the Broadmead members more humble, more spiritual, more repentant, more loving, and more grateful.[70] Despite our sins, Hardcastle encouraged his congregation, there is hope—hope that we will repent; that God will hear, forgive, and accept us; that the gospel will prosper; that our response to our persecution will encourage others to be strong; and that the spring of peace will follow the winter of persecution.[71]

Not only was there hope for individual sinners to change their ways; there was also the hope that the persecution would further the spread of the gospel message. Hardcastle proclaimed, "Beloved, my imprisonment preaches louder than ever I did."[72] The persecution of nonconformist churches in Bristol had "drawn the eyes of the whole nation after" them and had made everyone "turn aside to see the great sight, that the bush should be in the fire so long together, and yet not" be consumed (see Zeph 3:12–20).[73] Think about the thousands of people who are encouraged and emboldened by your standing firm in your faith, Hardcastle exhorted his congregation, yet also be aware of what faithlessness, even for one day, would do. When we suffer boldly for our faith, we show the world that we

---

[69] Hardcastle's sixth letter, 18 September 1675, 277.

[70] Hardcastle's fourth letter, 8 September 1675, 271–72.

[71] Hardcastle's second letter, no date, 263–64.

[72] Hardcastle's first letter, 18 August 1675, 257.

[73] Thomas Hardcastle's seventh letter, 25 September 1675, 281.

refuse to conform, not for self-interest or merely to cause dissention but for a "pure conscience."[74]

Christians who follow after us will reap the benefits of our faithful suffering. Believe me, Hardcastle declared, "we are sowing for posterity; the generation coming on will have the good fruit of this present persecution." When our persecution finally ends, many who were afraid to worship with us will flock to us, "either out of curiosity or conscience," and "fall in love with...those whom they have causelessly reproached, slandered, and traduced."[75] We can be confident, Hardcastle assured his flock, that even though our persecutors might bind us in prison, "the word of God is not bound; persecuting times have been converting times, and...in due time you will find that many will date their spiritual birth, their love to the things of God, their confirmation in the truths of God, from" the year of our persecution.[76]

Having focused in his first nine letters on the causes and the positive aspects of his church's persecution, Hardcastle then, in the remaining thirteen letters, contrasted true faith with false faith.[77] Following are several of Hardcastle's descriptions of these two opposite faiths.

1. As a gift from God, true faith is more precious than anything in the world. Such faith is amazing because God graciously gives it to some "weak wretched creatures" but not to others. True faith leads believers into a personal relationship with God.[78] In contrast, false faith can be earned by improving one's nature, acquiring a good education, or spending time in discussions with other people. Such faith abhors being in God's presence.[79]

2. True faith is precious; it knows that only the blood of Jesus can lift the burden of sins. People who understand that they are "filthy creatures" will cry out to God, "Give me faith, or else I die! Oh, for some precious faith!" Such faith is costly; it cost Christ his life.[80] Believers know that they

---

[74] Hardcastle's first letter, 18 August 1675, 259–60.

[75] Hardcastle's third letter, 3 September 1675, 264.

[76] Thomas Hardcastle's eighth letter, 2 October 1675, 285.

[77] Hardcastle used other colorful terms to describe the essence of false faith: seeming, counterfeit, common, cheap, traditional, notional, parochial, neighborhood, formal, and hypocritical.

[78] Thomas Hardcastle's tenth letter, 15 October 1675, 292–94.

[79] Ibid., 292–93.

[80] Thomas Hardcastle's eleventh letter, 23 October 1675, 297–98.

cannot cleanse themselves of sin because only the blood of Christ can purify their "polluted" and "vile" hearts. Only through true faith and by the light of Christ can a believer confess, "I have found my heart...to be a very sink and puddle of sin." False faith, however, "sees no such need of craving foreign aid."[81] Such faith ignores Christ's sacrifice because it does not want to be indebted to anyone, not even the Lord. Common faith is easy; it is cheap.[82] That is why people love and embrace it.

3. True faith abhors sin, and for a person of faith, "a wounded conscience will be a thousand times a greater torment...than any persecutor can inflict." By contrast, a "creed-faith, baptism-faith, [Lord's] supper-faith—in a word, this tradition, profession, conviction-faith"—does not care whether it sins or not.[83]

4. True faith is willing to have God scrutinize it. True believers are willing to show God "how vile" they are, for they fear God and throw themselves on God's mercy.[84] False faith shuns God, cares nothing for the things of God, and therefore remains dead.[85]

5. True faith, by looking beyond the present, evil world, keeps believers from being entangled by sin. Moreover, such faith will strengthen believers during times of persecution.[86] False faith is powerless; "it bears the name [of Jesus] in prosperity, but will not bear up the man in adversity."[87]

6. True faith makes believers compassionate; they long for the lost to be saved and for the poor to be clothed and filled.[88] False faith only cares about such things if it can gain the praise of others.[89]

7. True faith shields believers from the "fiery darts" of Satan, which tempt the conscience to sin, and from the darts of "wicked men" who revile

---

[81] Thomas Hardcastle's thirteenth letter, 6 November 1675, 308.

[82] Ibid., 298.

[83] Ibid., 299.

[84] Thomas Hardcastle's twelfth letter, 29 October 1675, 301–302. See also Thomas Hardcastle's twenty-first letter, 14 January 1676, 347.

[85] Hardcastle's twelfth letter, 29 October 1675, 302.

[86] Ibid., 302–303.

[87] Ibid., 303.

[88] Ibid.

[89] Ibid., 304.

and abuse believers.[90] True faith remembers the sufferings of Jesus and proclaims:

> What an honor he has put upon me, that I should be spoiled, and abused, and imprisoned for his cause!… And blessed be his name, which counts me worthy of such a privilege. Oh, sweet and precious cross! Lovely Jesus! What glory did he leave for me to take my sinful, infirm nature upon him! He made himself of no reputation and took upon him the form of a servant, who thought it not robbery to be equal to God [see Phil 2:5–11]. And I, a poor vile wretch, who is made of the same mold with the worms, and dust, and have a nature as vile as the vilest, and cannot say that I am worth a crumb of bread, or drop of water,—shall I think it hard to suffer a little loss, to bear a little reproach, to endure a little hardship?[91]

8. True faith raises believers "above the world…to frown at her smiles, and smile at her frowns; to endure her crosses, and despise her flatteries."[92] From such lofty heights, believers can see that nothing can hurt them, for God will never allow those whom he has saved to be harmed.[93]

9. True faith produces an everlasting joy, even in the midst of trials. Persecution is like the people who passed by the crucified Christ, wagging their heads (see Matt 27:39). Yet "those heads in a few days were quietly laid in the grave, where they could wag no more."[94] Persecution, too, will soon "wag no more," and for that, Hardcastle and his congregation could rejoice.

10. True faith considers the warnings of God and acts accordingly. During persecution, believers should confess their sins, put their trust in God, accept their punishment, and praise God for not punishing them even more.[95] A false, hypocritical faith ignores God's warnings and rests in a false security. Unbelievers foolishly put their hope in the "little props and leaning-stocks" of the world to keep them safe from the wrath of God.[96]

---

[90] Thomas Hardcastle's fourteenth letter, 12 November 1675, 313–14.

[91] Ibid., 314.

[92] Hardcastle's fifteenth letter, 20 November 1675, 319.

[93] Ibid., 319–20.

[94] Ibid., 323.

[95] Hardcastle's seventeenth letter, 3 December 1675, 324–26.

[96] Ibid., 326–27.

11. True faith reminds believers that they are pilgrims in the world. They know that in the world to come lies their true inheritance, which is the gift of God. A few worldly possessions help pilgrims on their way, but too many things become burdensome. "Heaven," however, "is the great deed of settlement; the earth is but the loose money to bear the charges;—the staff to walk to the kingdom."[97] False professors of the faith see the world as their true home; it is the center of their universe. They might talk about heaven, but they were none too eager to get there.[98]

12. True faith knows that it will overcome the world. Believers understand that they could be richer and safer by conforming to the Church of England's demands, but they know what is valuable and that what is valuable is costly. They would rather deprive themselves of the comforts and liberties of this life than deprive themselves of the riches and freedom of heaven. Believers also know that they could avoid persecution, but in doing so, they might find themselves in an even worse situation later. Therefore, it is better to "be condemned and destroyed by heathens" in God's way, Hardcastle affirmed, than to be persecuted in our own way.[99] Everyone, including me, Hardcastle confessed, would prefer not to suffer, "but I dare not sin against conscience to procure ease, and safety, and freedom, for the outward man."[100]

13. Finally, true faith listens for the command of God and then acts. A counterfeit faith plots and plans, reasons and calculates, but it never obeys; it never suffers for the gospel.[101]

Hardcastle's letters during his six-month imprisonment undoubtedly encouraged his church, for it continued to meet faithfully while waiting for the return of its imprisoned pastor. Hellier, too, remained faithful to his persecution of the church during those six months, but the Broadmead members fought back in their own way. During one service, the congregation lowered the preacher "down into a room under, through a trap made like a biffet-bench (buffet) against the wall, in a seat or a pew

---

[97] Thomas Hardcastle's eighteenth letter, no date, 332. See also 334–35.

[98] Ibid., 332–33, 335.

[99] Thomas Hardcastle's nineteenth letter, 25 December 1675, 337–38.

[100] Hardcastle's twenty-second letter, 22 January 1676, 353–54.

[101] Hardcastle's twentieth letter, 8 January 1676, 342. See also Hardcastle's twenty-second letter, 22 January 1676, 350.

enclosed" in order to escape Hellier and his friends.[102] During an afternoon service, Hellier and his men had to force their way up the stairs because people were sitting in the stairway, blocking access to the worship service. The intruders eventually made their way upstairs, took names, and left.[103] On another Sunday afternoon when some members again filled the stairway, Hellier became violent. As he worked his way up the stairs, he pulled Brother Dickason by his cloak until it ripped; grabbed a women who cried out, "Will you murder me?"; struck Martha Hawkins in her arm with his staff; and broke "a youth's head." When the persecutors entered the meeting, they arrested some worshipers and threw out others. They even threw Brother Ellis's Bible on the floor before they left.[104] When the persecutors returned later, they found the congregation listening to Ellis read one of Hardcastle's letters concerning the nature of true faith.[105]

Terrill noted with pride that on Sunday, 23 January 1676, Hardcastle left Newgate and immediately set out to preach openly at his church, arriving sometime between nine and ten a.m., which was the time he had been arrested six months earlier. Church members believed that praise was in order for the safe return of their pastor: "Praise be to the Lord, who discourages the adversary and gave such a spirit of courage to our pastor under all his circumstances of trouble, time after time, not only from foes, but from friends with arguments for prudence, so called." Despite the constant temptation to give up, Hardcastle had stood firm, constantly maintaining that perseverance "in open duty" was always "the best policy and safety."[106]

By all accounts, Hardcastle was a fearless, faithful preacher. For preaching the gospel, he spent approximately forty-one months of his life in jails and prisons. Such experiences undoubtedly harmed his health but not his passion to preach. Hellier and others tried on numerous occasions to bully him into silence, but what they could not do, death finally did on 29 September 1678. Early that morning the forty-one-year-old Hardcastle died following a brief illness. Though his death came suddenly, he was well

---

[102] *RCC*, 280.
[103] Ibid., 290–91.
[104] Ibid., 305–306.
[105] Ibid., 307.
[106] Ibid., 355.

prepared for it. One of the privileges of true faith, he had written in his eighteenth prison letter, was that death was "the door into glory; the way to be with Christ." Death's sting, which is sin, had been "disarmed of its terror by Christ, and its "fear...removed, which keeps hypocrites and unsound professors all their lifetime subject to bondage (Heb. 2:14–15; 1 Cor. 15:55–57)." Death is merely "a sleep; a giving up the ghost; a commending the spirit into the hands of the Lord; a going into the harbor.... [There are] none so full of joy as dying saints."[107]

Thomas Hardcastle paid a heavy price for his faith, yet his prison experiences were not unique; other Baptist pastors paid a similar price. Some were bi-vocational pastors; others, like Hardcastle, pastored full time, and like him, many spent their time in prison writing. Some wrote only prose; others, however, wrote prose and poetry. They were prison poets, prisoners who often aimed their messages at the heart rather than the head.

---

[107] Hardcastle's eighteenth letter, no date, 333–34.

Chapter 6

Prison Poets

Thou, whose sweet youth and early hopes enhance
Thy rate and price, and mark there for a treasure;
Hearken unto a verser, who may chance
Rhyme thee to good, and make a bait of pleasure.
    A verse may find him, who a sermon flies,
    And turn delight into a sacrifice.[1]

These words of the Anglican priest and poet George Herbert (1593–1633) expressed a belief held by several imprisoned Baptists: that truth can be expressed through poetry as well as through prose and propositions.

The Baptist poets discussed in this chapter did not neglect the preaching and writing of lengthy sermons or the writing of pedantic theological treatises, but they saw poetry as another means by which to preach the gospel. Thus, like the authors of the Psalms in the Bible, these prison poets spoke out against injustice, taught theology, eulogized fallen comrades, debated opponents, encouraged others, evangelized unbelievers, and told stories, for they found in poetry an "ally and evangelist" in their quest to be faithful servants of God's truth.[2]

Henry Adis: A Cleaner of Clothes and Souls

Henry Adis described himself as "a baptized believer, undergoing the name of a free-willer"; his opponents called him "a fanatic, or a mad man." Although he claimed that his enemies characterized him so "by the tongue

---

[1] George Herbert, "The Church-Porch," stanza 1, lines 1–6, http://www.ccel.org/h/herbert/temple/1p.html (accessed 15 July 2007).

[2] Morton Gledhill, "The Poet and the Preacher," *Baptist Quarterly* 7/2 (April 1934): 72.

of infamy," he seemed to accept their description proudly, as the titles of some of his sermons and pamphlets bear witness.[3] Along with being a baptized believer, Adis was a cleaner by trade and a London General Baptist pastor by calling.

In the aftermath of Thomas Venner's insurrection in January 1661, Adis noted that a meeting of his church had been interrupted by a mob, which included "rude and debauched soldiers."[4] Adis and two of his church members were arrested and taken to Westminster's Gatehouse Prison. This imprisonment was not the first for Adis, who had been jailed in 1648 in the Tower Chamber in Fleet Prison, forcing him to leave behind his wife and three small children.

Adis's opposition to the violent removal of King Charles I from power resulted in his being jailed in 1648. While in Fleet, Adis authored two documents, both of which were published in 1648: *A Cup for the Citie, and Her Adherents* and *A Spie, Sent out of the Tower-Chamber in the Fleet. A Cup for the Citie* is little more than a combination of approximately 123 passages of scripture that Adis used to prophesy the destruction of London, which was the seat of Parliamentary power against the king and, according to him, a cesspool of sin. "The rebellion," Adis concluded, "is as the sin of witchcraft, and stubbornness is an iniquity and idolatry."[5]

In *A Spie, Sent out*, Adis exhibited more creativity, for he used poetry to attack William Lenthall, Speaker of the House of Commons, whom he blamed for not allowing him to leave England and for ruining him financially.[6] Interested readers of *A Spie, Sent out* immediately noticed the title page, on which was printed the drawing of a naked man covered with eyes. In his left hand he held a torch and in his right, a lantern. The man represented Argus, the hundred-eyed monster of Greek mythology who

---

[3] Henry Adis, *A Fannaticks Letter Sent out of the Dungeon of the Gate-House Prison of Westminster* (London: printed by S. Dover for the author, 1660).

[4] Quoted in B. R. White, *The English Baptists of the Seventeenth Century*, A History of English Baptists 1 (London: The Baptist Historical Society, 1983) 97.

[5] Henry Adis, *A Cup for the Citie, and Her Adherents* (n.p., 1648) [10].

[6] [Henry Adis], *A Spie, Sent out of the Tower-Chamber in the Fleet* (n.p., 1648) 12; T. L. Underwood, "Adis, Henry (fl. 1648–1663)," *Biographical Dictionary of British Radicals in the Seventeenth Century*, ed. Richard L. Greaves and Robert Zaller, 3 vols. (Brighton England: Harvester Press, 1982) 1:2.

could see almost everything. From his cell in Fleet, Adis sent his spy Argus out "to see/ If any Justice in the Kingdom be."[7]

Before sending out Argus, Adis first recorded what his Maiden-Muse had already discovered. She wept when she heard people crying because they had been

> Plundered, Rob'd, and spoyl'd of all they have,
>   and of a Free-born subject made a slave.
> Life, Liberty, Estate, and Kingdomes Law
>   by greatness too unjustly kept in aw.

She was appalled

> to see that Christians worse then Heathens set
> Themselves to rob their God, of these his due,
>   Justice and Mercy, only by which two
> Most glorious Attributes he's pleas'd alone
>   To make himself to us most cleerly known?[8]

Despite the bleak picture Muse painted, Adis was confident that Argus could find justice, though it had been hidden by seven years of civil war. Argus was to search everywhere, and Adis warned him not to be duped by men who sit in the seats of justice, for "'tis not every he/ That sits in Justice seat, that just will be."[9] Remember my story, Adis instructed Argus, because I have been ruined by such men:

> Bereav'd of house, and goods, and remedy,
> And as unjustly caus'd in Goale to lie.
> Which maketh many think that I have spent all,
> Truth is, I'm ruin'd by unsavory Lenthall.
> That partial Judge, who with his Janus face,
> Relents no wrongs, blusheth at no disgrace,
> Whose will's his Law, and be it right or wrong,

---

[7] [Adis], *A Spie, Sent out*, 1.

[8] Ibid., 2.

[9] Ibid., 4.

He'll still be taking part with him that's strong.[10]

True justice, Adis informed Argus, is blind, and its "ears are open all complaints to hear,/ And from bribe taking both his hands are clear."[11] Although justice was a stranger in England, God still reigned, and he

...canst unlock the prisons, and canst see
The many poor oppressed, subjects free:
Where hundreds are enslav'd this instant houre
By tyrannie and arbytrarie power.[12]

Lenthall appeared to be a religious man, yet, Adis contended, the speaker's religion was a sham. He prays, observes fasts, and labors to destroy the superstitions of the Anglican Church,

...yet neglects the poor mans cry to hear,
All his religion's vain, 'tis plain and clear,
He wants the fear of God, and Charity,
And all his shews are but hypocrisie.[13]

Argus promised to fulfill his commission. He would search every home, every government committee, and every city to see if he could find the justice that Adis so desperately wanted. Whether the all-seeing spy found what he was searching for is unknown.

After eleven pages of poetry, or what can better be described as rhyming, Adis ended *A Spie, Sent out* with a section of prose. One might expect a clarion call for all Christians to fight the good fight, to keep the faith, to persevere, or to stand up for the justice for which Argus was searching. Adis issued no such call, but he did issue a two-page advertisement for his cleaning business. By his own account, he was an outstanding cleaner. Everyone who had used him had found his skills to be "very commodious and beneficial," for he had discovered a way to rid

---

[10] Ibid., 5.
[11] Ibid.
[12] Ibid., 7–8.
[13] Ibid., 9.

clothes of grease, wax, oil, wine, and other difficult stains without ruining the color of the clothes. If needed, Adis could provide next-day service. He could also restore worn clothes to such a condition that their owners could wear them proudly.[14] Adis was a rare man indeed; he knew how to cleanse people's souls of sin and their clothes of dirt.

When Adis gained his release from Fleet is unknown, but he apparently managed to stay clear of prison for several years because on 9 November 1660 he hand delivered a printed sermon to Charles II. In the preface to the sermon, Adis professed his loyalty to the king, but he maintained that he would neither swear to that loyalty nor fight for the king.[15] Moreover, because "one dram of downright honesty is of more true worth than a whole pound of fawning flattery," Adis promised to tell the truth to the king: "take it as you will, and do with me for it as you please."[16] Essentially, Adis told the king to permit people to have liberty of conscience, to reform the nation, and to flee debauchery.

Two weeks after giving the king his sermon, Adis was arrested following Venner's insurrection in 1661 and sent to Westminster's Gatehouse Prison. There, the Baptist minister wrote *A Fannaticks Letter Sent out of the Dungeon of the Gate-House Prison of Westminster*, in which he defended Baptists and himself against false accusations, rejected the use of force to establish Christ's kingdom on earth, and encouraged fellow Christians to stand firm in their faith. Contrary to the false reports about Baptists after Venner's insurrection, Adis rejoiced that no imprisoned Baptist could be "found an evil doer in what is charged upon us, as to plotting, contriving, or undermining, or in any act of hostility in disturbing the peace of the nation." With a clear conscience Baptists could proclaim:

> We are not guilty of what we are charged with, and that we are oppressed in judgment, and are injuriously torn from our callings and families, and most barbarously penned up in prison holes, and myself and some others of our society, thrust into a damp, dark,

---

[14] Ibid., 12–13.

[15] Henry Adis, "To Charles the II, of England, Scotland, France and Ireland, King," in *A Fannaticks Mite Cast into the Kings Treasury: Being A Sermon Printed to the King Because not Preach'd before the King*, by Henry Adis, 2nd ed. (London: printed by S. Dover for the author, 1660) [iv].

[16] Henry Adis, "An After-Writing to the King," ibid., [vi].

dirty dungeon, without either light or air, bed or bedding, first nine, and after twelve of us together, scarce[ly] able to lie down one by another; being thus used, NOT FOR WHAT WE HAVE DONE, BUT FOR WHAT WE ARE; NOT FOR WHAT IS FOUND IN OUR HOUSES, AS TO ARMS OR AMMUNITION.[17]

Adis vehemently denied the accusation of Hopping Jane, a notorious foul-mouthed drunkard, who claimed that she had heard him say that he "hoped to wash my hands in the king's blood." Nor did Adis ever confess in jail to the scandalous allegation that he had murdered a deputy, and the rumors that he had stored weapons and ammunition in his home were equally false. Authorities had searched his home nine times, six in one night, and found nothing.[18] Adis surmised that he been targeted for what he had written in his sermon to the king. If the authorities considered him vile for telling the truth, then Adis promised to "be yet more vile."[19]

Adis also stated his objections to using worldly weapons for spiritual ends, insisting that Jesus would establish his own kingdom, in his own time, and in his own way. Christians must strive for the faith, Adis declared, "not for WEALTH, POMP, PLEASURE,... POWER, nor DOMINIONS of the EARTH."[20] Encouraging his readers to resist the lust for political power, the Gatehouse prisoner reminded his readers, "we are yet in the kingdom of Christ's patience and not in the kingdom of his power, for if we may believe him, he tells us that his 'kingdom is not of this world' (John 18:[36])."[21]

Even if we wait patiently, Adis continued, we will still be busy "doing God's work, in God's way," fighting God's battles with "the sword of the Spirit, which is the word of God [Eph 6:17]." In the midst of one such battle, he found himself in a "dark, dolesome, drowsy, damp dungeon," completely bankrupt.[22] Yet whatever earthly goods he lost, he remained

---

[17] Henry Adis, *A Fannaticks Letter Sent out of the Dungeon of the Gate-House Prison of Westminster* (London: printed by S. Dover, 1660) 6. Despite its 1660 date, Adis probably wrote the pamphlet after Venner's rebellion in January 1661.

[18] Ibid., 7.

[19] Ibid., 8.

[20] Ibid., 11.

[21] Ibid., 12.

[22] Ibid., 14.

confident that God would repay him on judgment day. Therefore, he proclaimed, "O friends! let us hold fast our integrity so that we may be a blessing to our prince here and obtain the blessing hereafter."[23]

Adis concluded his pamphlet with a short poem:

> From my close constraint, the king's courtesie,
> For my Christian counsel, The Gate-House Dungeon;
> Damp and Dark, Void of Light, Darker than Night;
> Once a Den for Thieves, But now a House of Prayer;
> My Contented Castle, Till Christ Clear me.[24]

After Adis's release from prison on 25 March 1661, his family was among seven families that petitioned the king the following June for permission to emigrate to Surinam. They arrived in that country in 1663, and in December of that year Adis wrote a letter describing his freedom and the need for Surinamese Christians to take their faith more seriously.[25] He presumably died in Surinam, leaving the country a holier and cleaner place.

Abraham Cheare: A Children's Poet

Born to Christian parents, Abraham Cheare (1626–1668) earned a living as an iron worker in Plymouth, along the southwestern coast of England.[26] A year after being baptized in 1648 in a Plymouth Particular Baptist church, the twenty-three-year-old Cheare became the church's

---

[23] Ibid., 21.

[24] Ibid., 25.

[25] Michael Davies, "Adis, Henry (fl. 1641/2–1663," *Oxford Dictionary of National Biography* (Oxford: Oxford University Press, 2004), http://www.oxforddnb.com./view/article/69072 (accessed 16 July 2005).

[26] For biographical information on Cheare, see John C. Foster, "Early Baptist Writers of Verse. Cheare, Bunyan, Keach," *Transactions of the Baptist Historical Society* 3/2 (October 1912): 96–103; Joseph Ivimey, *A History of English Baptists*, 4 vols. (London: printed for the author, 1814) 2:104–16; B. R. White, "Cheare, Abraham (1626–1668)," in *Biographical Dictionary of British Radicals in the Seventeenth Century*, 1:139; and W. H. K. Wright, *West-County Poets: Their Lives and Works* (London: Elliot Stock, 1896), http://www.windeatt.f2s.com/poets/Cheare_A.html (accessed 11 February 2005).

pastor. One hundred and fifty members signed the invitation to call him as pastor.

In 1661, probably as a consequence of the Venner affair, Cheare spent three months in Exeter jail, thirty-six miles up the coast from Plymouth, for holding conventicles. More than a year after his release, he expressed his gratitude for his freedom in a letter to a friend, which was dated 26 June 1662. Cheare proclaimed that he had been freed only by God's grace, but he also noted that many others were being sent to prison, which he called "the place of ancient experience," where they would learn "to endure hardness as good soldiers." Though he was free, prison was never far from Cheare's mind: "I expect every day the same lot."[27] Shortly after writing this letter, he returned to Exeter jail, this time for three years, for holding conventicles and for refusing to take the Oath of Allegiance.

During his three years in Exeter, Cheare wrote several poems and letters. In a September 1662 letter, he thanked William Punchard for writing to him. The contents of Punchard's letter not only encouraged Cheare but also confirmed that God continued to minister to "his poor worms" even in prison. Cheare proclaimed that God had turned the prisoners' "holes of earth, where violence has thrust us as in so many slaughterhouses of men" into "the presence chambers of the great King, where he brings and feasts his favorites with the best things." Prison proved to be a great revealer of a person's character, Cheare noted, for "a week in a prison" reveals "a man's spirit" better "than a month in a church."[28] He also mentioned that his church, his "poor lambs," had "been visited by the constables again and again at their meetings, summoned by the mayor, [and] fined for not coming to church."[29]

Besides writing letters, Cheare authored several poems, many of which were designed to win children to the faith. The first stanza of "Remember now thy Creator in the dayes of thy Youth" perhaps summarizes Cheare's message to young people:

---

[27] Abraham Cheare to a friend, 26 June 1662, in *A History of English Baptists*, 2:104.

[28] Abraham Cheare to William Punchard, 17 September 1662, in *A History of English Baptists*, 2:105–106. Ivimey (*A History of English Baptists*, 2:105) said that this letter "smells of a prison."

[29] Ibid., 2:107.

Sweet children, Wisdom you invites
>   to harken to her Voice,
She offers to you rare delights
>   most worthy of your choice.
Eternal blessings in her wayes,
>   you shall be sure to find;
Oh! therefore in your youthful dayes,
>   your Great Creator mind.[30]

Cheare encouraged young people to be like Isaac, Samuel, Josiah, Obadiah, and Timothy, who followed God from their youth. Do not waste your youth satisfying your lusts; instead,

How worthy Christ is, could you learn,
>   to claim your Flower and Prime;
And how well pleasing 'tis, discern
>   to dedicate your time:
You pleasantly would make essayes,
>   to get your Souls enclin'd,
And gladly in your youthful dayes,
>   your Great Creator mind.[31]

Becoming a disciple of Christ, Cheare noted, was a decision children would never regret. If they would only "humbly bow without delayes," they would discover "Grace in his [Christ's] fight to find." Such a decision would help them not only in their youth but for the rest of their lives.[32]

In another poem, "Written to a young Virgin, Anno 1663," Cheare wrote from the standpoint of a young, beautiful girl pondering the usefulness of her beauty to gain eternity. As in the previous poem, which

---

[30] Abraham Cheare, "Remember Now Thy Creator in the Dayes of Thy Youth," in *A Looking-Glass for Children...Together, with Sundry Seasonable Lessons and Instructions to Youth, Calling Them Early to Remember their Creator: Written by Abraham Cheare, Late of Plymouth*, by Henry Jessey, 2nd ed. (London: printed for Robert Boulter, 1673) 23, stanza 1.

[31] Ibid., 26, stanza 13.

[32] Ibid., stanza 14.

ended with the common phrase "your Great Creator mind," Cheare ended each stanza of the poem about the beautiful virgin with a common theme in his children's poems: hell. People tell the young woman that she is beautiful, and she can tell by looking in a mirror that what they say is obviously true. God had indeed created her to be beautiful, with every part of her body almost perfect. " 'Tis pitty," she mused, "when I come to die/ all these should go to Hell."[33] Her parents could give her everything that she wanted, and many men might want to marry her, but what good are such things and compliments, she agonized, if I should go to hell?

The young maiden realized that she must resist the sin of pride and that she must shun pleasures, pastimes, and sports if she hoped to avert eternal damnation. She understood that by repenting and accepting Christ, he would lead her along a different path and, ultimately, to a different eternal home. For that she could sing of God's grace:

How first of goodness I was seiz'd
    from what a state I fell;
To what a glory God hath rais'd,
    a Fire-brand pluckt from Hell![34]

The poem of the young virgin articulated Cheare's concern for the eternal welfare of children, a concern he also expressed in poems to a cousin and two nephews. To his cousin W. L., Chreare wrote that God's presence with him in prison "doth this a Palace make;/ It makes the bitter of the Rod,/ be sweet for Jesus sake." However, for criminals who deserved their punishment, jail was a "dreadful place," especially if they did not repent of their sins. W. L. could avoid such a horrid fate if he heeded Cheare's advice: "Avoid those rude and wicked Boys" and "Love not their playes, and sinful Toys." Instead, study hard, read the Bible, learn to pray, obey your parents, and love others.[35]

Cheare advised his nephew A. L. to "remember well" that "wicked Children go to Hell." To avoid such a fate, the "pretty Child" must think

---

[33] Abraham Cheare, "Written to a Young Virgin, Anno 1663," in *A Looking-Glass for Children*, 27, stanza 2.

[34] Ibid., 29, stanza 10.

[35] Abraham Cheare, "To my Cousin W. L.," in *A Looking-Glass for Children*, 44.

about everything that he does because he "may be quickly sick, and die,/ and put into the Grave;/ From whence to judgment you must fly."[36] To little R. L., Cheare preached a similar message. Do not curse, fight, steal, lie, or waste your time playing games. Be careful of everything you do, Cheare counseled his young nephew, so that you will not destroy your soul:

> With wicked Children do not play,
>> for such to hell will go;
> The Devils Children sin all day,
>> but you must not do so.[37]

If you find the way to heaven, Cheare assured R. L., God will love you, your parents will rejoice, and your uncle will suffer more comfortably in prison.

Cheare finally left Exeter jail in August 1665, after his sister helped secure his release. He returned home to Plymouth and began preaching again, for which he was soon arrested and imprisoned in Plymouth's Guildhall Prison. A month later, authorities banished him to the Island of St. Nicolas (now Drake's Island) near Plymouth. Before leaving Guildhall, Cheare wrote a poem on the wall of his cell, in which he submitted himself to what he believed to be God's sovereign plan for his life. "Since my lines the Lord assigns/ In such a lot to be," Cheare declared, "I kiss the rod, confess my God/ Deals faithfully with me." Only God could judge him, and until that time, Cheare forgave his enemies and determined to live in God's peace.[38]

Shortly after arriving on the island, Cheare became seriously ill for about nine months. Upon recovering, he expressed his gratitude poetically "To his truly sacred Majesty, the High and Mighty Potentate, King of Kings, and Lord of Lords, Prince of Life and Peace, Heir of all things, and Head over all things to the Church."[39] Later that year, on 22 November 1667, Cheare, on behalf of himself and other prisoners, wrote a letter to

---

[36] Abraham Cheare, "To my Kinsman A. L.," ibid., 44.

[37] Abraham Cheare, "To my youngest Kinsman R. L.," ibid., 45.

[38] Abraham Cheare, "Verses Affixed to the Wall of the Prison at the Guildhall in Plymouth," in *A History of the English Baptists*, 2:109; Foster, "Early Baptist Writers of Verse," 99; and Wright, *West-County Poets*, http://www.windeatt.f2s.com/poets/Cheare_A.html.

[39] For the text of the poem, see Ivimey, *A History of the English Baptists*, 2:109–11.

some anonymous friends, describing the dependency of prisoners on their friends and family and thanking these friends for their gifts that supported the "poor undeserving creatures" in prison.[40] Despite being in prison and lacking the comforts of home, Cheare and his fellow prisoners confessed that they had not lacked anything of importance and had learned, like the apostle Paul, to be content in whatever circumstances they found themselves (Phil 4:11).[41] Though the prisoners could not speak for every prisoner of conscience, they expressed their gratitude for escaping "the sword" and, hopefully, "the pollutions of the adversary." Cheare and his companions also rejoiced that they had "found great grace in the wilderness."[42]

In January 1668 Cheare again was struck with an illness. This time, however, he did not recover. Cheare died on 5 March, and he did so, according to a friend who was with him, "without pang or considerable groan."[43]

Thomas Grantham: The Champion of the General Baptists

Thomas Grantham (1634–1692) was born near Spilsby, in Lincolnshire, 116 miles north of London.[44] He came from a poor family, and as a youth he worked as a tailor and then as a farmer. In 1653 Grantham professed his faith in Christ at a small General Baptist church in Boston, fourteen miles south of Spilsby, and was baptized. Three years later the

---

[40] Abraham Cheare to friends, 22 November 1667, in *The History of the English Baptists from the Reformation to the Beginning of the Reign of King George I*, by Thomas Crosby, 4 vols. (London: privately printed, [1739]) 3:17.

[41] Ibid., 3:19.

[42] Ibid., 3:20.

[43] Quoted in Ivimey, *A History of the English Baptists*, 2:113.

[44] For biographical information on Grantham, see Oscar C. Burdick, "Grantham, Thomas (1633/4–1692)," *Oxford Dictionary of National Biography*, http://www.oxforddnb.com./view/article/11298 (accessed 28 May 2005); Alexander Gordon, "Grantham, Thomas (1634–1692)," *Dictionary of National Biography*, ed. Leslie Stephen and Sidney Lee, 63 vols. (London: Smith, Elder, & Co., 1890) 22:410–12; W. L. Johnson, Jr., and R. L. Greaves, "Grantham, Thomas (1634–1692)," *Biographical Dictionary of British Radicals in the Seventeenth Century*, ed. Richard L. Greaves and Robert Zaller, 3 vols. (Brighton England: Harvester Press, 1983) 2:23–24; and the three-part article "A Memoir of Thomas Grantham," *General Baptist Repository and Missionary Observer* 4/44 (1 August 1825): 281–86; 4/45 (1 September 1825): 321–26; and 4/46 (1 October 1825): 361–67.

church called him as its pastor, and he began a long ministerial career, during which he would become "the first organized, comprehensive, published theologian of any of the Baptists."[45]

On 26 July 1660 Grantham and Joseph Wright presented Charles II with *A Brief Confession or Declaration of Faith*, describing the beliefs of the General Baptists in Lincolnshire and acknowledging their respect for civil magistrates. The king graciously accepted the confession, but he also expressed his dismay at the treatment Lincolnshire Baptists had experienced during Cromwell's protectorate and promised that things would go better for them in the future.[46] After Venner's insurrection, when things did not go better for Baptists, Grantham presented another confession to Charles on 23 February 1661, which the king gladly accepted.

After the passing of the Act of Uniformity in 1662, Grantham was arrested twice for preaching. Following his second arrest, he spent fifteen months in a Lincoln jail, where he authored two works. Grantham began his first prison publication, a lengthy poem titled *The Prisoner against the Prelate*, with an eight-page introduction stating that ministers needed no knowledge of Hebrew and Greek to understand the Bible, and he attached a poetic version of the General Baptists' *A Brief Confession* to the end of the poem. The poem itself narrated a dialogue between Jayle (Grantham) and Cathedral (the Lincoln Cathedral, symbolizing the Anglican Church). Whether Grantham intended it, his choice of names for the disputants in the poem was symbolic. Little Jayle's taking on the massive, majestic Lincoln Cathedral, which even Grantham confessed "did outwardly appear/ Right glorious, for to please both Eye and Ear," symbolized the titanic struggle Baptists and other dissenters faced when they would not violate their consciences by submitting to the demands of the Church of England.[47]

---

[45] William H. Brackney, *A Genetic History of Baptist Thought: With Special Reference to Baptists in Britain and North America* (Macon GA: Mercer University Press, 2004) 114.

[46] "A Memoir of Thomas Grantham," *General Baptist Repository and Missionary Observer* 4/44 (1 August 1825): 282–83.

[47] Thomas Grantham, *The Prisoner against the Prelate: or, A Dialogue between the Common Goal and Cathedral of Lincoln* ([London: n.p., 1662]) 9. Also available online at http://baptistlibraryonline.com/blo/content/view/13/. For photos depicting the massiveness of the Lincoln Cathedral, see http://www.freefoto.com/browse.jsp?id=1027–01–0; http://penelope.uchicago.edu/Thayer/E/Gazetteer/Places/Europe/

In the poem, the holy Cathedral at first did not want to disgrace himself by discussing religion with profane Jayle. Cathedral asked Jayle, where did you "Take thy degrees, the Liberal Arts to know" anything about religion? Jayle responded by stating that academic degrees do not make people spiritual:

Religion is not ty'd to Humane Learning,
For this is plain to all men of discerning,
That God hath chose the foolish, and the poor
Of this world, rich in Faith. Yea furthermore,
It seem'd well-pleasing to the Lord, that Babes
Should see true Light, whilest th' wise lie in dark shades.[48]

That was true long ago, Cathedral replied, but times have changed. Certainly Jayle understood that the Church of England "hath the eye of Learning bright," so "cease against the Church to fight."[49]

Determined not to surrender and having succeeded in drawing Cathedral into a debate, Jayle challenged the concept of a national church. In response, Cathedral replied that such a challenge was seditious and dangerous, for

The Land shall never quiet be, until
Rulers, by their Edicts, all sorts compel
To Uniformity, in things Religious;
And therefore thy Opinion is Prodigious.[50]

Jayle not only failed to see the danger in challenging a national church; he failed to see the benefits that compulsion in religion had produced. For example, the church at its beginning had few members, but now, Cathedral boasted, "Her Honour's great, her Members like the sands,/ As well in this as many other Lands." Moreover, church members were no longer the dregs

---

Great_Britain/England/Lincolnshire/Lincoln/churches/cathedral/tour/1.html; and
http://www.lincolncathedral.com/.

[48] Grantham, *The Prisoner against the Prelate*, 13.
[49] Ibid., 22.
[50] Ibid., 24.

of society. Now that society's "Nobler sort" had joined the church, "Her subeterranean places, and her Head/ Did lift up, as one risen from the dead."[51]

True, Jayle admitted, you have a large organization with beautiful buildings and important people. Nevertheless, such

> ...outward glory doth not prove
> That she from death to life doth nearer move
> ....
> And for the Nobler sort, it seems this day
> They'r too great strangers to the Gospel-way.[52]

The true church, as the apostle Peter noted, is a "Holy Nation" and is no sense a national church, confined by the borders of one country.[53]

The disputants then debated the Catholic Church. Jayle stated that he saw no difference between the Church of England and the Church of Rome. Cathedral, of course, denied any relationship with that "old Harlot" Rome. Read our scholars, he challenged Jayle, and you will see that we are not papists. Just because we received our baptism and ordination from Rome does not mean that we are Rome.[54] But, Jayle argued, you cannot divest yourself from the Catholic Church so easily. This organization that you call a whore is "thy Mother:/ She tells thee so, and thou canst shew no other."[55] You received your life and authority from Rome, Jayle reminded Cathedral, and if Rome is not a church as you profess, then neither are you.[56]

After establishing the unbroken link between Cathedral and Rome to his own satisfaction, Jayle moved on to debate baptism. You received your "Babeys-Sprinkling from Rome," Jayle taunted Cathedral, which proves that you are no church.[57] Such an argument shocked Cathedral: "Prodigious Jayle! where got'st thou this Objection?/ 'Tis some Anabaptistical

---

[51] Ibid., 25.
[52] Ibid.
[53] Ibid., 24. See 1 Peter 2:9.
[54] Ibid., 29–31.
[55] Ibid., 31.
[56] Ibid., 32.
[57] Ibid., 33.

infection."[58] With the curse of Anabaptism pronounced against his opponent, Cathedral then condemned Baptist Jayle's impudence for challenging the opinions of Anglican scholars concerning baptism: "Proud Jayle! How i'st thou darest thus contemn/ The expositions of my Learned men?"[59] With one voice, all of my doctors contend that the Bible supports the sprinkling of infants. Are you wiser than my scholars, Jayle?

Jayle responded: "Thy Learned men! why I have more than thou,/ Who do my sentence on these Texts allow,/...Thou hast no Baptisme, for thy Manner's badd."[60] "No BAPTISM No CHURCH," Jayle declared.[61] Therefore, since you have no baptism, Cathedral, you have no church.

The final argument debated by Jayle and Cathedral concerned the Church of England's use of civil authorities to punish heretics. Cathedral maintained that "if Kings did not assist by penalties/ My Church, I see men would me soon despise," which would enable heretics to destroy me. So with the power of the state behind me, "men readily obey/ My Discipline in whatsoere I say."[62]

To Jayle, however, such talk proved that the Church of England lacked spiritual power. You have bloodstained hands, Jayle reproached Cathedral. The true church

...for more than three hundred years
...had no defence from worldly Peers;
Yet Truth with purity did greatly prosper;
Errors they quash'd as fast as they did foster.[63]

---

[58] Ibid.

[59] Ibid., 35.

[60] Ibid.

[61] Ibid. 32.

[62] Ibid., 51.

[63] Ibid., 50. See also articles 24 and 25 in Grantham's confession, 72–73, for his understanding of the role of the magistrate in religion, at this point in his life. In a later work, Grantham contended that magistrates could punish idolaters. See Harry Leon McBeth, *English Baptist Literature on Religious Liberty to 1689* (Ph.D. diss., Southwestern Baptist Theological Seminary, 1961; repr., New York: Arno Press, 1980) 266–68.

On judgment day God will separate believers from heretics, Jayle assured his adversary. Until then, the king should stay out of the church's business and let the tares grow with the wheat.

Grantham's second prison publication, "The Baptist against the Papist" (1663), refuted the absurd accusation that he was a Catholic. In part one he defended the use of the Bible alone to settle religious questions. According to Grantham, "the only infallible and authoritative judge of…controversies in religion is the LORD himself, as he speaks by his Spirit in the holy scriptures, together with right reason."[64] Such a statement, however, did not preclude the judicious use of pastors, ancient Christian texts, or the biblical interpretations of individuals to settle church disputes. Grantham did, however, reject the belief "that the papal Church of Rome is the supreme judge and Catholic Moderatrix of all disputes in matters of faith, and that all are bound to hear and obey her voice under pain of damnation, and that the scriptures…is [sic] not the judge of controversies."[65]

In part two, Grantham presented ten reasons proving why Baptists, not the Catholic Church, constituted the true church of Christ:

1. The Catholic Church could not prove that it was the true church because it denied that the Bible is the sole arbiter in religious questions. Catholics could only rely on their own opinions and traditions to support their claim of being the true church.[66]

2. Catholics had no baptism. Grantham maintained that the baptism of believers by immersion constituted the biblical practice of baptism. Sprinkling "a few drops of water…on the face only from a man's finger ends or out of a glass in the midwife's pocket" could hardly be called baptism in the biblical sense of the word.[67]

3. The Catholic Church was a national church. National churches eliminate the need for individuals to be converted because they are automatically regenerated ("saved") when they are baptized as infants, established churches eradicate the distinction between believers and non-

---

[64] Thomas Grantham, "The Baptist against the Papist," in *Christianismus Primitivus*, by Thomas Grantham (London: printed for Francis Smith, 1678) book 4, part 1, p. 1. *Christianismus Primitivus* is available online at http://baptistlibraryonline. com/blo/content/view/13/.

[65] Ibid., 2.

[66] Ibid., 16.

[67] Ibid., 17.

believers, such churches become persecutors, national churches cannot practice church discipline without destroying a person's secular livelihood, and their existence implies that the primitive church was flawed because it neither had nor wanted secular power.[68]

4. The Church of Rome relied more on the sword of Caesar than on the sword of the Lord. According to Grantham, as "both experience shows and reason tells that it cannot be otherwise," Rome used "the terror of death and penal laws" to increase and maintain its membership.[69]

5. Rome labored to keep the world and the church in darkness by prohibiting people from reading the Bible, by preventing the scriptures from being translated into the languages of the people, and by using numerous ceremonies and repetitious prayers in its liturgy.[70]

6. The Catholic Church was (generally) comprised of unregenerate people. The gospel teaches that people must experience a new birth. "Where the Spirit of regeneration is, it is not without some demonstrable operation"; therefore, Grantham concluded, "the infants whom the papists say they baptize are not born of the Spirit, unless they can give some demonstrative sign of it."[71]

7. Catholic officials punished people who refuse to follow the church's "doctrine of devils." For example, Rome forbad its clergy to marry and prohibited, at times, the eating of some kinds of meat.[72]

8. The Catholic Church was the "Mystery Babylon" spoken of in Revelation 17:5. It claimed papal superiority over civil rulers (Rev 17:18), arrayed itself in "great riches and worldly pomp" (Rev 18:7), sat "upon nations, tongues, and peoples" (Rev 17:15), and enslaved "the souls of men and is drunk with blood" of the saints (17:6). Moreover, the Catholic Church even admitted that the Mystery Babylon was Rome, but the church identified the evil whore with the Roman Empire, not with itself. Thus, all of these wicked deeds committed by Rome constituted the marks of the Mystery Babylon.[73]

---

[68] Ibid., 29–30.
[69] Ibid., 30.
[70] Ibid., 31–33.
[71] Ibid., 34.
[72] Ibid., 34–35.
[73] Ibid., 35–37.

9. Being a national church, the Catholic Church lacked the marks of the true church, particularly, antiquity (because the primitive church was not a national church, it has to rely on force, which national churches must do, to make people Christians) and succession (because the Catholic Church was not the first church, its popes could not claim to be the successors of the primitive church).[74]

10. The current "assemblies of baptized believers" constituted the "true, visible church of Christ." Such a claim, Grantham explained, did not mean that non-Baptists were not Christians. Rather, the gospel of redemption and remission of sins must be preached, and people must first respond to that preaching before being baptized. "And," Grantham continued, "we do teach, as a most infallible doctrine, that without profession of faith, manifestation of repentance, and being baptized with water in the name of Jesus Christ, etc., no person can be orderly admitted into the church or kingdom of God on earth."[75]

Grantham left the Lincoln jail in spring 1664, but he was arrested again later that year after the passage of the Conventicle Act. In all, he was arrested ten times during his ministry. When he was free, Grantham preached, wrote, and started and nurtured churches wherever the need arose.[76] General Baptists considered him "their champion," who was always ready to expose himself to danger in their defense."[77]

After Grantham died on 17 January 1692, a friend who preached the funeral sermon expressed the sentiment of General Baptists: "This day is a very great man fallen in Israel."[78] The inscription on Grantham's headstone described him as:

A faithful confessor, and laborious servant of Christ;
Who with true Christian fortitude, endured persecution;

---

[74] Ibid., 37–40.

[75] Ibid., 41.

[76] "A Memoir of Thomas Grantham," *General Baptist Repository and Missionary Observer* 4/44 (1 August 1825): 281–86, and 4/45 (1 September 1825): 325–26.

[77] "A Memoir of Thomas Grantham," *General Baptist Repository and Missionary Observer* 4/45 (1 September 1825): 323.

[78] "Inscription on the Grave-Stone of the Late Mr. Thomas Grantham," *General Baptist Magazine*, January 1799, 216; Gordon, "Grantham, Thomas (1634–1692)," 22:411.

Through many perils, the loss of friends and substance,
    And ten imprisonments for conscience sake.

....

A man endowed with every Christian grace and virtue,

....

    A learned messenger of the baptized churches.[79]

Indeed, shortly before his death, Grantham exemplified why such statements could be made about him. An Anglican minister confessed to a judge that he had slandered Grantham by falsely stating that the Baptist minister had been punished in another town for stealing sheep. Instead of gloating about his legal victory and relishing the fact that an Anglican priest might experience the inside of a jail just as he had, Grantham paid the Anglican minister's fine, thereby saving him from being jailed.[80]

John Griffith: A Worthy Example to Follow

During part of the time Francis Bampfield and Thomas Delaune spent in London's Newgate Prison during the early 1680s, they enjoyed the company of several Baptists, including John Griffith (c. 1622–1700). Little is known about Griffith's early years.[81] Because he was usually known as Dr. John Griffith, he presumably had some formal education, perhaps in medicine. He began preaching around 1640 and started a General Baptist church in London, which ordained him as its pastor in 1646.

Griffith frequently ran afoul of the law for violating the Conventicle Act and for refusing to take the Oath of Allegiance. Arrested in 1661 for preaching illegally, he spent seventeen months in Newgate, where he wrote a poem recounting his call and his faith.[82] Griffith began his 148-page poem

---

[79] "Inscription on the Grave-Stone of the Late Mr. Thomas Grantham," 215.

[80] Gordon, "Grantham, Thomas (1634–1692)," 22:411; "A Memoir of Thomas Grantham," *General Baptist Repository and Missionary Observer* 4/45 (1 September 1825): 325–26.

[81] For biographical information on Griffith, see Alexander Gordon, "Griffith, John (1622?–1700)," *Dictionary of National Biography*, 23:233, and Beth Lynch, "Griffith, John (1621/2–1700)," *Oxford Dictionary of National Biography*, http://www.oxforddnb.com./view/article/11599 (accessed 28 May 2005).

[82] John Griffith, *Some Prison Meditations and Experiences: with Some Hints Touching the Fall of the Mother of Harlots, and the Exaltation of the Son of God upon the Throne of*

by challenging the Church of England, particularly its bishops, whom he sardonically called "Their Worships." These men "clapt" into prison anyone who, like Griffith, preached without their permission.[83] Despite being a "worthless worm," Griffith claimed that because God, by his mercy and grace, had called him to participate in a "mission" to preach, he did not need the blessing of Anglican bishops. Griffith also professed his innocence of anything with which authorities could charge him. Pass any law, he defiantly proclaimed, and sentence me to jail or to death, "I should contented be to lose my breath."[84]

The Baptist pastor acknowledged that some people might consider him to be a fool for opposing the powerful Church of England. To this accusation he pled guilty, but he reminded everyone that there were two kinds of fools. One kind ignores God, guzzling their

> ...bowls of Beer and Wine,
> Until they are as drunk as any Swine;
> With whoring, roaring, and their sports and play,
> That by them now are used ev'ry day,
> ....
> He then's a fool that for these earthly toys
> Doth lose eternal life and heav'nly joys.[85]

Griffith, however, proudly professed to be a fool of another kind; he was a fool for Christ:

> A crucified Christ these fools would know:
> As for the world, say these, tush, let it go.
> The world no peace nor comfort can afford,
> Like to a minutes presence of the Lord.[86]

David (n.p., 1663) title page. Griffith published these meditations after his release from Newgate.

[83] Ibid., 3. The poem also contains a lengthy tirade against the Catholic Church. See 9 and 69–118.

[84] Ibid., 4.

[85] Ibid., 6.

[86] Ibid., 6–7.

Christ's fools love their families, but they would lose even them willingly for him:

> And yet the Love of Christ is dearer far
> Unto their souls than wife or children are:
> The love of Jesus Christ surpasseth all:
> These fools are ready when their Lord doth call
> ....
> Such fools as these I therefore highly prise,
> For there are none but such that's truly wise.[87]

Such fools would also sacrifice their possessions, their country, and even their lives. Yet the faith that "What ever now I lose, I then shall find," comforted Griffith: "Oh how the thoughts of this contents my mind!"[88]

Griffith understood that he did not have to be in jail. Surrendering to the demands of "Their Worships" would mean freedom, but he would rather "dye in Jayle, than burn in Hell." Besides, prison was

> ...no unpleasant thing
> If Christ be there, that only blessed King;
> He with his Love doth make a Prison sweeter,
> (Tho unto sence it seems to be so bitter)
> Than any Princely Court, or stately Palace,
> When with his presence he the soul doth solace.
> If in Prison Jesus Christ be there,
> It's cause of joy to meet him any where.[89]

Turning to Christ for comfort and courage during the testing of his faith, Griffith proclaimed that

> In taking up, and bearing of the Cross,
> There can nor will be to my soul no loss;
> It is the certain way unto the Crown,

---

[87] Ibid., 7.
[88] Ibid., 9.
[89] Ibid., 11.

Christ went that way himself, 'twas his renown.

Christ's presence with him in jail encouraged Griffith to endure, despite not knowing whether God would deliver him from prison. Yet whether free or jailed, Griffith determined that he must follow Christ with the zeal with which the devil's followers obeyed his evil commands. Griffin persuaded himself:

> Do not quit thy self, thou'lt yield,
> And like a Coward saint and lose the field.
> Stand then upon thy watch, keep here thy guard,
> Lest thou be foild, and lose thy great reward.[90]

Griffith knew that he was engaged in a constant battle for his soul. Therefore, he sought to depend on his faith and on the Bible to overcome the hostilities he faced, for when one "fight doth end, there's in the room/ Another fight; one field's no sooner won,/ But presently another war's begun."[91]

To many outsiders, Griffith seemed to have been losing his battle with the devil. His imprisonment proved to some that he had joined a lost cause, yet he interpreted things differently. He reminded himself:

> ...think't no shame
> To lye in Newgate for the sake and Name
> Of thy dear Jesus, who hath thee esteem'd
> Worthy to bear his Name, and thee redeem'd.[92]

The cause for which Griffith was fighting and suffering was a righteous one. He knew that, one day, he would "see and meet with in the air,/ And all his [Christ's] Saints that dyed for his Word,/ And...be ever with the Lord."[93]

After his release from Newgate in 1662, Griffith returned to preaching in London, though little is known about his ministry until 1675. That year

---

[90] Ibid., 52.
[91] Ibid.
[92] Ibid., 63.
[93] Ibid.

approximately twenty members of a General Baptist church in Amersham, a few miles northwest of London, split off from their congregation because they believed that baptized believers should have hands laid on them. On 14 December Griffith assisted the group in starting a new church by laying hands on eighteen people.

Griffith returned to Newgate in 1683 for refusing once again to take the Oath of Allegiance. While in prison, he published an account of his and Bampfield's court appearance on 18 April 1683. In defending his refusal to take the oath, Griffith contended that the Bible stated that people who take oaths must do so "in truth and judgment, and in righteousness" (Jer 4:2). Griffith, however, could not take the oath in good conscience. He could not blindly obey all the king's laws, nor would he conform to the Church of England. Moreover, a Catholic might succeed King Charles and require that his subjects take another oath. Griffith promised never to swear allegiance to a Catholic monarch, either. "Do with me as you please," he dared his judges. "Come life, come death, the Lord assisting me, I will never take the Oath of Allegiance."[94] Once Griffith convinced the judges that he would not take the oath, they remanded him back to prison, where he remained "the Lord's prisoner," always ready to bear witness to the gospel.[95] The length of Griffith's stay in Newgate is unknown, though he was still in prison in January 1686 but free by 11 April 1687.[96]

Griffith died on 16 May 1700. In the funeral sermon for his fellow minister, Richard Allen described Griffith as a man of "sincere zeal" who had spent fourteen years "in sufferings, bonds, and imprisonments" solely for the "testimony of a good conscience."[97] Allen paid the deceased Baptist minister a great compliment, telling Griffith's family and friends, "I know of

---

[94] John Griffith, *The Case of Mr. John Griffith, Minister of the Gospel, and Now Prisoner in Newgate: Being a True and Impartial Account of What He Spake at the Sessions-house in the Old Bailey on the 18th of...April 1683*, reprinted in Crosby, *The History of the English Baptists*, 2:362–64.

[95] Ibid., 2:365.

[96] Gordon, "Griffith, John (1622?–1700)," 23:233; Lynch, "Griffith, John (1621/1622–1700)."

[97] Richard Allen, *A Gainful Death the End of a Truly Christian Life: A Sermon at the Funeral of Mr. John Griffith* (London: printed for Andr. Bell, 1700) 42–43.

no dishonor or blemish he brought upon our holy religion in his so long profession of it, but he was, I think, an ornament and reputation to it."[98]

Hercules Collins: A Christian Worthy of His Name

In 1684 another prominent Baptist, Hercules Collins (d. 1702), joined Bampfield, Delaune, and Griffith in Newgate. Little is known about Collins's early life, except that he probably did not receive a formal education and that he showed an interest in Christianity as a child. As with many early Baptist ministers, his lack of formal education did not prevent him from preaching. On 23 March 1677 Collins became pastor of London's Wapping Particular Baptist Church, which, a decade later, moved to Stepney.[99] Throughout his ministry, Collins was a prolific writer, authoring several pamphlets and tracts. Although he did not have a formal education, his publications reveal that he acquired a theological education, perhaps on his own.

Collins's violation of the Five Mile Act resulted in his imprisonment in 1684. One of his publications, *Some Reasons for Separation from the Communion of the Church of England, and the Unreasonableness of Persecution on that Account* (1682), also might have contributed to his arrest. In this publication, Collins crafted a dialogue between Conformist (the Church of England) and Nonconformist (a Baptist), in which the latter asserted that the Church of England was not an apostolic church and that persecution was as useless as it was ungodly. Obviously, such positions would not have endeared Collins with leaders in the government or in the Anglican Church.

Following his arrest and imprisonment in Newgate, Collins published two works, one of which was a funeral sermon that contained an elegy for two of his fallen friends, Francis Bampfield and Z. Ralphson, a Fifth Monarchist and Independent minister, both of whom died in Newgate.[100]

---

[98] Ibid., 42.

[99] Michael A. G. Haykin, "Collins, Hercules (d. 1702)," *Oxford Dictionary of National Biography*, http://www.oxforddnb.com./view/article/5939 (accessed 22 July 2005); Michael Haykin, "A Cloud of Witnesses: The Life and Ministry of Hercules Collins (d. 1702)," *Evangelical Times*, February 2001, http://www.evangelicaltimes. org/Articles/feb01/feb01a11.htm (accessed 12 February 2005).

[100] Ralphson was the alias of Jeremiah Marsden. See R. L. Greaves, "Marsden, (*alias* Ralphson), Jeremiah (1624–1684)," in *Biographical Dictionary of British Radicals in the Seventeenth Century*, 2:214–15.

Collins praised the men for "their great Worthiness/ ...their Refined Zeal, their Heart Contrite,/ ...their Compassions, with a publick Sp'rit/ Their Liberal Souls" and "their Stedfastness."[101] Even though death had removed them "from their Station,/ A signal loss both to the Church and Nation," they continued to preach the gospel, for their lives and writings "still doth Preach, although their Preaching's ended."[102]

Collins grieved the loss of his two friends and asked his readers to join him in mourning:

> Come join and mourn with me; O come, O come,
> And help me to express, now sitting dumb,
> In Melancholy Muteness, and in Tears,
> Sob forth our present loss, and ground of Fears.

Yet in the midst of their grief, Collins called the mourners to pause and remember the hope of the Christian faith:

> But stop a little, though there's Cause to weep,
> That those great Seers are both fallen asleep
> Yet they Transported in Triumphant Fame,
> Rejoicing praise the great JEHOVAHS Name.
> Free from all Cares, have now Eternal rest,
> With such Delights as cannot be exprest.
> Let none grudge this praise to their Memory,
> No Pen is fit to write their Elegy.[103]

With those two "Elijahs" gone, Collins called on Christians to pray:

> For some Elishas to appear, who shall
> Their Mantles take, and with a double measure

---

[101] Hercules Collins, "An Elegy on the Deaths of Mr. Bampfield and Mr. Ralphson, who Dyed Prisoners for Christ, in the Press Yard, Newgate," in *Counsel For the Living, Occasioned from the Dead: or, A Discourse on Job 3:17–18. Arising from the Deaths of Mr. Fran. Bampfield and Mr. Zach. Ralphson*, by Hercules Collins (London: printed by George Larkin for the author, 1684) 35.

[102] Ibid., 35–36.

[103] Ibid., 36

Of Holy Wisdom and Celestial Treasure,
Supply their place; Truth teach, and Truth defend,
And haste the Scarlet Whore to her last end.[104]

Collins published another work during his stay in Newgate, a thirty-four-page sermon titled *A Voice from the Prison*, in which he encouraged his congregation to stand firm in its faith during persecution. In this sermon on Revelation 3:11, Collins quoted or alluded to at least 213 passages and verses of scripture, all aimed at developing his theme, "hold fast what thou hast." He urged his church members to be patient and to endure their tribulations. If you do not endure your trials, he warned his flock, you will lose everything. If you "backslide from God, it may be wormwood and gall to your conscience all your time, and take away the comfort of all your enjoyments, and sting your conscience upon a death bed, as if you had had hell within you before death"; therefore, "hold fast what thou hast."[105]

When you are besieged by external forces and internal doubts to abandon your faith, Collins encouraged his congregation, "hold fast what thou hast." For if you do, Christ will say on judgment day:

These are they, Father, whose love to me many waters nor floods could not quench nor drown; these are they who chose me on my own terms, with the cross as well as the crown; these have made choice of me with reproaches, imprisonments, with fines, confiscation of goods, banishment, loss of limbs, life, and all; they have born all, endured all for my sake; in the greatest affliction, they kept from wavering, and the more they endured and lost for my sake, the more they loved me; as [with] some creatures, the more you beat them, the more they will love you, so a sincere soul, while God is afflicting him, he loves him.[106]

---

[104] Ibid., 37.

[105] Hercules Collins, *A Voice from the Prison, or, Meditations on Revelations 3:11, Tending to the Establishment of Gods Little Flock, in an Hour of Temptation* (London: printed by George Larkin for the author, 1684) 3.

[106] Ibid., 5.

We are waging a war with spiritual powers, Collins reminded his readers. Remember why you separated from the Church of England. Did you have good reasons, or did you merely pin "your faith upon another man's sleeves"? If you were sincere in your separation, you are duty bound to "hold fast what thou hast." To write such words implies that you can lose your crown, but ask yourselves this question: "What king would not tug hard to preserve an earthly crown?" Obviously, every king would. Therefore, "how much more should we endeavor to preserve an eternal one, by constant obeying the truth, and striving to enter in at the straight gate? For it is the will of your Father to lead you to a city of habitation..." (Ps 107:4, 7).[107]

Collins's release date from Newgate is unknown, but the man named for a pagan Greek hero noted for his strength and courage apparently "held fast" to his faith during several years in prison. A gifted preacher, Collins, at the time of his death in 1702, was preaching to a congregation of around 700 members.[108]

John Bunyan: A Baptist Pilgrim

The Baptist prisoners discussed earlier in this chapter all enjoyed various degrees of notoriety during their lifetimes, but history has relegated most of them to the pages of seldom-read history books. One Baptist prisoner who not only became well known during his lifetime but has remained famous for four centuries, was born in 1628 to Thomas Bunyan and his wife. The Bunyans named their son John. Of this well-known prisoner, W. Y. Fullerton observed, "If ever there was another man besides the forerunner of Jesus of whom it can truly said, 'There was a man sent from God whose name was John,' it was John Bunyan, and he too was a Baptist."[109]

John Bunyan was born at Elstow, near Bedford, forty-six miles north of London.[110] His father was a tinker (handyman) and was probably illiterate.

---

[107] Ibid., 10–11.

[108] Haykin, "Collins, Hercules (d. 1702)"; Haykin, "A Cloud of Witnesses."

[109] W. Y. Fullerton, "John Bunyan," *Review and Expositor* 25/3 (July 1928): 255. The New Testament quotation comes from John 1:6.

[110] Along with standard biographical entries in dictionaries, see Allen Smith, "John Bunyan (1628–1680)," in *The British Particular Baptists: 1638–1910*, ed.

While learning his father's trade, John also attended school. He learned to read and write, but he always claimed that he did not learn much more than that. Bunyan described himself as having been a great sinner who "had but few equals." He depicted his youth as being filled with sins that would make the heart of any Puritan shudder: "cursing, swearing, lying, and blaspheming the holy name of God."[111] Such sins haunted the young Bunyan, and he often had nightmares in which he dreamed that he was burning in hell. As a result of his hell-tormented youth, Bunyan turned against religion.

When he was sixteen, Bunyan joined the Parliament Army, where he encountered radical preachers, including Baptists like Henry Denne.[112] Bunyan probably did not participate in any fighting during his time (1644–1647) in the army.

After his discharge from the army, Bunyan returned to Elstow and earned a living as a tinker. In 1648 he married a poor girl, whose name he did not record. "We came together," Bunyan wrote, "as poor as poor might be, not having so much household stuff as a dish or spoon betwixt us both."[113] The only possessions his wife brought to the marriage were two religious books, which doubled Bunyan's library. The couple read these books, and they often discussed the life of his wife's pious father.

Slowly, Bunyan's faith rekindled, and he began attending church twice every Sunday. One Sunday afternoon, while playing a game, he heard a voice from heaven say, "Will you leave your sins and go to heaven, or have your sins and go the hell?" He ignored the voice, but during a break in the game, he "looked up to heaven, and was, as if I had, with the eyes of my

---

Michael A. G. Haykin, 3 vols. (Springfield MO: Particular Baptist Press, 1998) 1:79–92, and Clyde E. Fant, Jr., and William M. Pinson, Jr., "John Bunyan," in *20 Centuries of Great Preaching: An Encyclopedia of Preaching*, ed. Clyde E. Fant, Jr., and William M. Pinson, Jr., 13 vols. (Waco TX: Word Books, Publisher, 1971) 2:309–17.

[111] John Bunyan, *Grace Abounding to the Chief of Sinners*, in *Grace Abounding & The Life and Death of Mr. Badman*, by John Bunyan, Everyman's Library 85 (London: J. M. Dent & Sons Ltd, 1953) sec. 4, p. 8. Bunyan's spiritual autobiography resembles that of the apostle Paul's. See Rebecca Beal, "*Grace Abounding to the Chief of Sinners*: John Bunyan's Pauline Epistle," *Studies in English Literature* 21/1 (Winter 1981): 148–60.

[112] Roger Sharrock, "Bunyan, John (1628–1688)," in *Biographical Dictionary of British Radicals in the Seventeenth Century*, 1:105.

[113] Bunyan, *Grace Abounding to the Chief of Sinners*, sec. 15, p. 10.

understanding, seen the Lord Jesus looking down upon me, as being very hotly displeased with me, and as if he did severely threaten me with some grievous punishment for these and other my ungodly practices."[114] This experience set Bunyan on a tormented spiritual journey lasting perhaps as long as nine years, until late 1657 or early 1658.[115]

During his years of struggle, Bunyan attempted to change his lifestyle. He had some success, but he could not overcome his guilt-ridden conscience. One day while visiting Bedford to do some work, Bunyan overheard some women of a Separatist congregation talking about God. Being "a brisk talker" about religion himself, he drew nearer to hear what they had to say. The women confessed to being wretched sinners, yet they also marveled at God's saving them from their sins. As Bunyan listened to these women talk about God's grace, his "heart began to shake," and he realized that he had never even thought about the biblical teachings of the new birth or about the promises of God's redemption.[116]

The more Bunyan thought about spiritual things, the more despondent he became. He experienced brief periods of joy and peace, but he would soon fall like "a bird that is shot from the top of a tree, into great guilt and fearful despair."[117] Bunyan just could not settle the issue of whether he was a God-damned sinner or a God-saved sinner.

Bunyan, "still wandering in this psycho-spiritual maze," finally joined the Bedford Separatist congregation, pastored by John Gifford. According to tradition, sometime probably in 1655, Gifford baptized Bunyan in the Ouse River, at a spot called "The Ducking Place," near Bedford.[118] Gifford's church was an open-communion congregation; that is, as long as people led lives demonstrating true repentance and as long as they could verbalize God's work of salvation through Christ in their lives, the Bedford church

---

[114] Ibid., sec. 22, p. 12.

[115] Richard L. Greaves, "Bunyan, John (bap. 1628, d. 1688)," *Oxford Dictionary of National Biography*, http://www.oxforddnb.com./view/article/3949 (accessed 28 May 2005).

[116] Bunyan, *Grace Abounding to the Chief of Sinners*, sec. 37–39, p. 16.

[117] Ibid., sec. 140, p. 44.

[118] Greaves, "Bunyan, John (bap. 1628, d. 1688)"; Joseph D. Ban, "Was John Bunyan a Baptist? A Case Study in Historiography," *Baptist Quarterly* 30/8 (October 1984): 369–71; J. Hobson Thomas, "Bunyan the Baptist," *Baptist Quarterly* 4/3 (July 1928): 97.

accepted them as members.[119] The congregation believed that the gospel, not baptism, was the door through which believers entered the church.

Approximately nine months after joining the Bedford congregation, Bunyan began his preaching ministry. He described the first years of that ministry in these words:

> I went myself in chains to preach to them in chains, and carried that fire in my own conscience that I persuaded them to beware of. I can truly say, and that without dissembling, that when I have been to preach, I have gone full of guilt and terror even to the pulpit door, and there it has been taken off, and I have been at liberty in my mind until I have done my work, and then immediately, even before I could get down the pulpit stairs, I have been as bad as I was before; yet God carried me on, but surely with a strong hand, for neither guilt or hell could take me off my work.[120]

After two years of preaching as one spiritual prisoner to other spiritual prisoners, Bunyan recorded that "the Lord came in upon my own soul with some staid peace and comfort through Christ, for he did give me many sweet discoveries of his blessed grace through him."[121] After years of spiritual struggle and torment, Bunyan received the assurance that he was a God-saved sinner.

Bunyan preached wherever he could gather a congregation—in chapels, alleys, barns, or woods. People came "by hundreds" to hear him preach "the word."[122] His popularity, however, did not extend to Anglican clergymen, who condemned him. Some of Bunyan's opponents spread rumors that he was a witch, a Jesuit, a thief, a bigamist, and that he had several mistresses and whores with whom he had children. Bunyan bore such slanderous treatment proudly because, he said, "it belongs to my Christian

---

[119] Ban, "Was John Bunyan a Baptist?" 373.
[120] Bunyan, *Grace Abounding to the Chief of Sinners*, sec. 277, p. 85.
[121] Ibid., sec. 278, p. 85–86.
[122] Ibid., sec. 271, p. 84.

profession to be vilified, slandered, reproached and reviled.... I rejoice in reproaches for Christ's sake."[123]

Despite the vicious rumors and despite his wife's death in 1658, Bunyan continued to preach openly. With four children to care for, including one who was blind, Bunyan, in 1659, married woman named Elizabeth. Such a decision proved to be wise because Bunyan's days as a free man would soon come to an end.

Bunyan was scheduled to preach in a friend's home at Samsell in Bedfordshire on 12 November 1660. When he arrived, the friend suggested that the service be canceled because Justice Francis Wingate had issued a warrant for Bunyan's arrest. Bunyan refused, telling his friend, "Come, be of good cheer, let us not be daunted; our cause is good, we need not be ashamed of it; to preach God's word is so good a work that we shall be well rewarded, if we suffer for that...purpose." Retreating to a field, Bunyan mulled the matter over in his mind. If he fled from the authorities, he believed that the consequences would have been disastrous: new converts might think that, despite his bold preaching, he was really a coward; they and other Christians might follow his example and be afraid to stand for the gospel; and unbelievers might blaspheme the gospel. Finally, determined that he had to set a good example by obeying God rather than the state, Bunyan returned to the house, began the service, and was soon arrested for violating a conventicle act first enacted in 1593.[124]

Bunyan's trial was held in January 1661, while Thomas Venner and his Fifth Monarchists were terrorizing London. After Bunyan was found guilty, Justice John Keeling sentenced him to three months in the Bedford jail. If, after three months, Bunyan still refused to attend Anglican worship services and to stop preaching, he would be banished. If Bunyan then returned from banishment "without a special license from the king," Keeling threatened, "you must stretch by the neck for it."[125] In April, Bunyan refused to give in,

---

[123] Ibid., sec. 312, p. 93.

[124] John Bunyan, *A Relation of the Imprisonment of Mr. John Bunyan*, in *Grace Abounding & The Life and Death of Mr. Badman*, 104. *A Relation* consists of five letters Bunyan wrote to his church, describing his arrest, his encounters with the court, and Elizabeth Bunyan's attempts get her husband out of prison. See Richard L. Greaves, *Glimpses of Glory: John Bunyan and English Dissent* (Stanford CA: Stanford University Press, 2002) 130–45.

[125] Bunyan, *A Relation*, 116–17.

but instead of being banished, he was returned to jail, where, over the next eleven years, he wrote several poems and books, including his spiritual autobiography, *Grace Abounding to the Chief of Sinners*, and his most famous and beloved work, *The Pilgrim's Progress*.[126]

Although Bunyan could confidently proclaim, "I did meet my God sweetly in the prison,"[127] there was nothing sweet about leaving his family: "the parting with my wife and poor children has often been to me in this place as the pulling the flesh from my bones, and that not only because I am somewhat too, too fond of those great mercies, but also because I should have often brought to my mind the many hardships, miseries, and wants that my poor family was like to meet with, should I be taken from them." Particularly painful was leaving Mary, his blind daughter, "who lay nearer my heart than all I had besides; O the thoughts of the hardship I thought my blind one might go under, would break my heart to pieces."[128] Despite feeling like a man "pulling down his house upon the head of his wife and children," Bunyan concluded, "I must do it, I must do it."[129]

While in prison, Bunyan wrote four poems. Writing poetry served at least three purposes: it provided Bunyan with a respite in the writing of the more technical works he had written before being imprisoned; it helped break the monotony of prison life; and, along with the shoelaces he made, it helped support his family.[130] Three of the poems ("Profitable Meditations," "One Thing Is Needful," and "Ebal and Gerizzim") included doctrines steeped in Calvinism; the fourth ("Prison Meditations") contained a response to a friend who had written to encourage Bunyan.

---

[126] The exact number of poems and books that Bunyan wrote during this imprinment is hard to determine, but he wrote at least the following poems, books, and letters: "Profitable Meditations" (1661), "Prison Meditations" (1663), "One Thing Is Needful" (1665), "Ebal and Gerizzim" (1665), *I Will Pray With the Spirit* (1663), *Christian Behavior* (1663), *The Holy City* (1665), *The Resurrection of the Dead, and Eternal Judgment* (1665), *Grace Abounding to the Chief of Sinners* (1666), *Confession of Faith* (1672), *The Pilgrim's Progress* (not published until 1678), and *A Relation of the Imprisonment of Mr. John Bunyan* (posthumously published in 1765).

[127] Bunyan, *A Relation*, 111.

[128] John Bunyan, *Grace Abounding to the Chief of Sinners*, sec. 327, pp. 97–98.

[129] Ibid., sec. 328, p. 98.

[130] Graham Midgley, introduction to *The Poems*, in *The Miscellaneous Works of John Bunyan*, ed. Graham Midgley and Roger Sharrock, 13 vols. (Oxford: The Clarendon Press, 1980) 6:xv-xvi.

Bunyan began his first poem, "Profitable Meditations," by asking his readers not to take offence at his using poetry as a means for teaching theology. How truth is transmitted, he explained, is not as important as truth itself:

> Tis not the Method, but the Truth alone
> Should please a Saint, and mollifie his heart:
> Truth in or out of Meeter is but one;
> And this thou knowst, if thou a Christian art.[131]

Commenting on the use of poetry to express theology, F. Townley Lord observed:

> There is a place for intuition as well as reason, for poetry as well as prose, for imagination as well as logic.... He [Bunyan] recalls us to the power of poetry and imagination. He bids us be thankful that there were psalmists as well as legalists in the Hebrew race. He would argue that you cannot set out the grace of God in a syllogism, or in a series of propositions: you have to write a poem about it, or say it in an anthem. Our age is not likely to underestimate the advantages of scientific progress, and we must be careful lest the process of calculating, estimating, weighing arguments obscure the romance and poetry of life.[132]

Thus, just as physicians attempt to make their medicines easier to swallow, so Bunyan attempted to make theology more palatable by turning it into verse.[133] In doing so, "Man's heart is apt in Meeter to delight,/ Also in that to bear away the more:/ This is the cause I here in Verses write."[134]

In his three doctrinal poems, Bunyan addressed several themes, including the nature of humanity, the eternal destiny of sinners and saints,

---

[131] John Bunyan, "Profitable Meditations," in *The Miscellaneous Works of John Bunyan: The Poems*, ed. Graham Midgley, gen. ed. Roger Sharrock, 13 vols. (Oxford: The Clarendon Press, 1980) 6:4, lines 6-9. All citations of Bunyan's poems come from *The Poems*, vol. 6 of *The Miscellaneous Works of John Bunyan*.

[132] F. Townley Lord, "Bunyan's Message for To-day," *Baptist Quarterly* 4/4 (September 1928): 169-70.

[133] Bunyan, "Profitable Meditations," 6:4, lines 17–21.

[134] Ibid., lines 14–15.

the love of God, the sufferings of Christ, and the Christian life. God, according to Bunyan, created humanity for eternity, "For doubtless Man was never born/ For this Life and no more."[135] Everyone must

> ...tremble at that thought,
> That puts on God the Lie;
> That saith Man shall turn into nought
> When they be sick and die.[136]

Tragically, however, sin prevents people from realizing that an encounter with God awaits them after death, so they run headlong into the fires of hell. If only sinners could see the destruction that awaits them, they "would fly from Sin" their "mortal Foe."[137]

No one can escape death, which "is but as the Door/ Through which all men do pass,/ To that which they for evermore/ Shall have by *Wrath* or *Grace.*"[138] Death is an unprejudiced destroyer, snatching its victims from the powerful and the weak. It boasts:

> I am the King of Terrors, that's my name.
> I throw down Kingdoms, none can me withstand:
> Both Kings and Princes tremble at my fame,
> Thou fall'st when I upon thee lay mine hand.[139]

After death, sinners will spend eternity

> Either in Joy, in Bliss and Light,
> Or Sorrow, Woe, and Grief;
> Either with Christ and Saints in white,
> Or Fiends, without Relief.[140]

---

[135] John Bunyan, "One Thing Is Needful," 6:63, introduction stanza 3, lines 13–14.

[136] Ibid., 6:64, introduction stanza 11, lines 45–48.

[137] Bunyan, "Profitable Meditations," 6:5, stanza 2, lines 29–32.

[138] Bunyan, "One Thing Is Needful," 6:64, introduction stanza 12, lines 49–51.

[139] Bunyan, "Profitable Meditations," 6:25, stanza 124, lines 526–29. See also Bunyan, "One Thing Is Needful," 6:65–66, 68, section titled "Of Death," stanzas 1, 2, and 11, lines 62–65, 66–69, and 102–105.

Bunyan urged his readers not to postpone making a decision for Christ. Do not be seduced, Bunyan warned, into thinking that you have ample time to repent. Do not die thinking,

> I have so much imployment now that I
> Cann't tend it yet, to turn to thee for Grace:
> When I feel Death, then to thee I will flye,
> I may repent of Sin a little space.[141]

Life is fraught with uncertainty, and each sinner "hangeth by a thread/ Over the mouth of hell, as one half-dead;/ And O, how soon this thread may broken be!/ Or cut by death, is yet unknown to thee!"[142] Once an unrepentant sinner's thread breaks, his or her horrifying fate is sealed, for there is no "Repentance...within the grave,/ Nor Christ, nor grace, nor mercies for to save."[143]

Redeemed sinners, however, will experience a different fate. They can taunt death, saying, "O Death,...where is thy sting?/ Stir up thy strength & now make known thy might." The source of such boldness lies not within each saint but because "My JESUS hath me underneath his Wing,/ 'Tis he that triumph'd over thee in fight."[144]

Thus, salvation and eternal bliss lie beyond the power of any mortal, but God saves some sinners in spite of themselves. Each sinner freed from the fear of death and rescued from the flames of hell can only stand in awe

> Of God, who loved me when I was vile,
> And of sweet Jesus, who did reconcile
> Me unto justice, by his precious bloud,
> When no way else was left to do me good.[145]

---

[140] Bunyan, "One Thing Is Needful," 6:69, section titled "Of Death," stanza 29, lines 174–77.

[141] Bunyan, "Profitable Meditations," 6:19, stanza 86, lines 369–70.

[142] John Bunyan, "Ebal and Gerizzim," 6:106, lines 64–67.

[143] Ibid., lines 46–47.

[144] Bunyan, "Profitable Meditations," 6:25, stanza 125, lines 530–33.

[145] Bunyan, "Ebal and Gerizzim," 6:119, lines 544–47. See also Bunyan, "Profitable Meditations," 6:6–7, stanzas 13–14, lines 74–81.

Not because of good works does God save sinners, but because of "a bleeding Jesus, who did die./ The death," is "the reason why."[146] Christ's "bearing of our sins upon his back,/ By hanging on the Cross, as on a rack"[147] is the means by which "the Sinner" is "made a Saint."[148]

Even though good works do not save anyone, Bunyan contended that a sinner-turned-saint is expected to lead a holy life, one characterized by "Faith, hope, and love, true zeal, an upright heart,/ Right humbleness of mind, and every part."[149] God's Holy Spirit "now is come,/ And takes possession of thee as its home;/ By which a war maintained alwayes is,/ Against the old man, and the deeds of his."[150] Thus, saints are engaged in spiritual warfare until the end of their earthly lives. Periods of doubt and lapses of judgment will affect a saint's relationship with Christ, but Bunyan, no stranger to long periods of despondency, encouraged every troubled saint to

Hold up thy head..., thou doubting Saint,
Thy tender-hearted Christ is very sweet;
His loving-kindness will not let thee faint:
Look else upon his side, his hands and feet.[151]

In another prison poem, "Prison Meditations," Bunyan responded to a friend who had encouraged him to hold his "Head above the Flood."[152] This poem directly addressed Bunyan's prison situation, the cause of his imprisonment, his attitude at the time of writing the poem, and his confidence in final victory.

Unlike the conformist clergy who preached "*Fables*.../ Devis'd by cunning men,"[153] Bunyan maintained that he preached the gospel to people

---

[146] Bunyan, "Ebal and Gerizzim," 6:108, lines 124–27.

[147] Ibid., lines 135–37.

[148] Bunyan, "Profitable Meditations," 6:9, stanza 27, lines 131–34.

[149] Bunyan, "Ebal and Gerizzim," 6:117, lines 446–47.

[150] Ibid., 6:120, lines 580–83.

[151] Bunyan, "Profitable Meditations," 6:11, stanza 42, lines 191–94.

[152] John Bunyan, "Prison Meditations," 6:42, stanza 2, line 13.

[153] Ibid., 6:10, stanza 10, lines 43–44.

who were enslaved and haunted by their sins. "This was the work I was about," he declared,

> When Hands on me they laid,
> 'Twas *this* from which they pluck'd me out,
>   And vilely to me said,
>
> You Heretic, Deceiver, come,
>   To Prison you must go;
> You preach abroad, and keep not home,
>   You are the Church's foe.[154]

Prison did not coerce Bunyan into submitting to the government's demands; instead, it steeled his determination to persevere until he was liberated either by the king or by death. His enemies could lock him up physically, but he remained spiritually free:

> For though men keep my outward man
>   Within their Locks and Bars,
> Yet by the Faith of Christ I can
>   Mount higher than the Stars.
>
> Their *Fetters* cannot *Spirits* tame,
>   Nor tie up God from me;
> My Faith and Hope they cannot lame,
>   Above them I shall be.[155]

Threats of banishment and of hanging disturbed Bunyan, at least early in his imprisonment. In *Grace Abounding*, he admitted that he was not ready to die when he first entered jail. Worried about walking to the gallows, either shaking with fear or fainting, Bunyan confessed that he was "was ashamed to die with a pale face and tottering knees for" God's cause. The thought of being "on the ladder with a rope about my neck" horrified him. Another thought, however, encouraged him: he might have an opportunity

---

[154] Ibid., 6:44, stanzas 14–15, lines 60–67.
[155] Ibid., 6:43, stanzas 6–7, lines 24–31 .

to speak to the crowd assembled to watch him be hanged. If, through his dying words, "God will but convert one soul by my very last words, I shall not count my life thrown away, nor lost."[156] Thus, Bunyan's fear of death eventually passed, allowing him to proclaim that

> The Prison very sweet to me
>   Hath been, since I came here,
> And so would also hanging be,
>   If God would there appear.[157]

Whether he died a prisoner or a free man, Bunyan was assured of victory. Ultimately, "the sword would bow to the Spirit."[158] Despite being imprisoned and threatened with banishment and death, Bunyan challenged his tormentors to

> Consider…what I have said,
>   And judge of things aright;
> When all mens Cards are fully played,
>   Whose will abide the Light?

> Will *those* who have us hither cast?
>   Or *they* who do us scorn?
> Or *those* who do our Houses waste?
>   Or *us*, who this have borne?[159]

Bunyan's poems have never been considered great, perhaps not even good.[160] At times, he seemed to have been searching for words that rhyme, no matter how forced such rhyming was. One can imagine Bunyan sitting in

---

[156] Bunyan, *Grace Abounding to the Chief of Sinners*, sec. 334–35, p. 100.

[157] Bunyan, "Prison Meditations," 6:45, stanza 18, lines 76-79. "There" upon the gallows.

[158] Richard L. Greaves, "The Spirit and the Sword: Bunyan and the Stuart State," *Baptist Quarterly Review* 32/8 (October 1988): 375.

[159] Bunyan, "Prison Meditations," 6:51, stanzas 66-67, lines 268-275.

[160] For evaluations of his poetry, some of which are quite unflattering, see Midgley, introduction to *The Poems*, 6:xxv–xxx, and T. R. Glover, *Poets and Puritans*, 2nd ed. (London: Methuen & Co. Ltd., 1916) 112.

his cell, eyes closed, asking himself, "How many words rhyme with 'sin?'" Yet he did not write poetry for critics but for people who, like himself, were "unlettered and un-Latined."[161] Nor did he write to earn literary awards but to encourage the saved and to save the lost. For example, Isaac Backus, a Baptist pastor in the Massachusetts Bay Colony, writing almost sixty-five years after Bunyan's death, recorded in his diary, perhaps after reading "Prison Meditations," the following reaction: "Was something affected and quickened this morning in reading some of old father Bunyan's experiences. Oh! that I might follow him as he followed Christ."[162] Responses like this were what Bunyan sought to elicit from the readers of his poems.

The document that helped make Bunyan "without a doubt the most illustrious pastor of the English Baptist community of the seventeenth century" and "the most widely read Baptist of all times"[163] was his allegory about the Christian life, *The Pilgrim's Progress.* He probably wrote part one of the book during the latter portion of his lengthy imprisonment in the Bedford jail, but did not publish it until 1678. The book recounts the journey of a man named Christian as he encounters numerous trials and tribulations on the way from his home, the City of Destruction, to heaven, the Celestial City.

Bunyan began his allegory with the following:

> As I walked through the wilderness of this world, I lighted on a certain place, where was a den, and I laid me down in that place to sleep: and as I slept, I dreamed a dream. I dreamed, and, behold, I saw a man clothed with rags, standing in a certain place, with his face from his own house, a book in his hand, and a great burden upon his back (Isa. 64:6; Luke 14:33; Ps. 38:4; Hab. 2:2; Acts 16:31). I looked, and saw him open the book, and read therein; and, as he read, he wept and trembled; and not being able longer to contain,

---

[161] Glover, *Poets and Puritans,* 115.

[162] Isaac Backus, *The Diary of Isaac Backus,* ed. William G. McLoughlin, 3 vols. (Providence RI: Brown University Press, 1979), 1:199. Backus recorded these thoughts on Monday, 16 March 1752.

[163] Brackney, *A Genetic History of Baptist Thought,* 107.

he brake out with a lamentable cry, saying, "What shall I do?" (Acts 2:37).[164]

The story begins on a gloomy note. The dreamer found himself in a den (jail), wearied and seemingly defeated. This den was just another sinister place in the world, which he called a wilderness, suggesting that the world is a desolate place, a spiritual wasteland, filled with hostile people and dangerous traps designed to destroy God's people. The wilderness is more than geography, however; it is also a state of being, for Christian, the man in the dream dressed in rags and with a burden on his back, will struggle not only with external dangers but also with internal ones, such as doubts and fears.[165]

After finally deciding what he must do, Christian informed his wife and children that they must all leave their home or be destroyed by God's wrath. Thinking that Christian was crazy, his family tried to convince him not to leave. They ran after him, crying and pleading with him not to go. In order to shield himself from his family's fear, which was also a temptation, Christian stuck his finger in his ears and cried out, "Life! life! eternal life!"[166] He could not let even his family prevent him from heeding God's call.

As Christian began his journey, two neighbors, Obstinate and Pliable, joined him. Obstinate soon returned home, but Pliable continued on. When the two pilgrims fell into the Slough of Despond, Pliable became angry because he would not have begun the journey had he known that it was dangerous. After extracting himself out of the Slough, he too returned home. A man named Help offered his hand to Christian, who was sinking because of the burden on his back, and pulled him out of the mire. Help informed Christian that the Slough was the accumulation of "the scum and filth that attends conviction for sin, doth continually run, and therefore it is

---

[164] John Bunyan, *The Pilgrim's Progress* (repr., Grand Rapids MI: Baker Book House, 1984) 9.

[165] For helpful discussions of *The Pilgrim's Progress*, see Gordon Campbell, "The Theology of *The Pilgrim's Progress*," in *The Pilgrim's Progress: Critical and Historical Views*, ed. Vincent Newey (Liverpool: Liverpool University Press, 1980) 251-62; Greaves, *Glimpses of Glory*, 216-65; John R. Knott, Jr., "Bunyan's Gospel Day: A Reading of *The Pilgrim's Progress*," *English Literary Renaissance* 3/3 (Autumn 1973): 443-61; and Roger Pooley, "'The Wilderness of This World'—Bunyan's *Pilgrim's Progress*," *Baptist Quarterly* 27/7 (July 1978): 290-99.

[166] Bunyan, *The Pilgrim's Progress*, 12.

called the Slough of Despond; for still as the sinner is awakened about his lost condition, there ariseth in his soul many fears, and doubts, and discouraging apprehensions, which all of them get together, and settle in this place. And this is the reason of the badness of this ground."[167]

Christian continued his journey, despite being weighed down by his burden. Knowing that he could not unburden himself, he pressed on until he arrived at a hill on which there stood a cross. As the pilgrim approached the cross, his burden was "loosed from off his shoulders, and fell from off his back," tumbling into a sepulcher at the bottom of the hill, gone forever. Now unburdened by sin, Christian rejoiced that God "hath given me rest by His sorrow, and life by His death."[168]

Life for Christian, however, remained treacherous, for "A Christian man is never long at ease,/ When one fright's gone, another doth him seize."[169] Fortunately, he prepared himself for future battles by putting on the armor of God.[170] Though armed, when he encountered a hideous looking monster named Apollyon, Christian's guilt and fear caused him to debate whether to stand and fight or to flee. Realizing "that he had no armor for his back," he decided to stand his ground.[171] Apollyon proclaimed that he was the king of the land and that many who had followed Christ eventually "give him the slip and return again to me." If you do the same, Apollyon promised Christian, "all shall be well." Such a thing is unthinkable, Christian replied, for "how...can I go back from this [way], and not be hanged as a traitor?"[172] After that, a fierce battle ensued, with Apollyon getting the best of Christian. When the monster was about to inflict his fatal blow, Christian struck Apollyon with his sword, which symbolized the Bible, driving his enemy away.

Despite his great victory over such a mighty foe, Christian remained in danger. Fortunately, he did not have to journey alone because eventually he joined another pilgrim named Faithful. When they reached the town of Vanity, which was full of worldly things, games, and terrible sinners, the two

---

[167] Ibid., 17–18.

[168] Ibid., 45.

[169] Ibid., 55n.

[170] For the armor of God, see Ephesians 6:11–17.

[171] Bunyan, *The Pilgrim's Progress*, 68. Apollyon means "Destroyer." See Revelation 9:11.

[172] Ibid., 70.

pilgrims walked through the town's fair. The townspeople were "in a great hubbub" because of the men's odd clothes, their strange talk, and their bizarre values. Rather than buying things from the city's merchants, the two men proclaimed, "We buy the truth."[173] Because of the commotion caused by the two peculiar strangers, the town's authorities arrested the pilgrims for disturbing the peace and threw them into a cage.

When Faithful and Christian appeared in court, they heard the judge, Lord Hate-good, read the indictment: "That they were enemies to, and disturbers of their [the town's] trade; that they had made commotions and divisions in the town, and had won a party to their own most dangerous opinions, in contempt of the law of their prince."[174] After the testimony of three perjurers (Envy, Superstition, and Pickthank), the jury, led by Mr. Blind-man, returned a guilty verdict.[175]

The court sentenced the two pilgrims to die a cruel death, which Faithful did bravely. However, Christian, through divine intervention, escaped from prison and then sang the following as he continued his treacherous journey:

> Well, Faithful, thou hast faithfully profest
> Unto thy Lord: with whom thou shalt be blest;
> Are crying out under their hellish plights,
> Sing, Faithful, sing; and let thy name survive;
> For though they kill'd thee, thou art yet alive.[176]

Once again, Christian did not journey alone for long because he was soon joined by Hopeful. After becoming exhausted, they fell asleep near Doubting Castle. The owner of the castle, Giant Despair, captured them, threw them into a dark dungeon, and then abused them. When Christian became despondent and considered suicide, Hopeful encouraged him to remember that the Lord forbids suicide, and to remember that he had

---

[173] Ibid., 111.

[174] Ibid., 114–15.

[175] The names of the rest of the jury were: Mr. No-good, Mr. Malice, Mr. Love-lust, Mr. Live-loose, Mr. Heady, Mr. High-mind, Mr. Enmity, Mr. Liar, Mr. Cruelty, Mr. Hate-light, and Mr. Implacable.

[176] Bunyan, *The Pilgrim's Progress*, 121.

conquered other difficulties before. Christian eventually realized that he held within himself the key with which he could unlock any prison door. "What a fool...am I," he said, "thus to lie in a stinking dungeon, when I may as well walk at liberty! I have a key in my bosom, called Promise, that will, I am persuaded, open any lock in Doubting Castle."[177]

Once freed, Christian and Hopeful resumed their pilgrimage. After several more trials, they finally arrived at the Celestial City, but between them and the city's gate stood a river (death). With no bridge to cross the river, the two pilgrims entered the dangerous waters. Christian cried out in fear as waves engulfed him, yet Hopeful, who had gone first, called back: "Be of good cheer, my brother; I feel the bottom, and it is good."[178] With that word of encouragement, the beleaguered pilgrim crossed safely and arrived at his eternal home.

In *The Pilgrim's Progress* Bunyan portrayed the Christian pilgrimage as he had experienced it to be. Such a journey was beset with internal and external demons, all of which were intended to destroy a pilgrim's faith. According to Bunyan, God never promised that believers would have a life of ease, but God did promise to supply them with faith, hope, and encouragement. Such was Christian's message to By-ends (and therefore to all would-be pilgrims), who wanted to accompany Christian and Hopeful, and who professed to have never striven "against wind and tide." By-ends unashamedly confessed that he was "always most zealous when religion goes in his silver slippers."[179] To this deluded soul, Christian responded: "If you will go with us, you must go against wind and tide, the which, I perceive, is against your opinion: you must also own religion in his rags, as well as when in his silver slippers; and stand by him, too, when bound in irons, as well as when he walketh the streets with applause."[180]

Part of the power of *The Pilgrim's Progress* lay in Bunyan's ability to draw his readers into his story, to make them see what he saw, hear what he heard, and feel what he felt. Many dissenters of the seventeenth and eighteenth centuries in England and Colonial America could have related their experiences to those of Christian and therefore to those of Bunyan. For

---

[177] Ibid., 146.
[178] Ibid., 194.
[179] Ibid., 123.
[180] Ibid., 124.

anyone who had read his *Grace Abounding* knew that he, like Christian, had experienced the unburdening of his soul, the battle with fear and doubt, the use of the Bible to fight spiritual battles, the injustice of a biased judicial system, and the ministry of fellow pilgrims. Those whom God had truly called to salvation would face perilous physical and spiritual obstacles in life, but, as W. J. McGlothlin observed, "Christian always *gets through*, and though often sore and bruised he is usually on higher and firmer ground."[181] Bunyan's message to his fellow pilgrims was that they too would get through, for Christ is "a lover of poor pilgrims."[182]

As a consequence of Charles II's Declaration of Indulgence, Bunyan finally left prison sometime in 1672. His Bedford church had already called him as its pastor, so he applied for and was granted a license to preach. Also during the early 1670s, Bunyan had become embroiled in a controversy with other Baptists concerning the necessity of baptism for church membership.[183] Though a proponent of believer's baptism by immersion, Bunyan was an open-communion Baptist. For many Baptists such a position was traitorous because, they said, "'it is an ill bird that betrays his own nest.'" Bunyan, however, decried such "factious titles of Anabaptists, Independents, Presbyterians, or the like," and hoped that "if God should count me worthy, to be called a Christian, a Believer, or other such name which is approved by the Holy Ghost (Acts 11:26)."[184]

Bunyan enjoyed his freedom for a little more than four years before being jailed again near the end of December 1676 for about six months,

---

[181] W. J. McGlothlin, "Bunyan's 'Pilgrim's Progress': A Study," *Review and Expositor* 15/3 (July 1928): 290.

[182] Bunyan, *The Pilgrim's Progress*, 64.

[183] For the circumstances surrounding this controversy and whether Bunyan was a Baptist, see Ban, "Was John Bunyan a Baptist? A Case Study in Historiography," 367–76; Smith, "John Bunyan (1628–1680)," 89–90; Thomas, "Bunyan the Baptist," 97–103; Bill J. Leonard, *Baptist Ways: A History* (Valley Forge PA: Judson Press, 2003) 48, 51; H. Leon McBeth, *The Baptist Heritage: Four Centuries of Baptist Witness* (Nashville: Broadman Press, 1987) 81–83; Harry L. Poe, "John Bunyan's Controversy with the Baptists," *Baptist History and Heritage* 23/2 (April 1988): 25–35; G. Lyon Turner, "Bunyan's License under the Indulgence," *Transactions of the Baptist Historical Society* 6/2 (January 1919): 129–37; and A. C. Underwood, *A History of the English Baptists* (London: The Carey Kingsgate Press Limited, 1947) 103–104.

[184] John Bunyan, "Peaceable Principles and True," in *The Works of John Bunyan*, ed. George Offor, 3 vols. (Glasgow: Balckie and Son, 1854) 2:648–49.

probably for preaching at conventicles. Upon his release, he resumed his pastoral and preaching duties. During a preaching tour to London in 1688, he went out of his way to help heal a broken relationship between a father and son in Reading. On the journey to London, he rode through a downpour before arriving at a friend's home. Bunyan preached the following day, but he became seriously ill a few days later and died a free man on 31 August 1688. Throughout most of his ministry and prison experiences, Bunyan remained confident that the persecuted would triumphant over their persecutors. Had he lived a year longer, he would have reaped, at least to some extant, the fruit of that confidence.

The Glorious Revolution

In February 1685 Charles II died. He had converted to Catholicism on his deathbed, and his brother James II (r. 1685–1688), an avowed Catholic, succeeded him. His attempt to establish Catholicism in England failed, resulting in the Glorious Revolution of 1688, in which the king was deposed without bloodshed. To replace James, England invited William III, Prince of Orange, (whose wife was James's daughter Mary), from the Netherlands to rule England.

At the instigation of the new king, Parliament passed the Act of Toleration in 1689, granting most dissenters the freedom to worship. The act gave such freedom only to dissenters who believed in the Trinity and the divine inspiration of the Bible and who rejected the authority of Rome. The act also maintained the Church of England as the established church, and only Anglicans could hold public office.[185] Despite the inconsistencies and requirements in the act, at least English Baptists no longer had to fear being imprisoned for expressing their religious beliefs.

The Act of Toleration came too late for many English subjects because thousands of them had already fled in the previous decades to the New World. As George Herbert noted: "Religion stands on tip-toe in our land,/

---

[185] See "The Toleration Act, 1689," http://www.swan.ac.uk/history/teaching/teaching%20resources/Revolutionary%20England/TolerationAct.htm (accessed 12 December 2005). For the distinction between toleration and liberty, see Philip Wendell Crannell, "Tolerance and Company," *Review and Expositor* 24/1 (January 1927): 24–44, and George W. Truett, "Baptists and Religious Liberty," in *The Trophy of Baptists*, ed. J. Brent Walker (Macon GA: Smyth & Helwys, 2003) 30–31.

Ready to pass to the American strand."[186] These immigrants had preferred to take their chances with the uncertainties of an unsettled land than with the certainties of persecution by religious zealots like Archbishop William Laud.

---

[186] George Herbert, "The Church Militant," lines 234–35, http://www.ccel.org/h/herbert/temple/ChurchMilitant.html#tears (accessed 15 July 2007); Samuel Eliot Morison, *Builders of the Bay Colony* (Boston: Houghton Mifflin, 1930; repr. Boston: Northeastern University Press, 1981) 220.

Chapter 7

An Unforgettable Whipping

Historians have called the years from 1620 to 1640 in England the Great Migration because during that period of time thousands of English men and women fled to the New World. Writing from the Tower of London, Archbishop William Laud alluded to this exodus in his diary, claiming that he had never forced anyone from England. Those who did flee the country, the impeached Anglican leader maintained, "forsook it of themselves, being Separatists from the Church of England, as is more than manifest to any man who will but consider what kind of persons went to New England."[1] Of course, the "kind of persons" to which Laud referred were, in his opinion, troublemakers at best and heretics at worst. However, many of the approximately 20,000 people who fled to the New World during that twenty-year period would have named Laud as a primary reason for their leaving England.

Most of the people who fled England did not see themselves as troublemakers or heretics. For example, the Puritans who settled in the Massachusetts Bay Colony maintained that, despite leaving England, they had not left the Church of England. John Higginson, a minister at Salem, Massachusetts, expressed the Puritan attitude this way: "The generality of the people of God who came to this country [New England]...did not separate from the churches of England but came from the disorder there, with full desire of reformation without disturbance to any."[2] Thus, many of

---

[1] William Laud, *The History of the Troubles and Tryal of the Most Reverend Father in God, William Laud* (London: printed for Ri. Chilwell, 1694), in *The Works of the Most Reverend Father in God, William Laud, D.D.: Devotions, Diary, and History*, 7 vols. (Oxford: John Henry Parker, 1847) 3:420.

[2] Quoted in William G. McLoughlin and Martha Whiting Davidson, eds., "The Baptist Debate of April 14–15, 1668," in *Colonial Baptists: Massachusetts and Rhode Island*, The Baptist Tradition (Massachusetts Historical Society *Proceedings*, 1964; repr., New York: Arno Press, 1980) 117.

these immigrants still considered themselves as members in good standing with the Church of England. By establishing a church free from the impurities of its mother church, these immigrants hoped that the purity of the New England church would eventually be transported back to old England, thereby returning the English church to the truth. But once the Puritans had separated geographically from their ecclesiastical roots, they established Congregationalism, which emphasized individual church autonomy while attempting to remain theologically faithful to the Church of England.

Nathaniel Ward and the New England Way

One immigrant whom Laud helped forsake the English kingdom was Nathaniel Ward (c. 1578–1652). Isaac Backus, a Baptist minister and an early Baptist historian in the latter half of the eighteenth century, observed that, in Ward, we "may see the temper and language of paedobabtists in that day."[3] Ward preached and followed the "New England Way" in religion, a way that Baptists could not follow.

Born in Havervill, Suffolk County, England, and graduated twice from Emmanuel College, Cambridge, Ward embarked on a legal career.[4] After completing his legal training, he traveled in Europe, where he studied theology at the University of Heidelberg, under David Pareus, who

---

[3] Isaac Backus, *A History of New England with Particular Reference to the Denomination of Christians Called Baptists*, 2 vols., 2nd ed., ed. David Weston (Newton MA: The Backus Historical Society, 1871) 1:155.

[4] For biographical information on Ward, see Frederick S. Allis, Jr., "Nathaniel Ward: Constitutional Draftsman," *Essex Institute Historical Collections* 120/4 (October 1984): 241–263; K. Grudzien Baston, "Ward, Nathaniel (1578–1652)," *Oxford Dictionary of National Biography* (Oxford: Oxford University Press, 2004), http://www.oxforddnb.com/view/article/28700 (accessed 25 December 2005); Samuel Elliot Morison, *Builders of the Bay* (Boston: Houghton Mifflin Company 1930; repr., Boston: Northeastern University Press, 1981) 217–43; Simon P. Newman, "Nathaniel Ward, 1580–1652: An Elizabethan Puritan in a Jacobean World," *Essex Institute Historical Collections* 127/4 (October 1991): 313–26; Mary Rhinelander McCarl, "Ward, Nathaniel," *American National Biography Online* (Oxford: Oxford University Press, 2000), http://www.anb.org/articles/01/01–00934. html (accessed 4 January 2006); and Moses Coit Tyler, *A History of American Literature* (New York: G. P. Putnam's Sons, 1879) 227–41, also available online at http://www.dinsdoc.com/tyler_m–1–0a.htm.

convinced him to change careers. Ward's movements for the next decade are difficult to trace, but he eventually returned to England, became an Anglican priest in 1618, and then served as a chaplain aboard English merchant ships from 1620 to 1624. By 1626 he was back in England, where he served as the curate of a London church from 1626 to 1628. In 1628 or 1629 Ward, now a devout Puritan, became the rector of the parish of Stondon Massey in Essex County.

Ward's Puritanism soon attracted the attention of Laud, then the bishop of London, who interrogated Ward on 13 December 1631. The bishop demanded that Ward explain several of his aberrant practices, including not wearing the surplice (a white, loose-fitting, knee-length garment open at the sleeves) for two years; not reading prayers on Wednesdays, Fridays, and holidays; refusing to bow at the name of Jesus; and refusing to support the playing of games on Sundays.[5] The meeting with Laud frightened the Puritan priest. In a letter to his friend John Cotton, a minister in Boston, England, Ward expressed his fears:

> I was yesterday convented before the bishop, I mean to his court, and am adjourned to the next term. I see such giants turn their backs that I dare not trust my own weak heart. I expect measure hard enough and must furnish apace with proportionable armor. I lack a friend to help buckle it on. I know none but Christ himself in all our coast fit to help me, and my acquaintance with him is hardly enough of hope for that assistance my weak spirit will want, and the assaults of temptation call for. I pray, therefore, forget me not.[6]

Ward had good reason to fear the tenacious bishop, for Laud interviewed Ward again for three days in February 1632, admonished him in December, and then excommunicated him in 1633. He fled to Massachusetts in 1634, settling at Ipswich, where he pastored a church until poor health forced him to retire two years later.

---

[5] Tom Webster, *Godly Clergy in Early Stuart England: The Caroline Puritan Movement c. 1620–1643* (Cambridge: Cambridge University Press, 1997) 197–98; Baston, "Ward, Nathaniel (1578–1652)"; Newman, "Nathaniel Ward, 1580–1652: An Elizabethan Puritan in a Jacobean World," 319.

[6] Quoted in Allis, Jr., "Nathaniel Ward: Constitutional Draftsman," 244, and in Webster, *Godly Clergy in Early Stuart England*, 198.

Despite his retirement, Ward remained active in the colony's religious and political affairs. In 1641 he drafted *The Body of Liberties* for Massachusetts, a document comprised of ninety-five clauses delineating the basic rights and liberties of the colony's citizens.[7] Included in this document were several clauses that dealt with religion. Civil authorities, for example, had the "power and liberty to see [that] the peace, ordinances, and rules of Christ [are] observed in every church according to his word."[8] Also, one of "the liberties the Lord Jesus has given to the churches" granted that people not belonging to church, yet who were "orthodox in judgment and not scandalous in life," could start a church, "provided they do it in a Christian way, with due observation of the rules of Christ revealed in his word."[9] Massachusetts also opened its arms to people who professed "the true Christian religion" and were fleeing persecution or the devastation of natural disasters.[10]

Although the colony opened its arms to beleaguered souls, it also threatened to open its jails to anyone who was not "orthodox in judgment" or who lived a "scandalous life." According to their opponents, Baptists fit both categories. Just south of Massachusetts in the colony that was to become Rhode Island, a group of Massachusetts exiles formed a Baptist church in 1639, and then another group started a second Baptist church in 1644. Such alarming developments led the Massachusetts governor, John Winthrop, to note in his journal for 15 July 1644 that "Anabaptistry increased and spread in the country, which occasioned the magistrates, at the last court, to draw an order for banishing such as continued obstinate after due conviction."[11] Later, in November 1644, the General Court of Massachusetts enacted that order, which was aimed directly at "Anabaptistry." Claming that history had proven that Anabaptists had always

---

[7] For the text of this document, see John Beardsley, ed., "Liberties of New Englishmen." http://www.winthropsociety.org/liberties.php. For a discussion of the document, see Allis, Jr., "Nathaniel Ward: Constitutional Draftsman," 248–62, and Morison, *Builders of the Bay*, 226–34.

[8] Beardsley, "Liberties of New Englishmen," clause 58.

[9] Ibid., clause 95.1.

[10] Ibid., clause 89.

[11] John Winthrop, *The Journal of John Winthrop, 1630–1649*, ed. Richard S. Dunn, James Savage, and Laetitia Yeandle (Cambridge MA: Harvard University Press, 1996) 517.

been "the incendiaries of commonwealths, and the infectors of persons in main matters of religion, and the troublers of churches in most places where they have been," the court lamented that these heretics rejected infant baptism, denied that Christians could be magistrates, accepted pacifism, and rejected the right of civil authorities to punish offenders of the first table of the Ten Commandments. Therefore, because the presence of Anabaptists in the colony would produce "guilt…, infection, and trouble to the churches and hazard to the whole commonwealth," the General Court ordered the banishment of anyone holding Anabaptist beliefs.[12]

Two years after the law banishing Anabaptists from Massachusetts had been enacted, Ward returned to England, where he died six years later. Prior to leaving Massachusetts, however, he began writing *The Simple Cobler of Aggawam in America*, which he published in London under the pseudonym Theodore de la Guard. Although Ward aimed this work at the political and religious situation in England, which had been made safe for Puritans after the first civil war, he did not neglect to comment on the religious milieu in Massachusetts.

Ward spoke for many New Englanders when he took it upon himself "to be the herald of New England…to proclaim to the world, in the name of our colony," that heretics like Anabaptists would not be tolerated.[13] The idea of permitting different expressions of religion was just as repugnant to New Englanders as it was to the civil and ecclesiastical leaders who had run them out of old England. The devil himself, according to Ward, was the strongest advocate of "poly-piety" (religious liberty), which Ward called "the greatest impiety in the world," because such freedom would destroy both the true faith and good morals of real Christians.[14] Nowhere in the Bible, Ward maintained, does God permit "Christian states" to grant freedom to "adversaries of his truth, if" those states have the power to suppress Satan's

---

[12] "General Laws & Liberties 1641–1648," http://www.mayflowerfamilies.com/colonial_life/general_laws.htm (accessed 23 September 2005).

[13] Nathaniel Ward, *The Simple Cobler of Aggawam in America* (London: printed by John Dever & Robert Ibbitson for Stephen Bowtell, 1647) [2]. Also available online at http://puritanism.online.fr/puritanism/ward/ward.html. Aggawam was the Native American name given the town in which Ward lived before it was changed to Ipswich.

[14] Ibid., [3].

minions.[15] If such states do not quash heretics, "the simple cobbler" warned, "the church of...[God's] kingdom will soon become the devil's dancing school [rather] than God's temple."[16]

The retired Puritan priest considered "ignorant and tender conscienced Anabaptists" to be particularly loathsome because of their rejection of infant baptism: "What a cruelty it is to divest children of that only external privilege which their heavenly Father has bequeathed them, to interest them visibly in himself, his Son, his Spirit, his covenant of peace, and the tender bosom of their careful mother the church.... What an inhumanity it is to deprive parents of that comfort they may take from the baptism of their infants dying in their childhood."[17]

For readers unfamiliar with Anabaptist heretics, Ward provided the following analysis: They are devoid of spirituality, believing that "their religion began and ended in their opinion"; they express a sense of superiority in the way they look, the way they talk, and the way they walk; they are pathetically obstinate, for they seldom return to the truth; and they irrationally adopt any teaching that they believe will "keep them dry from the showers of justice." Anabaptists, however, cannot flee justice forever because, one day, "they will undoubtedly find God as jealous of his ordinances as [they] themselves are zealous of their opinions."[18]

If Ward's readers got the impression that Massachusetts only granted religious liberty to Puritans, they were greatly mistaken. All heretics, Ward proclaimed, "shall have free liberty to keep away from us, and such as will come to be gone as fast as they can, the sooner the better."[19] This statement summarizes succinctly the "New England Way." Archbishop Laud could not have stated the matter better himself, and he undoubtedly uttered something similar to Ward before "the simple cobbler" fled old England.

Roger Williams and Baptist Beginnings in America

During Ward's stay in Massachusetts, the colony had several clashes with people whom it considered to be a threat to its stability. Roger

---

[15] Ibid., [2].
[16] Ibid., [5].
[17] Ibid., [8–9].
[18] Ibid., [9].
[19] Ibid., [2].

Williams (c. 1603–1684), another Laudean exile, is perhaps the most famous of those miscreants. W. K. Jordan described the Leveller Richard Overton as "a vigorous, fearless, and refreshing thinker" who "must none the less be regarded as an incendiary who could probably never have lived happily in any ordered society."[20] That could also describe Williams, for he was a difficult man. Wherever he went, and he went many places, Williams was always seeking something else, something better, something purer. Although he did not walk in the Baptist way for long, this incendiary man is generally credited with (or in some circles damned for) being the founder of the Baptist tradition in America.

Born in London around 1603, Williams had a conversion experience sometime between the ages of ten to twelve, and he eventually accepted some Puritan teachings.[21] At the age of twenty-two he entered Cambridge University, from which he graduated with a B.A. in 1627. He then entered the master's program, but withdrew eighteen months later. By the time he married Mary Barnard in 1629, Williams had become a zealous Separatist, and he eventually withdrew from the Church of England and left his homeland for New England.

Williams and his wife left England on 1 December 1630 and arrived at Boston fifty-six days later. In a letter to a friend nearly twenty-two years later, Williams recalled that leaving England "was as bitter as death," but he apparently had little choice, for "Bishop Laud pursued me out of this land [England] and my conscience was persuaded against the national church and ceremonies and bishops."[22] Bostonians warmly welcomed the Williamses, and they soon asked Williams to be the town's minister. He refused the offer because he believed that the church consisted of "middle walkers," that is, people who were neither fully committed to the Church of England nor

---

[20] W. K. Jordan, *The Development of Religious Toleration in England: Attainment of the Theory and Accommodation in Thought and Institutions (1640–1660)*, 4 vols. (Cambridge MA: Harvard University Press, 1940) 4:190, n. 2.

[21] Edwin S. Gaustad, *Liberty of Conscience: Roger Williams in America*, Library of Religious Biography (Grand Rapids MI: William B. Eerdmans Publishing Company, 1991) 6.

[22] Roger Williams to Mrs. Anne Sadlier, ca. April 1652, in *The Correspondence of Roger Williams*, ed. Glenn W. LaFantasie, 2 vols. (Hannover RI: Brown University/University Press of New England, 1988) 1:358.

fully separated from it.[23] The Williamses settled at Salem for awhile and then at Plymouth, which was beyond the jurisdiction of the Massachusetts Bay authorities, before resettling at Salem in 1633.

At Salem and at Plymouth, Williams continued to advocate his Separatist views of complete severance from the Church of England. He castigated New Englanders for foolishly believing that they could be separate from and part of the Anglican Church at the same time ("middle walking"), which angered many colonists. He further angered them when he asserted that they could not take the Native Americans' land from them or occupy it without negotiating fairly with them. Furthermore, Williams contended that governments could legislate the outward actions of people, but not their consciences, which incensed many, particularly Puritan magistrates and ministers. Thus, in condemning many of the practices of the "New England Way," Williams declared that New Englanders were no different than old Englanders. Such scandalous opinions resulted in Williams being summoned before the Massachusetts Bay's General Court several times. According to Edwin Gaustad and Leigh Schmidt, "The Massachusetts authorities listened, at first with patience, then with incredulity, and finally with horror. Here was a man gone mad, a zealot who heeded neither the voice of reason nor the voice of God. Williams had gone so far as to declare that their churches were impure, their title to the land unclear, their enforcement of true religion both cruel and absurd."[24] Finally, in October 1635, after exhausting all of its patience, the court ordered that the stubborn Salem preacher leave the colony within six weeks. Realizing that Williams would neither leave nor repent, the court then decided to have him sent back to England. Upon learning of the court's decision, Williams fled the colony in January 1636.

Native Americans, who appreciated Williams treating them like human beings, provided him with food and shelter. In spring 1636, he purchased land from these benefactors near the top of Narragansett Bay, built a shelter, and then sent for his wife and two small children. Several people from Salem

---

[23] Gaustad, *Liberty of Conscience*, 25.

[24] Edwin Gaustad and Leigh Schmidt, *The Religious History of America: The Heart of the American Story from Colonial Time to Today*, rev. ed. (San Francisco: HarperSanFrancisco, 2002) 66.

soon joined the Williams family in this new settlement, which Williams had named Providence.

Even though the colony had finally rid itself of its problem child, Massachusetts authorities still kept a wary eye on what was happening to their south, and what they saw disturbed them. In December 1638, Governor Winthrop recorded in his diary that "the devil was not idle" in Providence, for Williams and his followers believed "that no man should be molested for his conscience."[25] The following March, the Massachusetts governor recorded that the situation in Providence had deteriorated because Catherine Marbury Scott, who was "infected with Anabaptistry," had convinced Williams "to make open profession thereof, and [he] was re-baptized by" Ezekiel Holliman.[26] Williams then baptized Holliman and approximately eighteen others, thereby forming the first Baptist church in America.[27] Williams, however, did not remain long with his Baptist congregation. As Glenn W. LaFantasie observed, "For the rest of his life, he would pray with his wife, but in his heart he was a congregation of one."[28]

Because neighboring colonies began claiming the land on which Providence and other nearby towns had been built, Williams traveled to England in 1643 to obtain a charter for the colony of Providence Plantations (later named Rhode Island) and then returned home in 1644. After William Coddington of Portsmouth received a charter for part of Providence Plantations and was named governor for life, his opponents sent Williams and John Clarke, a Baptist pastor in the nearby town of Newport, to England in 1651 to obtain a charter uniting all of Rhode Island. After obtaining a nullification of Coddington's charter, Williams returned home in 1654, where he died in 1683. Clarke, however, remained in England nine more years.[29] In his second attempt in 1662 to obtain a charter from Charles

---

[25] Winthrop, *The Journal of John Winthrop*, 276.

[26] Ibid., 286.

[27] The mode of these baptisms has been debated. See Pamela R. Durso and Keith E. Durso, *The Story of Baptists in the United States* (Brentwood TN: Baptist History and Heritage Society, 2006) 40, n. 2.

[28] Glenn W. LaFantasie, "Williams, Roger," in *American National Biography Online*, http://www.anb.org/articles/01/01-00983.html (accessed 25 December 2005).

[29] Gaustad, *Liberty of Conscience*, 129–32; Edwin S. Gaustad, *Roger Williams*, Lives and Legacies (Oxford: Oxford University Press, 2005) 63–70; Francis J. Bremer,

II, Clarke requested that Rhode Islanders "be permitted to hold forth a lively experiment, that a most flourishing civil state may stand...and best be maintained, and that among English spirits, with a full liberty in religious concernments, and that true piety rightly grounded upon gospel principles will give the best and greatest security to the sovereignty, and will lay in the hearts of men, the strongest obligation to true loyalty."[30] In 1663, a year after Parliament passed the Act of Uniformity and a year before it passed the Conventicle Act, both of which were designed to eliminate religious dissent, Charles granted Rhode Island its charter providing, among other things, religious liberty to the colony's citizens.

John Clarke and His Pastoral Visit to Massachusetts

In accompanying Williams to England, Clarke returned to the place of his birth. Born at Westhorpe, Suffolk County, in 1609, Clarke (1609–1676) received a formal education either at Cambridge or at Oxford.[31] He was well versed in Hebrew and Greek. He probably received medical training,

---

"Williams, Roger (c. 1606–1683)," *Oxford Dictionary of National Biography*, http://www.oxforddnb.com/view/article/29544 (accessed 25 December 2005).

[30] John Clarke, "Second Address from Rhode Island to King Charles the Second," in *Records of the Colony of Rhode Island and Providence Plantations, in New England*, ed. John Russell Bartlett, 10 vols. (Providence RI: A. Crawford Greene and Brother, State Printers, 1856) 1:490–91.

[31] Along with articles in various dictionaries, biographical material on Clarke can be found in the following: Thomas W. Bicknell, *Story of John Clarke*, 2nd ed. (Providence RI: privately printed, 1915); John Clarke, *Ill Newes from New-England*, in *Colonial Baptists: Massachusetts and Rhode Island*, The Baptist Tradition (London: H. Hills, 1652; repr., New York: Arno Press, 1980); Sydney V. James, *John Clarke and His Legacies: Religion and Law in Colonial Rhode Island 1638–1750*, ed. Theodore Dwight Bozeman (University Park: The Pennsylvania State University Press, 1993); Wilbur Nelson, *The Life of Dr. John Clarke* ([Newport RI: privately printed,] 1924; repr., [Newport RI: privately printed,] 1963); Wilbur Nelson, *The Ministry of Dr. John Clarke* (Newport RI: privately printed, 1927); Wilbur Nelson, "The Ministry of Dr. John Clarke," *Chronicle* 1/2 (April 1938): 32–38; and George Selement, "John Clarke and the Struggle for Separation of Church and State," *Foundations* 15/2 (April-June 1972): 111–25.

perhaps at the University of Leyden in Holland, for he often identified himself as a "physician of Rhode Island in America."[32]

With his wife, sister, and two brothers, Clarke immigrated to Boston, Massachusetts, arriving there in November 1637. Their reason for leaving England is unknown, but it would not be too far-fetched to surmise that they left to escape religious persecution.

If Clarke and his family had hoped that, by fleeing England, they were fleeing religious persecution, their hopes were dashed immediately when they set foot in Boston. The town was embroiled in a religious controversy with Anne Hutchinson, the sister of Catherine Marbury Scott. On Monday mornings in her home, Hutchinson taught theology to women and led discussions concerning politics and the previous day's sermons preached by the Reverends John Wilson and John Cotton, co-pastors of the Boston church. The attendance at her Thursday afternoon meetings was even larger than the attendance at the Sunday services at the town's established church.[33] That women would assemble at the Hutchinson home to discuss the weighty subjects of religion and politics was bad enough, but the civil and ecclesiastical authorities were even more concerned about the content of Hutchinson's teaching. In November 1637 Massachusetts authorities tried her for "traducing the ministers." Rather than accepting everything that her spiritual masters told her that she must believe, Hutchinson claimed that she had received direct revelations from God, which often contradicted the teachings of her ministers. In fact, during her trial, she informed the court that her latest revelation was that God would destroy the colony if its leaders continued to persecute her for speaking the truth.[34] Unfazed, the court banished Hutchinson and a dozen of her closest followers from the colony in spring 1638, and threatened others who accepted Hutchinson's teachings with the same fate.

The Hutchinson controversy seemed to baffle Clarke: "I thought it not strange to see men differ about matter of heaven, for I expect no less upon earth. But to see that they were not able so to bear with each other in their

---

[32] Clarke, *Ill Newes*, 1. Clarke also referred to himself a physician in his will and in the addendum to that will. See James, *John Clarke and His Legacies*, 159, 163–64.

[33] William G. McLoughlin, *Rhode Island: A Bicentennial History* (New York: W. W. Norton & Company, Inc., 1978), 18; Bicknell, *Story of John Clarke*, 57–60.

[34] McLoughlin, *Rhode Island*, 20.

different understandings and consciences, as in those utmost parts of the world to live peaceably together" was troubling.[35] Had they not all "fled from the persecuting hands of the lordly bishops"?[36] Indeed, they had, but that apparently did not matter. Therefore, Clarke joined the Hutchison group, not because he agreed with all of its theology, but, having lived under Charles I's reign and William Laud's watchful eyes, he knew that when the righteous rule, the rule is seldom righteous.

The Massachusetts exiles eventually located on Aquidneck Island (later Rhode Island), where they established the town of Portsmouth in 1638. The following year Clarke helped found Newport, where he became the pastor of the town's church. By 1644 that church had identified itself as a Particular Baptist church. At what point in his life he became a Baptist is unknown. Unlike Roger Williams, however, Clarke remained a Baptist for the rest of his life, pastoring his Newport church for forty years and proving to be a devoted and capable Baptist leader. In fact, Clarke, not Williams, was the most important and influential seventeenth-century colonial American Baptist and therefore deserves the title "Father of American Baptists."[37]

In the year following his and Williams's arrival in England in 1651 to obtain a better charter for their colony, Clarke published his *Ill Newes from New-England*, which Edwin Gaustad called a "well known (not necessarily well read)...book."[38] With Charles I and Archbishop Laud resting peacefully in their graves and a more tolerant attitude toward dissenters, at least in some circles, permeating England, Clarke took the opportunity to define who New England Baptists were rather than to let their enemies, like Nathaniel Ward, define them. *Ill Newes* included Clarke's narrative of his pastoral visit to Lynn, Massachusetts, and his prison writings related to an incident in that town, an incident that William Estep characterized as "the most notorious case of persecution against Baptists in New England."[39]

---

[35] Clarke, *Ill Newes*, 23–24.

[36] Ibid., [3].

[37] Walter B. Shurden, "Ill News from Twenty-First Century America," *Baptist History and Heritage* 39/2 (Spring 2004): 6.

[38] Edwin S. Gaustad, "John Clarke: 'Good Newes from Rhode Island,'" *Baptist History and Heritage* 24/4 (October 1989): 23.

[39] William R. Estep, *Revolution within the Revolution: The First Amendment in Historical Context, 1612–1789* (Grand Rapids MI: William B. Eerdmans Publishing Co., 1990) 89.

Clarke began the narrative of his July 1651 pastoral visit to an elderly church member living near Lynn with these words: "It came to pass." Modern readers familiar with the King James Version of the Bible will recognize these words immediately because they often introduce stories in that translation of the Bible. Modern translators, however, leave the sentence out because it adds nothing to the narratives it introduces. Readers of Clarke's *Ill Newes*, however, would have understood immediately the symbolism of the phrase. What Clarke was about to describe was significant. The description of the events that followed those words was more than just a presentation of meaningless historical facts; it portrayed the struggles between truth and error, good and evil, freedom and tyranny, and justice and injustice. These events sadly described how, according to the subtitle of the book, *while old England is becoming new, New-England is become Old.*[40] Thus, when he wrote, "It came to pass," Clarke began describing the events that have been included in every American-published Baptist history textbook and every American Baptist history class for the past several hundred years.

The incident at Lynn, seventy miles from Clarke's home in Newport, Rhode Island, occurred as a result of a pastoral visit by Clarke, Obadiah Holmes, and John Crandall to a fellow church member, William Witter.[41] When the blind, sixty-seven-year-old Witter became a member of the Newport congregation is unknown. The reason for his doing so is clear, for he had run afoul of the Massachusetts authorities on more than one occasion. On 28 February 1643, Witter appeared before the Quarterly

---

[40] Clarke, *Ill Newes*, 1.

[41] It is interesting to note how authors have characterized this visit. William McLoughlin described it as "the invasion from Rhode Island," implying that the visit, whatever the pastoral concerns the Baptists had, was intended to cause a political crisis. Henry Melville King, in the title of one of his books, called it a "summer visit" with an "innocent purpose" but with "painful consequences," suggesting that the visit was not intended to create a political showdown between the Rhode Islanders and the Massachusetts authorities. See William G. McLoughlin, *New England Dissent, 1630–1833: The Baptists and the Separation of Church and State*, 2 vols. (Cambridge MA: Harvard University Press, 1971) 1:19 and *Soul Liberty: The Baptists' Struggle in New England, 1630–1833* (Hanover NH: University Press of New England, 1991) 31. Also see Henry Melville King, *A Summer Visit of Three Rhode Islanders to the Massachusetts Bay in 1651: An Account of the Visit of Dr. John Clarke…: Its Innocent Purpose and Its Painful Consequences* (Providence RI: Preston and Rounds, 1896).

Court at Salem and was charged with speaking offensively about infant baptism. The court ordered him to confess his sin on a lecture day and to ask the pardon of his pastor, Thomas Cobbett.[42] Whether Witter obeyed the court is unknown, but three years later, on 18 February 1646, he was back in court again for disparaging infant baptism, having stated that people "who stayed while a child is baptized does worship the devil."[43] The court ordered him again to confess his error publicly before his congregation or else be reprimanded.[44] The court remained patient with him to see if he would remain "obstinate" or change his ways. Witter apparently remained obstinate because the court records for 24 June 1651 state that his church excommunicated him "for absenting himself from the public ordinances nine months or more and for being re-baptized."[45]

On Saturday evening, 19 July 1651, the three Rhode Island Baptists arrived at Witter's home. The next day, the Baptists held a worship service in the elderly man's home, which was attended by four or five townspeople who showed up unexpectedly. Apparently, "the scent of heresy was marvelously acute" in Massachusetts because informers had notified the magistrate of the Rhode Islanders' presence at Witter's.[46] During the worship service, two constables, "with their clamorous tongues," interrupted Clarke and "uncivilly disturbed" the worshipers. When he asked to see a warrant, one of the constables, "with a trembling hand," which Clarke interpreted as reflecting a guilty conscience, produced it, the substance of which follows: "By virtue hereof, you are required to go to the house of William Witter, and so to search from house to house for certain erroneous persons, being strangers, and them to apprehend, and in safe custody to keep, and to morrow morning by eight of the clock to bring before me, Robert Bridges."[47]

---

[42] Joseph B. Felt, *Ecclesiastical History of New England: Comprising Not Only Religious, But Also Moral, and Other Relations*, 2 vols. (Boston: Congregational Library Association, 1855) 1:482.

[43] Quoted ibid., 1:568

[44] Ibid., 1:569.

[45] Joseph B. Felt, *Ecclesiastical History of New England: Comprising Not Only Religious, But Also Moral, and Other Relations*, 2 vols. (Boston: Congregational Library Association, 1862) 2:46.

[46] King, *A Summer Visit of Three Rhode Islanders*, 47.

[47] Clarke, *Ill Newes*, 28.

Clarke assured the constables that he and the others would go peacefully and then requested to finish the service. The constables refused, took the "erroneous persons" to lunch at a tavern, and then escorted them to a church service being led by Cobbett. Before going to the service, Clarke warned one of the constables that if the Baptists were forced to attend the service, they would be compelled to testify, by word and deed, that they were dissenters. Nevertheless, a constable took them anyway.

As Clarke, Holmes, and Crandall entered the church, the congregation was praying, and after taking off their hats and greeting the worshipers, the Baptists sat down and put their hats back on. Clarke began to read a book, probably his Bible. Observing Clarke's actions, a magistrate, Robert Bridges, ordered the constable to remove the Baptists' hats, which he did. Clarke let his hat lay where it fell and sat quietly during the rest of the service. At the conclusion of the service, he asked to address the congregation, but Bridges refused. Clarke responded by claiming that he did not want to evaluate the service but to explain his actions when he had entered the church. He had not intended to offend anyone; rather, he had intended to emphasize two points. First, the Baptists could not faithfully worship with strangers, and what is not of faith is sin. Second, Clarke had no way of knowing whether the congregants were Christians. Following these explanations, the constable returned the Baptists to the tavern, where they were watched over night like "thieves and robbers."[48]

Clarke recorded that the next day (Monday) the authorities transferred the three Baptists to a Boston jail. However, he might have gotten his days wrong because the authorities apparently permitted the three men to go free on Monday, which allowed them to return to Witter's, where they observed the Lord's Supper and baptized some converts.[49] Then, on Tuesday, 22 July, the authorities transferred Clarke, Holmes, and Crandall to Boston, having charged the men with holding an unlawful worship service, disturbing a church's worship service, alleging that the church at Lynn was not a true church, "seducing and drawing aside of others after their erroneous

---

[48] Ibid., 29–30.

[49] McLoughlin, *New England Dissent*, 1:19–20, n. 24. See also the sentence of the Boston court in Clarke, *Ill Newes*, 32.

judgments and practices, and for suspicion of having their hands in the re-baptizing of one or more" persons.[50]

At their trial on Thursday morning, 31 July, the governor of Massachusetts, John Endicott, examined the Baptists "without producing either accuser, witness, jury, [or] law of God or man." During the examination, Endicott accused Clarke, Holmes, and Crandall of being Anabaptists, denying their own baptisms, and nullifying the worship of the established church. Clarke denied being an Anabaptist and stated that if what he and his companion had testified to was true, then perhaps the governor should examine his own relationship with God, not theirs.[51]

To the surprise of no one, the court found the three Baptists guilty of worshiping illegally at Witter's home, disrespecting the laws and worship of God by keeping their hats on during a worship service, claiming that the established church was not Christian, observing the Lord's Supper with excommunicated persons, lying about not re-baptizing people, and denying the legitimacy of infant baptism. For these crimes the court fined Clarke £20; Holmes, £30; and Crandall, £5. Failure to pay the fines would require that they "be well whipped."[52]

After being sentenced in the afternoon, Clarke informed the court that he and his friends had never been told which laws they had broken. Having appeared at court, having been found guilty, and having been sentenced, Clarke wondered whether they could now learn exactly what laws they had supposedly transgressed. After all, he told Endicott, your laws protect you from being mistreated. Certainly, you would not treat strangers any differently than you yourself would want to be treated. Could it be, Clarke surmised, that no laws have been produced to condemn us because no laws, either God's or man's, exist that would?[53]

Incensed, Endicott declared that the Baptists had denied the legitimacy of baptizing infants, that Clarke "deserved death," and that he would not allow "such trash brought into their jurisdiction." The governor was just getting started: "You go up and down, and secretly insinuate [heresy] into those who are weak, but you cannot maintain it before our ministers." Then

---

[50] Clarke, *Ill Newes*, 30–31.
[51] Ibid., 31.
[52] Ibid., 32.
[53] Ibid., 33.

he appeared to challenge Clarke, stating, "You may try, and discourse or dispute with them."[54] Clarke wanted to respond, but Endicott had him returned to jail.

Whether the governor was sincere about his challenge is unknown, but Clarke jumped at the invitation to debate the colony's ministers. From his cell on 1 August, Clarke wrote to the court, stating that he was available to debate anyone publicly, so why not hold the debate now? Just name the time, place, and person to be debated, Clarke requested, and he would show up. He also requested that he be granted immunity for anything he said during the debate.[55]

The court decided, "after much ado," that a debate should be held in five days. News of the impending event caused "no small stir" among Congregational ministers. However, the magistrates, perhaps desiring not to give Clarke a public forum in which to espouse his heresy and hoping that their problem might return quietly to Rhode Island, rescheduled the debate for two weeks later and requested that Clarke draft a statement of the beliefs he would defend. This statement, which he titled "the testimony of John Clarke, a prisoner of Jesus Christ at Boston, in the behalf of my Lord and of his people," consisted of four "conclusions": (1) Jesus is the anointed Priest, the anointed Prophet, the anointed King, and the Lord; (2) Baptism, "or dipping in water," is one of the Lord's commandments, "and that a visible believer, or disciple of Christ Jesus (that is, one who manifests repentance towards God and faith in Jesus Christ), is the only person that is to be baptized, or dipped"; (3) All believers have the freedom, even the duty, to use their spiritual gifts to edify their congregations; and (4) "No...believer...has any liberty, much less authority from his Lord, to smite his fellow servant...with outward force, or arm of flesh, [or] to constrain or restrain his conscience, [or even] his outward man for conscience sake, or worship of his God."[56]

After some anonymous friends of Clarke paid his fine, the court ordered his release on 11 August; he was free to go home. In a note to the magistrates, Clarke noted that his friends had acted "without my consent and contrary to my judgment." Even so, he still wanted to debate and

---

[54] Ibid.
[55] Ibid., 34.
[56] Ibid., 36–37.

promised to return to Massachusetts "lest the cause should hereby suffer, which I profess is Christ's."[57]

Clarke, however, received a note signed by five magistrates, informing him that he had misunderstood Endicott's comments at his sentencing. The governor had not challenged him to a debate; he had merely informed the prisoner that if he were to debate, any Massachusetts minister would be able to prove him wrong. Nevertheless, the magistrates notified Clarke that if he still wanted a debate, one would be held and he would not be held criminally liable for anything he said.[58] If Clarke had his date correct, he was still in jail on 14 August when he responded to the magistrates. He was confident that he had understood the governor's words correctly at his sentencing, and he was ready to debate.[59]

The debate, however, was never held. Clarke attributed the cancellation to one of two reasons: either the Massachusetts authorities were embarrassed to have their treatment of the Baptists discussed openly, or they feared having their theology and practices judged publicly by arguments from the Bible.[60] With no one to debate, Clarke returned to Rhode Island, confident that, by his words and deeds, he had borne witness to the biblical command that faith "belongs to the Holy Spirit of promise and to the sword of that Spirit, which is the word (not of man, but) of God" and that civil authorities cannot compel people to worship God "contrary to their minds and consciences."[61]

John Crandall (1612–1676) also returned home without being whipped. He had posted bail and returned to his family. Plagued by a guilty conscience for leaving his brethren behind, however, Crandall returned to Massachusetts, but was allowed to return home with Clarke.[62]

Back in Rhode Island, Clark and Crandall continued their ministries. Clarke went with Roger Williams to England for twelve years to secure a charter for Rhode Island. After returning from England in 1664, Clarke pastored his church for eight more years, worked as a physician, served

---

[57] Ibid., 38.
[58] Ibid., 39.
[59] Ibid., 39–40.
[60] Ibid., 40.
[61] Ibid., 41.
[62] Ibid., 42–42.

several years in the colony's general assembly, and was elected three times as
the colony's deputy governor. He died on 20 April 1676. Crandall helped
found the town of Westerly in 1665 and pastored a church there. On 14 and
15 April 1668, he participated in a Baptist-Puritan debate in Boston.[63]
Sometime around 1669 he became a Seventh Day Baptist and continued to
work for the civil and religious liberty for all people. He died in Newport on
29 November 1676.[64]

Obadiah Holmes and His Unforgettable Whipping

Whereas Clarke and Crandall escaped their "well whippings," Obadiah
Holmes (c. 1607–1682) received his and was proud of it. Such a fate would
not have surprised people who knew Holmes, whom one modern historian
described as "a pugnacious man [and] a hot-tempered fault-finder."[65]

Born in northern England near Manchester, Holmes was one of three
sons who attended Oxford University.[66] Whether he graduated from the
university is unknown, but he eventually returned home to earn a living as a
glass worker and a weaver. Despite the influence of his godly parents,
Holmes confessed to caring for "nothing but folly and vanity."[67] After
several years of spiritual struggle, he determined "to avoid the popish relics
of the bishops and that filthy, hellish rabble, and to separate from them and
all those who mentioned them and were fully known in my own country."
Therefore, in 1638 he and Catherine, his wife, braved "the dangers of the

---

[63] For more on this debate, see McLoughlin and Whiting Davidson, "The Baptist
Debate of April 14–15, 1668," 91–133; McLoughlin, *New England Dissent*, 1:61–70;
and McLoughlin, *Soul Liberty*, 37–92.

[64] See Paul E. Crandall, "John Crandall and 17th Century Seventh Day Baptists,"
Baptist History and Heritage 2/2 (July 1967): 114–16, and Don A. Sanford, *A Choosing
People: The History of Seventh Day Baptists* (Nashville: Broadman Press, 1992) 97, 115.

[65] James, *John Clarke and His Legacies*, 44.

[66] For biographical information on Holmes, see Judson Boyce Allen, "Holmes,
Obadiah," in *Encyclopedia of Southern Baptists*, ed. Norman Wade Cox and Judson
Boyce Allen, 2 vols. (Nashville: Broadman Press, 1958) 1:629–30; O. Knott,
"Obadiah Holmes, of Newport, R. I.," *Transactions of the Baptist Historical Society* 5/3
(April 1917): 169–71; and Edwin S. Gaustad, ed., *Baptist Piety: The Last Will &
Testimony of Obadiah Holmes*, Religion and American Culture (Grand Rapids MI:
Christian University Press, 1978; repr., Tuscaloosa: The University of Alabama
Press, 2005).

[67] Obadiah Holmes, "On My Life," in Gaustad, *Baptist Piety*, 73.

seas to come to New England," where they "tried all things in several churches." The Holmeses lived in Salem for approximately six years before moving to Rehoboth in the Plymouth Colony. Yet neither the move from England nor the move to Rehoboth calmed Holmes's troubled soul, for his "spirit was like a wave tossed up and down."[68] He became embroiled in several controversies with the pastor of Rehoboth's church and eventually, along with several others, began worshiping apart from the town's congregation. Holmes finally became convinced that salvation was by grace alone. In 1649 John Clarke and Mark Lucar, a recent immigrant from England, visited the dissident congregation in Rehoboth, and, as a result, Holmes was baptized by immersion.[69]

The spiritual peace Holmes experienced soon gave way to civil strife because "immediately the adversary cast out a flood against us and stirred up the spirits of men."[70] In June, Plymouth's General Court received four petitions (one signed by several citizens of Rehoboth, one by most of the ministers in Plymouth, one by the congregation of a neighboring church, and another by the General Court at Boston) demanding that action be taken against the Holmes group. The Plymouth Court summoned Holmes and two others and ordered them "to desist, and neither to ordain, nor to baptize, nor to break bread together, nor yet to meet on the first day of the week." The men refused to be intimidated, informing the court that "it was better to obey God rather than man," and they continued to practice their faith.[71] In October, Holmes and nine others appeared before the Plymouth Court for violating its previous order. The court's sentence has been lost, but, whatever it was, the Holmes family moved to Newport, Rhode Island, in 1651, where they could worship freely. Shortly after the move, Holmes joined John Clarke and John Crandall on their pastoral visit to William Witter and to their showdown with Massachusetts authorities.

In a letter to London Baptists, which Clarke included in *Ill Newes*, Holmes recounted his sentencing on Thursday, 31 July 1651, and his flogging the following September. After his sentence had been read, Holmes

---

[68] Ibid., 75–76.

[69] Gaustad, *Baptist Piety*, 17–18.

[70] Obadiah Holmes to John Spilsbury, William Kiffin et al., 1651, in Clarke, *Ill Newes*, 46.

[71] Ibid., 46–47.

told his readers, he proclaimed, "I bless God [that] I am counted worthy to suffer for the name of Jesus." At that point, Pastor John Wilson of Boston struck Holmes and shouted, "The curse of God or Jesus go with you." Returned to prison and separated from his two friends, Holmes confessed to being dejected for about an hour, but "then the Lord came in and sweetly relieved" his spirits.[72]

Holmes noted in his letter that friends offered to pay his fine. He acknowledged that he would have accepted "their love to a cup of cold water," but not their money, even though his refusal ensured that he would be flogged.[73] Holmes slept well the night before his punishment, and the following morning friends visited him and offered him wine so that he could endure his whipping. Once again, Holmes refused aid because, he reasoned, if he "had more strength, courage, and boldness than ordinarily could be expected, the world should either say, 'He is drunk with wine,' or else that 'the comfort and strength of the creature has carried him through.'" Taking leave of his friends, Holmes retreated to his cell to pray. The devil tempted him with thoughts of his family, with concerns for his reputation, and with fears that he might be doing this to make a name for himself rather than for God's sake. Holmes, however, refused to yield to the devil's enticements:

> After awhile there was…a voice from heaven in my very soul, bearing witness with my conscience, that it was not for any man's case or sake in this world, that so I had professed and practiced, but for my Lord's case and sake, and for him alone, whereupon my spirit was much refreshed; as also in the consideration of these three scriptures, which speak on this matter: "Who shall lay anything to the charge of God's elect?" [Rom 8:33.] "Although I walk through the valley and shadow of death, I will fear none evil, thy rod and thy staff they shall comfort me" [Ps 23:4]. "And he that continueth to the end, the same shall be saved" [Matt 10:22].[74]

After being assured to his own satisfaction that his motives were pure, Holmes prayed for the strength and courage to endure the excruciating pain that awaited him. When the jailor came for him, Holmes picked up his Bible

---

[72] Ibid., 47.

[73] Ibid.

[74] Ibid., 48.

and went confidently to his punishment, where he would receive his unforgettable whipping.

While waiting to be whipped, Holmes asked to say a few words to the crowd that had gathered to witness Massachusetts justice in all of its bloody glory. Encrease Nowell, a magistrate standing next to Holmes, refused, but Holmes spoke anyway, challenging anyone to a debate. I am no debater, he told the spectators, but as I am about to shed my blood for what I believe, "I am ready to defend it by the Word, and to dispute that point with any who shall come forth to withstand it." Nowell told him that this was no time to debate, but when Holmes proclaimed, "I am to suffer for...the Word of God and testimony of Jesus Christ," Nowell retorted, "No, it is for your error and going about to seduce the people."[75] The debate was on. What error? Holmes asked. No minister visited me in prison in order to convince me of my supposed errors. And what about that public debate the governor had promised to have? Holmes received no reply and continued speaking as the executioner ripped off his clothes. "I have now come to be baptized in afflictions by your hands," Holmes proclaimed, "so that I may have further fellowship with my Lord." The executioner then lashed him thirty times with a three-corded whip, one lash for every pound he was fined.[76]

When the bloody spectacle was over, and after Holmes was loosed from the whipping post, he uttered his famous words: "You have struck me as with roses.... Although the Lord has made it easy to me, yet I pray to God [that] it may not be laid to your charge." Several people rushed to his aid, two of whom were arrested for shaking his hand.[77]

After receiving aid from a friend, Holmes left Boston, but, he proudly noted, not before "some submitted to the Lord and were baptized, and many were put upon the way of inquiry."[78] As a result, warrants were issued for his arrest, but Holmes, whipped in body but not in spirit, returned triumphantly to Rhode Island, where his friends and family were waiting four miles outside of Newport, and there they "rejoiced in the Lord."[79]

---

[75] Ibid., 49.

[76] Ibid., 50.

[77] Ibid., 51. The two were John Spur and John Hazel. See Clarke, *Ill Newes*, 55–62.

[78] Holmes to Spilsbury, Kiffin et al., 1651, 51–52.

[79] Ibid., 52.

During the next several years, Holmes served as pastor of the Newport church while Clarke was in England and then again after Clarke's death in 1676. In his last will and testament, dated 20 December 1675, Holmes discussed thirty-five articles that constituted his faith. Immediately after this discussion, he referred to that unforgettable whipping he had received twenty-four years earlier: "For this faith and profession I stand and have sealed the same with my blood at Boston in New England."[80] Holmes died on 15 October 1682.

The Spin on the Incident at Lynn

News, particularly ill news, travels fast. Soon after Clarke, Holmes, and Crandall received their sentences at Boston, Roger Williams noted in a letter to Governor John Winthrop, Jr., of Connecticut that he had heard about the sentences and the proposed debate between Clarke and representatives of the Massachusetts Congregational church.[81] In another letter to Winthrop shortly thereafter, Williams informed the governor, "I met Mr. John Clarke at Providence," who had just been released from prison. "There was great hammering about the disputation, but they could not hit. And although (my much lamented friend)...Governor [Endicott] told" Clarke "that he was worthy to be hanged, etc., yet he [Clarke] was as good as thrust out without pay, or whipping, etc. But Obadiah Holmes remains."[82]

With Holmes still in prison awaiting his whipping, Williams wasted no time in writing Endicott a scathing letter, chastising him and the other magistrates for involving themselves "in matters of conscience and religion" and for "persecuting and hunting any[one] for any matter merely spiritual and religious."[83] Endicott, Williams reminded his friend, "the Maker and

---

[80] Obadiah Holmes, "Of My Faith," in Gaustad, *Baptist Piety*, 91.

[81] Roger Williams to John Winthrop, Jr., ca. early August 1651, in *The Correspondence of Roger Williams*, 1:332–33.

[82] Roger Williams to John Winthrop, Jr., ca. late August 1651, in *The Correspondence of Roger Williams*, 1:336.

[83] Roger Williams to Governor John Endicott, ca. August–September 1651, in *The Correspondence of Roger Williams*, 1:339. This letter can also be found in Roger Williams, *The Bloody Tenent yet More Bloody*, by Roger Williams (London: printed for Giles Calvert, 1652) 303–13, and a modernized version in Perry Miller, *Roger*

Searcher of our hearts knows with what bitterness I write, as with bitterness of soul I have heard" all the arguments justifying persecution "from yourself and others, who formerly have fled from (with crying out against) persecutors!" You belittle the experiences of people who have been persecuted for their consciences, telling them, "'you are conventiclers, heretics, blasphemers, seducers. You deserve to be hanged.'" Governor, you rail at them, shouting that you want to rid the colony of every heretic and that you would rather have "'many whores and whoremongers and thieves'" live in your midst.[84]

Pause for a moment, Endicott, from your persecuting ways and listen, Williams suggested. If you listen closely, you will hear a voice, the "dreadful voice from the King of kings, the Lord of lords, [saying], 'Endicott, Endicott, why huntest thou me? Why imprisonest me? Why finest, why so bloodily whippest, why wouldst thou (did not I hold your bloody hands) hang and burn me?'" Ask yourself, governor, as you go about your heretic hunting, "'Is it possible...that since I hunt, I hunt not the life of my Savior and the blood of the Lamb of God? I have fought against many several sorts of consciences. Is it beyond all possibility and hazard that I have not fought against God, that I have not persecuted Jesus in some of them?'"[85] You and others have declared that "heretics, blasphemers, [and] seducers ought to be" executed.[86] Well, here is what I say: it is "impossible for any man or men to maintain their Christ by the sword and to worship a true Christ!—to fight against all conscience opposite to theirs, and not to fight against God in some of them, and to hunt after the precious life of the true Lord Jesus Christ."[87]

Williams: His Contribution to the American Tradition, Makers of the American Tradition (Indianapolis IN: The Bobbs-Merrill Company, Inc., 1953) 158–64.

[84] Williams to Endicott, ca. August–September 1651, in *The Correspondence of Roger Williams*, 1:343.

[85] Ibid., 1:344. In asking Endicott to listen and to reflect, Williams was alluding to two passages from the New Testament: Acts 9:4–5 and Matthew 25:41–46.

[86] Ibid., 1:345. According to Clarke, Endicott said this at the Rhode Island Baptists' trial, and according to John Spur, John Cotton, in a sermon prior to their sentencing, denounced them as "soul-murderers" who deserved death. See Clarke, *Ill Newes*, 33, 56.

[87] Williams to Endicott, 1:344–45.

Endicott and other Massachusetts authorities were well accustomed to Williams's outbursts of "heresy" and probably did not give his opinions much thought. However, when Clarke published in England his account of the incident at Lynn and its aftermath, he guaranteed that the persecution of the three Newport Baptists and, perhaps more importantly, the whipping of Holmes would never be forgotten. No longer was the ill news concerning that persecution merely known locally; it had become known internationally.

After hearing or reading about the incident, Richard Saltonstall shot off a letter to the two Boston pastors, John Cotton and John Wilson. A former Massachusetts magistrate who had returned to London, Saltonstall rebuked the two ministers for their "tyranny and persecutions in New England." He chastised the ministers for forcing people to attend worship services against their consciences and then threatening to punish them if they objected. All this does, Saltonstall maintained, is make hypocrites who conform to your ways because they fear being punished. I pray that you would stop committing those acts there "in a wilderness, which you went so far to prevent."[88] But I am not the only one praying for you, Saltonstall informed Cotton and Wilson, for many people "in the public assemblies" are praying "that the Lord would give you meek and humble spirits, [so that you will] not...strive so much for uniformity as to keep the unity of spirit in the bond of peace." I hope that you do not consider yourselves to be infallible judges of people, for even "the most learned of the apostles confessed he knew but in part and saw but darkly as through a glass."[89]

Whether Governor Endicott replied to Williams's rebuke is unknown. Cotton, however, responded to Saltonstall's chastisement, informing the former Massachusetts magistrate that he could see quite clearly and that he did not consider himself infallible. After explaining to Saltonstall that he and Wilson had no part in forcing the Newport Baptists to attend the Lynn church or in determining their punishment, Cotton then justified the punishments levied against them. No one forced Holmes, "an excommunicate person," to visit Massachusetts and to re-baptize Christians. He knew well that such acts violated the colony's laws, which were based on

---

[88] Richard Saltonstall to John Cotton and John Wilson, c. 1652, in *A Collection of Original Papers Relative to the History of the Colony of Massachusets-Bay*, ed. Thomas Hutchinson (Boston: printed by Thomas and John Fleet, 1769) 401.

[89] Ibid., 402. See 1 Corinthians 13:12.

God's law. Therefore, no one can fault Massachusetts for whipping him, Cotton reasoned, because "it was more voluntarily chosen by him than inflicted on him." Like Clarke, Holmes could have accepted his friends' offer to pay his fine, "but he chose rather to be whipped." Besides, Cotton sarcastically noted, we actually did the Baptists a favor by jailing them because "I believe they fared neither of them better at home, and I am sure that Holmes had not been so well clad of many years before."[90] As for Saltonstall's rebuke that forcing people to attend worship services produces hypocrites, so what? It is better to be a hypocrite than a profane person, for at least "hypocrites give God part of his due, the outward man, but the profane person gives God neither outward nor inward man."[91]

Much could be written about Cotton's justification of forcing people to worship against their consciences and of Holmes's whipping. However, Joseph Ivimey's comment is sufficient: "We have happily arrived at the period when arguments are not necessary to prove the absurdity of this reasoning."[92]

Another response to the incident at Lynn came from Thomas Cobbett, pastor of the Lynn church, who, after receiving a copy of Clarke's book, responded with *A Brief Answer to a Certain Slanderous Pamphlet Called* Ill News from New-England. The title summarizes succinctly Cobbett's spin on the whole affair. As a participant in the incident, Cobbett had an even greater stake than did Cotton in defending Massachusetts's actions against the Baptists.

---

[90] John Cotton to Richard Saltonstall, c. 1652, in *A Collection of Original Papers Relative to the History of the Colony of Massachusets-Bay*, 404.

[91] Ibid., 405. Cotton often defended the punishing of heretics. Around 1635 he received a copy of John Murton's *A Most Humble Supplication*, against which Cotton wrote *The Controversie Concerning Liberty of Conscience in Matters of Religion, Truly Stated, and Distinctly and Plainly Handled,...By Way of Answer to Some Arguments to the Contrary Sent unto Him* (London: printed for Thomas Banks, 1646). Whereas Murton proudly (but incorrectly) claimed Martin Luther as a champion of religious liberty, Cotton proudly (but, unfortunately, correctly) cited John Calvin, "who procured the death of Michael Servetus for pertinacity in heresy and defended his fact by a book written of that argument." See Colton, *The Controversie*, 14.

[92] Joseph Ivimey, *A History of English Baptists*, 4 vols. (London: printed for the author, 1811) 1:216.

Civil magistrates, Cobbett contended, have the authority and the responsibility to punish people who violate the two tables of the Ten Commandments. Such punishment originates not from a vindictive heart but from a loving one. "Is it not," Cobbett asked his readers, "...an act of love in civil or church rulers, ruling according to God,...seasonably to restrain and punish others under their charge, for transgressing the laws and rules of God, civilly or ecclesiastically?"[93] Indeed, it is because godly magistrates always punish violators for "their best welfare."[94]

Moreover, Cobbett reasoned, true saints of God, those who pray for the coming of God's kingdom and who yearn to lead a godly life, will welcome being corrected if they begin to lead a life displeasing to God. Therefore, "the saints, willed by a right-guided will, [will desire] their own corporal punishment by others for their own erroneous corruptions in religion."[95] Thus, the Massachusetts civil and ecclesiastical authorities, true saints that they were, only did to the Baptists what they would have wanted done to themselves, thereby fulfilling Jesus' command to treat others as they want to be treated (Matt 7:12).

When Cobbett moved from justifying the punishment of heretics to speaking about the character of the heretics, he had nothing good to say. Clarke, according to the Puritan pastor, was a hypocrite for dedicating his "scandalous pamphlet" to Parliament and the Council of State (a group that directed domestic and foreign policy) while, at the same time, decrying the use of civil power (the "sword of steel") in deciding religious matters.[96] Yet, Cobbett asked, how did Parliament and Cromwell, Clarke's heroes, "condemn and damn episcopal government in the church and all their trash?"[97] They did so by using the "sword of steel" in the same manner for which Clarke condemned the Massachusetts authorities.

---

[93] Thomas Cobbet, *A Brief Answer to a Certain Slanderous Pamphlet Called Ill News from New-England...By John Clark of Road-Island, Physician*, in *The Civil Magistrates Power in Matters of Religion Modestly Debated, Impartially Stated according to the Bounds and Grounds of Scripture*,...(London: printed by W. Wilson for Stephens, 1653; repr., New York: Arno Press, 1972) 9. The pagination starts over with *A Brief Answer*.

[94] Ibid., 10.

[95] Ibid., 14.

[96] See Clarke, *Ill Newes*, [3]–9.

[97] Cobbet, *A Brief Answer*, 25.

Clarke, asserted Cobbett, was not only a hypocrite; he was also a liar and a coward. He falsely claimed that, at his sentencing, Governor Endicott offered to hold a public debate. According to Cobbett, Endicott made no such offer at the sentencing, as the governor and four other magistrates made clear in their 11 August letter to Clarke.[98] In that same letter, however, the magistrates did accept Clarke's offer to debate publicly, yet he placed so many conditions on the debate that Cobbett could only conclude that the Rhode Island heretic, not the Massachusetts authorities, was the one who feared having the debate.[99]

Obadiah Holmes did not fare any better than Clarke. In Cobbett's opinion, Holmes also was a liar, for in his letter to London Baptists he accused Pastor Wilson of striking and cursing him. Wilson never struck Holmes, Cobbett countered; he merely "laid his hand softly and gently upon Holmes's shoulder as he passed by [and]...said this, 'You go away under the curse of the Lord'" because Holmes "was an excommunicated person."[100]

As for Holmes's whipping, Cobbett, like Cotton, also put the blame for that squarely on the criminal's back. The Puritan pastor emphasized that the Massachusetts court had given Holmes a clear choice: he could either pay his fine "OR ELSE...be well whipped."[101] Cobbett surmised that Holmes freely chose the "or else" because he wanted to make a name for himself and to shed his blood for his cause.[102]

To many observers, the justification of the civil magistrates' punishment of the Rhode Island Baptists smacks of hypocrisy because Cobbett and other Puritans had come to New England to escape being persecuted for their religious beliefs. In fact, during a debate with Baptists on 14 April 1668 in Boston, Cobbett stated he that he and other Puritans "came over here [New England] for liberty of conscience."[103] After all, they could not, in good conscience, worship according to the *Book of Common Prayer* and accept all of the tenets of the Church of England. Of course, the Rhode Island Baptists had demanded the same liberty; they wanted the

---

[98] Ibid., 29. See Clarke, *Ill Newes*, 39, for the text of this letter.

[99] Cobbet, *A Brief Answer*, 30–32.

[100] Ibid., 33.

[101] Ibid., 42.

[102] Ibid., 41.

[103] McLoughlin and Davidson, "The Baptist Debate of April 14–15, 1668," 118.

liberty to worship God according their consciences in Newport, in Witter's home, or wherever they chose.

Thus, were Puritans hypocrites for demanding liberty of conscience while denying it to others? Not according to Gaustad and Schmidt:

> The Puritans came to create a pure church and to conduct a holy experiment free of opposition, distraction, and error. They were not hypocrites who demanded freedom of religion then denied that same freedom to others. Freedom of religion across the board was never the plan, never the commission or errand. They came to prove that one could form a society so faithful, a church so cleansed, that even old England itself would be transformed by witnessing what determined believers had managed to achieve many thousands of miles away. That was the vision to be steadily pursued, without weakening or wavering, without transgressing or backsliding, without ever forgetting the awesome obligations of a covenant with God.[104]

Therefore, in Cobbett's opinion, far from being hypocritical, Massachusetts authorities had acted with integrity. Everyone knew, including the Rhode Island Baptists, that Massachusetts had always punished and would continue to punish heretics. Had they let the Baptists go unpunished, then the Massachusetts authorities would have been hypocrites who would have deserved the wrath of God.

But why did the Massachusetts magistrates insist on whipping Holmes? Was it sincerely out of a loving concern for a wayward brother? If it was, why then did the Massachusetts magistrates not fulfill the "or else" in the case of Holmes's friend John Hazell? After Holmes's flogging, Hazell shook his friend's hand, for which he was arrested immediately and ordered to "pay 40 shillings or be well whipped." He refused to pay the fine, which meant that, like Holmes, he should have been whipped. Yet, after languishing in jail for five days, Hazell was told to go home.[105] Why, it could be asked, did the magistrates insist on fulfilling the "or else" of Holmes's sentence but not of Hazell's? The answer to this question is probably this: believing that the Plymouth Colony earlier had failed to punish Holmes adequately in 1649

---

[104] Gaustad and Schmidt, *The Religious History of America*, 54.
[105] See Clarke, *Ill Newes*, 59–62.

after he and several others began worshiping on their own, the Massachusetts authorities whipped him in 1651 because they wanted him whipped. Moreover, they wanted to send a message to anyone who even considered advocating religious beliefs contrary to those held by Congregationalist Puritans. Such a message, the authorities hoped, would end any discussion of Baptists beliefs among Massachusetts citizens. Holmes's whipping, however, did not stop the discussion. As Sydney James observed, "The [Holmes] episode probably did not achieve what the magistrates intended: the public whipping called attention to the ideas it was meant to suppress."[106] Indeed, in 1653 President Henry Dunster of Harvard College, perhaps as a result of Holmes's flogging, refused to have his infant son baptized, thereby continuing the public discussion of the legitimacy of infant baptism that the Massachusetts authorities wanted to suppress.[107]

Martha Kimball and Her Taxing Experience

Despite their legal and ecclesiastical efforts at preventing the cancerous presence of Baptists from taking root in their colony, the Massachusetts authorities ultimately failed. In 1655 Thomas Goold (Gould), a friend of Henry Dunster, refused to have his second child baptized. His church in Charlestown censured him and excluded him from its fellowship. In 1663 Goold began holding private religious meetings, which, in 1665, led to the formation in Boston of the first Baptist church in Massachusetts.[108]

Even with the advent of Baptist churches in Massachusetts, Congregationalism remained strong, but the Puritan authorities eventually had to loosen their grip on the religious lives of their citizens. Fearing the loss of its charter under King Charles II, Massachusetts finally relented in 1682 to allow Boston Baptists to worship freely, although the colony continued taxing its citizens to support the Congregational churches and their ministers. In 1723, however, King George I ordered Massachusetts to

---

[106] James, *John Clarke and His Legacies*, 48.

[107] See Henry S. Burrage, *A History of the Baptists in New England* (Philadelphia: American Baptist Publication Society, 1894) 38; McLoughlin, *Soul Liberty*, 32–34; and David Porter, "The Baptist Struggle for Religious Freedom in the Massachusetts Bay Colony, 1650–1670," *Foundations* 14/1 (January–March 1971): 26–28.

[108] Durso and Durso, *The Story of Baptists in the United States*, 34; Bill Leonard, *Baptist Ways: A History* (Valley Forge PA: Judson Press, 2003) 79–80.

stop forcing dissenters to support Congregationalism, and five years later the colony exempted Anglicans, Quakers, and Baptists from religious taxes.[109] Members of these groups could obtain a certificate signed by their ministers stating that they attended regularly and contributed financially to their church.[110]

When a new group of Baptists called Separate Baptists formed in the mid-1700s in Massachusetts during the revival known as the First Great Awakening, authorities claimed that these Baptists, who were more revivalistic than other Massachusetts Baptists, were not exempt from paying religious taxes. Separates, however, claimed the exemption and were often punished for being "tax dodgers."[111]

Even possessing an exemption certificate, however, did not prevent some Separate Baptists from being forced to pay religious taxes. For example, in 1774 Martha Kimball, a member of a Baptist church in Haverville, Massachusetts, wrote to Isaac Backus, a Baptist minister in Middleborough, describing her arrest for not paying her religious taxes. Kimball, who described herself as "a poor widow woman," contacted Backus because she knew that he was preparing a history of Baptists in New England, and she wanted "to let the public know how the Baptists have been oppressed in Massachusetts Bay." She described for Backus how on a cold, winter night in 1768, the town's tax collector arrested her, forcing her to leave three small children at home. Before taking her to a jail several hours away, the collector stopped at a tavern where Kimball was "advised" to pay the "ministerial rate." She refused to pay it, she said, "because I was a Baptist, and belonged to the Baptist society in Haverhill, and had carried...a certificate to the assessors,...according to [the] law." After reluctantly paying the tax, she returned to her "poor fatherless children through the snow, on foot, in the dead of the night, exposed to the severity of the cold."[112]

---

[109] McLoughlin, *Soul Liberty*, 5.

[110] Ibid., 252.

[111] Ibid., 164. For example, Esther White, a member of Backus's Middleborough church, spent thirteen months in jail for refusing to pay her religious taxes. See Pam Durso, "Baptist Women in America, 1638–1800," in *Distinctively Baptist: Essays on Baptist History: A Festschrift in Honor of Walter B. Shurden*, ed. by Marc A. Jolley with John D. Pierce (Macon GA: Mercer University Press, 2005) 215–16.

[112] Martha Kimball to Isaac Backus, 2 September 1774, in *A History of New England*, 2:145, n. 1. See also Durso, "Baptist Women in America, 1638–1800," 216.

The case of Martha Kimball shows that Congregationalism, despite being forced to tolerate some dissenters, still attempted to cling to its privileged position in Massachusetts, a position that was not legally eliminated until 1833. Dissenters like Kimball, who obeyed the law requiring the acquisition of certificate of tax exemption, remained at the mercy of Massachusetts authorities, who often deemed it their privilege to decide who were real Baptists, and therefore exempt from religious taxation, and who were not real Baptists, and therefore required to pay religious taxes.

In 1768 Kimball was in a vulnerable position, making her a prime target for men who deemed it necessary to persecute a widow and single mother in order to maintain the ministries of Congregational churches. She could not afford to leave her three children to fend for themselves during the harsh winter. In her case, intimidation worked, and whether it worked in other cases is unknown. Despite Kimball's frightening experience, the persecution of Massachusetts Baptists was declining in 1768; however, the persecution of Baptists was just beginning to become more violent in the southern colony of Virginia.

Chapter 8

Prison Pulpits

Englishmen first set foot in what is now Virginia near the end of April 1607. They named their first permanent settlement, Jamestown, for King James I, and their colony, Virginia, for the "virgin queen," Elizabeth I. Among the colonists' reasons for coming to the New World, foremost was their desire to spread the gospel. The Royal Charter of Virginia stated that the whole "adventure was to be carried on only 'by the providence of God,' and the propagation of the Christian religion to those who 'as yet live in darkness and miserable ignorance of the true knowledge and worship of God.'"[1] To that end the colony established the Church of England as the foundation of this new society.

The Establishment of the Church of England in Virginia

The Church of England officially became Virginia's established church in 1619. The colony's legislature created parishes, set apart glebe lands (lands used to raise crops to pay clergy and support the church), and promised to support Anglican ministers financially. With the English church officially established, the colony required that all clergymen arriving in Virginia present their Anglican credentials to the governor.[2]

---

[1] Edwin Gaustad and Leigh Schmidt, *The Religious History of America: The Heart of the American Story from Colonial Time to Today*, rev. ed. (San Francisco: HarperSanFrancisco, 2002) 37. See also Sanford H. Cobb, *The Rise of Religious Liberty in America: A History* (New York: Macmillan, 1902) 74–75. Available online at http://www.dinsdoc.com/cobb-1-0a.htm. The text of the charter can be found in William Waller Hening, *The Statutes at Large: Being a Collection of All the Laws of Virginia, from the First Session of the Legislature in the year 1619*, 13 vols. (Philadelphia: printed for the auther by Thomas Desilver, 1823) 3:58–66. Available online http://vagenweb.rootsweb.com/hening/.

[2] Gaustad and Schmidt, *The Religious History of America*, 38–39.

To help ensure that Virginians received their weekly dose of religion, the legislature passed a law in April 1699 penalizing all persons over twenty-one years old who absented themselves from "their parish church or chapel once in two months to hear divine service upon the Sabbath day."[3] Absentees were to be fined five shillings or fifty pounds of tobacco. People could avoid the fine if they could prove that they had good reasons for being absent, or if they could prove that, being dissenters, they were exempted under the English Act of Toleration, which had been passed in 1689.[4] In October 1705 the legislature reduced the allowable time for absence to one month and, perhaps to close a loophole in the law, added that congregants must remain "in a decent and orderly manner" until the end of the worship service.[5] Also in 1705 the legislature further entrenched the Anglican Church in Virginia by passing several laws that criminalized denials of monotheism, the Trinity, the existence of God, the truth of Christianity, and the authority of the Bible. A second offense for any of these crimes carried a three-year prison sentence.[6]

In passing such laws, colonial Virginians were doing nothing new; they were merely replicating what they had learned and lived with back in England. Thus, just as all English men and women were expected to be Anglicans, so too all Virginians were expected to be Anglicans. According to Richard Hooker, an Anglican priest and theologian during the reign of Elizabeth I, "We hold that...there is not any man of the Church of England but the same man is also a member of the commonwealth; nor any man a member of the commonwealth, who is not also of the Church of England."[7]

---

[3] Hening, *The Statutes at Large*, 3:170.

[4] Ibid., 3:171.

[5] Ibid., 3:360. For an example of Baptists receiving the exemption to this law, see Lewis Peyton Little, *Imprisoned Preachers and Religious Liberty in Virginia: A Narrative Drawn Largely from the Official Records of Virginia Counties, Unpublished Manuscripts, Letters, and Other Original Sources* (Lynchburg VA: J. P. Bell Co., Inc., 1938) 92.

[6] Hening, *The Statutes at Large*, 3:358–59.

[7] Richard Hooker, *The Laws of Ecclesiastical Polity*, in *The Works of that Learned and Judicious Divine Mr. Richard Hooker with an Account of His Life and Death by Isaac Walton*, 7th ed., 3 vols. (Oxford: Clarendon Press, 1888) 3:330. Available online at http://oll.libertyfund.org/Intros/Hooker.php. See also Thomas E. Buckley, "Keeping Faith: Virginia Baptists and Religious Liberty," *American Baptist Quarterly* 22/4 (December 2003): 423.

The Act of Toleration made such an assumption more difficult to enforce, but Virginia authorities and ministers did their best to ensure that anyone who attempted to undermine the authority of the Church of England, or who did not follow the letter of law concerning religion, paid a heavy price.

The Persecution of Virginia Baptists

Baptists began entering Virginia in the late seventeenth century and settled in the southeastern part of the colony. By 1699 Thomas Bonger, a General Baptist preacher, was holding meetings, and three years later these Baptists began requesting that the Baptist General Assembly in England send ministers. Not until 1714, however, did a minister arrive, after which the Baptists constituted a church across the James River from Jamestown. A group of Maryland Baptists, comprised mostly of Particular, or Regular, Baptists settled in the northwest part of the colony in 1743. In the 1760s, Separate Baptists from New England began entering the colony.[8]

As Baptists began arriving in Virginia, most people paid little attention to them because, according to Robert Semple, a pastor and an early Virginia Baptist historian, "they were viewed, by men in power, as beneath their notice. None, said they, but the weak and wicked join them; let them alone, they will soon fall out among themselves and come to nothing."[9] Left to themselves, though, the number of Baptists began to increase, forcing people in power to take notice of them. As they and other dissenting groups increased, Baptists started beating "against that stout wall that surrounded and protected the Anglican Church."[10] However, with the help of local magistrates, Anglicans beat back.

Although all Baptist groups suffered some abuse, the General Baptists died out several years after their beginning in Virginia, thereby escaping the widespread persecution that began in earnest in the 1760s. Most Particular Baptists attempted to obey the laws passed by the Virginia legislature, which

---

[8] Reuben Edward Alley, *A History of Baptists in Virginia* (Richmond: Virginia Baptist General Board, [1973]) 18–19; H. Leon McBeth, *The Baptist Heritage: Four Centuries of Baptist Witness* (Nashville: Broadman Press, 1987) 221.

[9] Robert B. Semple, *History of the Rise and Progress of the Baptists in Virginia*, rev. and exp. by G. W. Beale (Richmond: Pitt & Dickinson, Publishers, 1894) 24–25. Hereafter cited as Semple, *History* (1894).

[10] Gaustad and Schmidt, *The Religious History of America*, 47.

spared most of them from abuse. Separates, however, suffered the most, for they interpreted Virginia laws in ways that led to their persecution. Several social, religious, and civil factors contributed to their persecution.[11]

Socially, many Baptists were poor and uneducated. Thus, most Virginians considered them to be an "ignorant illiterate set—and of the poor and contemptible class of people."[12] Even William Fristoe, a Virginia Baptist pastor in the mid-eighteenth to the early-nineteenth centuries, admitted, "In a general way, those among us who have been wrought upon under the preaching of the gospel, and professed conversion to Christ, have been of the mediocrity, or poorer sort among the people." But that fact did not embarrass Baptists; rather, it helped assure them of the legitimacy of their religious experience. As Fristoe observed, "We have been encouraged to believe that it gave clearer proof the genuine quality of religion among us—for in times of the promulgation of the gospel it was the common people that heard the truth preached with gladness."[13]

Perhaps worse, in the minds of Virginians, than Baptists being made up of a bunch of uneducated and uncouth, poor white folk, was their success in converting slaves to the Baptist way. Baptists even called their converted slaves "brothers" and "sisters."[14] Slaves caught worshiping with Baptists at their outdoor meetings were often treated harshly. A visitor to one such meeting observed with horror as persecutors unleashed their fury on the black congregants: "as the congregation was very large, amongst them there were abundance of Negroes[;] the patrollers were let loose upon them, being urged thereto by the enemies and opposers of religion. Never having seen

---

[11] See Wesley M. Gewehr, *The Great Awakening in Virginia, 1740–1790* (Durham NC: Duke University Press, 1930) 128–33; Buckley, "Keeping Faith," 424–25; and William Fristoe, *The History of the Ketocton Baptist Association, 1766–1808* (Staunton VA: William Gilman Lyford, 1808) 62–85. These pages from Friscoe can be found at http://www.geocities.com/baptist_documents/persecution.va.index.html.

[12] Fristoe, *The History of the Ketocton Baptist Association*, 64.

[13] Ibid., 148. See also John Leland, "The Virginia Chronicle," in *The Writings of the Late Elder John Leland, Including Some Events in His Life, Written by Himself, with Additional Sketches*, ed. L. F. Greene (New York: G. W. Wood, 1845; repr., Gallatin TN: Church History Research and Archives, 1986) 105, and David Thomas, *The Virginian Baptist* (Baltimore: printed by Enoch Story, 1774) 54–55.

[14] Rhys Isaac, *The Transformation of Virginia, 1740–1790* (Chapel Hill: Published for the Institute of Early American History and Culture, Williamsburg, Virginia, by the University of North Carolina Press, 1982; repr., 1999) 171.

such a circumstance before, I was equally struck with astonishment and surprise, to see the poor Negroes flying in every direction, the patrollers seizing and whipping them, while others were carrying them off prisoners, in order, perhaps, to subject them to a more severe punishment."[15] These patrols consisted of "a mounted highway guard that arrested and punished Negroes found away from their homes without written passes from their owners."[16] Undoubtedly, the raucous atmosphere of the Separate Baptist meetings and the knowledge that Baptists aggressively evangelized slaves helped the patrollers find their prey.

Along with the social factors that contributed to Baptists being despised by their Virginia neighbors was the way in which Separates expressed their religion. Their preaching styles and worship services scandalized Anglicans, and even some Particular Baptists, who preferred a more subdued worship experience. Separate worship services were anything but subdued. Their ministers often wept as they preached, and the sound of their voices, rising and falling, shouting and whispering, has been described as a "holy whine."[17] Preachers used this tone, particularly during their outdoor meetings, to relieve the strain on their voices.

The passion with which Separate ministers preached was contagious, and their services were characterized by an outpouring of emotions. John Leland, a Virginia Baptist minister from 1776 to 1792, noted that "the work among" Separatists "was very noisy." Congregants "would cry out, 'fall down,' and, for a time, lose the use of their limbs, which exercise made the bystanders marvel; some thought they were deceitful, others, that they were

---

[15] James Ireland, *The Life of The Rev. James Ireland* (1819 ed.), in *Esteemed Reproach: The Lives of Reverend James Ireland and Reverend Joseph Craig*, ed., Keith Harper and C. Martin Jacumin (Macon GA: Mercer University Press, 2005) 103–104.

[16] Garnett Ryland, *The Baptists of Virginia: 1699–1926* (Richmond: The Virginia Baptist Board of Missions and Education, 1955) 57, n. 73.

[17] John A. Broadus, "American Baptist Ministry of 100 Years Ago," *Baptist Quarterly* 9/1 (January 1875): 18–19; Gewehr, *The Great Awakening in Virginia*, 114; Semple, *History* (1894), 15; John S. Moore, "The Baptist March across Virginia," *Virginia Baptist Register* 18 (1979): 880.

bewitched, and many being convinced of all, would report that God was with them of a truth."[18]

As Baptists worshiped, their ministers preached on the depravity of humanity, the necessity of experiencing the "new birth," and the evils of infant baptism. Naturally, Separates only baptized believers. Such a practice defied a December 1662 Virginia law that called for punishing people who refused to have their children baptized by fining them 2,000 pounds of tobacco. Although the Act of Toleration superseded this law, Baptists, by insisting on believer's baptism, proved to most Virginians that they were, in the words of the 1662 law, "schismatical persons" who, "out of their averseness to the orthodox established religion, or out of the new fangled conceits of their own heretical inventions," continued to threaten the existence of the established church of Virginia and even of the colony itself.[19]

Not content to keep their religion to themselves or confine their passion to their worship services on Sundays, Separate Baptists practiced what many considered to be a confrontational religion. Their evangelistic zeal led them to witness to their faith in their workplaces, in homes, in stores, and even to their slaves. For Virginians who had been baptized as infants, such aggressiveness was demeaning, paternalistic, and contemptible.

Baptists attacked not only the religion of the Church of England but also the character and preaching of its ministers. In a letter to Nathaniel Saunders, a Baptist pastor in Orange County, William Green, an Anglican minister, commented on a heated confrontation between members of Saunders's congregation and those of the county's established church. Green had been informed "that some of your sect were the aggressors, by abusing the minister of this parish, and uttering many indecent and scandalous invectives and reflections against the [Anglican] Church and its

---

[18] John Leland, "The Virginia Chronicle," 105. See also Thomas, *The Virginian Baptist*, 63. Charles Woodmason, an itinerant Anglican minister in North Carolina, also lamented the boisterous worship of North Carolina Baptists. See Richard J. Hooker, ed., *The Carolina Backcountry on the Eve of the Revolution: The Journal and Other Writings of Charles Woodmason, Anglican Itinerant* (Chapel Hill: The University of North Carolina Press, 1953) 101–102.

[19] Hening, *The Statutes at Large*, 1:165–66.

members."[20] Green remarked that if the information he had received was true, "worse could not be said of the pagans and idolaters, who sacrificed their children to Moloch, than has been said by some of your society, concerning the church and its members; the ministers not excepted."[21]

Leland noted that Anglican clergymen saw nothing wrong with spending time on worldly amusements, and he described their preaching as "dry and barren, containing little else but morality."[22] Despite their sermonizing about morality, the established ministers, according to Semple, were best known for their "loose and immoral deportment,"[23] and Baptists used their moral shortcomings against them and their church.

The Baptists' attitude toward Anglican ministers was not merely the biased evaluation of disgruntled dissenters. Virginia governors and bishops often lamented both the poor quality and the immorality of ministers sent to the colony.[24] In 1705 even the Virginia legislature had to address the immorality of some clergymen. In "an act for the effectual suppression of vice, and restraint and punishment of blasphemous, wicked, and dissolute persons," legislatures felt compelled to inform Virginians that nothing contained in the act "shall be construed to exempt any clergyman within this colony, who shall be guilty of any of the crimes herein before-mentioned."[25] As Sanford Cobb observed, "To suppose that the moral character of the clergy did not give reason for that provision, changes the statue into a monstrous and gratuitous insult to the [established] church and its ministry,—an impossible thing for a legislature with reverence for the [Anglican] Church and its orders."[26] Thus, many Baptists, despite being

---

[20] William Green to Nathaniel Saunders, 7 February 1767, in *Imprisoned Preachers*, 78.

[21] Ibid., 80–81. Moloch (Molech) was the national god of the Ammonites, to whom adherents sacrificed their children. See Leviticus 18:21; 20:2–5; 1 Kings 11:7; 2 Kings 23:10; Jeremiah 32:35.

[22] Leland, "The Virginia Chronicle," 108.

[23] Semple, *History* (1894), 43. See also pages 39, 44; and Robert Boyte C. Howell, *The Early Baptists of Virginia: An Address, Delivered in New York, before the American Baptist Historical Society, May 10th 1856* (Philadelphia: Press of the Society, 1857) 36.

[24] See Cobb, *The Rise of Religious Liberty in America*, 94–96, and Howell, *The Early Baptists of Virginia*, 37.

[25] Hening, *The Statutes at Large* 3:358, 362. See also 2:384

[26] Cobb, *The Rise of Religious Liberty in America*, 94.

uneducated, were savvy enough to use the moral failures of many of the Anglican clergy to beat away successfully at the established church, whereas Anglican ministers were ultimately unsuccessful in their attempt to beat Baptists into submission.

Another factor fueled the Anglican ire against Baptists: many Virginians believed that Baptists threatened the stability of civil society. At a minimum, they considered Baptists to be lawbreakers. Particular Baptists, more than Separates, attempted to obey Virginia laws. For example, they obtained the required licenses to preach at specific meeting places.[27] They also submitted to being interviewed by Anglican ministers to determine their fitness to minister. The colony based these requirements on the Act of Toleration, which stated "that no congregation or assembly for religious worship shall be permitted or allowed by this act, until the place of such meeting shall be certified" by a bishop, archdeacon, or justice of the peace.[28] Separates, however, claimed that the act gave them the right to preach wherever they wanted. Yet, as an anonymous author (probably a lawyer) wrote in *Virginia Gazette*, "You must perform the condition before you can claim the exemption; that is, among other qualifications, you must preach and assemble at registered or licensed houses only." If you obey the laws as they are written and not as you want them to be written, the author continued, "you will meet with protection, and not interruption, from magistracy here, but if you break those limits, and *everyone* undertakes to preach *everywhere*, you may expect to be proceeded against as the law directs, and can derive no advantage from the Act of Toleration."[29]

Baptists, however, maintained that their religious practices harmed no one. The author of the *Gazette* article saw things differently and claimed that Baptists attempted to "terrify and frighten many honest and...pious" people into converting to their faith. Even worse, the author claimed, they taught "'that after conversion a man cannot sin unto death.'" Such a teaching, he warned, removes "all religious restraints from men of

---

[27] Semple, *History* (1894), 383. See also Fristoe, *The History of the Ketocton Baptist Association*, 85.

[28] "The Toleration Act, 1689." Available online at http://www.swan.ac.uk/history/teaching/teaching%20resources/Revolutionary%20England/TolerationAct.htm.

[29] "An Address to the Anabaptists imprisoned in Caroline County, August 8, 1771," *Virginia Gazette*, 20 February 1772, [2].

abandoned principles, who, having been once dipped in your happy waters, are let loose to commit upon us murders and every species of injury, when they can do it secretly so as to avoid temporal punishment."[30]

Such talk of Baptist brigands roaming the countryside frightened Virginians who believed that, once Baptists grew numerically stronger, they would massacre non-Baptists and take over the colony. Yet, as Fristoe noted, "Groundless and stupid as this conjecture was, it was spoken of from one to the other, until many of the old bigots would feel their tempers inflamed, and their blood run quick in their veins, and declare they would take up arms and destroy" the Baptists first.[31] "Groundless and stupid" as such thinking might have been to Baptists, many Virginians considered it to be the gospel truth.

Many Virginians further inflamed the belief that Baptists sought to conquer the colony by calling them Anabaptists. In "A Recipe to make an Anabaptist Preacher in Two Days Time," which appeared in the 31 October 1771 issue of the *Virginia Gazette*, another anonymous author mocked Baptists for their obstinacy, arrogance, delusions of grandeur, and conspiratorial nature:

> Take the herbs of hypocrisy and ambition, of each a handful; of the spirit of pride two drams; of the seed of dissention and discord one ounce; of the flower of formality three scruples, of the roots of stubbornness and obstinacy four pounds; and bruise them altogether in the mortar of vainglory, with the pestle of contradiction, putting amongst them one pint of the spirit of self-conceitedness. When it is lukewarm, let the dissenting brother take two or three spoonfuls of it, morning and evening before exercise; and while his mouth is full of the electuary, he will make a wry face, wink with his eyes, and squeeze out some tears of dissimulation. Then let him speak as the spirit of giddiness gives him utterance. This will make the schismatic endeavor to maintain his doctrine, wound the church, delude the people, justify their proceedings of

---

[30] Ibid., [1].
[31] Fristoe, *The History of the Ketocton Baptist Association*, 66.

illusions, foment rebellion, and call it by the name of liberty of conscience.[32]

Thus, most Virginians considered Baptists, particularly Separates, to be a group of ignorant losers comprised mainly of people from the dregs of society who, through their fanatical, mean-spirited religion, were determined to destroy Virginia's established church and take over the colony. In his letter to Nathaniel Saunders, William Green promised to do what he could to convince Anglicans to "live in peace, brotherly love and charity," but he was honest in his assessment of what lay ahead for Baptists if they did not temper their zeal: "I think men who will behave in such a manner cannot reasonably expect to be treated with common decency or respect."[33] Baptists did not soften their attacks on the established church or its ministers, nor did they care whether Anglicans respected them. Consequently, they were not treated with decency or respect. During the 1760s and 1770s, at least seventy-eight Virginia Baptists suffered some kind of physical or verbal abuse.[34] Many of them suffered more than once, and several spent some time in jail. Three men left first-hand accounts of their prison experiences.

John Waller: A Persecutor, a Preacher, and a Persecuted Preacher

If someone had told the friends of John Waller (1741–1802) prior to 1767 that a plaque praising their friend for his ministry would one day be placed on a church named Wallers Baptist Church in Spotsylvania County, Virginia, they would have been dumbfounded.[35] That Waller would be a preacher would have been unimaginable; after all, someone had dubbed him

---

[32] "A Recipe to make an Anabaptist Preacher in Two Days Time," *Virginia Gazette*, 31 October 1771, [2] ; Little, *Imprisoned Preachers*, 233–34.

[33] Green to Saunders, 81.

[34] For a list of seventy-eight Virginia Baptists who were persecuted, the counties in which they were persecuted, and the nature of their persecutions, see the appendices in Harper and Jacumin, *Esteemed Reproach*, [207]–13, and Little, *Imprisoned Preachers*, 516–20. Little's lengthy book chronicles the persecution of Virginia Baptists. See also his "Imprisoned Preachers and Religious Liberty in Virginia," *Chronicle* 1/2 (April 1938): 23–31.

[35] The church is located in Parlow, Virginia. The website for Wallers Baptist Church is http://wallersbaptist.com/templates/System/default.asp?id=37451 (accessed 16 July 2007).

"Swearing Jack" and his lifestyle was anything but godly. He gambled, and his volatile temper "brought him to many a scrape."[36]

Waller, however, was destined to become more than a gambling brawler. Because of John's talent for satire, William Waller believed that his nephew should be a lawyer, so he enrolled John in a grammar school to prepare him for a legal career. His uncle's death, however, prevented John from continuing his formal education, so he then spent much of his time learning how to gamble and causing trouble, for which he became infamous. If there was any devilry being committed in Spotsylvania County, people assumed that the "Devil's Adjutant," another of Waller's notorious epithets, was the instigator.[37]

Despite his foul mouth, his gambling, and his mischievous and combative spirit, Waller possessed one virtue that endeared him to his Virginia neighbors: he hated Baptists. He loved making Baptists miserable, often unleashing "his fury toward" them and "presenting" them "to the court as nuisances."[38] In the eyes of many Virginians, anyone who hated Baptist could not be all bad. Thus, even if Waller's friends could have been convinced that he would become a preacher one day, they still would have had difficulty believing that he would become a Baptist.

Waller's journey from a persecutor of Baptists to a persecuted Baptist preacher began in an unlikely place: a tavern. In 1766, while a member of a Spotsylvania County grand jury, Waller heard the case of Lewis Craig, a

---

[36] Morgan Edwards, *Materials towards a History of The Baptists in the Provinces of Maryland, Virginia, North Carolina, South Carolina, Georgia* (n.p., 1772) 72. For biographical information on Waller, see Edwards, *Materials*, 72–78; Robert B. Semple, *History of the Rise and Progress of the Baptists in Virginia* (Richmond: privately printed, 1810) 403–11, hereafter cited as Semple, *History* (1810); Jack Manly, "Waller, John," in *Encyclopedia of Southern Baptists*, 2 vols. ed. Norman Wade Cox and Judson Boyce Allen (Nashville: Broadman Press, 1958) 2:1476; John Moore, "John Waller (1741–1802), 'A Man Worthy of Notice'," *Virginia Baptist Register*, 1995, 1745–53; John S. Moore, ed., "Morgan Edwards' 1772 Virginia Notebook: Edited with Notes and Comments," *Virginia Baptist Register*, 1978, 854–56; and James B. Taylor, *Lives of Virginia Baptist Ministers*, 2nd ed. (Richmond: Yale & Wyatt, 1838) 77–84. Material on Waller from the first edition of Taylor's *Lives* is available online at http://www.geocities.com/baptist_documents/waller.john.by.taylor.html (28 August 2005).

[37] Semple, *History* (1810), 404; Taylor, *Lives of Virginia Baptist Ministers*, 77.

[38] Edwards, *Materials*, 73.

Baptist preacher who had been arrested for holding illegal religious meetings. After indicting Craig for illegal preaching, the members of the jury retired to a tavern to celebrate their part in keeping Virginia safe from the Baptist menace. Craig followed them and bought them drinks, which got their attention.

Craig thanked the men for the "honor" they had done him: "While I was wicked and injurious, you took no note of me, but since I altered my course of life and endeavored to reform my neighbors, you concern yourselves much about me. I have gotten this mug of grog, to treat you with, and shall take the spoiling of my goods joyfully."[39] The content of Craig's testimony and the manner in which he delivered it affected Waller deeply. He sensed that this pathetic Baptist preacher possessed something that he had never seen in another person. Morgan Edwards, an early American Baptist historian, described the result of Craig's testimony this way: "The arrow, which Craig shot at a venture, struck in Waller's mind, until a fixed seriousness took place and a conversion came on."[40]

After Craig's speech in the tavern, Waller began attending Baptist meetings, searching for the happiness and strength he had witnessed in the indicted Baptist preacher. Yet Waller experienced a spiritual crisis, not happiness. Finally, after seven or eight months of inner turmoil, his conversion finally "came on." He described the fateful moment in these words:

I had long felt the greatest abhorrence of myself and began almost to despair of the mercy of God. However, I determined never to rest until it pleased God to show mercy or cut me off. Under these impressions, I was at a certain place, sitting under preaching. On a sudden, a man exclaimed that he had found mercy and began to praise God. No mortal can describe the horror with which I was seized at that instant. I began to conclude my damnation was certain. Leaving the meeting, I hastened into a neighboring wood and dropped on my knees before God to beg for mercy. In an instant, I felt my heart melt, and a sweet application of the Redeemer's love to my poor soul. The calm was great, but short.[41]

---

[39] Quoted in Semple, *History* (1810), 404.
[40] Edwards, *Materials*, 74.
[41] Quoted in Taylor, *Lives of Virginia Baptist Ministers*, 78.

With his spiritual struggle over, Waller traveled to Orange County, where James Read, an evangelist, baptized him in 1767.

The calm that Waller experienced after his conversion ended after he became a member of a group that Semple called "the young prophets in Orange and Spotsylvania" who, having been "animated by an ardent desire for their Master's kingdom, sallied forth in every direction, spreading the tidings of peace and salvation."[42] Not everyone, however, welcomed these new prophets.

Waller's troubles began on 4 June 1768, when he, Lewis Craig, James Chiles, James Read, and William March were arrested in Spotsylvania County for preaching. At their trial, the prosecutor charged them with disturbing the peace and emphasized the aggressiveness for which Separate Baptists despised: "May it please your worships, these men are great disturbers of the peace; they cannot meet a man upon the road but they must ram a text of scripture down his throat."[43] Found guilty, the Baptists refused an offer to be freed if they promised not to preach anymore in the county. Consequently, Craig spent four weeks in the Fredericksburg jail; Waller and the others, forty-three days. These incarcerations were the first known imprisonments of Baptist preachers in Virginia.[44]

Further persecution of Waller occurred in Caroline County in April 1771. The parish minister, Mr. Morton; his clerk, Thomas Buckner; and the sheriff, William Harris, rode up to the stage on which Waller was singing. Morton used his horsewhip to turn the pages of the hymnal, but Waller kept his place by placing his thumb on the page. After Waller finished the song and as he began to pray, Morton rammed the end of his whip into Waller's mouth. Then Buckner rode up and yanked the preacher off the stage. The men proceeded to beat Waller's head on the ground, after which the sheriff whipped him, leaving him "in a gore of blood" and scarred for life. According to Edwards, Waller then stood up, "remounted the stage and preached a most extraordinary sermon, thereby showing that beaten oil is best for the sanctuary."[45]

---

[42] Semple, *History* (1894), 24–25.
[43] Quoted in Semple, *History* (1894), 30.
[44] Edwards, *Materials*, 74; Little, *Imprisoned Preachers*, 93–103.
[45] Edwards, *Materials*, 75; Little, *Imprisoned Preachers*, 229–31.

Two weeks later, Waller recounted his harrowing experience to a group of fellow Baptists, telling how he had experienced "liberty...under the lash."[46] According to Pastor John Williams, who recorded Waller's narrative in his diary, when someone asked Waller how he was able to control himself while being whipped and humiliated, the former persecutor, in words similar to those of Obadiah Holmes, "answered that the Lord stood by him of a truth and poured his love into his soul without measure, and the brethren and sisters about him singing praises to Jehovah, so that he could scarcely feel the stripes for the love of God, rejoicing with Paul that he was worthy to suffer for his dear Lord and Master."[47]

On another occasion while Waller was preaching in Hanover County, "a huge fellow" pulled him off the platform and dragged him around by his hair. This incident turned into a tug-of-war when a man of equal size came to Waller's rescue. As the persecutor pulled on Waller's arm, the friend pulled on the other. Edwards commented that "poor Waller was like to lose both [arms]; the hurt stuck to him for many weeks."[48]

In summer 1771 Waller and three other preachers spent forty-six days in a Middlesex County jail for preaching. While in jail on 12 August 1771, he described in a letter to someone only identified as "dear brother" the events surrounding his arrest on Saturday, 10 August, for holding an illegal worship service at James McCain's home. While William Webber was preaching on James 2:18, several men, including the parish parson and James Montague, a county magistrate, "in a most furious rage" burst in on the meeting. The intruders arrested Waller, Webber, Thomas Wafford, Robert Ware, Richard Faulkner, and James Greenwood and took them to Urbana Prison. Before leaving McCain's, one man whipped Wafford severely and hit another worshiper once before his companions stopped him.[49]

---

[46] This phrase is Rhys Isaac's. See Isaac, *The Transformation of Virginia*, 163.

[47] Quoted ibid., 163, and in Little, *Imprisoned Preachers*, 231.

[48] Edwards, *Materials*, 76.

[49] John Waller to a "Dear brother in the Lord," 12 August 1771, in *History* (1894), 481–82. This letter can also be found in Little, *Imprisoned Preachers*, 275–56; William Estep, *Revolution within the Revolution: The First Amendment in Historical Context, 1612–1789* (Grand Rapids MI: William B. Eerdmans Publishing Co., 1990) 180–81; and Garnett Ryland, *The Baptists of Virginia: 1699–1926* (Richmond: The Virginia Baptist Board of Missions and Education, 1955) 70–71.

Waller then described how the men took the prisoners "one by one, into a room, and examined our pockets and wallets for firearms, etc., charging us with carrying on a meeting against the authority of the land." After determining that the Baptists were unarmed, the magistrate asked for the men's preaching licenses, which none had. Montague demanded that the prisoners "give bond and security not to preach any more in the county, which," Waller noted proudly, "we modestly refused to do."[50]

Because Wafford and Faulkner were laymen, Montague released them, but he had the other prisoners taken "to the sheriff and sent to close jail, with a charge not to allow" them "to walk in the air until court day." The sheriff and jailor treated them kindly, for which Waller asked that "the Lord reward them for it."[51]

According to Semple, Urbana Prison "swarmed with fleas." Once in their cell, the Baptists borrowed a candle from the jailor, sang "praises of that Redeemer whose cross they bore and from whose hands they expected a crown in the end," thanked God "that it was a prison and not hell that they were in," prayed "for themselves, their friends, their enemies and persecutors," and then went to sleep. The next day (Sunday) several of the prisoners' friends visited them, and Greenwood preached to them. Waller recorded this event in his letter: "Yesterday we had a large number of people to hear us preach, and among others many of the great ones of the land, who behaved well while one of us discoursed on the new birth. We find the Lord gracious and kind to us beyond expression in our afflictions." Not knowing how long he would be in prison, Waller asked his "dear brother" and "the church" to pray for the prisoners, their benefactors, and even their persecutors.[52]

On Monday, 26 August, the day of their trial, Waller and his friends had no expectation of winning their case, and they were right. The court noted that the Baptists had been arrested under a warrant for "teaching and preaching the gospel under the pretence of the exercise of religion, in [an]other manner than according to the liturgy of the Church of England and without having Episcopal ordination to teach and preach the same

---

[50] Waller to a "Dear brother in the Lord," 482. By "meeting," Waller possibly meant "mutiny."

[51] Ibid.

[52] Ibid.

according to the canons of the said Church of England." The justices rejected the Baptists' defense that they were "Protestant dissenters" and found them guilty because "they had not qualified themselves as teachers or preachers, either according to the laws of this colony or of Great Britain or the canons of the Church of England."[53] The court ordered each of the Baptists to pay bonds of £50 and securities of £25 and to promise not to preach in the county for six months. The Baptists refused and were returned to prison.

After several weeks in prison, Webber became seriously ill. On 20 September 1771, Waller wrote to Justice James Mills, one of the men who had passed judgment on the Baptists, in an attempt to get medical attention for his "poor brother prisoner." Waller emphasized the gravity of the situation by noting that Webber was "in a very low state of health, and without divine interposition" would soon "launch off the shores of mortality." Waller hoped that Miles would consider that Webber was a young man who lived with his mother in Goochland County, and that he was only in Middlesex County because Waller had asked him to come. The young preacher, like Waller, could not promise to refrain from preaching if he was released "for fear of sinning against God." Nevertheless, Waller assured the justice that "it is more than probable" that if Webber was permitted to return home to be nursed by friends, "he would never be under obligations of coming into this county again, for he has not the care of a church here." Therefore, Waller hoped that Miles would do what he could to help the sick, twenty-four-year-old Baptist preacher. Ironically, Waller signed his letter to one of the magistrates who had sentenced him to six months in prison, "I am your friend, John Waller Jr."[54] Whether Webber gained an early release is unknown, though he did not "launch off the shores of mortality" until thirty-eight years later.

When they began their imprisonment, the Baptists announced that they would preach every Sunday and Wednesday, and crowds of supporters and detractors gathered to hear them. Ironically, the prison became a secure pulpit from which the Baptists preachers could share the gospel without fear

---

[53] The entire sentence of the court can be found in Little, *Imprisoned Preachers*, 280.

[54] John Waller to James Mills, 20 September 1771, *The Baptists of Virginia*, 73. The letter can also be found in Little, *Imprisoned Preachers*, 285.

of persecution. Eventually, the county authorities began to question the wisdom of keeping the preachers in their jail. According to Semple, their captors learned "that the imprisonment of the preachers tended rather to the furtherance of the gospel" because "the preaching seemed to have double weight when coming from the jail." On 26 September, after spending forty-six days in prison, the Baptists paid their bonds for good behavior and were set free, much to the relief of Middlesex County authorities, who were "desirous to be rid of" them.[55]

After being freed from Urbana Prison, Waller continued to preach in other Virginia counties and was incarcerated two more times. In 1772 he probably spent ten days in a Caroline County jail for preaching in the home of Henry Goodloe.[56] Two years later, on 13 March, Waller and three other Baptists were arrested during a worship service in Essex County. One was freed because he had not preached in the county, but Waller and the other two were sent to jail. The three men spent their time preaching twice a week, counseling people who sought their advice, reading, and praying.[57] The court records for 21 March 1774 note that Waller and the other two "Anabaptist preachers" had been arrested for "preaching and expounding the scriptures contrary to [the] law" and that they had confessed to doing so.[58] Two of the men posted bond and were freed. Waller, however, refused and was returned to jail. Semple recorded that Waller, dejected and alone except for the drunks with him in jail, "had no alternative but to commit himself to the hands of Omnipotence and wait for deliverance."[59] Six days later, he posted bond and returned home, never to spend another day in jail.

In November 1793 Waller resigned as pastor of the church that he and 154 others had started on 2 December 1769.[60] Originally named the Lower Spotsylvania Church, by 1774 it had become known as Waller's meetinghouse, and now it is called Wallers Baptist Church.[61] Waller left Virginia, where, during his ministry, he had spent 113 days in jail. He

---

[55] Semple, *History* (1894), 35–36.

[56] Little, *Imprisoned Preachers*, 324–25.

[57] Semple, *History* (1894), 39–40.

[58] Little, *Imprisoned Preachers*, 400.

[59] Semple, *History* (1894), 40.

[60] Ibid., 24, 197.

[61] See ibid., 79.

relocated in South Carolina, where he pastored until his death on 4 July 1802.

James Ireland: An Example of Grace during Adversity

Perhaps the most famous Virginia Baptist to be imprisoned was James Ireland (1748–1806).[62] Although Ireland was only confined to jail once for his faith, the time he spent in the Culpeper County jail (November 1769 to April 1770) proved to be adventurous and dangerous. During his prison term, he wrote many letters, undoubtedly detailing the adventures he experienced in jail. Unfortunately, these letters have not survived. Near the end of his life, however, Ireland, being in "a low state of health and weak habit of body" and "confined to a bed with a languishing sickness," narrated his life story to a friend.[63] Ireland included several stories of his being persecuted, including three attempts to kill him in jail. These incidents were but a few of Ireland's sufferings, for he assured his readers that he could have "added a hundred circumstances more."[64]

Ireland was born at Edinburgh, Scotland, in 1748. His parents provided him with an opportunity to receive a good education, and as good Presbyterians, they taught him right from wrong, even though they were unacquainted "with vital and experimental religion."[65] Ireland described himself as having a "tenacious and retentive memory," which made him an excellent student.[66] Although teachers did not have to correct his schoolwork, he confessed to receiving "severe corrections for my wildness and wickedness."[67]

Ireland soon became bored with school, and when he saw one of his friends who had joined the navy decked out in a flashy uniform, he "felt a

---

[62] For biographical information on Ireland, see Ireland, *Life*, 1–175; Semple, *History* (1810), 425–27; Levering Evans, "Ireland, James," in *Encyclopedia of Southern Baptists*, 1:690–91; Little, *Imprisoned Preachers*, 150–80, 182–91; and Taylor, *Lives of Virginia Baptist Ministers*, 114–25. Material on Ireland from the first edition of Taylor's *Lives* is available online at http://www.geocities.com/baptist_documents/ireland.james.va.ministrs.html (28 August 2005).

[63] Ireland, *Life*, 13.

[64] Ibid., 128.

[65] Ibid., 15.

[66] Ibid.

[67] Ibid., 22.

glow of ambition."[68] Although Ireland's father did not want him to go to sea, he allowed his son, still a teenager, to leave school to become a sailor. After making four voyages, James decided to leave Scotland for America because he had committed "an act of juvenile indiscretion" and feared "the rigor of the penal laws of the government under which I was born and raised." He never identified the nature of this "indiscretion," but he did characterize his immigration to America "as the most auspicious and fortunate epoch of my life. It pleased my Great Deliverer to bring good out of evil, and I was destined to exchange a land of tyranny and sanguinary oppression for a country of liberty, reason, and humanity."[69]

When the eighteen-year-old Ireland arrived in Virginia, he settled in Shenandoah County and became a schoolmaster. Near the end of his life, he commented that, when he arrived in Virginia, the country "groaned under the tyranny of a rigorous religious intolerance.... From this rigorous intolerance arose many of my severe trials and cruel persecutions in the early part of my gospel labors."[70] Such intolerance did not affect him when he arrived in Virginia because, at that time in his life, he did not care much about faith. He soon made a name for himself because of his dancing skills and his teaching abilities. Although he confessed to reading "profane and jest books," Ireland would not tolerate in his students the behavior he had exhibited back home in Scotland: "I would reprove sin in those who were under my tuition and instruction; I set an orderly example before my scholars and prided myself in a conformity to orderly and regular rule, by which I acquired a general esteem as a teacher."[71]

Along with being a dancer and a disciplinarian, Ireland, according to the editor of his autobiography, "was no mean poet."[72] His poetry caught the attention of Nicholas Fain, a member of a Separate Baptist church near Ireland's school. Fain challenged Ireland to write a poem on charity or brotherly love, which he did. Then Fain challenged him to write another poem on a subject of his own choosing. Again, Ireland accepted the challenge, choosing as his topic "the natural man's dependence for

---

[68] Ibid., 24.
[69] Ibid., 35–36.
[70] Ibid., 36.
[71] Ibid., 43.
[72] Ibid., 163.

heaven."[73] One of the final lines from the poem nagged him: "The law does breathe nothing but death to slighters of salvation."[74] To erase these words from his mind, Ireland "began to sing wicked and lascivious songs, of which" he "had a great number." That line, however, so haunted him that he proclaimed to his friends that he would never dance again.[75]

About a year later, Ireland joined the Freemason Brethren. He had also been reading his Bible and attending meetings of Particular Baptists, who also called themselves brethren, despite their scandalous reputation. After attending a Baptist meeting with a Freemason friend, the friend proclaimed, "We will stick to our own profession," and together they swore that they would never become Baptists.[76]

Despite his determination to remain a heathen, Ireland was reading the Bible one night when the words of Isaiah 65:1 "bolted in upon my mind: 'I am found of them that sought me not.'"[77] This passage deepened his spiritual struggle that had begun with his writing the second poem for Fain. News of his struggle spread throughout the county, and the rumor was that "James Ireland was going to be mighty good now, for he is going to get converted."[78] Realizing that they were about to lose their party favorite, two friends promised to convert him back to a life of frivolity, only to be converted with him to the path of righteousness.[79]

Ireland was not the only person in his area struggling with his spirituality, so he began holding religious meetings in his home. Those who gathered for worship soon invited John Pickett, a Separate Baptist minister, to preach to them. He preached for two days and then left to hold meetings in other areas. Ireland's two friends who had tried to convert him back to a life of frivolity traveled to hear Pickett preach. Upon their return home, they told Ireland about the meetings, and then all three went to a cornfield to pray. During the prayer, Ireland recalled, "*that* was the time when God

---

[73] Ibid., 49.

[74] Ibid., 54. The complete text of the poem is on 50–53.

[75] Ibid., 55.

[76] Ibid., 59.

[77] Ibid., 61.

[78] Ibid., 66.

[79] See ibid., 66–68, 89–90.

converted my soul, [and] removed my burden of sin and guilt, giving me to possess that peace which was beyond understanding."[80]

Pickett accepted another invitation to preach to Ireland's group, but when he failed to arrive for the service, the group decided that Ireland should preach in Pickett's stead, which he did "in fear and much trembling."[81] His sermon had such an effect on the congregation that many asked if he would preach in their homes, which he did several times a week. Thus began Ireland's preaching ministry. It would not be long, however, before his ministry caught more than the attention of his friends; others also took notice. As Semple observed, "Mr. Ireland was a man of too much distinction to escape the notice of the enemies of the cross."[82]

Ireland eventually concluded that immersion was the proper mode of baptism, and he and several others decided to join the Separate Baptists because, of all the Baptists, they "had the warmest preachers and the most fire among them."[83] Samuel Harris of Pittsylvania County baptized Ireland after Ireland preached a trial sermon and the members of the Dan River church heard his testimony. The next day the church presented him with his credentials to be an itinerant Separate Baptist preacher.[84]

In November 1769, after preaching in Carter's Run, Ireland stayed at the home of Thomas McClanahan in Culpeper County. Knowing that Ireland was scheduled to preach the following day at a Mr. Manfia's house, McClanahan informed Ireland that he would be arrested. Because of this ominous warning, Ireland had to weigh his options carefully: "I sat down and counted the cost, freedom or confinement, liberty or a prison; it admitted of no dispute. Having ventured all upon Christ, I determined to suffer all for him."[85]

Arriving at Manfia's the next day and receiving once again the news of his imminent arrest, Ireland preached on top of a table. After the sermon and while Ireland was praying, two men pulled him off the table by his collar

---

[80] Ibid., 94.

[81] Ibid., 98.

[82] Semple, *History* (1810), 426–27.

[83] Ireland, *Life*, 105. Ireland later joined the Particular Baptists. Fristoe (*The History of the Ketocton Baptist Association*, 62) said that Ireland joined them "for convenience."

[84] Ireland, *Life*, 118.

[85] Ibid., 121.

and demanded to know who gave him the authority to preach. "He who was the author of the gospel," Ireland replied.[86] He then promised to appear at court a few days later.

On court day, Ireland knew from the outset that his fate was sealed. He recounted that eleven magistrates "brow-beat me, mall treated me, and threw out the most opprobrious appellations against me—would admit no defense I could make, but ordered me to hold my tongue, and let them hear no more of my vile, pernicious, abhorrible, detestable, abominable, diabolical doctrines, for they were nauseous to the whole court." Realizing that "imprisonment was inevitable, and [that] they were determined to make an example of" him, Ireland remained silent. The sheriffs took him to jail, where many people verbally harassed him throughout the night.[87]

Soon after being jailed, Ireland began to doubt that God had called him to preach. He asked friends to post his bond, but as he was explaining his reasons for wanting to be out of prison, "it pleased God to let in a glimmering ray of comfort upon my mind; I grasped at it like a man when drowning, grasping at a twig, and immediately told the brethren, I could not sign the bond for my liberation."[88] Yet relief from his doubts did not last, for soon he once again plunged into "deep distress." One day while lying on his bed with his Bible in his hand, Ireland asked God for a sign that he had been called to preach. Opening his Bible to John 8:31–32, Ireland read, "If you continue in my word, you shall know the truth, and the truth shall set you free." Immediately, he recalled, "my chains...dropped off, my heart bounded with comfort, and if all the ministers and people of God upon earth had said I had run before I was sent, it would have had no influence upon me. That passage opened to me thus: that it was my duty to continue in preaching his word, and while so doing, he would make manifest to me the truth of what I prayed for, and the truth would make me free from such temptations."[89] Henceforth, Ireland never doubted that God had truly called him to preach the gospel.

While Ireland struggled with his calling, his jailor struggled with how he could benefit from the Baptist's incarceration. Knowing that many people

---

[86] Ibid.

[87] Ibid., 122.

[88] Ibid., 124.

[89] Ibid.

wanted to visit his prisoner, the jailor began charging them eight shillings and four pence. Ireland said that he paid the fee, called "commitment and release money," more than once so that people could have the "opportunity of laying open to me the state of their souls." The jailor, who also owned a tavern, permitted some people to visit Ireland for free. When customers became unruly, he threw them into jail with Ireland. These drunks could stay with Ireland for free on the condition that they abuse Ireland, which they did gladly.[90]

Convinced now of his call to preach, Ireland determined not to let his persecutors and a bunch of drunks prevent him from doing so, and he continued his ministry by preaching "through the little iron grate" in his cell to the multi-racial crowds that assembled outside his window. Such boldness, however, proved to be dangerous for him and his congregations: "The wicked and persecutors would ride up at a gallop among my hearers, until I have seen persons of respectability under their horse's feet: clubs have been shaken over the heads of other individuals, with threatenings if ever they attended there again, while the poor Negroes have been stripped and subjected to stripes, and myself threatened with being shut up in total darkness if ever I presumed to preach to the people again." On at least one occasion while he was preaching, "these miscreants" stood on something outside of Ireland's window in order to urinate in his face.[91]

When intimidation did not silence Ireland, his enemies turned to even more violent methods. A group assembled at a nearby tavern, owned by a Mr. Stewart, and plotted to blow up Ireland's cell. The plotters could only procure a half-pound of gunpowder, which they placed under his cell. Fortunately, Ireland was not sitting above the bomb when it exploded, pushing up one plank in the floor. Uninjured, unfazed, and uninterrupted, he continued singing a hymn he had begun before the blast.[92]

Another unfriendly group tried to suffocate him by burning Indian pepper pods filled with brimstone that had been placed at the base of his cell door. The smoke filled the entire jail, forcing Ireland to press his nose into cracks in the jail wall in order not to suffocate.[93]

---

[90] Ibid., 126.
[91] Ibid., 127.
[92] Ibid.
[93] Ibid.

Having survived these attempts on his life, Ireland next survived being poisoned by his jailor and a physician. When the physician then offered to care for him, for a price, at his home, Ireland knew that "avarice was at the bottom of this scheme, and I saw through it, and of consequence rejected it with horror."[94]

During his stay in jail, Ireland kept up a lengthy correspondence with ministers and churches. Through these letters, which have not survived, fellow Baptists strengthened their imprisoned brother, and he, in turn, strengthened them. Much to his joy, Ireland noted that some of his letters to people wanting to know why he was jailed and how he could withstand his sufferings led to their conversions.

Ireland's letters were not the only means of transforming lives. His kindness and patient counsel led to the conversion of a man with whom he shared a cell early in his incarceration and who had threatened to kill him.[95] The Baptist minister also turned another enemy into his friend. Mr. Stewart, the owner of the tavern where men had plotted to blow up Ireland and one of the men who had ridden his horse into Ireland's congregations assembled outside of the jail, also became the imprisoned Baptist's friend. One day when Stewart and his friends were outside Ireland's window cursing him, the Baptist prisoner overheard the tavern owner ask to borrow some money from his companions. When no one gave Stewart any money, Ireland handed him some through his window, which dumbfounded his persecutor. Ireland described the effect that this incident had on Stewart: "I perfectly gained him over to be my friend from that instant, neither would he suffer any person to throw out a word of insult against me from that time, without his resenting it. He and his companion would repeatedly apply to the jailor for the key, in order to come in and visit me, at which times we often spent many hours together in friendly conversation."[96]

Despite being physically and psychologically abused, and despite struggling spiritually during the first few days of his imprisonment, Ireland stayed strong through five months in prison. He took no credit for such strength, preferring instead to attribute his steadfastness to God's presence: "My prison then was a place in which I enjoyed much of the divine presence;

---

[94] Ibid., 128.
[95] Ibid., 130–33.
[96] Ibid., 135.

a day seldom passed without some signal token and manifestation of the divine goodness towards me, which generally led me to subscribe my letters, to whom I wrote them, in these words, 'From my palace in Culpeper.'"[97]

In April 1770 Ireland left his palace because he and his friends had determined that his spending more time in jail would be fruitless; therefore, he posted bond and agreed to attend his trial in May. Once free, Ireland wrote a petition, which he presented to the Virginia governor. The petition requested permission to construct a church building in Culpeper County, in which Ireland could preach without fear of persecution. After being examined by an Anglican minister, Ireland received a license for his building.[98]

At his trial in May, Ireland pled not guilty to his alleged crimes and attempted to defend himself. Realizing that he would be unable to convince the court of his innocence, he produced his license, signed by the governor, granting him permission to have a meeting house and "to preach there without molestation." That document stunned the courtroom. Ireland obviously enjoyed seeing the expressions on his judges' faces: "Never was a people so chagrined as the bench of magistrates." Once the magistrates recovered from their shock, they were more than determined to send him to prison. The trial from that point went badly for Ireland, and a friend suggested that he hire an attorney named Bullet, who had been observing the proceedings. Once Bullett assured Ireland that he could win the case, the Baptist minister hired him for $16.66.[99]

Bullett argued that the court had prosecuted Ireland on laws that had been dead for seventy years, that the magistrates could be held criminally liable for their conduct toward Ireland, and that the conventicle acts for which the court was prosecuting the Baptist preacher had been repealed by the Act of Toleration. Seeing that the magistrates were losing their case, the Anglican parson of Culpeper County came forward to help the court attempt to rebut Bullett's arguments. Ireland also wanted to rejoin the fray and requested that Bullett ask the court to allow him to debate the parson. If he lost the debate, Ireland promised to go to prison voluntarily. Amused, Bullett replied that the magistrates would not permit the Bible to be debated. Ireland knew that; otherwise, he told his lawyer, "they would not

---

[97] Ibid., 129.
[98] Ibid., 135–36.
[99] Ibid., 136.

imprison those who preach it."[100]

Realizing that they had lost their case, the magistrates, in order to save face, adjourned the court and ordered Ireland to await being recalled for another trial. Everyone knew that he would never be called back, and everyone knew that the established church and those who supported it had suffered a humiliating defeat. Ireland summed up that momentous day with these words: "Thus ended this great sham trial, to the mortification of the bench and their abettors; while on the other hand, the pious followers of the dear Redeemer were overjoyed at their disappointment and the prospect of having a meeting house for themselves."[101]

Now free to preach, Ireland started several churches, pastored three churches in Frederick and Shenandoah counties, and went on several mission tours. He married Jane Burgess in 1771, and together they had eight children. After Jane died in 1790, Ireland married Ann Pollard the next year. They had one child.

In June 1792, for some unknown reason, Betsy Southerlin, a houseguest of the Irelands, and Sucky, their servant, poisoned almost the entire family. Ireland became deathly ill, but survived; however, his three-year-old son, William, died. Despite the women's confessions and the fact that poison was eventually found under a plank in Southerlin's room, both women were acquitted.[102] Ireland recovered enough to resume preaching, but the poisoning affected him the rest of his life.

In 1804 Ireland fell from his horse when a drunk rider rammed him. Two years later his carriage overturned, severely injuring him and confining him to his bed for most of the remainder of his life. He died on 5 May 1806. According to Keith Harper and C. Martin Jacumin, Ireland's "graceful response to adversity is one of the most evocative episodes in American Baptist history."[103]

Joseph Craig: A Reluctant Prisoner for the Lord

Another imprisoned Baptist preacher who left an autobiographical account of his ministry and prison experiences was Joseph Craig (1741–c.

---

[100] Ibid., 136–37.

[101] Ibid., 137.

[102] Ibid., 150–57.

[103] Keith Harper and C. Martin Jacumin, introduction to *Esteemed Reproach*, 3.

1827).[104] John Taylor, an acquaintance of Craig, described his fellow Baptist preacher as "a very singular man" whose "great eccentricity drew the attention of all who knew him. No man in the bound of our acquaintance manifested more zeal in the cause of religion than Joseph Craig. At times his zeal seemed intemperate, as if the man had not common sense. And yet there was something in him more original than was found in other men."[105] Like Ireland and Waller, Craig often found himself at odds with Virginia's religious establishment. Unlike them, however, he saw no disgrace in escaping his bonds whenever the opportunity arose.

Born in Virginia in 1741 to an Anglican father and a Presbyterian mother, Craig spent thirteen to fourteen years "under a sense of condemnation" until one day a man told him to go hear David Thomas, a Baptist preacher.[106] He went often, sometimes traveling twenty miles to listen to Thomas's sermons. One day, while traveling with the preacher, Craig, then twenty-three years old, "felt some solemn and awful impressions" on his mind and was converted to the Baptist way. He then began preaching to friends, to family, and even to his Anglican priest, who was infuriated and shook his fist at Craig.[107]

Craig traveled extensively throughout Virginia with several Baptist evangelists, and he had several run-ins with the law, most of which are undated. In Caroline County, he was arrested four times for preaching without a license. Once when he was incarcerated, he sat in his cell singing "about one hour, exceedingly happy." After that hour, the authorities permitted him to walk in the jail yard, and he experienced a sense of assurance that he was doing the will of God. He prayed to God, "'Lord, I have left all and followed thee,' and 'proved my faith by my work'—and it seemed as if he had said, face-to-face, 'I can believe you have.'" Such

---

[104] For biographical information on Craig, see Joseph Craig, *A History of Rev. Joseph Craig* (1813), in Harper and Jacumin, *Esteemed Reproach*, 181–205; Leo T. Crismon, "Craig, Joseph," in *Encyclopedia of Southern Baptists*, 1:327; and John Taylor, *Baptists on the American Frontier: A History of Ten Baptist Churches of which the Author Has Been Alternately a Member*, ed. Chester Raymond Young, annotated 3rd ed. (Macon GA: Mercer University Press, 1995) 105–107, 151, n. 175

[105] Taylor, *Baptists on the American Frontier*, 106.

[106] Craig, *A History*, 181.

[107] Ibid., 182–83.

assurance did not last long, however. After spending three weeks in jail, Craig, having become homesick, sat down in the jail yard and cried.[108]

The date of Craig's release is unknown, but, having proved once that he was willing to be jailed for preaching, he concluded that he did not have to prove it twice. Once after preaching in a home, a constable arrived with a warrant for his arrest, but Craig and another man sneaked out of the house. When a magistrate arrived, he and his men "hunted the closets and the rooms, but," Craig noted proudly, they "found me not."[109]

On another occasion, Craig traveled to Essex County to preach and, feeling emboldened for some reason, he thought, "if war was fashionable,…I would try and war a good warfare, and, as I had gotten into it, I did not care how much I suffered for the Lord's sake; and I concluded that they might do their worst, and I would try and do what I could for the Lord. And surely I did cry aloud that day! And we had a good time."[110]

Craig's "war" with the authorities did not occur that day, but it did the following day at a church called Guinea's Bridge in Essex County. While the congregation was singing, a constable grabbed Craig and stood by him until the hymn was finished. The constable and "some big men" took the preacher to a house three miles away and lodged him in an upper room. Craig noted that they took his little knife from him "for fear that I would kill some of them!" The next morning, while the men were on the front porch, he decided to escape, for, according to Semple, Craig considered "it no dishonor to cheat the devil."[111] When he got about fifty yards from the house, the Baptist fugitive heard someone shout, "Craig is gone."[112]

Men on horseback and others with dogs pursued Craig into the woods and recaptured him. Treating him roughly, they returned him to the house and put him on a horse, with one man sitting behind him. He announced that he had to "keep my conscience clear, or I should fall into keen despair—I did not care about life or death." The man behind him told him to do what he needed to do, so Craig slipped off the horse and stood still. When the constable asked him why he was so sullen, Craig responded, "I

---

[108] Ibid., 189.
[109] Ibid., 190.
[110] Ibid., 190.
[111] Semple, *History* (1894), 205.
[112] Craig, *A History*, 190.

will have no hand in carrying Joseph Craig to prison." The constable then put Craig back on the horse, tied his feet together under the animal, and took him to jail. By the time the group arrived at the jail, the rope had become untied, which Craig interpreted as a sign from God that he would be freed. When he discovered that the door of his cell would not lock, Craig, later that evening, took off for home, a free man.[113]

In 1781 Craig moved to Kentucky with his family and his brother Lewis, the preacher whose testimony started John Waller on his spiritual journey. In Kentucky, Joseph pastored two Separate Baptist churches in Fayette County before giving up the pastoral ministry.[114] He continued ministering, however, as an exhorter—that is, someone who, at the end of a worship service, encouraged people to make a decision. A hard worker, Craig became a wealthy farmer.[115] He died sometime between 1819 and 1827.

The End of the Anglican Establishment

In May 1790 Isaac Backus, a Baptist pastor in Middleborough, Massachusetts, wrote to his brother about his recent four-month trip to North Carolina and Virginia, during which he traveled 1,200 miles and preached 117 sermons in 29 counties. Backus told his brother about how Anglicans had held all the power in Virginia and how they had "imprisoned Baptist ministers for preaching without their leave." Those days were gone, Backus noted, for "in 1786 their establishment was demolished, and the Church of England has very little if any more influence in Virginia." He then informed his brother about the growth Baptists had experienced in Virginia and about their current reputation among government officials there: "Before 1768 there were but about five Baptist churches in the state, and now they have more than a hundred churches, some of which have five or six hundred members; and they are the most esteemed by government of any denomination therein."[116]

---

[113] Ibid., 191

[114] Frank M. Masters, *A History of Baptists in Kentucky* (Louisville: Kentucky Baptist Historical Society, 1953) 39, 63.

[115] Taylor, *Baptists on the American Frontier*, 107. See also Craig, *A History*, 203.

[116] Isaac Backus to Elijah Backus, 25 May 1790, in *Notes of the Baptists, and Their Principles, in Norwich, Conn., from the Settlement of the Town to 1850*, by Frederic Denison (Norwich: Manning, 1857) 47.

In the eighteenth century, Virginia Baptists transitioned from being considered an obnoxious, ignorant, seditious group of pests to, in Backus's words, "the most esteemed...denomination," at least in the eyes of some government officials. Undoubtedly, many Virginians, particularly Anglicans, held a different opinion, for, as Backus noted, 1786 had been a particularly bad year for them. That year, the Virginia legislature enacted Thomas Jefferson's Bill for Establishing Religious Freedom, part of which stated: "Be it enacted by the General Assembly, That no man shall be compelled to frequent or support any religious worship, place, or ministry whatsoever; nor shall be enforced, restrained, molested or burdened in his body or goods, nor shall otherwise suffer on account of his religious opinions or belief; but that all men shall be free to profess, and by argument to maintain, their opinions in matters of religion, and that the same shall in no wise diminish, enlarge or affect their civil capacities."[117]

Baptists were not the only people of faith who had rebelled against the Virginia religious establishment and who fought for religious liberty. They were, however, the most persecuted, and like imprisoned Baptists in Massachusetts and England, they did not allow prison to silence them. Near the end of his massive book on imprisoned Virginia Baptist preachers, Lewis Peyton Little emphasized the irony and the futility of imprisoning those preachers: "What seemed to shut them in was in reality the means of opening them out. If the strong arm of the law had not seized these men and confined them in the county gaols of Colonial Virginia, some of them would never have been heard of beyond the narrow confines of their own immediate neighborhood. But their confinement was their enlargement."[118] Indeed, Virginia Baptists turned their prisons into pulpits, proving once again that the best way for a government to kill a religion is not to imprison adherents of that religion but to make them its friends.

---

[117] "Bill for Establishing Religious Freedom," in Estep, *Revolution within the Revolution*, 195.

[118] Little, *Imprisoned Preachers*, 499.

Chapter 9

Living in Two Worlds

In his sermon "Christians in Spite of Everything," Harry Emerson Fosdick, the longtime Baptist pastor of New York City's Riverside Church, marveled at how people like John Bunyan could maintain their faith even in the most dreadful circumstances. The key to their perseverance, Fosdick remarked, lay in their ability to live simultaneously in two worlds. He noted that numerous

> great books...have been written in prison!... When one considers how they [the prisoners] could do that, it is evident that they must have concentrated their attention on their interior resources rather than on their outward circumstances. Like all the rest of us, they lived in two worlds: first, the external system of circumstances alien to their wishes, antagonistic to their finest aspirations, a veritable prison house; but, on the other side, the inner world where a man's mind may be his kingdom, where there are doors of the spirit which a man can open and which then no man or circumstance can shut—realms, principalities, and dominions of the soul where one walks at liberty. As between these two, they so minimized the outer and maximized the inner that they proved to themselves and to mankind that
>> Stone walls do not a prison make,
>> Nor iron bars a cage.[1]

---

[1] Harry Emerson Fosdick, "Christians in Spite of Everything (Philippians 4:22)," in *20 Centuries of Great Preaching: An Encyclopedia of Preaching*, ed. Clyde E. Fant, Jr., and William M. Pinson, Jr., 13 vols. (Waco TX: Word Books, Publisher, 1971) 66. The poem Fosdick quoted is Richard Lovelace's "To Althea, from Prison (IV)," which can be found at http://www.poetry-archive.com/l/to_althea_from_prison.html.

Indeed, the imprisoned Baptists of the seventeenth and eighteenth centuries lived in two worlds. They lived in a world where established churches were the norm and persecution was the means these churches and the civil governments that supported them dealt with religious dissenters. Yet these Baptists simultaneously lived in another world, one in which God's kingdom ruled and the sword of the Spirit (the Bible), not the sword of Caesar, settled religious disputes. Bunyan himself proclaimed the effect these two worlds had on Baptist prisoners:

> This Goal to us is as a Hill,
>   From whence we plainly see
> Beyond this World, and take our fill
>   Of things that lasting be.
>
> From hence we see the emptiness
>   Of *all* this world contains;
> And here we feel the Blessedness
>   That for us yet remains.[2]

In both worlds, fear reigned. In "the external system of circumstances," as Fosdick described it, fear produced fantasy and persecution, yet in "the inner world where a man's mind may be his kingdom," the fear of God reigned, producing courage and freedom.

The Fear that Produced Fantasy and Persecution

All imprisoned Baptists of the seventeenth and eighteenth centuries would have identified with the bewilderment of the Baptist authors of *Sion's Groans for Her Distressed*, who wondered "why...the Christian religion should be built and supported by violence and cruelty, when the foundation was laid, and the work carried on all the apostles' days, and some hundreds of years after, by quite contrary means." The authors concluded that the

---

[2] John Bunyan, "Prison Meditations," in *The Miscellaneous Works of John Bunyan: The Poems*, ed. Graham Midgley, gen. ed. Roger Sharrock, 13 vols. (Oxford: The Clarendon Press, 1980) 6:47, stanzas 34–35, lines 140–47.

"strongest argument" of those who used force to "support...their religion is, TAKE HIM, JAILOR."[3]

The civil and ecclesiastical authorities in England, Massachusetts, and Virginia would have disagreed vehemently with the authors of *Sion's Groans*. These authorities quoted the Bible, particularly passages from the Old Testament, to demonstrate the divine right of kings and the responsibility of civil magistrates to protect their established churches and to punish religious dissenters. Thus, "Take him, jailor" was not an argument at all; rather, the threat of punishment and, if necessary, the use of force were necessary to ensure that unity was established and maintained. National or colonial unity and survival depended largely on religious uniformity. If people believed the same doctrines and worshiped the same way, or at least acted as if they did, the state would prosper. Civil magistrates and ministers of established churches regarded religious liberty, which Baptists advocated from their genesis, to be the root of all heresy and a threat to the existence of the state. Therefore, in the minds of civil and ecclesiastical authorities, strong, and at times deadly, measures had to be used against advocates of religious freedom.

Though no magistrate or minister would have admitted it, fear was the foundation of such arguments, and, according to Rhys Isaac, "Fear breeds fantasy."[4] During the seventeenth and eighteenth centuries, many people considered Baptists to be an evil and an odd group, against which wild and bizarre rumors were often spread. For example, David Benedict, a nineteenth-century Baptist pastor and historian in Rhode Island, recounted a conversation he had had with an elderly woman at the beginning of his ministry. Part of the conversation concerned the absurd observation of how the physical characteristics of Baptists had changed, for the better, over the years. The woman noted that when she was young, some Baptists lived "in the back part of our town, and an outlandish set of people they certainly were.... As it was told to me, you could hardly find one among them but

---

[3] Thomas Monck et al., *Sion's Groans for Her Distressed, or Sober Endeavours to Prevent Innocent Blood* (n.p., 1661), in *Tracts on Liberty of Conscience and Persecution, 1614–1661*, ed. Edward Bean Underhill, Elibron Classics Series (London: J. Haddon, 1846; repr., [Chestnut Hill MA]: Adamant Media Corporation, 2003) 362.

[4] Rhys Isaac, *The Transformation of Virginia, 1740–1790* (Chapel Hill: Published for the Institute of Early American History and Culture, Williamsburg, Virginia, by the University of North Carolina Press, 1982; repr., 1999) 175.

what was deformed in some way or other. Some of them were hair-lipped, others were blear-eyed, or hump-backed, or bow-legged, or clump-footed; hardly any of them looked like other people. But they were all strong for plunging, and let their poor ignorant children run wild, and never had the seal of the covenant put on them."[5] Whether many people believed such a description is uncertain, but the outlandish and exaggerated portrayals of Baptist practices and beliefs surely skewed the way many people perceived and treated Baptists.

The Baptists' insistence on baptizing believers only by immersion frightened many people. Some of their opponents accused them of child abuse for not baptizing infants. Others emphasized the physical danger of believer's baptism. In his book *Anabaptism*, Robert Baillie, a Church of Scotland minister, noted that many adults living in warm climates could not "be plunged over their heads in cold water" without jeopardizing their lives. He based his opinion on the "experience" of Scots "in that short time wherein this noisome ceremony has been brought in fashion."[6]

---

[5] David Benedict, *Fifty Years among the Baptists*, The Michigan Historical Reprint Series (New York: Sheldon & Company, 1860; repr., [Ann Arbor]: The Scholarly Publishing Office, The University of Michigan, n.d.) 93.

[6] Robert Baillie, *Anabaptism, the True Fountaine of Independancy, Antinomy, Brownisme, Familisme, and Most of the Other Errours, which for the Time Doe Trouble the Church of England, Unmasked* (London: printed by M. F. for Samuel Gellibrand, 1647) 171. In *Plain Scripture Proof of Infants Church-membership and Baptism* (London: printed for Robert White, 1651) 136–38, Richard Baxter, a Presbyterian minister, also decried the baptizing of people in the nude. See also Charles Woodmason's harangue against Baptists in *The Carolina Backcountry on the Eve of the Revolution: The Journal and Other Writings of Charles Woodmason, Anglican Itinerant*, ed. Richard J. Hooker (Chapel Hill: The University of North Carolina Press, 1953) 95–117. An itinerant Anglican minister in North Carolina in the eighteenth century, Woodmason, in a sermon, accused Baptists of causing the increase in numerous social evils. Who has not noticed, he asked his congregation, the increase in drunkenness, slanders, swearing, fornication, adultery, theft, murders, and prostitution (to name only a few) since Baptists entered North Carolina? (Woodmason, *The Carolina Backcountry*, 95–101). Woodmason also claimed that in the late 1760s "a thousand persons of the dissenting tribe were...under the hands of surgeons for the venereal distemper" (Woodmason, *The Carolina Backcountry*, 95n25). But what else could be expected of such "rambling fanatics," "vermin of religion," "ignorant wretches," and "lascivious persons" who worshipped at "schism shops"? (Woodmason, *The Carolina Backcountry*, 99, 101, 103, 95). See also *The Leacherous*

Believer's baptism by immersion not only threatened the health and lives of baptismal candidates, but, according to several opponents of Baptists, it also jeopardized the essence of public decency because Baptists supposedly performed this rite in the nude. According to Baillie, such a practice was not limited to a fringe sect, for "most of our dippers" did so.[7] "For men and women to stand up naked, as they were born, and naked men...to go into the water with naked women, holding them in their arms until they have plunged them in the water" was nothing less than scandalous.[8]

Readers of Daniel Featley's *The Dippers Dipt: or, The Anabaptists Duck'd and Plung'd over Head and Eares* did not have to use their imagination to picture the Baptists' baptismal practice, for the author provided a sketch of such a ceremony. The center of one page in his book has a drawing of two naked "dippers" and their naked baptismal candidates, three of whom are women. One of the dippers appears to be whispering something to a woman, and the reader is left to wonder what salacious suggestions he is making to one of the "virgins of Sion."[9] Even if a small number of Baptists did baptize in the nude, Featley's depiction of a Baptist baptismal service was obviously meant to portray all Baptists as sexual perverts.

The unflattering portrayals of Baptists, however, fueled a greater fear—that Baptists would destroy the church and the state. What would become of Christianity if Baptists, whom Featley contemptuously described as "an ignorant and sottish sect," were permitted to spread their heresy and stupidity?[10] And what would become of the quality of churches if they followed the Baptist example of calling uneducated ministers like Thomas

---

Anabaptist, or The Dipper Dipt: A New Protestant Ballad (London: printed for Benjamin Harris, 1681).

[7] Baillie, *Anabaptism*, 173. Baptists vehemently denied this accusation. See Samuel Richardson, *Some Brief Considerations on Doctor Featley His Book, Intitled* The Dipper Dipt (London: n.p., 1645) 5, and Henry Haggar, *The Foundation of the Font Discovered* (London: printed for Giles Calvert, 1653) 100.

[8] Baillie, *Anabaptism*, 171.

[9] Daniel Featley, *The Dippers Dipt: or, The Anabaptists Duck'd and Plung'd over Head and Eares, at a Disputation in Southwark*, 4th ed. (London: printed for Nicholas Bourn and Richard Royston, 1646). This drawing is located two pages prior to the title page.

[10] Featley, *The Dippers Dipt*, 121.

Ewins, Henry Adis, John Bunyan, and John Waller? Obviously, in the opinion of Baptist opponents, nothing good.

Church and state officials created a more powerful fantasy by constantly warning of the dire consequences of permitting religious liberty. When Baptists had to worship secretly during the early years of their existence, their opponents fantasized that the heretics met clandestinely because they were plotting, under the pretext of liberty of conscience, the overthrow of the civil government. Consider the language of the following example.

Thomas Cobbett, the Puritan pastor of the church at Lynn, Massachusetts, when John Clarke, Obadiah Holmes, and John Crandall made their famous incursion into Massachusetts, well expressed the fear that civil and ecclesiastical authorities had of religious liberty. Cobbett argued that any civil court had the right "to restrain and punish civilly" anyone who attempted "to disturb our peace, to undermine our churches and the ministration of church ordinances," and "to undermine our civil state, whose foundations shake, with those of the churches." Permitting heretics like Baptists to run free in the land meant that "both civil government and state and churches...would soon be blown up, and we should become a very chaos."[11]

As Cobbett's words reveal, Baptists represented radical religious and political change, and the leaders of the governments and of the established churches in England, Massachusetts, and Virginia equated such change with religious and social catastrophe. To prove that their fears were warranted, they pointed to the bloody rebellion of Anabaptist radicals in Münster, Germany, in the 1530s, to the beheadings of William Laud in 1645 and of Charles I in 1649, and to Thomas Venner's 1661 insurrection in London. Yet no matter how much Baptists denied being Anabaptists or being interested in destroying the civil government, few people believed them. Honesty was not enough to destroy the fear built on fantasy.

---

[11] Thomas Cobbett, *A Brief Answer to a Certain Slanderous Pamphlet Called* Ill News from New-England...*By John Clark of Road-Island, Physician*, in *The Civil Magistrates Power In Matters of Religion Modestly Debated, Impartially Stated according to the Bounds and Grounds of Scripture*,...(London: printed by W. Wilson for Stephens, 1653; repr., New York: Arno Press, 1972) 40.

Essentially, church and political leaders feared losing control, and in such fear they could not envision an environment in which they could maintain the people's trust and loyalty by persuasion and argument rather than by political power and persecution. Ecclesiastical and civil leaders could not fathom a world in which common people could make religious and political decisions for themselves. Consequently, they let themselves be controlled by their fear of losing control.

Fear, however, breeds more than fancy; it often breeds persecution. In Baptists, and in other dissenters, the civil and ecclesiastical authorities in England, Massachusetts, and Virginia saw people who threatened their power and authority. These authorities sincerely believed that too much freedom, particularly religious freedom, would destroy both church and state. The fear of losing control thus led to the use of fear as a means of controlling dissenters like Baptists. Civil and religious authorities believed that if they imprisoned Baptists, or sometimes physically beat them, they would submit, at least outwardly, which would then be a step toward civil and ecclesiastical stability.

Such was the world in which Baptists lived, but that was not their only world. As their writings reveal, most imprisoned Baptists did not submit to threats, persecutions, or incarcerations, for they feared not the Church of England, the Puritan Congregationalists, or the civil magistrates, but God.

The Fear that Produced Faith and Courage

Fear is often not a cowardly or paralyzing reaction to one's world, for, as Aristotle taught, "to fear some things is even right and noble, and it is base not to fear them—e.g., disgrace."[12] Imprisoned Baptists, however, feared more than disgrace; they feared God. Francis Bampfield, sitting in his cell in Salisbury, England, wrote about "the holy fear of God," which "would either prevent or remedy the sinful fear of men. Christ's ministers and messengers should not decline any duty through carnal fear. It is one great design of the persecuting enemy to hurry us into that distempered passion. They would put us in fear that we might sin, and [that] they might

---

[12] Aristotle, *Nicomachean Ethics*, 3.6, in *Classics of Philosophy*, 2nd ed., ed. Louis P. Pojman (New York: Oxford University Press, 2003) 312.

have matter for an evil report [so] that they might reproach us and, what is worse, [so] that they might reproach our God."[13]

Henry Adis, writing in Gatehouse Prison in London, emphasized the benefits to the nation if Christians lived in the fear of God. Adis encouraged his readers to follow the path of Christians who had gone before them,

> not at all fearing what man can do to us, for this is the requirement of our Lord and Master, who said, "Fear not him that can kill the body only, and afterwards can do no more, but rather fear him, that after he hath killed the body, can cast both the body and soul into hell; I say, fear him" ([Luke 12:5]; Matt. 10:28). And in his fear, let us be found in well doing, endeavoring as much as in us lies, to see the peace and welfare of the nation be secured. For if every man's particular interest is involved in the general good, then it stands every particular man in hand, to study the good, peace, safety, and welfare of the whole.[14]

And from his cell in London's Newgate Prison, Hercules Collins proclaimed the liberating effect the fear of God had on prisoners: "O! Blessed state to be delivered from the fear of men, the fear of evil, the fear of prison, the fear of poverty, the fear of flames, as many have experienced through grace. And if they may be believed, [they] can speak experimentally, which is more than to read it, that Christ's yoke is easy, and...notwithstanding all [that] befalls the saints; his burden is a light burden [Matt 11:30], and his ways are pleasant, and his paths are peace [Prov 3:17]."[15]

The "holy fear of God" described by imprisoned Baptists, however, did not completely eliminate the concerns for the welfare of their families and friends, but only John Bunyan admitted being fearful of death. He also acknowledged experiencing periods of despondency, as did John Waller and James Ireland. It would be unbelievable, however, to think that the other incarcerated Baptists did not experience some fear or moments of terror at

---

[13] Francis Bampfield, *Open Confessor and the Free Prisoner* (London: n.p., 1675) 4.

[14] Henry Adis, *A Fannaticks Letter Sent out of the Dungeon of the Gate-House Prison of Westminster* (London: printed by S. Dover, 1660) 10.

[15] Hercules Collins, *A Voice from the Prison, or, Meditations on Revelations 3:11, Tending to the Establishment of Gods Little Flock, in an Hour of Temptation* (London: printed by George Larkin for the author, 1684) 31.

the hands of their persecutors. But even if they had such experiences, their faith kept them focused on the world in which their persecutors ultimately had no power. "True faith," Thomas Hardcastle reminded his Bristol congregation, "keeps the soul much in serious, distinct thoughts of its passage into another world."[16] Such "faith gives the soul a clear view of the glory to come, reigning with Christ, that exceedingly and eternal weight of glory, for a few, light, momentary afflictions. The clouds are hastening away, sorrow and mourning fleeing apace, praise waiting for the Lord in Zion."[17]

The fear of God not only led imprisoned Baptists to hold fast to their faith when facing persecution; it also gave them the courage to endure their persecutions. Bunyan encouraged his readers not to let anything or anyone hinder them because "the Crown is at the end,/ Let's run, and strive, and fly, and let's contend/ With greatest courage, it for to obtain;/ 'Tis life, and peace, and everlasting gain."[18] From the Tower of London, Richard Overton courageously spoke for many Baptists when he declared: "I bid defiance to what all the men and devils in earth or hell can do against me in the discharge of my understanding and conscience for the good of the commonwealth, for I know that my Redeemer lives [Job 19:25], and that after this life I shall be restored to life and immortality and receive according to the innocency and uprightness of my heart." Without that assurance, Overton confessed that he would have led a radically different life: "I would not thus put my life and well being in jeopardy, and expose myself to those extremities and necessities that I do. I would creaturize, be this or that or anything else, as were the times, eat, drink, and take my pleasure, turn Judas or anything to flatter great men for promotion: but blessed be the God of heaven and earth, [for] he has given me a better heart and better

---

[16] Thomas Hardcastle's eighteenth letter, no date, in *The Records of a Church of Christ, Meeting in Broadmead, Bristol, 1640–1685*, ed. Edward Bean Underhill (London: J. Haddon, 1847) 333. Hereafter cited as *RCC*.

[17] Thomas Hardcastle's fourteenth letter, 12 November 1675, in *RCC*, 315–16.

[18] John Bunyan, "Ebal and Gerizzim," in *The Miscellaneous Works of John Bunyan: The Poems*, ed. Graham Midgley, gen. ed. Roger Sharrock (Oxford: The Clarendon Press, 1980) 6:108, lines 112–15. See also Bampfield, *Open Confessor and the Free Prisoner*, 5, and Thomas Grantham, *The Prisoner against the Prelate: or, A Dialogue between the Common Goal and Cathedral of Lincoln* ([London: n.p., 1662]) 4.

understanding."[19] Overton and many other Baptists, however, did place their trust in God, even though such trust could have cost them their earthly lives. Even so, the Leveller leader proclaimed, "I know that my life is hid in Christ [Col 3:3], and if upon this account I must yield it—welcome, welcome, welcome by the grace of God."[20]

Overton's last statement highlights an important aspect of the Baptists' understanding of their faith. They never claimed that their courage was the product of their own inner resources; rather, their courage to endure persecution was the product of grace. Bampfield emphasized this point:

> I would not write thus out of any self-confidence, but to declare that which is Jehovah's command and our duty, for who or what am I, if left to myself, any longer than I have supplies of grace and of strength from the Holy Spirit? I cannot stand before my own fears, even those...that are causeless ones, [for] my own thoughts would quickly overbear and overwhelm me, every difficulty would be too hard, and every cross would be too hard. If at any time I stand, it is by faith; I may not be high-minded but must fear, with a holy fear, with the fear of Jehovah in my heart, that I may not depart from him. Peter's eminent grace was holy boldness for Christ, and yet he quickly failed in this grace, wherein he did so excel, and that shortly after he put forth some choice expressings and actings of that grace. As much as Paul was a man of courage in the cause of Christ, yet he humbly acknowledged his own weakness and nothingness in all his laborings and sufferings for his LORD, denying himself as to any sharing in any of that honor, which in the whole of it was due to Christ: "I," says he, "yet not I, but the grace of God which was with me [1 Cor 15:10]; I am crucified with Christ ; nevertheless, I live, yet not I, but Christ liveth in me" [Gal 2:20]. It was in the grace that is in Christ Jesus that Paul was strong; it was Christ's grace.[21]

---

[19] John Lilburne, Thomas Prince, and Richard Overton, *The Picture of the Councell of State, Held forth to the Free People of England* ([London:] n.p., 1649), in *The Leveller Tracts, 1647–1653*, ed., William Haller and Godfrey Davies (Gloucester MA: Peter Smith, 1964) 228.

[20] Ibid., 230.

[21] Bampfield, *Open Confessor and the Free Prisoner*, 4.

With such "fearful" faith and courage, many Baptists preached themselves into prison. Preaching a believers' church, Baptists insisted that only people who could confess their faith in Christ and then express such faith could become members of a church. Rejecting infant baptism and worship based on any book other than the Bible, Baptists contended that a living God demanded a living faith, one that each person must experience himself or herself. As William Brackney observed, the early Baptist emphasis on experience compelled them "to move beyond liturgical confessionalism to a form of Christianity that was fully experiential."[22] Consequently, Baptists detested the Church of England and what they considered to be its ungodly dependence on the state to protect and promote its ministry, its unbiblical practice of baptizing infants, its highly educated but completely unspiritual clergy, its spiritually suffocating *Book of Common Prayer*, and its narcoleptic liturgical worship. In rejecting such practices, Baptists rejected the Church of England's official teachings and interpretations of the Bible, which infuriated those people who claimed to be their spiritual masters. For such convictions, Baptists suffered the wrath of kings, governments, bishops, clergy, and anyone else who demanded that they bow to their authority.

Because they preached a gathered church and practiced a congregational form of church government, Baptists argued that not only should people choose rather than be forced to attend church; they should also choose whom they wanted to be their ministers. Overton expressed such a position in his baptismal confession, in which he wrote that Christ's church should be "assembled together *cordially* and *unanimously*, to choose persons to bear offices in this church."[23] Baptists contended that such cordial gatherings be assembled by God's Spirit, not by the magistrate's sword. Moreover, once gathered, Baptists claimed the responsibility of choosing their ministers, even if their leaders had not received a formal, university education or a proper ordination by "the church."

---

[22] William H. Brackney, *A Genetic History of Baptist Thought: With Special Reference to Baptists in Britain and North America* (Macon GA: Mercer University Press, 2004) 530. See Woodmason's mocking of the Baptist emphasis on religious experience in Hooker, *The Carolina Backcountry on the Eve of the Revolution*, 103–104.

[23] [Richard Overton's Baptismal Confession], in *The Early English Baptists*, by Benjamin Evans (London: J. Heaton & Son, 1862) 1:255.

Imprisoned Baptists also advocated religious liberty. They denied the state's and the established church's attempts to compel people to worship in ways that violated their consciences. To Baptists, the idea of a forced fellowship was an oxymoron as much as it was a heresy. According to English and Virginia Anglicans, English Presbyterians, and Massachusetts Congregationalists, however, religious liberty was heretical and seditious. Baptist prison writings of the seventeenth and eighteenth centuries are replete with arguments against the accusation of heresy, noting that the early Christian church prospered without any help from civil authorities. Baptist prison writings also contain numerous professions of loyalty to the Crown. Even though Baptists denied that the king, or any magistrate for that matter, had the authority to meddle in religious affairs, none denied the right and responsibility of civil authorities to legislate the outward actions of people and to punish people when their actions threatened the lives or property of others. Consequently, most Baptists considered themselves to be members of the king's or of the government's loyal opposition.[24] Civil authorities, however, rejected such professions of loyalty, considering them a ruse to hide Baptists' true motive—destroying the state. These authorities could not live with the Baptist "but": we affirm your right to manage our civil affairs, "but" we deny your right to control our religious lives. Most civil authorities considered this position to be seditious. They had to control every aspect of people's lives, even people's relationship with God.

Conclusion

In discussing Bunyan's understanding of suffering for liberty of conscience, Richard Greaves presented an interpretation with which most, if not all, imprisoned Baptists would have agreed. Imprisonment "was not merely something to be endured but virtually an act of worship, calling for the active participation of the believer through willing acceptance. In the confrontation with the Stuart state, victory was only possible for those who could find 'joy under the cross,' the spiritual experience of suffering for the right cause in the right way."[25] Imprisoned Baptists of the seventeenth and

---

[24] See Edwin S. Gaustad, "Baptists and Experimental Religion," *Chronicle* 15/3 (July 1952): 118.

[25] Richard L. Greaves, "The Spirit and the Sword: Bunyan and the Stuart State," *Baptist Quarterly Review* 32/8 (October 1988): 375.

eighteenth centuries believed that by defying civil and religious authorities and suffering the consequences, they were suffering for the right cause and in the right way.

During the seventeenth and eighteenth centuries, Baptists knew that they could avoid unimaginable hardships if they bowed to the pressure to conform. Many Baptists considered such yielding as a retreat from their cause and their God, and they moved forward in their faith because they believed that retreating would have been spiritually fatal. Faith in God provided no reason to turn back, or, as Thomas Hardcastle encouraged his Bristol congregation: "Religion is still for standing and going forward." Thus, they advanced, some into prison and then back to freedom, others into jail and then into the grave. All, however, did so because they knew what Hardcastle knew: "There is no armor for the back."[26]

---

[26] Thomas Hardcastle's first letter, 18 August 1675, in *RCC*, 258.

Bibliography

Primary Sources

Adis, Henry. *A Cup for the Citie, and Her Adherents*. N.p., 1648.

————. *A Fannaticks Letter Sent out of the Dungeon of the Gate-House Prison of Westminster*. London: printed by S. Dover for the author, 1660.

————. *A Fannaticks Mite Cast into the Kings Treasury: Being a Sermon Printed to the King Because Not Preach'd before the King*. 2nd edition. London: printed by S. Dover for the author, 1660.

[————.] *A Spie, Sent out of the Tower-Chamber in the Fleet*. N.p., 1648.

Against Universall Libertie of Conscience, Being Animadversions upon Two Letters Written to a Friend Pleading for It. London: printed for Thomas Underhill, 1644.

Backus, Isaac. *A History of New England with Particular Reference to the Denomination of Christians Called Baptists*. Edited by David Weston. 2nd edition. 2 volumes. Newton MA: The Backus Historical Society, 1871.

Bagshaw, Edward. *The Life and Death of Mr. Vavasor Powell*. [London : n.p., 1671].

Baillie, Robert. *Anabaptism, the True Fountaine of Independancy, Antinomy, Brownisme, Familisme, and Most of the Other Errours, Which for the Time Doe Trouble the Church of England, Unmasked*. London: printed by M. F. for Samuel Gellibrand, 1647.

Bampfield, Francis. *A Continuation of a Former Just Appeal, From Lower Courts on Earth, to the Highest Court in Heaven*. [London: n.p., 1684].

————. Francis Bampfield to William Benn, c. 1672. In *The Judgment of Mr. Francis Bampfield, Late Minister of Sherborne in Dorsetshire for the Observation of the Jewish, or Seventh Day Sabboth*, by William Ben, 3–8. London: printed by W. Godbid for Sarah Nevill, 1677.

————. *A Just Appeal, From Lower Courts on Earth, to the Highest Court in Heaven*. London: printed for the author, 1683.

————. *The Lords Free Prisoner*. London: printed for W. T., 1683. Also available online at http://www.seventh-day-baptist.org.au/library/books/prisoner.htm.

———. *A Name, an After-one.* London: printed for John Lawrence, 1681.

———. *Open Confessor and the Free Prisoner.* London: n.p., 1675.

Massachusetts Historical Society, Boston.

Barber, Edward. *To the Kings Most Excellent Majesty, and the Honourable Court of Parliament.* [London:] n.p., 1641.

Bartlett, John Russell, editor. *Records of the Colony of Rhode Island and Providence Plantations, in New England.* Volume 1. Providence RI: A. Crawford Greene and Brother, State Printers, 1856.

Baxter, Richard. *More Proofs of Infants Church-membership and Consequently their Right to Baptism.* London: printed for N. Simmons and J. Robinson, 1675.

———. *Plain Scripture Proof of Infants Church-membership and Baptism.* London: printed for Robert White, 1651.

Beardsley, John, editor. "Liberties of New Englishmen." The Winthrop Society. http://www.winthropsociety.org/liberties.php.

Bettenson, Henry, editor. *Documents of the Christian Church.* 2nd edition. London: Oxford University Press, 1963.

A Brief Narration of the Imprisonment of Mr. Francis Bampfield. N.p., 1662.

Bunyan, John. *Grace Abounding & The Life and Death of Mr. Badman.* Everyman's Library 85. London: J. M. Dent & Sons Ltd., 1953.

———. *The Miscellaneous Works of John Bunyan.* Volume 6. *The Poems,* edited by Graham Midgley and Roger Sharrock (general editor). Oxford: The Clarendon Press, 1980.

———. "Peaceable Principles and True." In *The Works of John Bunyan,* edited by George Offor, 2:648–57. Glasgow: Balckie and Son, 1854.

———. *The Pilgrim's Progress.* Reprint, Grand Rapids MI: Baker Book House, 1984.

Burrage, Champlin. *The Early English Dissenters in the Light of Recent Research.* 2 volumes. Cambridge: University Press, 1912.

Cheyney, Edward P., editor. *Readings in English History Drawn from the Original Sources.* New York: Ginn and Company, 1922.

Clarke, John. *Ill Newes from New-England.* In *Colonial Baptists: Massachusetts and Rhode Island.* The Baptist Tradition. London: H. Hills, 1652. Reprint, New York: Arno Press, 1980.

Cobbet, Thomas. *The Civil Magistrates Power in Matters of Religion Modestly Debated, Impartially Stated according to the Bounds and Grounds of Scripture,…Together with a Brief Answer to a Certain Slanderous Pamphlet*

Called Ill News from New-England... *By John Clark of Road-Island, Physician.* London: printed by W. Wilson for Stephens, 1653. Reprint, New York: Arno Press, 1972.

Collins, Hercules. "An Elegy on the Deaths of Mr. Bampfield and Mr. Ralphson, who Dyed Prisoners for Christ, in the Press yard, Newgate." In *Counsel For the Living, Occasioned from the Dead: or, A Discourse on Job 3:17–18. Arising from the Deaths of Mr. Fran. Bampfield and Mr. Zach. Ralphson*, by Hercules Collins, 34–37. London: printed by George Larkin for the author, 1684.

———. *Some Reasons for Separation from the Communion of the Church of England, and the Unreasonableness of Persecution on that Account.* London: printed for John How, 1682.

———. *A Voice from the Prison, or, Meditations on Revelations 3:11, Tending to the Establishment of Gods Little Flock, in An Hour of Temptation.* London: printed by George Larkin for the author, 1684.

Cotton, John. *The Controversie Concerning Liberty of Conscience in Matters of Religion, Truly Stated, and Distinctly and Plainly Handled,...By Way of Answer to Aome Arguments to the Contrary Sent unto Him.* London: printed for Thomas Banks, 1646.

"The Declaration of Indulgence, 1672." http://www.swan.ac.uk/history/teaching/teaching%20resources/Revolutionary%20England/Indulgence.htm.

Delaune, Thomas. *A Narrative of the Tryal and Sufferings of Thomas DeLaune.* N.p.: printed for the author, 1683. Reprint, n.p., 1704. Reprinted in *A Plea for the Non-Conformists*, by Thomas Delaune, 56–68. London: n.p., 1704.

———. *A Plea for the Non-Conformists.* [Reprint], London: n.p., 1704.

———. *Two Letters to Dr. Benjamin Calamy, One in English, the Other in Latine.* N.p., n.d.

Denne, Henry. *Antichrist Unmasked in Two Treatises. The First, An Answer unto Two Paedobaptists, Dan. Featly, D.D. and Stephen Marshall, B.D....* N.p., 1645.

———. *The Levellers Designe Discovered.* London: n.p., 1649. Also available online at http://baptistlibraryonline.com/blo/content/view/33/25.

Edwards, Thomas. *Gangraena.* In 3 parts. London: printed by T. R. and E. M. for Ralph Smith, 1645–1646.

Featley, Daniel. *The Dippers Dipt: or, The Anabaptists Duck'd and Plung'd over Head and Eares, at a Disputation in Southwark*. London: printed for Nicholas Bourn and Richard Royston, 1645.

———. *The Dippers Dipt: or, The Anabaptists Duck'd and plung'd Over Head and Eares, at a Disputation in Southwark*. 4th ed. London: printed for Nicholas Bourn and Richard Royston, 1646.

Gardiner, Samuel Rawson, editor. *The Constitutional Documents of the Puritan Revolution 1625–1660*. 3rd edition. Revised edition. Oxford: Oxford University Press, 1906. Also available online at http://www.constitution.org/eng/conpur013.htm.

Gee, Henry, and William John Hardy, editors. *Documents Illustrative of English Church History*. London, Macmillan and Co., Ltd., 1914.

Grantham, Thomas. *Christianismus Primitivus*. London: printed for Francis Smith, 1678. Also available online at http://baptistlibraryonline.com/blo/content/view/13/.

———. *The Prisoner against the Prelate: or, A Dialogue between the Common Goal and Cathedral of Lincoln*. [London: n.p., 1662]. Also available online at http://baptistlibraryonline.com/blo/content/view/13/.

Griffith, John. *The Case of Mr. John Griffith, Minister of the Gospel, and Now Prisoner in Newgate: Being a True and Impartial Account of What He Spake at the Sessions-house in the Old Bailey on the 18th of...April 1683*. In *The History of the English Baptists from the Reformation to the Beginning of the Reign of King George I*, by Thomas Crosby, 2:361–66. London: privately printed, 1739.

———. *Some Prison Meditations and Experiences: with Some Hints Touching the Fall of the Mother of Harlots, and the Exaltation of the Son of God upon the Throne of David*. N.p., 1663.

Haggar, Henry. *The Foundation of the Font Discovered*. London: printed for Giles Calvert, 1653.

Hardcastle, Thomas. *Christian Geography and Arithmetick*. London: printed for Richard Chiswell, 1674.

Harper, Keith, and C. Martin Jacumin, editors. *Esteemed Reproach: The Lives of Reverend James Ireland and Reverend Joseph Craig*. Macon GA: Mercer University Press, 2005.

Hell Broke Loose: or, a Catalogue of the spreading Errors, Heresies and Blasphemies of these Times, for Which We Are to Be Humbled. London: printed for Tho. Underhill, 1646.

Helwys, Thomas. *An Advertisement or Admonition unto the Congregations.* N.p., 1611. Also available online at http://www.baptistlibraryonline.com/library/Helwys/admonition.pdf.

———. *A Short Declaration of the Mystery of Iniquity (1611/1612)*, edited by Richard Groves. Macon GA: Mercer University Press, 1998. Also available online at http://www.baptistlibraryonline.com/library/Helwys/mystery.pdf.

Hening, William Waller. *The Statutes at Large: Being a Collection of All the Laws of Virginia, from the First Session of the Legislature in the Year 1619.* Volumes 1 and 3. Available online at http://vagenweb.rootsweb.com/hening/.

Hooker, Richard. *The Laws of Ecclesiastical Polity.* Volume 3 of *The Works of that Learned and Judicious Divine Mr. Richard Hooker with an Account of His Life and Death by Isaac Walton.* 7th edition. Oxford: Clarendon Press, 1888. Also available at http://oll.libertyfund.org/Intros/Hooker.php.

Hooker, Richard J., editor. *The Carolina Backcountry on the Eve of the Revolution: The Journal and Other Writings of Charles Woodmason, Anglican Itinerant.* Chapel Hill: The University of North Carolina Press, 1953.

Hutchinson, Thomas, editor. *A Collection of Original Papers Relative to the History of the Colony of Massachusets-Bay.* Boston: printed by Thomas and John Fleet, 1769.

James I. *The Workes of the Most High and Mightie Prince, James.* London: printed by Robert Barker and John Bill, 1616.

Janz, Denis R., editor. *A Reformation Reader: Primary Texts and Introductions.* Minneapolis: Fortress Press, 1999.

Jessey, Henry. *A Looking-Glass for Children...Together, with Sundry Seasonable Lessons and Instructions to Youth, Calling Them Early to Remember Their Creator: Written by Abraham Cheare, Late of Plymouth.* 2nd edition. London: printed for Robert Boulter, 1673.

———. *The Lord's Loud Call to England.* London: printed for Francis Smith, 1660.

LaFantasie, Glenn W., editor. *The Correspondence of Roger Williams.* Volume 1. Hannover RI: Brown University/University Press of New England, 1988.

Laud, William. Epistle dedicatory to *A Relation of the Conference between William Laud, Late Lord Archbishop of Canterbury, by the Command of King*

James, of Ever Blessed Memory.... 6th edition. Oxford: John Henry
     Parker, 1849. Available online at
     http://justus.anglican.org/resources/pc/lact/laud/v2/dedicatory.html.
————. *The Works of the Most Reverend Father in God, William Laud, D.D.* 7
     volumes. Oxford: John Henry Parker, 1847–1860.
The Leacherous Anabaptist, or The Dipper Dipt: A New Protestant Ballad.
     London: printed for Benjamin Harris, 1681.
A Letter of the Ministers of the City of London...against Toleration. London:
     printed for Samuel Gellibrand, 1645.
Lilburne, John, and Richard Overton. *The Out-cryes of Oppressed Commons.*
     2nd edition. [London:] n.p., 1646.
Lilburne, John, Thomas Prince, and Richard Overton. *The Picture of the
     Councell of State, Held forth to the Free People of England.* [London:] n.p.,
     1649. In *The Leveller Tracts, 1647–1653*, edited by William Haller and
     Godfrey Davies, 190–246. Gloucester MA: Peter Smith, 1964.
————. *The Picture of the Councell of State, Held forth to the Free People of
     England.* 2nd ed. [London:] n.p., 1649.
Lumpkin, William L., editor. *Baptist Confessions of Faith.* Philadelphia:
     Judson Press, 1959.
McIlwain, Charles Howard, editor. *The Political Works of James I.* London:
     N.p., 1616. Reprint, Cambridge MA: Harvard University Press, 1918.
     Available online at http://www.perseus.tufts.edu/cgi-
     bin/ptext?doc=Perseus%3Atext%3A1999.03.0071.
McLoughlin, William G., and Martha Whiting Davidson, editors. "The
     Baptist Debate of April 14–15, 1668." In *Colonial Baptists: Massachusetts
     and Rhode Island.* The Baptist Tradition. Massachusetts Historical
     Society *Proceedings* (1964), 91–133. Reprint, New York: Arno Press,
     1980.
Murton, John. *A Description of What God hath Predestinated Concerning Man,
     in his Creation, Transgression, & Regeneration.* N.p., 1620.
Overton, Richard. *An Arrow against All Tyrants and Tyranny, Shot from the
     Prison of New-gate into the Prerogative Bowels of the Arbitrary House of
     Lords and All Other Usurpers and Tyrants Whatsoever.* [London:] n.p.,
     1646. In *The English Levellers*, edited by Andrew Sharp, 54–72.
     Cambridge Texts in the History of Political Thought. Cambridge:
     University Press, 1998. Also available at online
     http://www.constitution.org/lev/eng_lev_05.htm.

———. *The Baiting of the Great Bull of Bashan Unfolded*. London: n.p., 1649.

———. *The Commoners Complaint*. London: n.p., 1646. In *Tracts on Liberty in the Puritan Revolution, 1638–1647*, edited by William Haller, 373–95. New York: Octagon Books, Inc., 1965.

———. *Overton's Defyance of the Act of Pardon*. London: n.p., 1649.

Powell, Vavasor. *Common-Prayer-Book No Divine Service*. London: printed for Livewell Chapman, 1660.

———. *The Bird in the Cage, Chirping Four Distinct Notes to His Consorts Abroad*. London: printed for L. C. 1661.

Religions Lotterie, or the Churches Amazement.... London: printed by T. F., 1642.

Rhodes, Neil, Jennifer Richards, and Joseph Marshall, editors. *King James VI and I: Selected Writings*. Aldershot, Hants England: Ashgate Publishing Company, 2003.

Richardson, Samuel. *Some Brief Considerations on Doctor Featley His Book, Intitled* The Dipper Dipt. London: n.p., 1645.

Robinson, John. *The Works of John Robinson, Pastor of the Pilgrim Fathers, with a Memoir and Annotations* by Robert Ashton. 3 volumes. London: John Snow, 1851. Also available online at http://oll.libertyfund.org/ToC/0064.php.

Thomas, David. *The Virginian Baptist*. Baltimore: printed by Enoch Story, 1774.

"To the Reader." In *A Sermon Preached at Shadwell-Chapell in Yorkshire*, by Thomas Hardcastle. London: n.p., 1665.

"The Toleration Act, 1689." Available online at http://www.swan.ac.uk/history/teaching/teaching%20resources/Revolutionary%20Englan d/TolerationAct.htm.

Underhill, Edward Bean, editor. *The Records of a Church of Christ, Meeting in Broadmead, Bristol. 1640–1687*. London: J. Haddon, 1847.

———. *Tracts on Liberty of Conscience and Persecution, 1614–1661*. Elibron Classics Series. London: J. Haddon, 1846. Reprint, [Chestnut Hill MA]: Adamant Media Corporation, 2003.

Ward, Nathanial. *The Simple Cobler of Aggawam in America*. London: printed by John Dever & Robert Ibbitson for Stephen Bowtell, 1647. Also available online at http://puritanism.online.fr/puritanism/ward/ward.html.

Wilkinson, John. *The Sealed Fountaine Opened to the Faithfull, and Their Seed. Or, A Short Treatise, Shewing, That Some Infants Are in the State of Grace, and Capable of the Seales, and Others Not. Being the Chief Point, wherein the Separatists Doe Blame the Anabaptists. By John Wilkinson, prisoner at Colchester, against John Morton Prisoner at London*. [London : n.p., 1646].

Williams, Roger. *The Bloody Tenent Yet More Bloody*. London: printed for Giles Calvert, 1652.

———. *The Bloudy Tenent of Persecution, for Cause of Conscience*, edited by Richard Groves. Macon GA: Mercer University Press, 2001.

Winthrop, John. *The Journal of John Winthrop, 1630–1649*, edited by Richard S. Dunn, James Savage, and Laetitia Yeandle. Cambridge MA: Harvard University Press, 1996.

Wolfe, Don M., editor. *Leveller Manifestoes of the Puritan Revolution*. New York: Thomas Nelson and Sons, 1944.

Wood, Anthony. *Athenæ Oxonienses: An Exact History of all the Writers and Bishops Who Have Had Their Education in the Most Ancient and Famous University of Oxford*. Volume 2. London: printed for Tho. Bennet, 1692.

Secondary Sources

Alley, Reuben Edward. *A History of Baptists in Virginia*. Richmond: Virginia Baptist General Board, [1973].

American National Biography Online. Oxford University Press, 2000. http://www.anb.org.

Bagshaw, Edward. *The Life and Death of Mr. Vavasor Powell*. [London : n.p., 1671].

Benedict, David. *Fifty Years among the Baptists*. The Michigan Historical Reprint Series. New York: Sheldon & Company, 1860. Reprint, [Ann Arbor]: The Scholarly Publishing Office, University of Michigan, n.d.

Bicknell, Thomas W. *Story of John Clarke*. 2nd edition. Providence RI: privately printed, 1915.

Brackney, William Henry. *A Genetic History of Baptist Thought: With Special Reference to Baptists in Britain and North America*. Macon GA: Mercer University Press, 2004.

Burgess, Walter H. *John Smith the Se-Baptist, Thomas Helwys and the First Baptist Church in England, with Fresh Light upon the Pilgrim Fathers' Church*. London: James Clarke & Co., 1913.

Burrage, Henry S. *A History of the Baptists in New England*. Philadelphia: American Baptist Publication Society, 1894.

Calamy, Edmund. *The Nonconformist's Memorial*. 3 volumes. London: printed by J. Cundee, 1802–1803.

Campbell, Gordon. "The Thology of *The Pilgrim's Progress*." In *The Pilgrim's Progress: Critical and Historical Views*, edited by Vincent Newey, 251–62. Liverpool: Liverpool University Press, 1980.

Carlisle, John C. *The Story of the English Baptists*. London: James Clarke & Co., 1905.

Cathcart, William, editor. *The Baptist Encyclopaedia*. Philadelphia: Louis H. Everts, 1881.

Child, Robert L., and C. E. Shipley. *Broadmead Origins: An Account of the Rise of Puritanism in England, and of the Early Days of Broadmead Baptist Church, Bristol*. London: The Kingsgate Press, [1940].

Clifford, John, editor. *The English Baptists: Who They Are, and What They Have Done*. London: E. Marlborough & Co., 1881.

Cobb, Sanford H. *The Rise of Religious Liberty in America: A History*. New York: Macmillan, 1902. Also available online at http://www.dinsdoc.com/cobb-1-0a.htm.

Coggins, James Robert. *John Smyth's Congregation: English Separatism, Mennonite Influence, and the Elect Nation*. Studies in Anabaptist and Mennonite History. Waterloo, Ontario: Herald Press, 1991.

Cox, Norman Wade, and Judson Boyce Allen, editors. *Encyclopedia of Southern Baptists*. 2 volumes. Nashville: Broadman Press, 1958.

Crosby, Thomas. *The History of the English Baptists from the Reformation to the Beginning of the Reign of King George I*. 4 volumes. London: privately printed, 1738–1740.

Davies, David. *Vavasor Powell: The Baptist Evangelist of Wales*. London: Alexander and Shepheard, 1896.

Defoe, Daniel. Preface to *A Plea for the Non-Conformists*, by Thomas Delaune. London: printed for John Marshall, 1720.

Dexter, Henry Martyn. *The True Story of John Smyth, the Se-Baptist as Told by Himself and His Contemporaries*. Boston: Lee and Shepard, 1881.

Durant, Will. *The Story of Civilization*. Part 6, *The Reformation: A History of European Civilization from Wyclif to Calvin: 1300–1564*. New York: Simon and Schuster, 1957.

Durant, Will, and Ariel Durant. *The Story of Civilization*. Part 7, *The Age of Reason Begins: A History of European Civilization in the Period of Shakespeare, Bacon, Montaigne, Rembrandt, Galileo, and Descartes: 1558–1648*. New York: Simon and Schuster, 1961.

Durso, Pam. "Baptist Women in America, 1638–1800." In *Distinctively Baptist: Essays on Baptist History: A Festschrift in Honor of Walter B. Shurden*, edited by Marc A. Jolley with John D. Pierce, 193–218. Macon GA: Mercer University Press, 2005.

Durso, Pamela R., and Keith E. Durso. *The Story of Baptists in the United States*. Brentwood TN: Baptist History and Heritage Society, 2006.

Edwards, Morgan. *Materials towards a History of the Baptists in the Provinces of Maryland, Virginia, North Carolina, South Carolina, Georgia*. N.p., 1772.

Estep, William R. *The Anabaptist Story*. Grand Rapids MI: William B. Eerdmans Publishing Company, 1975.

———. "The English Baptist Legacy of Freedom and the American Experience." In *Pilgrim Pathways: Essays in Baptist History in Honour of B. R. White*, edited by William H. Brackney and Paul S. Fiddes, 263–81. Macon GA: Mercer University Press, 1999.

———. *Revolution within the Revolution: The First Amendment in Historical Context, 1612–1789*. Grand Rapids MI: William B. Eerdmans Publishing Co., 1990.

Evans, Benjamin. *The Early English Baptists*. 2 volumes. London: J. Heaton & Son, 1862–1864.

Fant, Clyde E., Jr., and William M. Pinson, Jr. "John Bunyan." In *20 Centuries of Great Preaching: An Encyclopedia of Preaching*, edited by Clyde E. Fant, Jr., and William M. Pinson, Jr., 2:309–17. Waco TX: Word Books, Publisher, 1971.

Felt, Joseph B. *Ecclesiastical History of New England: Comprising Not Only Religious, But Also Moral, and Other Relations*. 2 volumes. Boston: Congregational Library Association, 1855–1862.

Fosdick, Harry Emerson. "Christians in Spite of Everything (Philippians 4:22)." In *20 Centuries of Great Preaching: An Encyclopedia of Preaching*, edited by Clyde E. Fant, Jr., and William M. Pinson Jr., 9:63–69. Waco TX: Word Books, Publisher, 1971.

Frank, Joseph. *The Levellers: A History of the Writings of Three Seventeenth-Century Social Democrats: John Lilburne, Richard Overton, William Walwyn*. Cambridge MA: Harvard University Press, 1955.

Fristoe, William. *The History of the Ketocton Baptist Association, 1766–1808*. Staunton VA: William Gilman Lyford, 1808.

Gaustad, Edwin S. *Liberty of Conscience: Roger Williams in America*. Library of Religious Biography. Grand Rapids MI: William B. Eerdmans Publishing Company, 1991.

———. *Roger Williams*. Lives and Legacies. Oxford: Oxford University Press, 2005.

Gaustad, Edwin S., editor. *Baptist Piety: The Last Will & Testimony of Obadiah Holmes*. Religion and American Culture. Grand Rapids MI: Christian University Press, 1978. Reprint, Tuscaloosa: University of Alabama Press, 2005.

Gaustad, Edwin, and Leigh Schmidt. *The Religious History of America: The Heart of the American Story from Colonial Time to Today*. Revised edition. San Francisco: HarperSanFrancisco, 2002.

Gewehr, Wesley M. *The Great Awakening in Virginia, 1740–1790*. Durham NC: Duke University Press, 1930.

Glover, T. R. *Poets and Puritans*. 2nd edition. London: Methuen & Co. Ltd., 1916.

Goldie, Mark. "The Search for Religious Liberty, 1640–1690." In *The Oxford Illustrated History of Tudor & Stuart Britain*, edited by John Morrill, 293–309. Oxford: Oxford University Press, 1996.

González, Justo L. *A History of Christian Thought: From the Protestant Reformation to the Twentieth Century*. 3 volumes. Nashville: Abingdon Press, 1979.

———. *The Story of Christianity*. 2 volumes. San Francisco: HarperSanFrancisco, 1984–1985.

Gordon, Charles. *The Old Bailey and Newgate*. New York: James Pott & Company, 1902.

Greaves, Richard L. *Glimpses of Glory: John Bunyan and English Dissent*. Stanford CA: Stanford University Press, 2002.

———. *Saints and Rebels: Seven Nonconformists in Stuart England*. Macon GA: Mercer University Press, 1985.

Greaves, Richard L., and Robert Zaller, editors. *Biographical Dictionary of British Radicals in the Seventeenth Century*. 3 volumes. Brighton England: Harvester Press, 1982–1984.

Griffiths, Arthur. *The Chronicles of Newgate*. London: Chapman and Hall, 1884.

Hill, Christopher. *The Century of Revolution, 1603–1714*. The Norton Library History of England. New York: W. W. Norton & Company, Inc., 1961.

Howell, Robert Boyte C. *The Early Baptists of Virginia: An Address, Delivered in New York, before the American Baptist Historical Society, May 10th 1856*. Philadelphia: Press of the Society, 1857.

Isaac, Rhys. *The Transformation of Virginia, 1740–1790*. Chapel Hill: Published for the Institute of Early American History and Culture, Williamsburg, Virginia, by the University of North Carolina Press, 1982. Reprint, 1999.

Ivimey, Joseph. *A History of English Baptists*. 4 volumes. London: printed for the author, 1811–1830.

James, Sydney V. *John Clarke and His Legacies: Religion and Law in Colonial Rhode Island 1638–1750*, edited by Theodore Dwight Bozeman. University Park: Pennsylvania State University Press, 1993.

Jones, R. Tudur. "The Sufferings of Vavasor." In *Welsh Baptist Studies*, edited by Mansel John, 77–91. Llandysul: The South Wales Baptist College, 1976.

Jordan, W. K. *Development of Religious Toleration in England*. 4 volumes. Cambridge MA: Harvard University Press, 1932–1940.

King, Henry Melville. *A Summer Visit of Three Rhode Islanders to the Massachusetts Bay in 1651*. Providence RI: Preston and Rounds, 1896.

Lee, Jason K. *The Theology of John Smyth: Puritan, Separatist, Baptist, Mennonite*. Macon GA: Mercer University Press, 2003.

Leland, John. "The Virginia Chronicle." In *The Writings of the Late Elder John Leland, Including Some Events in His Life, Written by Himself, with Additional Sketches*, edited by L. F. Greene. New York: G. W. Wood, 1845. Reprint, Gallatin TN: Church History Research and Archives, 1986.

Leonard, Bill J. *Baptist Ways: A History*. Valley Forge PA: Judson Press, 2003.

Little, Lewis Peyton. *Imprisoned Preachers and Religious Liberty in Virginia: A Narrative Drawn Largely from the Official Records of Virginia Counties, Unpublished Manuscripts, Letters, and Other Original Sources*. Lynchburg VA: J. P. Bell Co., Inc., 1938.

Lyon, T. *The Theory of Religious Liberty in England, 1603–39*. Cambridge: The University Press, 1937.

Manning, Brian. "The Levellers and Religion." In *Radical Religion in the English Revolution*, edited by J. F. McGregor and B. Reay, 65–90. Oxford: Oxford University Press, 1984.

Masters, Frank M. *A History of Baptists in Kentucky*. Louisville: Kentucky Baptist Historical Society, 1953.

McBeth, Harry Leon. *The Baptist Heritage: Four Centuries of Baptist Witness*. Nashville: Broadman Press, 1987.

———. *English Baptist Literature on Religious Liberty to 1689*. Ph.D. dissertation, Southwestern Baptist Theological Seminary, 1961. Reprint, New York: Arno Press, 1980.

McGregor, J. F. "The Baptists: Fount of All Heresy." In *Radical Religion in the English Revolution*, edited by J. F. McGregor and B. Reay, 23–63. Oxford: Oxford University Press, 1984.

McLoughlin, William G. *New England Dissent, 1630–1833: The Baptists and the Separation of Church and State*. Volume 1. Cambridge MA: Harvard University Press, 1971.

———. *Rhode Island: A Bicentennial History*. New York: W. W. Norton & Company, Inc., 1978.

———. *Soul Liberty: The Baptists' Struggle in New England, 1630–1833*. Hanover NH: University Press of New England, 1991.

McLoughlin, William G., editor. *The Diary of Isaac Backus*. Volume 1. Providence RI: Brown University Press, 1979.

Miller, Perry. *Orthodoxy in Massachusetts, 1630–1650: A Genetic Study*. Cambridge MA: Harvard University Press, 1933.

———. *Roger Williams: His Contribution to the American Tradition*. Makers of the American Tradition. Indianapolis IN: The Bobbs-Merrill Company, Inc., 1953.

Morgan, Edmund S. *Visible Saints: The History of the Puritan Idea*. Ithaca NY: Cornell University Press, 1963.

Morison, Samuel Eliot. *Builders of the Bay Colony*. Boston: Houghton Mifflin, 1930. Reprint, Boston: Northeastern University Press, 1981.

Nelson, Wilbur. *The Ministry of Dr. John Clarke*. Newport RI: privately printed, 1927.

Nelson, Wilbur. *The Life of Dr. John Clarke*. [Newport RI: privately printed], 1924. Reprint [Newport RI: privately printed], 1963.

Oxford Dictionary of National Biography. Oxford: Oxford University Press, 2004. http://www.oxforddnb.com.

Pamphilus, Eusebius. "Church History." In *A Select Library of the Nicene and Post-Nicene Fathers of the Christian Church*. Ed. Philip Schaff and Henry Wace. 2nd series. 14 volumes. Grand Rapids MI: Wm. B. Eerdmans Publishing Company, n.d. http://www.ccel.org/ccel/schaff/npnf201.iii.xvi.v.html.

Poe, Harry. "John Bunyan." In *Baptist Theologians*, edited by Timothy George and David S. Dockery, 26–48. Nashville: Broadman Press, 1990.

Robinson, H. Wheeler. *The Life and Faith of the Baptists*. Revised edition. In *British Baptists*. The Baptist Tradition. London: The Kingsgate Press, 1946. Reprint, New York: Arno Press, 1980.

Ryland, Garnett. *The Baptists of Virginia: 1699–1926*. Richmond: The Virginia Baptist Board of Missions and Education, 1955.

Sanford, Don A. *A Choosing People: The History of Seventh Day Baptists*. Nashville: Broadman Press, 1992.

Schama, Simon. *A History of Britain*. Volumes 1 and 2. New York: Hyperion, 2000–2001.

Semple, Robert B. *History of the Rise and Progress of the Baptists in Virginia*. Richmond: privately printed, 1810.

———. *History of the Rise and Progress of the Baptists in Virginia*. Revised and expanded by G. W. Beale. Richmond: Pitt & Dickinson, Publishers, 1894.

Shurden, Walter B. *The Baptist Identity: Four Fragile Freedoms*. Macon GA: Smyth & Helwys Publishing, Inc., 1993.

———. *Not an Easy Journey: Some Transitions in Baptist Life*. Macon GA: Mercer University Press, 2005.

———, editor. *Religious Liberty*. Proclaiming the Baptist Vision 4. Macon GA: Smyth & Helwys, 1997.

Smith, Allen. "John Bunyan (1628–1680)." Volume 1 in *The British Particular Baptists: 1638–1910*, edited by Michael A. G. Haykin, 79–92. Springfield MO: Particular Baptist Press, 1998.

Smith, W. Harvey. "Some Seventeenth Century Baptists: Denne—Keach—Bunyan; and Others." In *The English Baptists: Who They Are, and What They Have Done*, edited by John Clifford, 74–99. London: E. Marlborough & Co., 1881.

Stassen, Glenn H. *Just Peacemaking: Transforming Initiatives for Justice and Peace*. Louisville KY: Westminster/John Knox Press, 1992.

Stephen, Leslie, and Sidney Lee, editors. *Dictionary of National Biography*. 63 vols. London: Smith, Elder, & Co., 1885–1900.

Swaish, John. *Chronicles of Broadmead Church, Bristol: 1640–1923: A Brief Narrative*. Bristol: Young & Humphrys, [1927].

Taylor, Adam. *The History of the English General Baptists*. 2 volumes. London: printed for the author, 1818.

Taylor, James B. *Lives of Virginia Baptist Ministers*. 2nd edition, revised. Richmond: Yale & Wyatt, 1838.

Taylor, John. *Baptists on the American Frontier: A History of Ten Baptist Churches of Which the Author Has Been Alternately a Member*, edited by Chester Raymond Young. Annotated 3rd edition. Macon GA: Mercer University Press, 1995.

Torbet, Robert G. *A History of the Baptists*. 3rd edition. Valley Forge PA: Judson Press, 1963.

Truett, George W. "Baptists and Religious Liberty." In *The Trophy of Baptists*, edited by J. Brent Walker, 29–32. Macon GA: Smyth & Helwys, 2003.

Tull, James E. *Shapers of Baptist Thought*. Valley Forge PA: Judson Press, 1972.

Tyler, Moses Coit. *A History of American Literature*. New York: G. P. Putnam's Sons, 1879. Also available online at http://www.dinsdoc.com/tyler_m-1-0a.htm.

Underwood, A. C. *A History of the English Baptists*. London: The Carey Kingsgate Press Limited, 1947.

Vedder, Henry C. *A Short History of the Baptists*. Revised edition. Philadelphia: American Baptist Publication Society, 1897. Also available online at http://www.reformedreader.org/history/vedder/preface.htm.

Watts, Michael R. *The Dissenters*. Volume 1. Oxford: Clarendon Press, 1978.

Webster, Tom. *Godly Clergy in Early Stuart England: The Caroline Puritan Movement c. 1620–1643*. Cambridge: Cambridge University Press, 1997.

White, B. R. *The English Baptists of the Seventeenth Century*. A History of the English Baptists 1. London: The Baptist Historical Society, 1983.

————. "Introduction: The English Puritan Tradition." In *The English Puritan Tradition*, Christian Classics, edited by Barrington R. White, 9–28. Nashville: Broadman Press, 1980.

Whitley, William T. *A Baptist Bibliography, Being a Register of the Chief Materials for Baptist History, Whether in Manuscript or in Print, Preserved in Great Britain, Ireland, and the Colonies*. Volume 1. London: The Kingsgate Press, 1916.

————. "Biography." In *The Works of John Smyth, Fellow of Christ's College, 1594–8*, edited by W. T. Whitley, 1:xvii–cxxii. Cambridge: University Press, 1915.

————. *A History of British Baptists*. London: Charles Griffin & Company, Limited, 1923.

Wright, W. H. K. *West-County Poets: Their Lives and Works*. London: Elliot Stock, 1896. Available at http://www.windeatt.f2s.com/poets/Cheare_A.html.

Articles

Allis, Jr., Frederick S. "Nathaniel Ward: Constitutional Draftsman." *Essex Institute Historical Collections* 120/4 (October 1984): 241–63.

"An Index to Notable British Baptists." *Transactions of the Baptist Historical Society* 7/3–4 (January–December 1921): 182–239.

Ban, Joseph D. "Was John Bunyan a Baptist? A Case Study in Historiography." *Baptist Quarterly* 30/8 (October 1984): 367–76.

"Baptists in Literature till 1688." *Transactions of the Baptist Historical Society* 1/2 (April 1909): 114–20.

"Baptists in the State Papers." *Transactions of the Baptist Historical Society* 5/3 (April 1917): 144–53.

Barber, J. H. "Constantine in Relation to Christianity." *Review and Expositor* 9/1 (January 1912): 63–82.

Beal, Rebecca. "*Grace Abounding to the Chief of Sinners*: John Bunyan's Pauline Epistle." *Studies in English Literature* 21/1 (Winter 1981): 148–60.

Broadus, John A. "American Baptist Ministry of 100 Years Ago." *Baptist Quarterly* 9/1 (January 1875): 1–20.

Brown, Harold. "The History of the Baptists in England to 1644." *Chronicle* 8/1 (January 1945): 1–14.

Buckley, Thomas E. "Keeping Faith: Virginia Baptists and Religious Liberty." *American Baptist Quarterly* 22/4 (December 2003): 421–33.

Burrage, Champlin, editor. "Early Welsh Baptist Doctrines, Set forth in a Manuscript, Ascribed to Vavasor Powell." *Transactions of the Baptist Historical Society* 1/1 (November 1908): 3–20.

Clayton, J. Glenwood. "Thomas Helwys: A Baptist Founding Father." *Baptist History and Heritage* 8/1 (January 1973): 2–15.

Clonts, F. W. "Thomas Helwys and His Book, *The Mistery of Iniquity*." *Review and Expositor* 41/4 (October 1944): 372–87.

Coulton, Barbara. "Vavasor Powell and His Baptist Connections." *Baptist Quarterly* 40/8 (October 2004): 477–87.

Crandall, Paul E. "John Crandall and 17th Century Seventh Day Baptists." *Baptist History and Heritage* 2/2 (July 1967): 114–16, 126.

Crannell, Philip Wendell. "Tolerance and Company." *Review and Expositor* 24/1 (January 1927): 24–44.

Estep, William R. "Anabaptists and the Rise of English Baptists." *Quarterly Review* 28/4 (October–December 1968): 43–53 and 29/1 (January–March 1969): 50–62.

———. "On the Origins of English Baptists." *Baptist History and Heritage* 22/2 (April 1987): 19–26.

———. "Thomas Helwys: Bold Architect of Baptist Policy on Church-State Relations." *Baptist History and Heritage* 20/3 (July 1985): 24–33.

Farrer, Augustine J. D. "Cromwell as Dictator." *Baptist Quarterly* 7/5 (January 1935): 193–201.

Foster, John C. "Early Baptist Writers of Verse. Cheare, Bunyan, Keach." *Transactions of the Baptist Historical Society* 3/2 (October 1912): 95–110.

Fullerton, W. Y. "John Bunyan." *Review and Expositor* 25/3 (July 1928): 255–77.

Gaustad, Edwin S. "Baptists and Experimental Religion." *Chronicle* 15/3 (July 1952): 110–20.

———. "John Clarke: 'Good Newes from Rhode Island.'" *Baptist History and Heritage* 24/4 (October 1989): 20–28.

———. "A Livelie Experiment." *Foundations* 7/2 (April 1964): 102–10.

Gibbons, B. J. "Richard Overton and the Secularism of the Interregnum Radicals." *Seventeenth Century* 10/1 (Spring 1995): 63–75.

Gledhill, Morton ."The Poet and the Preacher." *Baptist Quarterly* 7/2 (April 1934): 69–78.

Greaves, Richard L. "The Spirit and the Sword: Bunyan and the Stuart State." *Baptist Quarterly Review* 32/8 (October 1988): 358–79.

Hannen, Robert B. "Historical Notes on the Name 'Baptist.'" *Foundations* 8/1 (January 1965): 62–71.

Harkness, R. E. E. "The Price of Freedom." *Chronicle* 16/3 (July 1953): 151–57.

———. "These Baptists: Ignominiously Called Mad Men." *Chronicle* 14/1 (January 1951): 27–39.

Hayden, Roger. "Broadmead, Bristol in the Seventeenth Century." *Baptist Quarterly* 23/8 (October 1970): 348–59.

Haykin, Michael. "A Cloud of Witnesses: The Life and Ministry of Hercules Collins (d. 1702)." *Evangelical Times*, February 2001. http://www.evangelical-times.org/Articles/feb01/feb01a11.htm.

Himbury, D. Mervin. "The Religious Beliefs of the Levellers." *Baptist Quarterly* 15/6 (April 1954): 269–76.

Hudson, Winthrop S. "Baptists Were Not Anabaptists." *Chronicle* 16/4 (October 1953): 171–79.

"Inscription on the Grave-Stone of the Late Mr. Thomas Grantham." *General Baptist Magazine*, January 1799, 215–16.

Jordan, M. Dorothea. "John Smyth and Thomas Helwys: The Two First English Preachers of Religious Liberty. Resemblances and Contrasts." *Baptist Quarterly* 12/6–7 (April–July 1947): 187–95.

Kerr, Norman. "John Clarke—Architect of Freedom." *Chronicle* 19/4 (October 1956): 147–59.

Kingsley, Gordon. "Opposition to Early Baptists (1638–1645)." *Baptist History and Heritage* 4/1 (January 1969): 18–30, 66.

Kliever, Lonnie D. "General Baptist Origins: The Question of Anabaptist Influence." *Mennonite Quarterly Review* 36/4 (October 1962): 291–321.

Knott, John R., Jr. "Bunyan's Gospel Day: A Reading of *The Pilgrim's Progress*." *English Literary Renaissance* 3/3 (Autumn 1973): 443–61.

Knott, O. "Obadiah Holmes, of Newport, R. I." *Transactions of the Baptist Historical Society* 5/3 (April 1917): 169–71.

Little, Lewis Peyton. "Imprisoned Preachers and Religious Liberty in Virginia." *Chronicle* 1/2 (April 1938): 23–31.

Lord, F. Townley. "Bunyan's Message for To-day." *Baptist Quarterly* 4/4 (September 1928): 166–70.

Manley, Kenneth Ross. "Origins of the Baptists: The Case for Development from Puritanism-Separatism." *Baptist History and Heritage* 12/4 (October 1987): 34–46.

McBeth, Leon. "Baptist Origins." *Baptist History and Heritage* 15/4 (October 1980): 36–41.

McGlothlin, W. J. "Bunyan's 'Pilgrim's Progress': A Study." *Review and Expositor* 15/3 (July 1928): 278–91.

———. "The Struggle for Religious Liberty." *Review and Expositor* 8/3 (July 1911): 378–94.

"A Memoir of Thomas Grantham." *General Baptist Repository and Missionary Observer* 4/44 (1 August 1825): 281–86; 4/45 (1 September 1825): 321–26; 4/46 (1 October 1825): 361–67.

Miller, Robert T. "Religious Conscience in Colonial New England." *Journal of Church and State* 1 (November 1959): 19–36.

"Ministers Charged with Holding Posts in the Established Church While Being Baptists, Grouped in Eleven Classes." *Transactions of the Baptist Historical Society* 1/1 (November 1908): 38–41.

Moore, John. "The Baptist March Across Virginia," *Virginia Baptist Register* 18 (1979): 879–89.

———. "John Waller (1741–1802), 'A Man Worthy of Notice.'" *Virginia Baptist Register* 34 (1995): 1745–53.

Moore, John S., editor. "Morgan Edwards' 1772 Virginia Notebook: Edited with Notes and Comments." *Virginia Baptist Register* 17 (1978): 845–71.

Mosteller, James D. "Baptists and Anabaptists: I: The Genius of Anabaptism." *Chronicle* 20/1 (January 1957): 3–27.

———. "Baptists and Anabaptists II: John Smyth and the Dutch Mennonites," *Chronicle* 20/3 (July 1957): 100–14.

Mullins, E. Y. "The Practical Value of Poetry." *Review and Expositor* 11/4 (October 1914): 536–50.

Nelson, Wilbur. "The Ministry of John Clarke." *Chronicle* 1/2 (April 1938): 32–38.

Newman, A. H. "Baptist Pioneers in Liberty of Conscience." *Review and Expositor* 6/2 (April 1909): 239–55.

Newman, Simon P. "Nathaniel Ward, 1580–1652: An Elizabethan Puritan in a Jacobean World." *Essex Institute Historical Collections* 127/4 (October 1991): 313–26.

Payne, Earnest A. "Who Were the Baptists?" *Baptist Quarterly* 16/8 (October 1956): 339–42.

Poe, Harry L. "John Bunyan's Controversy with the Baptists." *Baptist History and Heritage* 23/2 (April 1988): 25–35.

Pooley, Roger. "'The Wilderness of This World'—Bunyan's *Pilgrim's Progress*." *Baptist Quarterly* 27/7 (July 1978): 290–99.

Porter, David. "The Baptist Struggle for Religious Freedom in the Massachusetts Bay Colony, 1650–1670." *Foundations* 14/1 (January–March 1971): 24–32.

Renihan, James M. "An Examination of the Possible Influence of Menno Simons' *Foundation Book* upon the Particular Baptist Confession of 1644." *American Baptist Quarterly* 15/3 (October 1996): 190–207.

Roper, Cecil M. "Henry Denne and the Fenstanton Baptists in England." *Baptist History and Heritage* 16/4 (October 1981): 26–38.

Selement, George. "John Clarke and the Struggle for the Separation of Church and State." *Foundations* 15/2 (April–June 1972): 111–25.

Shrader, Wesley. "The Struggle for Religious Freedom in Early Virginia." *Review and Expositor* 53/2 (April 1956): 168–73.

Shurden, Walter B. "Ill News from Twenty-First Century America." *Baptist History and Heritage* 39/2 (Spring 2004): 6–7.

Slawson, Myra E. "The Writing of *Grace Abounding to the Chief of Sinners*." *Quarterly Baptist* 42/2 (January–March): 59–63.

Stassen, Glen H. "Anabaptist Influence in the Origin of Particular Baptists." *Mennonite Quarterly Review* 36/4 (October 1962): 322–48.

Thomas, J. Hobson. "Bunyan the Baptist." *Baptist Quarterly* 4/3 (July 1928): 97–103.

Thompson, Philip E. "People of the Free God: The Passion of Seventeenth-Century Baptists." *American Baptist Quarterly* 15/3 (September 1996): 223–41.

Tonks, A. Ronald. "The Impact of Religious Toleration on English Baptists in the 17th and 18th Centuries." *Quarterly Baptist* 34/1 (October–December): 46–60.

Turner, G. Lyon. "Bunyan's License under the Indulgence." *Transactions of the Baptist Historical Society* 6/2 (January 1919): 129–37.

"Two Hardcastles, Presbyterian and Baptist." *Transactions of the Baptist Historical Society*. 4/1 (April 1914): 33–45.

Vedder, Henry. "Baptists and Liberty of Conscience: The English Baptists, 1500–1643." *Baptist Quarterly Review* 6/21 (January–March 1884): 111–29.

———. "Baptists and Liberty of Conscience: The English Baptists, 1644–1689." *Baptist Quarterly Review* 6/22 (April–June 1884): 223–39.

————. "Baptists and Liberty of Conscience: The Opposition of Presbyterians and Independents." *Baptist Quarterly* 6/23 (July–September 1884): 347–68.

Watner, Carl. "'Come What, Come Will!': Richard Overton, Libertarian Leveller," *Journal of Libertarian Studies* 4/4 (Fall 1980): 405–32. Also available online at http://64.233.161.104/search?q=cache:_9isBTSYcz4J:www.mises.org/journals/jls/4_4/4_4_7.pdf+%22Come+what,+come+will!%22&hl=en.

White, Barrie. "Early Baptist Arguments for Religious Freedom: Their Overlooked Agenda." *Baptist History and Heritage* 24/4 (October 1989): 3–10.

————. "The English General Baptists and the Great Rebellion 1640–1660." *Baptist History and Heritage* 8/1 (January 1973): 16–27.

————. "Samuel Eaton (d. 1639): A Particular Baptist Pioneer." *Baptist Quarterly* 24/1 (January 1971): 10–21.

Whitley, W. T. "Bunyan's Imprisonment: A Legal Study." *Transactions of the Baptist Historical Society* 6/1 (January–December 1918): 1–24.

————. "Henry Denne." *Baptist Quarterly* 11/3–4 (July and October 1942): 124.

————. "Early English Baptists." *Chronicle* 1 (January 1938): 15–22.

————. "Thomas Helwys of Gray's Inn and of Broxtowe Hall, Nottingham." *Baptist Quarterly* 7/6 (April 1935): 241–55.

Wolfe, Don M. "Unsigned Pamphlets of Richard Overton: 1641–1649." *Huntington Library Quarterly* 21/1–4 (1957/1958): 167–201.

Newspaper Articles

"An Address to the Anabaptists Imprisoned in Caroline County, August 8, 1771." *Virginia Gazette*, 20 February 1772, [1–2].

"A Recipe to Make an Anabaptist Preacher in Two Days Time." *Virginia Gazette*, 31 October 1771, [2].

Ritter, L. M. "James Ireland—Martyr." *Religious Herald*, 30 January 1830, 8.

Winfrey, E. W. "James Ireland." *Religious Herald*, 13 February 1830, 11.

Index